# China Hands
# and Old Cantons

# China Hands and Old Cantons

## Britons and the Middle Kingdom

John M. Carroll

ROWMAN & LITTLEFIELD
*Lanham • Boulder • New York • London*

Published by Rowman & Littlefield
An imprint of The Rowman & Littlefield Publishing Group, Inc.
4501 Forbes Boulevard, Suite 200, Lanham, Maryland 20706
www.rowman.com

86-90 Paul Street, London EC2A 4NE

Copyright © 2021 by The Rowman & Littlefield Publishing Group, Inc.

*All rights reserved.* No part of this book may be reproduced in any form or by any electronic or mechanical means, including information storage and retrieval systems, without written permission from the publisher, except by a reviewer who may quote passages in a review.

British Library Cataloguing in Publication Information Available

**Library of Congress Cataloging-in-Publication Data**

Names: Carroll, John M. (John Mark), 1961- author.
Title: China hands and old Cantons : Britons and the Middle Kingdom / John M. Carroll.
Other titles: Britons and the Middle Kingdom
Description: Lanham : Rowman & Littlefield, [2021] | Includes bibliographical references and index.
Identifiers: LCCN 2021023698 (print) | LCCN 2021023699 (ebook) | ISBN 9781538157572 (cloth) | ISBN 9781538157589 (epub)
Subjects: LCSH: Great Britain—Commerce—China—History—19th century. | China—Commerce—Great Britain—History—19th century. | British—China—History—19th century. | Guangzhou (China)—Social life and customs—19th century. | Guangzhou (China)—Commerce—History—19th century. | China—History—Qing dynasty, 1644-1912.
Classification: LCC HF3508.C5 C37 2021 (print) | LCC HF3508.C5 (ebook) | DDC 382.0941051—dc23
LC record available at https://lccn.loc.gov/2021023698
LC ebook record available at https://lccn.loc.gov/2021023699

∞™ The paper used in this publication meets the minimum requirements of American National Standard for Information Sciences—Permanence of Paper for Printed Library Materials, ANSI/NISO Z39.48-1992.

# Contents

| | | |
|---|---|---:|
| Acknowledgments | | vii |
| Introduction | | 1 |
| 1 | The Crying Abuses: Explanations | 27 |
| | Restricted China | 29 |
| | Stationary China | 32 |
| | Despotic China | 35 |
| | The Tartars and Their Empire | 42 |
| | Not Entirely Unreasonable | 46 |
| | Themselves to Blame | 49 |
| | Hood-winked | 53 |
| 2 | The Crying Abuses: Solutions | 61 |
| | Visitors Weigh In | 62 |
| | Intimidation or Restraint? | 67 |
| | At Home | 74 |
| | Improving Their Own Situation | 81 |
| | Somewhere Else | 88 |
| 3 | Being There | 99 |
| | Challenging the Jesuits | 102 |
| | A Peculiar Monopoly | 107 |
| | Interesting Evidence | 113 |
| | Opinions Grounded upon Experience | 118 |
| | The Terms Controversy | 122 |

|   |   |   |
|---|---|---|
|   | Setting the Record Straight | 125 |
|   | War, Hong Kong, and Beyond | 130 |
| 4 | Sizing Up China | 139 |
|   | An Immense and Unparalleled Population | 140 |
|   | A Horrid Practice | 150 |
|   | So Extraordinary a Custom | 155 |
|   | Footbinding and the War to Open China | 167 |
| 5 | The Opium Debates | 183 |
|   | Opium Mania | 187 |
|   | Opium in the Press | 193 |
|   | The Issues | 196 |
|   | James Innes | 201 |
|   | Setting the Record Straight, Again | 206 |
|   | Opium and War | 211 |
| Epilogue: China Freed | | 221 |
| Bibliography | | 243 |
| Index | | 259 |

# Acknowledgments

"The question is, what will we learn about the opium?" It was the kind of query I had received many times while conducting the research for this book. On this particular occasion, it came from an immigration officer at Heathrow Airport whose family originally hailed from Bihar, the region of India where much of the opium sold to China in the late 1700s and early 1800s was processed. I did not have the heart to tell him that the opium trade and the war it led to in 1839 are both well-trodden topics in British imperial history and modern Chinese history. Like my last book, *Canton Days: British Life and Death in China*, this one shows how the relationship between Britain and China during this period involved much more than opium and war.

Because this book evolved alongside *Canton Days*, everyone acknowledged there should consider themselves thanked again here. Some, and several not mentioned there, deserve special thanks. Robert Bickers once again read the entire manuscript; Paul Cha, Kendall Johnson, Julia Kuehn, James St. André, and Tim Weston read various chapters. Many colleagues at conferences and workshops also offered useful comments. They include Song-Chuan Chen, Hao Gao, Henrietta Harrison, Richard Horowitz, Peter Kitson, Keith McMahon, Caroline Reeves, Patricia Sieber, Rosalien Van der Poel, and John Wong. Robert Bickers, Grace Chou, James Fichter, Mark Hampton, Loretta Kim, and Matthew Mosca organized conferences in 2011, 2012, and 2015 where I was able to present sections of chapters 1 and 2. Lorna Carson and the Trinity Centre for Asian Studies at Trinity College Dublin invited me to present a preliminary version of chapter 4 in May 2016, as did the Hong Kong Museum of Medical Sciences in March 2018.

I am also indebted to the many archivists and librarians in the India Office Records and Private Papers at the British Library, the Archives and Special Collections at the School of Oriental and African Studies Library, the

Archives and Manuscripts at the Wellcome Library, the National Archives of the UK, the Jardine Matheson Archive at the Cambridge University Library, and the Special Collections at the University of Hong Kong Library.

Research and writing require financial support, for which I thank the Louis Cha Fund for China Studies, the Hsu Long-sing Research Fund, the University Research Seed Funding Programme for Basic Research (all at the University of Hong Kong), and the Hong Kong Research Grants Council General Research Fund (grant number HKU 740912H).

Parts of the book appeared earlier in *Britain and China: Empire, Finance and War, 1840–1970*, edited by Robert Bickers and Jon Howlett, and in *The Cultural Construction of the British World*, edited by Barry Crosbie and Mark Hampton. I am obliged to the editors and publishers for letting me use some of that material here. For illustrations and maps, I thank the Library of Congress Geography and Map Division, Martyn Gregory Gallery, Barry Lawrence Ruderman Antique Maps Inc., the Harvard Map Collection, the National Portrait Gallery in London, the Government Art Collection of the UK, the Wellcome Collection, and the Hong Kong Maritime Museum. The Syndics of Cambridge University Library and Jardine, Matheson kindly granted permission to quote from letters in the Jardine Matheson Archive.

My thanks go to Susan McEachern, Katelyn Turner, Alex Schwartz, Haley White, Chris Fischer, Emily Natsios, and the entire editorial and production team at Rowman & Littlefield. This is my third book with Susan and my second with Katelyn, so I am triply and doubly appreciative of their support.

As always, I am grateful most of all to my family, especially Katie and Emma.

# Introduction

"Ramrod" knew how the hostilities with the Great Qing should be conducted. In early October 1839, aboard a ship anchored off the island of Hong Kong, the anonymous British merchant submitted a long letter to the *Canton Press*, its operations recently moved from Canton (Guangzhou) to the Portuguese territory of Macao. The object should be trade rather than conquest: opening new markets to "British enterprize." No matter what measures the British took against the government of China, they would have to "protect, cherish, and refrain from injuring the Chinese *people*." And victory must be certain. For if the Chinese were to win, "our *prestige* of superiority is gone, and our cause lost, even before we have well begun it." He then proceeded to explain his strategy, dismissing one by one the other solutions being debated among the British community in China.

A land invasion was out of the question. Hauling ten thousand troops from British India across the "stupendous" mountains of Nepal and Tibet would be nigh impossible. "The wandering of the Children of Israel in the wilderness would be nothing to theirs!" Trekking through Assam would mean crossing deserts where "the foot of civilized man never yet trod, thro' jungle the abode of wild beasts, and swamps the abode of sickness and pestilence." A "pretty good road" led from Burma into Yunnan, and "Ramrod" saw no reason why an Anglo-Burmese army could not march into China. But surely the Burmese would "like much better to defend their feudal superior, the Emperor of China, than to aid us in attacking him."

If the assault were by sea, the object must be the capital at Peking (Beijing). But even this would be impractical, and the British must not try to colonize China. Neither the European nor the native soldiers who had lived in India for so long could survive the winter of Peking, "a place as cold as the North Pole." How were these "jolly old bull dogs" to take a city of two million inhabitants, defended by the "best and bravest of China and Tartary, all of whom are sworn to conquer or die"? If the British lost, "not a man would probably return to tell the tale."

Blockading the entire coast seemed the cheapest and most obvious solution, especially for a great naval power. But other foreign states would hardly respect such a blockade, and the Qing government might simply open more ports to the Americans and, even worse, the French. A blockade was "a dangerous way of making war, the time required for its operations being so uncertain." And what were the British to tell the Chinese people they would encounter along the coast? That men from "the most civilized point in the world" had come to blockade their ports, sink their ships, and starve them to death—all to make their emperor pay for two million pounds of the "healthful and exhilarating Drug Opium" Imperial Commissioner Lin Zexu had destroyed in June? Who would not "shudder" at the idea of "being employed on such a degrading service as the depriving of women and children of their little meals"? Such a policy would be more befitting of "the States of Barbary and Tunis" than "the Empire of Great Britain."

The easiest and most effective way, "Ramrod" continued, would be to occupy and fortify several islands along the China coast, including Hong Kong. With "offers of protection and the kindest of treatment," the British would manage the inhabitants so well that the Qing authorities could never dislodge them. "Thus then by a simple process would the Chinese government be humbled and taught our importance in the scale of nations; their military would be defeated and made to confess the superiority of European discipline; an excellent security would be afforded against oppression in the future; the ports of China would be thrown open to our manufactures." Above all, the millions of people the British could finally trade with on "an extended scale" would "meet us as *kind friends*, not as *rancorous enemies*."[1]

We are unlikely ever to know the identity of "Ramrod." His was only one of many competing "expert" voices offering opinions about Britain's position in China. Like many of the names in this book, he may even have been an editorial device rather than an actual source, vividly bellicose and evoking military precision and discipline. But there is no doubt about the "oppression" he hoped to see eliminated: the Canton System, which since the mid-1700s had confined China's trade with the West to Macao and a tiny section of Canton. Foreigners were required to leave Canton each year when the trading season ended. All goods were to be bought and sold through a group of specially licensed Chinese merchant houses, known to the foreigners as "hongs" and organized as the Cohong. Western women were not allowed to live anywhere in China except for Macao, though occasionally some managed to slip from

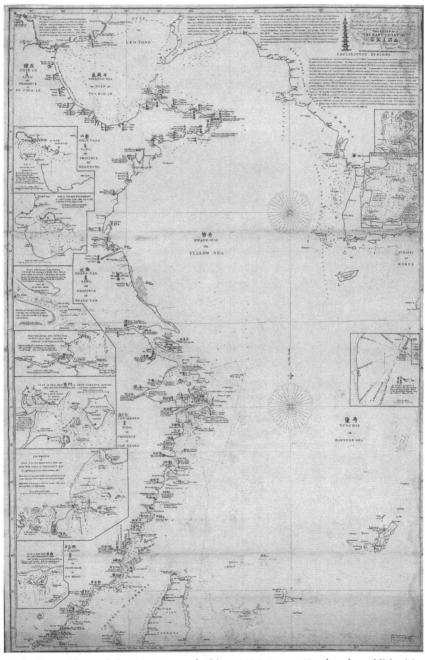

Figure I.1. *Chart of the East Coast of China*, 1835, James Horsburgh, published by J. & C. Walker. Library of Congress Geography and Map Division

there into Canton. The magnitude of the trade, perhaps unparalleled anywhere else in the world, was so great and the system worked well enough for the merchants to return each year to their "factories" after spending the off-season in Macao. Yet they complained increasingly loudly about its restrictions—especially when the East India Company's monopoly on trade with China ended in 1834 and more private traders flocked to Canton.[2]

The calls for a more aggressive British policy toward China became even more strident after the death in October 1834 of Lord Napier, dispatched that summer as the first chief superintendent of British trade. Though many Britons in China had opposed the Napier mission, his detention by the local authorities, first in Canton and then as he lay ill with typhus while trying to reach Macao by boat, made him a martyr. In January 1836 the Scottish trader James Matheson, who had lived in China for seventeen years and had accompanied Napier's widow, Elizabeth, and her husband's remains back to Britain, published a lengthy pamphlet from London warning that the government's weak China policy threatened to make it "the laughing-stock of the world."[3] One month earlier, Matheson had tried to draw foreign secretary Lord Palmerston's attention to the "unprotected state of our commercial relations with that Empire."[4] That March, Hugh Hamilton Lindsay, a former Company supercargo who had since become a private trader, wrote a public letter (also

Figure I.2. *Canton: The Hongs or Factories*, ca. 1779, Chinese artist, reverse-glass painting. *Photo*: Martyn Gregory Gallery

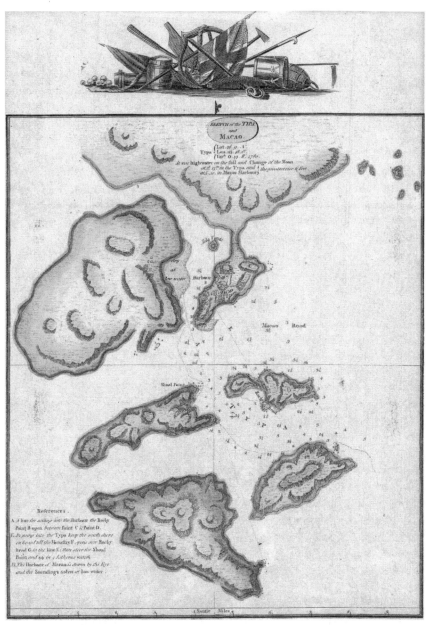

Figure I.3. *Sketch of the Typa and Macao*, ca. 1780, by Alexander Hogg. Harvard Map Collection, Harvard Library

from London) to Palmerston outlining his plan for an expedition powerful enough to "coerce the Chinese empire, with its countless millions of inhabitants." By "combining energetic measures with judicious policy," a "comparatively small" naval force would do the trick. The whole thing could be over in less than four months, without causing any "serious inconvenience" to trade.[5]

At the heart of this Canton System lay two commodities: Chinese tea, introduced to Britain in the early 1600s, and Indian opium, mostly from Bengal. By the mid-1700s, the balance of trade overwhelmingly favored China. Tea had become the national drink of Britain and was imported in enormous quantities, but no British good could create a similar demand in China. The British responded by selling opium, cultivated and prepared in India, where the East India Company, functioning as the government of British India, drew much of its revenue from its monopoly on the production and sale of opium. Exports rose dramatically after 1773, when the Company was granted its own opium monopoly in eastern India and began to subcontract the shipping of opium through "country traders"—private merchants who delivered it to the China coast in small "country ships."

As the Chinese demand for opium increased, British traders became even more frustrated with the restrictions of the Canton System and the Qing ban on opium. Even if, as the *Press* argued in August 1836, some of these grievances were "more nominal than real" and none so "glaring" as to justify the use of violence, few Britons in China disagreed something had to be done to improve their situation. "One thing is certain," the paper declared, "to obtain the end desired, considerable risk must be run, and probably guilt incurred on our side."[6]

Everything came to a head in March 1839 when Lin Zexu, recently appointed to suppress the opium trade, required all foreign traders to surrender their opium and promise never to import it again. Three months later, Lin ceremoniously destroyed twenty thousand chests of this "foreign mud." The result was the Opium War. The Qing forces put up a tougher fight than many Britons, in China and at home, had expected, but the British were able to send enough troops from India (though by sea rather than by land). And they had important advice and information from James Matheson's business partner William Jardine, who had lived in China for almost twenty years and knew the coast well. A former Company surgeon, Jardine had become the most powerful opium trader in East Asia. He had left China in January 1839, before the crisis erupted, but on his way to England he learned from Matheson that the opium had been destroyed.[7]

Jardine reached London in September, only to discover that both official and public opinion seemed to be against the China traders. Palmerston even refused to meet him, not once but several times. When Jardine was finally able to see Palmerston on September 27, he provided as much information as possible on how to pursue the expedition against China. When Palmerston's cabinet met on October 1 to set a China policy, it was almost exactly what Jardine had recommended (and "Ramrod" had rejected): blockading the coast from the river to the capital at Peking down to the Canton coast. And when the expedition, on which Palmerston had never consulted Parliament (and of which even his prime minister, Lord Melbourne, remained skeptical), was debated in the House of Commons in April 1840, one of the most persuasive proponents of war ended up being George Thomas Staunton, a former Company officer considered by many British traders to be too soft on China.[8]

Urging Palmerston to send an expedition was a group of British merchants in London and manufacturers, mostly in the northern cities of Liverpool, Manchester, and Glasgow, determined not only to obtain compensation for the lost opium but also to expand British trade with China. Some of these merchants had lived and worked in China, even spending most of their professional lives there. Canton was far from London—several months by sea—but Britons at home also had reasonably up-to-date information about China through the English-language press at Canton. Even if the influence of Jardine and Matheson on British policy has often been exaggerated, there is little doubt they were important for Palmerston's decision and for encouraging some Britons to support a more aggressive policy.[9] And the press frequently featured editorials and letters demanding a punitive mission against China, sometimes while arguing against outright war.

As this book shows, however, these calls for action were hardly the only suggestions for improving Britain's position in China. And Britons who spent time in China from the late 1700s through the 1830s—"China hands" or "old Cantons" as they were sometimes called—wrote about far more than how to open it. The encounters that transpired in Canton between Britain and China are known best for resulting in the Opium War, as if some eighty years of commercial and cultural contacts could be understood through the several years leading up to the war. Yet these encounters also produced an enormous archive of writings on China.

Long before anyone ever considered the idea of going to war with China, Britons, frustrated with the restrictions of the Canton System and unable to live or travel elsewhere in China apart from Macao, devoted thousands of pages in memoirs, travel accounts, ethnographic studies, narratives of military action, translations, and newspapers and other periodicals to understanding China, its people, and their civilization. Well before the American missionary Samuel Wells Williams wrote *The Middle Kingdom* (1848), often considered the first comprehensive study of China in English, Britons compiled detailed and often thoughtful accounts of China. They discussed almost everything they saw and speculated about much of what they did not or could not see. Whether writing memoirs, monographs, or newspaper pieces, they claimed their firsthand experience gave them and their publications an advantage over those in Britain and elsewhere.

As should be expected—but often is not—from such a wide and diverse range of authors and genres often aimed at different readerships, opinions differed. (And the British public was of course never a constant: to some extent, it was the audience these authors imagined when writing, and when idealizing, specific controversies related to China.) Although Jardine and Matheson had been in China longer than many Company officers, they never had a monopoly on knowledge or on opinion. Everyone hoped China might be opened to more trade. But there was rarely any agreement on how this should happen. Nor was there ever a consistently "pacific" or "warlike" party in Canton.[10] Views were never static over these fifty-odd years, and confusing times bred confused explanations and solutions. Each new generation of Britons in Canton also meant a changing relationship with China. In the late 1700s, for example, Britons in China often wrote matter-of-factly about the Canton System and its restrictions; by the late 1830s they usually wrote about how it had to go.

Who were these men and why were they in China? Where and what were they writing? Some were members of the two British embassies to Peking—Lord Macartney's in 1792–1794 and Lord Amherst's in 1816–1817—both sent to secure better trading and diplomatic concessions from the Qing government, and both unsuccessful. The first member to recount the Macartney embassy was neither its leader nor its official secretary, George Leonard Staunton, but Aeneas Anderson, Macartney's valet, who put out his version in 1795, shortly after returning to Britain.[11] In 1797 came one by Staunton and then in 1798 another by a guard named Samuel Holmes. Macartney, who died in 1806, never published his journals. But they were compiled the following year by his private secretary on the embassy, John Barrow, who had released his own narrative in 1804. Even more members of the Amherst embassy published accounts: Staunton's son, George Thomas, first commissioner and head of the East India Company's Select Committee at Canton; Henry Ellis, second commissioner; Robert Morrison, the first British missionary to China and the embassy's principal interpreter; Clarke Abel, the chief medical officer and naturalist; and naval officers Basil Hall and John McLeod, who sailed to China with the embassy but did not accompany it to Peking.[12]

These embassy members had something in common that most Britons in China lacked: they had traveled far beyond the confines of Canton and Macao. Many of their countrymen were traders associated with the Company's establishment at Canton, a few of whom were also able to venture into the hinterland with the Amherst embassy. The younger Staunton had first gone to China as Lord Macartney's page. He returned in 1799 as a Company writer and soon distinguished himself as one of Britain's first sinologists. In 1810 he published a translation of the Qing legal code. Staunton left China forever in January 1817 after the Amherst embassy reached Canton from Peking. John Francis Davis went to China in 1813 as a Company writer. Like Staunton and Morrison, he accompanied the Amherst embassy (and published his account, though not until much later) and became one of Britain's greatest sinologists. After the death of Lord Napier in October 1834, Davis became the superintendent of British trade but soon resigned and left China in January 1835 (returning in 1844 as governor of Hong Kong and plenipotentiary and superintendent of trade at Canton). He wrote several books that became pillars of the British literary canon on China.

With the Company officers in Canton were private traders, who by the 1820s began to outnumber the Company men. Some, like Jardine and Matheson and their rivals Thomas Dent and his brother Lancelot, had gone to China that way. Others had previously worked for the Company but then gone into private service. One was Hugh Lindsay, whose voyage up the China coast in 1832 had convinced him Chinese people everywhere were eager to trade and the main obstacle to expanding trade was the Qing government. Both Company and private ships docked downriver at Whampoa (Huangpu) had surgeons who often recorded their observations. Among them was Charles Toogood Downing, who wrote three volumes on his experience there as a *fan qui* (Cantonese for "foreign devil" and more often written "fan-kwei").

A handful of these British "foreign devils" were missionaries, though their number remained tiny because of the Qing government's proscription of Christianity and the East India Company's policy against missionaries, as well as the hostility of the Catholic authorities in Macao toward Protestantism. Robert Morrison arrived in Canton in 1807 with the London Missionary Society and soon started translating and interpreting for the Company. He died in Canton in August 1834, shortly after being appointed chief interpreter to Lord Napier. Walter Henry Medhurst went to Malacca in 1818 to work in the Anglo-Chinese College established by Morrison and fellow missionary William Milne. He then worked mainly among the overseas Chinese communities in Penang and Batavia, hoping they might in turn convert their compatriots in China, though he later made several expeditions up the China coast to investigate the possibilities for missionary work there. George Tradescant Lay had first gone to China in the mid-1820s as a naturalist on HMS *Blossom* and returned in 1836 as a missionary with the British and Foreign Bible Society.

Figure I.4. *Whampoa, in China,* 1835, by Edward Duncan, after William John Huggins, hand-colored engraving. Hong Kong Maritime Museum. Copyrights by Hong Kong Maritime Museum

British travelers often passed through Canton and Macao en route to and from other parts of Asia. Naval officer James Johnson of HMS *Caroline* visited in December 1804. The artists, Thomas Daniell and his nephew William, spent time there on their way to Calcutta and in 1810 published their *Picturesque Voyage to India; By the Way of China.* Daniel Tyerman and fellow missionary George Bennet visited in autumn 1825 as part of their travels to China, Southeast Asia, and India. Tyerman died in 1828 in South Africa on the way home, but Bennet published a two-volume account of their journey. The physician and naturalist George Bennett (not to be confused with the missionary George Bennet) visited in the early 1830s as part of his three-year "wanderings" in China, Southeast Asia, and New South Wales. James Holman, the first blind person known to have circumnavigated the globe, went in late 1830 at the beginning of the trading season and later published a four-volume account of his travels. Military men and naval soldiers who went to China as part of the British expedition during the Opium War, such as John Elliot Bingham, Edward Cree, Keith Stewart Mackenzie, and Duncan McPherson, also left detailed records.[13]

These are only the men for whom we have names: like "Ramrod," most Britons in Canton expressed their opinions under pseudonyms and through the local English-language press. The *Canton Register*, the first English-language newspaper in China to last more than a few issues, was established in 1827 by James Matheson's nephew Alexander and edited by an American trader, William Wightman Wood. It was soon taken over by Matheson himself and placed under British editorship—first the Anglo-Irish merchant Arthur Saunders Keating and then John Slade, who went to China in 1816 and understood some Chinese, and who edited the paper for ten years until his death in August 1843.

The *Register* was critical of China from the start. An early issue announced that although the paper had "perfect good will" toward China and no "malicious design of exposing only the dark side of her character," its news about China would "very generally be, a record of crime."[14] Several issues later, the paper defended its practice of accepting articles "unfolding the disgusting depravity which exists in the Empire of China"—because it aimed to "furnish a faithful picture of China, not only for amusement, but for moral and philosophical purposes, that the student of human nature may see, how the institutions, opinions, and usages of this country, operate on the morals and peace of society."[15]

The *Register* soon became so notorious for its negative coverage that in October 1828 one "Hardface" criticized it for never providing a "comparative estimate" of the "moral and physical condition" of the Chinese against other Asians or even with Europeans, and for judging them "barbarians because they wear long hair, wide dresses, and thick shoes, instead of crops, cocked hats, tights, stiff cravats, pumps, and shoe buckles."[16] Undaunted, and frustrated by the British government's complacency, the *Register* constantly exhorted Britons in China and at home of the need for better trading conditions. In April 1835 it reminded its readers that by sending a superintendent and "publicly and pressingly" inviting the Qing authorities to enter into free trade, the British government had "already passed the Rubicon." Fear was the "single passion" the British had left to convince the Qing they were serious.[17]

The other two news outlets, the *Chinese Repository* and the *Canton Press*, generally urged more peaceful modes of engagement. Although the *Repository*, established in May 1832 and soon available almost worldwide, is often erroneously cited as an example of a British periodical in Canton, it was edited by the American missionary Elijah Coleman Bridgman and bankrolled by his compatriot David Washington Cincinnatus Olyphant, a fierce critic of the opium trade.[18] Still, like the *Register*, it initially focused on improving Britain's position in China (many of the articles written by Bridgman and by Olyphant's associate, Charles W. King, also an American). The *Press*, founded in 1835, was funded by Lancelot Dent following a controversy among the private traders after the end of the Company's monopoly. On one side were Jardine, Matheson, Lindsay, and the fiery James Innes. The other side was represented by former Company servants such as James Frederick

Nugent Daniell and John Claremont Whiteman, and by Dent, who then funded an alternative publication. The *Press* was edited first by W. H. Franklyn and then until 1844 by Edmond Moller, who although originally Danish or German was fluent in English and appears to have been a naturalized British citizen.[19]

These periodicals were part and parcel of Western commercial and religious expansion in China. The merchants and missionaries who supported them and contributed articles were committed to opening China, sometimes by force. And the relationship between knowledge and power was abundantly clear: to be opened, China had to be understood. All three publications arose from the weakening of the East India Company, as the decline of Company control and the rise of free trade saw not only the expansion of the foreign community in Canton and Macao, from private traders to missionaries, but also an expansion of information. All three were also made possible by the loosening of the Canton System, which they eventually helped end by giving foreigners the upper hand over the Chinese. Beginning with the establishment of the *Register*, for the first time all foreign traders enjoyed the same access to information on China and on the latest commercial terms.[20]

As in other British communities overseas, these publications were started with local readers in mind and were outlets for expressing both rivalry and cooperation. They were soon used for obtaining support at home and for imagining the China Britons into a wider trans-imperial British identity.[21] Although they were sojourners, like the settlers in South Africa, Australia, and New Zealand these Britons constructed a discourse around the need to defend their practices—especially selling opium—from the charges leveled against them by critics at home. The press not only reflected the attitudes of editors and owners, and attempted to influence opinion both in Canton and abroad, but also enabled local British residents to voice their views on a variety of matters. It helped shape a British "maritime public sphere" that stretched from Canton to Singapore and India and all the way to Britain.[22] And it hoped to convince politicians, merchants, and industrialists at home that Britain's position was in dire need of improvement.

Many public debates drew on information from books and pamphlets by Britons who had been in China, and from these periodicals. In 1840, during the early stages of the Opium War, Hugh Lindsay wrote from London (as "A Resident in China") that it was "hardly necessary" to note how "very useful" the Canton press had been from the start of the "very serious" disputes with China. "Without these contributions from the pens of very competent and intelligent individuals on the spot, we should all have been very much in the dark as to what has been going on in China, whereas the whole is now spread out before us."[23] Yet the press was also a place where Britons in

China debated and argued about how to resolve disputes and effect change. Well into the Opium War and after the occupation of Hong Kong in January 1841, the *Register* and *Press* in particular reflected and sometimes reinforced the differences among the community, bickering constantly with each other though rarely with the *Repository*, whose scholarly aura generally kept it above reproach.

Many of these men never met or even lived in the same era. And there was a huge difference between a Briton of Macartney's era and one of "Ramrod's"— between the early days of the French Revolution and the world of steam and the post-Waterloo years. But they all lived in or passed through the port of Canton. Boasting a population of more than 750,000, Canton was not just one of the largest cities in the world: except for Macao, it was the only place in China where Europeans and Chinese encountered each other regularly. The city was mainly a place for trading, but it was also one for observing and learning. The conventional emphasis on politics and diplomacy when studying early Sino-British relations has obscured some of the cultural and social aspects of these encounters, preventing us from seeing Canton as a place and a process: a place from where China could be observed and interpreted; and a process for doing this observing and interpreting. For these Britons, Canton was both physical and epistemological.

No one was naive enough to assume that China could be understood entirely through Canton. As Basil Hall of the Amherst embassy reminded his readers, it would be as unfair to judge China by the "state of society as the great sea-port of Canton" than to assess England from its grimy shipyards or dockyards.[24] And despite their frequent complaints about the low moral character of the inhabitants of Canton, these Britons often warned against making assumptions about China based on Canton. John Davis insisted that the Chinese had been "under-estimated" or "despised" because of their "moral attribute." This, he cautioned, made as much sense as trying to "form an estimate of our national character in England" from "some commercial sea-port." If the British judged the Chinese solely on their experience at Canton, "we in fact become as illiberal as themselves."[25]

Still, even though working and living there meant being confined to a small section of the city, with few opportunities to explore the surrounding countryside, Canton provided a firsthand understanding of China. According to Hall, the members of the Amherst embassy, after traveling more than one thousand miles in China, had in only several days in Canton not only seen "everything they had met with before, but could observe it to better purpose than during the journey."[26] Chief physician and naturalist to the embassy, Clarke Abel was particularly interested in Chinese medicine and botany.

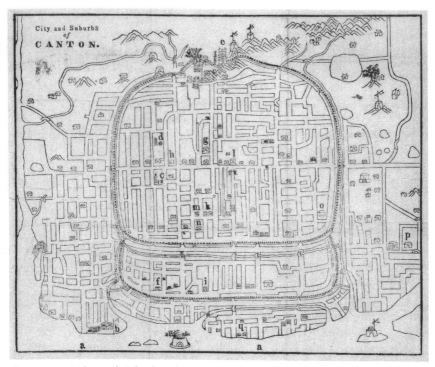

Figure I.5. "City and Suburbs of Canton." In *Chinese Repository* 2, no. 4 (August 1833). The foreign factories are marked with "b" in the lower left-hand corner; "a" denotes the Pearl River. Barry Lawrence Rudman Antique Maps Inc.

From the coast to and from Peking, he paid especially close attention to plants and insects and to illness and disease. His stay in Canton, however, provided the opportunity for much deeper and sustained contact. There he could visit pharmacies, learning how Chinese medicine was sold and administered. With a Company physician as interpreter, Abel met one of the "most respectable native practitioners of Canton."[27]

Canton was also a place for scrutinizing Chinese religious practices. Abel recalled how the Amherst embassy's time there provided its only chance to see Buddhist rites on "a great scale," for the embassy was housed in parts of a large Buddhist temple.[28] John Davis described a Buddhist temple in a suburb beyond the city walls, with one hundred priests and "several spacious halls" and another "very large" temple and monastery across the river from the foreign factories.[29] Charles Downing regretted how "the present limited state of our intercourse" prevented "the transient visitor" from learning much about Chinese religious beliefs and practices. Fortunately, although most visitors to Canton had little chance to become "personally acquainted" with

Confucianism, Downing had ample opportunity to observe the "ceremonies of other sects" and "idolatrous practices"—not to mention *fengshui* ("the pains which are taken to appease the spirits of the wind and waters by the native sailors").[30]

In Canton, they could witness how opium was consumed, as well as the effects of what they often called this "pernicious drug." Opium smokers, wrote Abel, had "a very peculiar, sottish, and sleepy physiognomy, in consequence of the whole visage being turgid with blood."[31] While John Barrow in 1804 explained that opium was "too expensive to be used by the common people," and Abel in 1818 wrote that "no opium is exposed for sale in the shops, probably because it is a contraband article," those who were in Canton in the 1830s saw a very different situation.[32] John Davis observed how the consumption of opium had "pervaded all classes" and had spread with "astonishing rapidity through the country." The "engrossing taste of all ranks and degrees" of Chinese people meant the importation of opium had in recent years "exceeded the aggregate value of every other English import combined."[33] They could also see the conniving and corruption associated with the opium trade. Walter Medhurst wrote in 1838 that "no one makes a secret of the business or the practice, and though the officers of government are loud in denouncing the indulgence in public, they privately wink at what is patronised by their own example, or subservient to their own interests."[34]

Britons never simply lived in or traveled through Canton, however: they understood and interpreted it for their own purposes. Canton became a place for refining, correcting, or even refuting existing images of China. Charles Downing explained how it was entirely different from the painted Chinese porcelain he had seen in England, which "would make you imagine that the whole country was laid out as a parterre, with gravel walks and grottos; that you could not move one step without danger of running against a crockery-ware pagoda, or into a canal, filled with gold and silver fish." He warned against the "very erroneous opinions" that "have prevailed in Europe with regard to the character of the Chinese, and the degree of civilization to which they have arrived." Even in England, a "great proportion of the more unenlightened classes" looked upon "the sons of Han as a peculiar and odd kind of savages or barbarians, and are almost unwilling to believe that such outlandish people possess any useful or praiseworthy institutions."[35]

These men's curiosity rarely started or ended with China. Indeed, scholars have rarely asked what knowledge of the fabled Middle Kingdom foreigners took with them to China, or how it changed along the way and once they arrived—especially since no one went directly from England to China but via many other places, including South America, Africa, India, and the East Indies.[36] And British knowledge of China was shaped partly by British experiences and networks in South and Southeast Asia.[37] China thus existed along a spectrum of foreign locales, and no one who went to China did so without making comparisons with other places. We often forget what happened in China was part of the larger and longer process of British encounters with "indigenous" peoples.[38]

Several main themes emerge from these writings, forming a British network of information about China that was circulated and often recirculated: the lack of morality among Chinese people; their hostility and contempt for foreigners; their backward technology and despotic government; and their superstition and idolatry. Yet not everything in these accounts was condemnatory or disparaging. In what became a standard trope of Chinese industriousness and commercial honesty, John Davis described the Chinese as "the most steady, considerate, and matter-of-fact people in the world, who in grave matters of business are often a match for the best of Europeans." He observed "a business-like character about the Chinese which assimilates them in a striking manner to the most intelligent nations of the west, and certainly marks them out, in very prominent relief, from the rest of Asiatics." Odd as it might seem, Davis argued, "in every thing which enters into the composition of actively industrious and well-organized communities, there is vastly less difference between them and the English, French, and Americans than between these and the inhabitants of Spain and Portugal, whose proneness to stolid bigotry and oriental laziness were perhaps in part imbibed from the Arabs."[39]

Political and ideological agendas also differed. The members of the Macartney and Amherst embassies, for example, had different reasons for being in China and writing about it than missionaries and other long-term residents did. And these Britons often asked important questions. To be sure, exposure to China and its people often reinforced British attitudes of superiority. There is little evidence to suggest their time in China caused Britons to question their own civilization, identities, or ideologies, let alone the righteousness of the British presence there. The writings betray no shortage of confidence and disdain. Yet they also contain plenty of wondering and questioning, ambivalence and sometimes even self-doubt. Some Britons hoped China could be opened without force. Charles Downing aimed in his three volumes to reveal "the absurdity of prejudice" Chinese and Europeans in Canton had for each other. "The foreigners there regard the natives with dislike and contempt, as if they were of an inferior nature. The Chinese, in their turn, call the strangers barbarians and Fan-quis, and seem to loathe them as real demons and infernal spirits. They have no kind of sympathy or fellow-feeling with the inhabitants of other nations."[40]

Like the men who made the long journey to China to make their fortunes or convert the Chinese to Christianity, attitudes came and went. They also changed over time. In a letter to a friend at home, an anonymous Irishman explained in 1804 that he had finally learned the Chinese could no more be judged through Western standards than Europeans could be through Chinese ones; his long residence in Canton had given its inhabitants "so warm a place in my heart, that I am almost enthusiastic about them."[41] In October 1807, shortly after arriving in China, Robert Morrison complained in a letter home how in Canton "the grossest idolatry prevails."[42] Ten years later he wrote that although the Chinese had imported many of their divinities from India, at least they had omitted the "gross indecent parts" of Indian "superstitions."[43] In early 1834 he confided to his son John Robert, who had become the chief interpreter for the British private traders in Canton, that he found his studies in the Chinese "and other" scriptures "very interesting and edifying." Morrison now advised his son to read the Confucian classics, which "though pagan," were "exhibitions of the highest morality of the human mind" in China and, unlike the Greek and Roman classics, would neither lower nor lead to the loss of "the moral sense."[44]

Missionaries such as Morrison have often been criticized for aiding British expansion in China.[45] But this does not mean they all supported the use of force in opening China; some of their writings can be read as attempts to decrease the likelihood of conflict with China, partly by encouraging a greater appreciation of China and its people. Even if missionaries were critical of Chinese idolatry (as they saw it), they respected and admired certain aspects of Chinese culture. In his *View of China* (1817), Morrison argued that although in China there was "much to blame," there was also "perhaps something from which to learn." For one, they preferred reason to violence. "A Chinese would stand and reason with a man, when an Englishman would knock him down, or an Italian stab him. It is needless to say which is the more rational mode of proceeding." Morrison described the Chinese as "selfish, cold-blooded, and inhumane" and "haughty, insolent, fraudulent and inhospitable" to foreigners. But he praised them for their mildness, urbanity, and industry, and for their respect for parents and the aged.[46]

Walter Medhurst also lauded China for its advanced civilization. Dividing the peoples of the world into savage and civilized, he placed the Chinese in the latter category: they were a "quiet, orderly, well-behaved nation, exhibiting many traces of civilization, and displaying them at a period when the rest of mankind were for the most part sunk in barbarism." He especially admired their love for propriety and reciprocity. "In no unchristian country do we find such attention paid to ceremony, such polish in daily intercourse, and so many compliments passing to and fro, as among the Chinese." This civilization could be seen "in a more substantial form" in the Chinese discovery of paper, gunpowder, and the compass—long before they had "given an extraordinary impulse to the progress of civilization in Europe."[47] Even George Lay, who wrote at length about the moral and physical deficiencies of the Chinese people, was impressed by the tolerance of Buddhism, Taoism, and Confucianism. "Worshipers of all sects and parties seem to bear and forbear . . . content to leave the sword of persecution in its peaceful scabbard."[48]

No one suggested that understanding China was a straightforward process. Aware of the contemporary European interest in China, Charles Downing explained that in an empire of "such vast extent, and the three hundred millions of inhabitants composed of so many nations, Chinese, Tartars, Monguls [sic], Indian Lolos, and savage Miaos from the mountains, it cannot be supposed that they should all have the same ideas on these subjects."[49] They realized understanding China meant confirming, correcting, or even refuting previous knowledge and the many ideas about China circulating in Europe, some influenced by the pronouncements of the Jesuit missionaries (who had been operating in China since the 1500s and continued to enjoy some influence in the imperial capital), some in direct opposition to them, and some derived from Chinese or Chinese-like artwork. "People in Europe," John Davis lamented, "have been strangely misled, in their notions of Chinese physiognomy and appearance, by the figures represented on those specimens of manufacture which proceed from Canton, and which are commonly in a style of broad caricature."[50]

Nor were Britons in China as ignorant of Chinese languages and culture as has often been assumed—including, as we shall see, by some contemporary observers. Chinese porcelain, painting, and furniture fascinated Britons in China as they did those at home.[51] Aeneas Anderson, Lord Macartney's valet, described the porcelain warehouses in Canton as superior to any in the world, "for extent, grandeur, and stock in trade."[52] Other trade goods also stimulated an interest in Chinese horticulture, especially among British naturalists.[53] And the Company's factory at Canton played a far more active role in the development of British knowledge of China than is usually assumed.[54] Almost all the major British sinologists of the early 1800s were "products of, or associated with," the factory, which had better resources for studying Chinese culture than contemporary libraries in Europe and was "a key site of knowledge production" about China.[55] From 1808, when Select Committee president John William Roberts appointed Robert Morrison as interpreter and supported his studies, to the final days of the Company's monopoly, the Select Committee promoted the study of Chinese, often against the views of the Court of Directors in London.[56]

The end of the East India Company's monopoly destroyed the "promising future" of Britain's "earliest school of Chinese studies."[57] This was "a major blow" for British sinology, for the new Canton Chamber of Commerce, which replaced the Select Committee to manage British affairs in China, had little interest in sponsoring knowledge of China.[58] Yet learning about China, and transmitting this knowledge home, did not end with the closure of the Company's factory. John Robert Morrison contributed articles to the *Repository*, as did Robert Hugh Inglis, a Company officer who became a private trader. John Davis wrote several books after leaving China in early 1835.[59] Charles Downing published his three volumes in 1838, the same year as Walter Medhurst's *China: Its State and Prospects*. George Lay published *The Chinese as They Are* in 1841, during the Opium War.

As the following chapters show, long-term residents and short-term visitors alike offered an array of explanations for how China had become the kind of place it had. There was never one single or unified approach. For those with a knowledge of Chinese history, we see in chapter 1, the Canton System and its restrictions were an anomaly, which meant they might be ended. Some blamed the Manchus for amplifying traditional Chinese concerns about relations with the outside world, while others realized the Qing government's attitudes toward foreign trade were driven by the rise of British power elsewhere in Asia. Others blamed the restrictions on China's stagnation and despotism, which by confining Western trade to Canton not only hampered the improvement of relations with the outside world but also deprived China of the rewards more trade could bring. Ending the Canton System would thus benefit everyone: free trade would ensue and the Chinese people would welcome being liberated from Manchu despotism. Yet these Britons sometimes acknowledged that foreigners, even the British, had done little to commend themselves to the Chinese.

The solutions for improving this sorry state of affairs, the subject of chapter 2, were as diverse as the explanations. Even after the end of the Company's monopoly and the Napier fiasco, there was never any consensus. The most commonly proposed solution was for Britain to take a more aggressive stance. But these approaches varied and were never accepted by all members of the British community in China. And even those who called for a tougher policy often urged caution and restraint. Private traders such as James Matheson and Hugh Lindsay hurried back to Britain to drum up support for their cause. But other China hands, both in Canton and in Britain, had different opinions. For George Thomas Staunton, the Canton System worked well and needed only minor changes. And even when Britons blamed the problems they faced in Canton primarily on the Qing authorities, they often admitted they could do more to improve their own situation. Many believed they had weakened their position by failing to convince their compatriots at home and in India how much the Chinese needed foreign trade. Some suggested trying to open a second port in China, though only in the 1830s did anyone call seriously for an alternative to Canton.

No one professed to be the only reliable source of information on China. Still, whether embassy members, merchants, or missionaries, Britons who spent time in China believed that only those who had been there could truly understand it. As chapter 3 shows, they also disagreed on the best way to do so, which could be as much about having different opinions as about highlighting the originality of their own work. Books, pamphlets, and other writings on China invariably opened by declaring their authors' credentials, and even visitors found ways to distinguish their accounts. Until the end of the Company's monopoly, the issue the China hands tried the hardest to exert their experience and authority upon was whether the monopoly should be extended. Many, especially those who had worked for the Company, stressed how little the British public—and even the government—knew about China or appreciated the hardships British traders there faced. Those who returned to Britain after a long service in China were particularly irritated by the lack of understanding and support. The belief that only those with direct experience could understand what was happening in China deepened during the Opium War and after the British occupied the island of Hong Kong in January 1841.

Most Britons who wrote about China during or after their time there were interested in improving Britain's position and opening the empire to more trade. Opening China, however, required understanding it. Chapter 4 examines three frequently discussed and interrelated subjects: the size of China's population, the extent of infanticide (especially among girls), and the origins and practice of footbinding. The huge population offered an almost unlimited market for British exports. For some, it also explained how China functioned—or failed to function as they thought it should. Assessing the size of China's population was also a way of showing expertise, which became especially important with the growing number of Western works on China. Determining the extent of infanticide was likewise a matter of claiming experience and authority, as was attempting to figure out why footbinding came about and was so prevalent. The Opium War and the opening of China to British soldiers, naval officers, and military surgeons provided unprecedented opportunities for Britons to encounter women and girls with bound feet, though greater exposure to more Chinese people did not necessarily mean more reliable information about footbinding.

By the late 1830s, the topic Britons in China debated and argued about the most was the opium trade. Chapter 5 shows how these disputes reflected a wide range of opinions, not only about China's right to prohibit opium and Britain's to import it, but also about the British presence in China. While Qing scholar-officials waged what has been called "the inner Opium War"—deciding how to cope with the opium crisis and the British threat—Britons in Canton disagreed with each other and those at home about how to respond to the Chinese government's efforts to curb the opium trade. Especially after the surrender and destruction of the opium in 1839, they paid close attention to the debates in Britain and India regarding the opium and China crises. And they waged another campaign as part of their own inner Opium War: obtaining compensation from the British government for the surrendered "healthful and exhilarating" drug "Ramrod" had extolled.

## NOTES

1. *Canton Press* 5, no. 2 (12 October 1839): n.p.; original emphasis.
2. On the Canton System, see: Paul Van Dyke, *The Canton Trade: Life and Enterprise on the China Coast, 1700–1845* (Hong Kong: Hong Kong University Press, 2005); Li Guorong, Qin Bo, and Li Bing, eds., *Diguo shanghang: Guangzhou shisanhang* [Imperial Trading Houses: Guangzhou's Thirteen Hongs] (Beijing: Jiuzhou chubanshe, 2007); Leonard Blussé, *Visible Cities: Canton, Nagasaki, and Batavia and the Coming of the Americans* (Cambridge, MA: Harvard University Press, 2008); Zhang Wenqin, *Guangdong shisanhang yu zaoqi Zhongxi guanxi* [The Thirteen Hongs of Canton and Early Sino-Western Relations] (Guangzhou: Guangdong jingji chubanshe, 2009); Tan Yuanheng, *Guangzhou shisanhang: Ming-Qing 300 nian jiannan quzhe de waimao zhi lu* [The Thirteen Hongs of Guangzhou: The Ming-Qing's 300-Year-Long Difficult and Winding Road of Foreign Trade] (Guangzhou: Guangdong jingji chubanshe, 2015); John M. Carroll, *Canton Days: British Life and Death in China* (Lanham, MD: Rowman & Littlefield, 2020), chap. 1, and "The Canton System: Conflict and Accommodation in the Contact Zone," *Journal of the Hong Kong Branch of the Royal Asiatic Society* 50 (2010): 51–66.
3. James Matheson, *The Present Position and Prospects of the British Trade with China: Together with an Outline of Some Leading Occurrences in Its Past History* (London: Smith, Elder, 1836), 51. On Napier's mission and death, see Priscilla Napier, *Barbarian Eye: Lord Napier in China, 1834, Prelude to Hong Kong* (London: Washington Brassey's, 1995); Carroll, *Canton Days*, 259–72.
4. Matheson to Palmerston, 21 December 1835, FO 17/12/407–10, The National Archives of the UK.
5. Hugh Hamilton Lindsay, *Letter to the Right Honourable Viscount Lord Palmerston on the British Relations with China* (London: Saunders and Otley, 1836), 12–13, 18.
6. "Brito-Chinese Polities," *Canton Press* 1, no. 49 (13 August 1836): 388–89. On British attitudes toward China and the decision to go war, see: Glenn Melancon, "Peaceful Intentions: The First British Trade Commission in China, 1833–5," *Historical*

*Research* 72, no. 180 (2000): 33–74; Harry G. Gelber, *Opium, Soldiers and Evangelicals: Britain's 1840–42 War with China, and Its Aftermath* (Basingstoke, UK: Palgrave Macmillan, 2004); Hao Gao, "Prelude to the Opium War? British Reactions to the 'Napier Fizzle' and Attitudes towards China in the Mid Eighteen-Thirties," *Historical Research* 87, no. 237 (2014): 491–509, "Going to War against the Middle Kingdom? Continuity and Change in British Attitudes towards Qing China (1783–1840)," *Journal of Imperial and Commonwealth History* 45, no. 2 (2017): 210–31, and *Creating the Opium War: British Imperial Attitudes towards China, 1792–1840* (Manchester: Manchester University Press, 2020), especially chaps. 4–5.

7. On Jardine and Matheson, see: Alain Le Pichon, ed., *China Trade and Empire: Jardine, Matheson & Co. and the Origins of British Rule in Hong Kong, 1827–1843* (Oxford: Published for the British Academy by Oxford University Press, 2006); Richard J. Grace, *Opium and Empire: The Lives and Careers of William Jardine and James Matheson* (Montreal: McGill-Queen's University Press, 2014).

8. Stephen R. Platt, *Imperial Twilight: The Opium War and the End of China's Last Golden Age* (New York: Knopf, 2018), 382–88.

9. On the limited extent of Jardine and Matheson's influence, see: Glenn Melancon, "Honour in Opium? The British Declaration of War on China, 1835–1840," *International History Review* 21, no. 4 (1999): 854–74, and *Britain's China Policy and the Opium Crisis: Balancing Drugs, Violence and National Honour, 1833–1840* (Aldershot, UK: Ashgate, 2003). Palmerston had already begun to make his own plans for dealing with the China crisis, soon after the news that Lin had blockaded the foreign factories reached England in August 1839.

10. Cf. Song-Chuan Chen, *Merchants of War and Peace: British Knowledge of China in the Making of the Opium War* (Hong Kong: Hong Kong University Press, 2017), chap. 2.

11. On the Macartney embassy, see: James L. Hevia, *Cherishing Men from Afar: Qing Guest Ritual and the Macartney Mission of 1793* (Durham, NC: Duke University Press, 1995); Robert Bickers, ed., *Ritual and Diplomacy: The Macartney Mission to China, 1792–1794* (London: British Association for Chinese Studies and Wellsweep Press, 1993); Xiaoqing Ye, "Ascendant Peace in the Four Seas: Tributary Drama and the Macartney Mission of 1793," *Late Imperial China* 26, no. 2 (2005): 89–113; and Henrietta Harrison, "Chinese and British Diplomatic Gifts in the Macartney Embassy of 1833," *English Historical Review* 133, no. 560 (2018): 65–97.

12. On the Amherst embassy, see: Eun Kyung Min, "Narrating the Far East: Commercial Civility and Ceremony in the Amherst Embassy to China (1816–1817)," in *Interpreting Colonialism*, ed. Byron R. Wells and Philip Steward (Oxford: Voltaire Foundation, 2004), 160–80; Hao Gao, "The Amherst Embassy and British Discoveries in China," *History* 99, no. 337 (2014): 568–87, and "The 'Inner Kowtow Controversy' during the Amherst Embassy to China, 1816–1817," *Diplomacy and Statecraft* 27, no. 4 (2016): 595–614; Peter J. Kitson, "The Dark Gift: John Francis Davis, Thomas De Quincey and the Amherst Embassy to China of 1816,'" in *Writing China: Essays on the Amherst Embassy (1816) and Sino-British Cultural Relations*, ed. Peter J. Kitson and Robert Markley (Cambridge: D.S. Brewer, 2016), 56–82, and "The 'Catastrophe of This New Chinese Mission': The Amherst Embassy to China of

1816," in *Early Encounters between East Asia and Europe: Telling Failures*, ed. Ralf Hertel and Michael Keevak (Abingdon, UK: Routledge, 2017), 67–83; John M. Carroll, "The Amherst Embassy to China: A Whimper and a Bang," *Journal of Imperial and Commonwealth History* 48, no. 1 (2020): 15–38.

13. On travel accounts and firsthand experience, see Nicholas Clifford, *"A Truthful Impression of the Country": British and American Travel Writing in China, 1880–1949* (Ann Arbor: University of Michigan Press, 2001).

14. *Canton Register* 1, no. 7 (11 February 1828): 26.

15. *Canton Register* 1, no. 11 (15 March 1828): 41.

16. *Canton Register* 1, no. 37 (18 October 1828): 151.

17. *Canton Register* 8, no. 14 (7 April 1835): 54.

18. Elizabeth L. Malcolm, "The *Chinese Repository* and Western Literature on China 1800 to 1850," *Modern Asian Studies* 7, no. 2 (1973): 165–78; Murray Rubinstein, "The Wars They Wanted: American Missionaries' Use of *The Chinese Repository* before the Opium War," *American Neptune* 48 (1988): 271–82; Kendall A. Johnson, *The New Middle Kingdom: China and the Early American Romance of Free Trade* (Baltimore: Johns Hopkins University Press, 2017), chap. 4.

19. Prescott Clarke, "The Development of the English Language Press on the China Coast, 1827–1881," MA dissertation, University of London, 1961, 1–71, especially 40–41, 44–45; Frank H. H. King, ed., and Prescott Clarke, *A Research Guide to China-Coast Newspapers, 1822–1911* (Cambridge, MA: East Asian Research Center, Harvard University, 1965), chap. 2.

20. Van Dyke, *Canton Trade*, 108, 174–75.

21. Alan Lester, "British Settler Discourse and the Circuits of Empire," *History Workshop Journal* 54 (2002): 24–48.

22. Song-Chuan Chen, "The British Maritime Public Sphere in Canton, 1827–1839," PhD dissertation, University of Cambridge, 2008, and *Merchants of War and Peace*, 16–20.

23. A Resident in China [Hugh Hamilton Lindsay], *Remarks on Occurrences in China, since the Opium Seizure in March 1839, to the Latest Date* (London: Sherwood, Gilbert, and Piper, 1840), 100.

24. Basil Hall, *Voyage to Loo-Choo, and Other Places in the Eastern Seas, in the Year 1816; Including an Account of Captain Maxwell's Attack on the Batteries at Canton; and Notes of an Interview with Buonaparte at St. Helena, in August 1817* (Edinburgh: A. Constable, 1826), 40–41.

25. John Francis Davis, *The Chinese: A General Description of That Empire and Its Inhabitants* (London: Charles Knight, 1836), vol. 1, 237–38.

26. Hall, *Voyage to Loo-Choo*, 298.

27. Clarke Abel, *Narrative of a Journey in the Interior of China, and of a Voyage to and from That Country, in the Year 1816 and 1817: Containing an Account of the Most Interesting Transactions of Lord Amherst's Embassy to the Court of Pekin, and Observations on the Countries Which It Visited* (London: Orme and Brown, 1818), 216.

28. Abel, *Narrative of a Journey*, 226.

29. Davis, *Chinese*, vol. 2, 20.

30. Downing, *Fan Qui*, vol. 2, 288, vol. 3, 18.

31. Abel, *Narrative of a Journey*, 215.

32. John Barrow, *Travels in China, Containing Descriptions, Observations, and Comparisons, Made and Collected in the Course of a Short Residence at the Imperial Palace of Yuen-Min-Yuen, and on a Subsequent Journey through the Country from Pekin to Canton in Which It Is Attempted to Appreciate the Rank That the Extraordinary Empire May Be Considered to Hold in the Scale of Civilized Nations* (London: Cadell and Davies, 1804), 152; Abel, *Narrative of a Journey*, 214.

33. Davis, *Chinese*, vol. 2, 432, 436.

34. Walter Henry Medhurst, *China: Its State and Prospects, with Special Reference to the Spread of the Gospel; Containing Allusions to the Antiquity, Extent, Population, Civilization, Literature, and Religion of the Chinese* (London: J. Snow, 1838), 87.

35. Downing, *Fan Qui*, vol. 1, 66–67.

36. Important exceptions include Clifford, *"Truthful Impression of the Country,"* and Robert Bickers, *The Scramble for China: Foreign Devils in the Qing Empire, 1832–1914* (London: Allen Lane, 2011).

37. Ulrike Hillemann, *Asian Empire and British Knowledge: China and the Networks of British Imperial Expansion* (New York: Palgrave Macmillan, 2009).

38. See, for example: Martin Daunton and Rick Halpern, eds., *Empire and Others: British Encounters with Indigenous Peoples, 1600–1850* (London: University College of London Press, 1999), 42–78; and Philippa Levine, "Naked Natives and Noble Savages," in *The Cultural Construction of the British World*, ed. Barry Crosbie and Mark Hampton (Manchester: Manchester University Press), 17–38.

39. Davis, *Chinese*, vol. 1, 237–38, 251, 359.

40. Downing, *Fan Qui*, vol. 3, 316–17.

41. Anon., *An Intercepted Letter from J— T—, Esq. Writer at Canton, to His Friend in Dublin, Ireland*, 3rd ed. (Dublin: N. M. Mahon, 1804), 41. This is an English retranslation of a letter originally written in English, sent home on the East India Company's ship *Althea*, but captured along with a collection of others and taken to Mauritius by the French, who translated and published the correspondence.

42. Letter to Thomas Wilson, Esq., 9 October 1806, in Eliza Morrison, *Memoirs of the Life and Labours of Robert Morrison, Compiled by His Widow, with Critical Notices of His Chinese Works, by Samuel Kidd* (London: Longman, Orme, Brown, Green and Longmans, 1839), vol. 1, 172.

43. Robert Morrison, *A View of China, for Philological Purposes: Containing a Sketch of Chinese Chronology, Geography, Government, Religion & Customs* (Macao: Printed at the Honorable East India Company's Press by P. P. Thoms, 1817; London: Black, Parbury, and Allen, 1817), 112.

44. Robert Morrison to John Robert Morrison, 18 February 1834, MS5829, Wellcome Library. On Morrison's life in China, see Carroll, *Canton Days*, chap. 7.

45. For example: Gu Changsheng, *Cong Malisun dao Situ Leideng: Laihua xinjiao chuanjiaoshi pingzhuan* [From Robert Morrison to Leighton Stuart: Critical Biographies of Missionaries to China] (Shanghai: Shanghai renmin chubanshe, 1985), chap. 1.

46. Morrison, *View of China*, 121–22, 124–25.

47. Medhurst, *China*, 97, 99, 101, 141. On Medhurst's respect for Chinese culture, see Elizabeth H. Chang, "Converting Chinese Eyes: Rev. W. H. Medhurst, 'Passing,' and the Victorian Vision of China," in *A Century of Travels in China: Critical Essays on Travel Writing from the 1840s to the 1940s*, ed. Douglas Kerr and Julia Kuehn (Hong Kong: Hong Kong University Press, 2007), 27–38.

48. G. [George] Tradescant Lay, *The Chinese as They Are: Their Moral, Social, and Literary Character* (London: W. Ball, 1841), 100.

49. Downing, *Fan Qui in China*, vol. 2, 287.

50. Davis, *Chinese*, vol. 1, 250–51.

51. Elizabeth Hope Chang, *Britain's Chinese Eye: Literature, Empire, and Aesthetics in Nineteenth-Century Britain* (Stanford: Stanford University Press, 2010); David Porter, *The Chinese Taste in Eighteenth-Century England* (Cambridge: Cambridge University Press, 2010).

52. Aeneas Anderson, *A Narrative of the British Embassy to China in the Years 1792, 1793, and 1794; Containing the Various Circumstances of the Embassy, with Accounts of Customs and Manners of the Chinese, and a Description of the Country, Towns, Cities, &c. &c.* (London: J. Debrett, 1795), 258.

53. Fa-ti Fan, *British Naturalists in Qing China: Science, Empire, and Cultural Encounter* (Cambridge, MA: Harvard University Press, 2004), 13–14.

54. T. H. Barrett, *Singular Listlessness: A Short History of Chinese Books and British Scholars* (London: Wellsweep Press, 1989), 53–58.

55. Peter J. Kitson, *Forging Romantic China: Sino-British Cultural Exchange 1760–1840* (Cambridge: Cambridge University Press, 2013), 81, 83.

56. Susan Reed Stifler, "The Language Students of the East India Company's Canton Factory," *Journal of the North China Branch of the Royal Asiatic Society* 69 (1938): 67–69.

57. Stifler, "Language Students," 69.

58. Kitson, *Forging Romantic China*, 93.

59. Tamara S. Wagner, "Sketching China and the Self-Portrait of a Post-Romantic Traveler: John Francis Davis's Rewriting of China in the 1840s," in Kerr and Kuehn, *Century of Travels in China*, 13–26.

*Chapter One*

# The Crying Abuses
## *Explanations*

The most common complaints by Britons who visited or lived in China were about what the *Canton Register* called the "crying abuses" of the Canton System.[1] "As soon as a foreign vessel arrives in China her submission to the Government begins," an anonymous merchant wrote in late 1829.[2] In December 1830 more than forty British traders petitioned the House of Commons, claiming they were subjected to "privations and treatment to which it would be difficult to find a parallel in any part of the world."[3] It was useless to "sit down quietly and hope for better times," a contributor to the *Register* contended in August 1831. Nor was it only the Chinese government that required convincing of the need for change: "the more fully acquainted those at home become with the *real* state of things in this country—the oftener and the stronger this is forced on their attention—the greater is our rational hope of redress."[4]

Calling for the restrictions on foreign trade to be ended meant understanding how they had come into existence in the first place, and why they continued to be enforced. These Britons realized the rulers of China who had devised a sophisticated mechanism for confining foreigners to a tiny section of Canton were not Chinese but Manchus. Well aware that the Canton System, far from simply a mechanism for regulating trade, reflected both external and domestic political concerns, they often noted how tensions on China's other borders and within the empire itself could have repercussions for foreigners in Canton. They hoped that developments on China's other frontiers might lead to favorable results in Canton. In March 1833 the *Chinese Repository* offered promising news from Kashgar, on China's western frontier. As the missionary and frequent contributor Robert Morrison explained, the Daoguang Emperor had recently freed the "Booriats" (presumably the Kirghiz, known in Qing sources as Burut), from "all imposts whatsoever," allowing them to bring their horses, sheep, and other livestock to sell without having to pay any duty or tax to the Qing government.[5]

Both subjects and participants in their own expanding empire in Asia, where the East India Company had often been an agent of disruption, many Britons appreciated the peace and order the Manchus had brought to China. It was a mistake, the private trader Robert Hugh Inglis argued in May 1835 in the *Repository*, to assume that the "Tartars," like the Goths, were "mere barbarians, who brought nothing but courage and energy of character into their new possession."[6] Others believed that by closing China to the Western world the Manchus had violated the "natural" tide of history, both Chinese and otherwise. The idea that the Canton System was "unnatural" became a common theme, especially after the end in 1834 of another unnatural system: the Company's monopoly, increasingly under siege in a nation becoming obsessed with free trade.[7]

Some blamed the restrictions of the Canton System on the perversion and corruption of the "Chinese character." Just as often, however, they offered more thoughtful and reasoned—though not necessarily accurate—explanations, including fear, jealousy, and xenophobia. "The government of China is bitter against everything European," Morrison wrote in April 1815 to the directors of the London Missionary Society, "except the profits of trade."[8] Others attributed the Canton System to China's traditional isolation. Struck by the "innocent" and "universal" joyfulness of the local population during the Lunar New Year festivities in February 1828, the *Register* saw evidence of a "disposition of freedom" that would have allowed a "friendly intercourse" had they not been restrained by the "peculiar" customs so "repulsive to the cultivation of social intimacy, and so inconsistent with a civilized nation."[9] An anonymous *Register* correspondent argued in January 1835 that the Qing government's "narrow policy" toward trade stemmed from the Confucian education system, which, because the great sage had lived at a time when China was "still in a low state of civilisation, without trade and manufactures," emphasized political wisdom at the expense of commerce.[10]

Still others believed Manchu rule had accentuated this exclusivity. In August 1830 the *Register* printed translations of correspondence from the 1770s between the governor-general of Guangdong and the hong merchants explaining the rules and regulations of the Canton System. These documents proved the system was designed to maintain "a constant, oppressive, and degrading espionage on all foreign merchants."[11] In August 1834 a frustrated Lord Napier, sent to superintend British trade in China after the end of the Company's monopoly, wrote that in its "extreme degree" of "mental imbecility" and "moral degradation," the Qing government was "entirely ignorant" of international law and hardly deserved to be treated by "civilized nations" according to the same rules they applied to themselves.[12] John Francis Davis, who had worked for the Company in Canton for twenty years and accompanied Lord Amherst's embassy to Peking, argued in 1836 that "the Tartars are at all times extremely jealous of any intimate connection arising between their Chinese subjects and foreigners; and this lies at the bottom of their rigid system of exclusion."[13] In January 1838 the *Canton Press* suggested that the "extreme reluctance" of the Chinese to allow foreigners to enter China resulted partly from their "peculiar manners" and the pride such "a long course of prosperity" had created, and partly from being ruled by "foreign conquerors" who feared "every collision with foreign nations as threatening the subversion of their power."[14]

## RESTRICTED CHINA

The Canton System was sometimes considered a historical anomaly. Although an argument against its restrictions, this also offered the possibility they might be ended. In 1833, shortly after the decision to end the Company's monopoly in China, former Select Committee president Charles Marjoribanks explained in a public letter to Charles Grant, president of the Board of Control that managed British affairs in India, how in the early years of British trade with China "all the different ports of the empire were open to our ships." It was only after the Manchu conquest in 1644 that the trade was restricted to Canton and controlled by the hong merchants.[15] In an October 1836 article on the dilapidated tombs of two foreigners (one a Spanish priest) he had discovered while "strolling over the hills" on the island of Honam (Henan), opposite the factories, a *Press* correspondent predicted that if foreigners were granted more freedom in China, "doubtless there would be discovered in many parts of it, various relicks [sic] of people from the western Nations, who, during the commencement of the present dynasty, were permitted to go whither they liked, and settled where they pleased."[16]

If only the rulers and people of China better understood their own history. In October 1833 a correspondent to the *Register* recommended that "one of our Anglo-Chinese sinalogues [sic]" take up the task in a "plain treatise" showing the "liberal sentiments of the ancient sages" toward foreign trade. Starting as far back as the Han Dynasty some two thousand years earlier, "we would be able to convince the Chinese, that the ancients, whom they wish to imitate in every thing, were very liberal in their intercourse with foreign nations." The records of the Tang and Song dynasties could "make the present narrow-minded generations blush." The Mongol emperors had been "decidedly in favor of foreign intercourse." And who had not heard of the "liberal principles" of the great Kublai Khan? "No true Chinaman could be offended by being obliged to acknowledge the principles of his ancestors as the true ones, nor could the most inquisitorial policy oppose the spread of ancient opinions upon this subject."[17] In July 1834, Robert Morrison's son John Robert remarked in the *Repository* how Chinese in the Tang, Song, and Ming dynasties had all demonstrated "far more commercial enterprise than their posterity of the present age." Although thousands of Chinese went to India each year to trade, this number would be three times larger, "were it not for the utter contempt with which the Celestial Empire treats all intercourse with foreign nations."[18]

John Davis argued that Chinese historical records provided "abundant evidence" that a "much more liberal as well as enterprising disposition once existed, in respect to foreign intercourse, than prevails at present." Their statistical records showed a "perfect knowledge" of the advantages of foreign trade, "a striking contrast to the indifference which the present Tartar Government affects to feel towards it." Before the Europeans arrived, the Chinese government had given "every encouragement to foreign commerce." Neighboring countries had sent missions "with a view to inviting mutual intercourse," while Chinese junks had even reached the Indian peninsula. Only after the Manchu conquest was European trade limited to Canton. Since then, the "jealous and watchful Tartar dominion" created by this "handful of barbarians" had "unquestionably occasioned many additional obstacles to an increased commerce with the rest of the world."[19]

Despite their resentment of the Manchus, for some Britons trying to understand the origins of the Canton System the early years of Qing rule became a golden age. They used their knowledge of this history to critique the current regime. Robert Morrison explained (correctly) that although for more than a century almost all European trade with China had been restricted to Canton and Macao, "it was not always so." At various points during the Ming Dynasty, the ports of Amoy (Xiamen), Ningpo (Ningbo), and nearby Chusan (Zhoushan) were opened to European trade and became "large ports for their commerce." In his twenty-third year on the throne, the Kangxi Emperor had reopened "all the ports of his empire, and allowed a *free trade* to his own subjects and to all foreign nations." Even after foreign trade and emigration were prohibited some thirty years later, the Qing government had occasionally made allowances. Early in the reign of Yongzheng, Kangxi's son, following population increases in the coastal provinces, merchants were allowed to trade with nations in Southeast Asia; some junk owners were even rewarded with official honors and titles for importing rice from Siam.[20]

James Goddard, a merchant who in December 1833 called for an embargo to help end the Canton System, also suggested the new British superintendent

Figure 1.1. Robert Morrison, 1824, by John Robert Wildman, oil on canvas, engraved. National Portrait Gallery, London

should use Kangxi's edicts opening the empire to trade to support his case. The "folly" of the Jesuits and their "speculative doctrines" had eventually forced the Qing authorities to change this policy, forcing commerce to "pay the debts of ecclesiastical arrogance."[21] Lord Napier explained to prime minister Earl Grey that Kangxi ("the first and greatest of all the Tartar race") had encouraged foreign trade and "invited the learned of all Europe to settle in his dominions." Had the Qianlong Emperor, Kangxi's grandson, never confined foreign trade to Canton, and had British trade not been conducted according to a monopoly that privileged the Company and the Chinese government—"without any reference to the convenience, comfort, or advantage of the people"—British trade would have spread far beyond Canton. Instead, the Company's willingness to concede to the Chinese "on every case of aggression" had only reinforced the Manchus' belief that the British depended on the trade with China.[22]

## STATIONARY CHINA

Those who did not eulogize Kangxi and his reign often argued that the Manchus had not only absorbed but also magnified China's traditional fear of foreigners and relative isolation compared to other empires. The *Register* regretted how the Manchus, even though foreigners themselves, had become the "stanchest [sic] advocates" of the Chinese policy of viewing foreign states as either "objects of dread or contempt."[23] China had historically spread "not by conquering, but by being conquered," the missionary Walter Henry Medhurst put it. Although the Manchus had subjugated China, by retaining rather than changing its political institutions and conforming themselves to its laws and customs, they had been "in fact, subdued by the Chinese: while China remained what China was, having only changed its rulers, and gained a great accession of territory."[24] Robert Inglis explained how what had mostly contributed to the "integrity and stability" of the empire was China's "isolated locality and peculiar language, which cut her off from communication with other large empires." What had originally been accidental had since under the Manchus become a "principle of safety by the government, which endeavors to introduce the character of *isolation* into all its departments." By "shrinking from communication with the rest of the world," China had "stood still, whilst Europe passed her in the career of knowledge."[25]

The notion of China having "stood still" for centuries—even millennia—had by the late eighteenth century become a common theme in European discourse.[26] It invariably figured in writings by foreigners who visited or resided there, and who often tried to show how this stagnancy, like the decline of the Qing Empire, was partly the result of China's limited contact with the outside world. Sometimes it was reinforced even by writers who could be otherwise sympathetic to China. George Thomas Staunton's decision to translate only one section of the Qing legal code, for example, created "an ossified image of China or Chinese law by fixing it with a single text." Staunton's translation "helped rekindle the already popular idea of a stationary or regressive China."[27] In his *View of China, for Philological Purposes*, published in 1817 in Macao by the Company, Robert Morrison explained that the Chinese had undergone "as many revolutions as any people on the earth." But he also emphasized China's stagnation, which he blamed on the "inflexible nature" of its language.[28]

Comparing the Qing and Russian empires ("the greatest indeed that exist in the world"), John Barrow, Lord Macartney's personal secretary on the first embassy, explained in 1804 why the two were now turning out so differently. Russia had emerged from its "state of barbarism" only one century earlier, but within another would "make a conspicuous figure among European nations, both in arts and arms"—even though the Russians' "natural genius" was "cramped in some degree" by their frigid climate. China's civilization, however, remained at the "same degree, or nearly so" as it had been two thousand years earlier. The reason was their different relations with the outside world:

> Russia invites and encourages foreigners to instruct her subjects in arts, sciences, and manufactures. China, from a spirit of pride and self-importance, as well as from jealousy, rejects and expels them. The language of Russia is easily acquired, and her subjects as easily learn those of other countries, whilst that of China is so difficult, or their method of learning it so defective, as to require the study of half the life of man to fit him for any of the ordinary employments of the state, and they have no knowledge of any language but their own. The one is in a state of youthful vigour, advancing daily in strength and knowledge; the other is worn out with old age and disease, and under its present state of existence is not likely to advance in any kind of improvement.[29]

Henry Ellis, second commissioner on the Amherst embassy, likewise believed China had become "stationary." The size of the empire, the "barbarism" of the neighboring tribes, and the infrequent of contact with other nations were partly to blame. But an even more significant and more deeply rooted cause was the "very nature" of China's "system of polity and morals," which had produced a "plausible exterior and apparent superiority" over other nations, thus creating a sense of complacency among philosophers and rulers alike. The result had been a "continued political aggregation, rather than union." Although the government had "readily" changed hands many times, each succeeding dynasty had preserved the civil institutions of its predecessor. The maxims of public administration and the habits of domestic life were so favorable to despotic rule that it would require either "uncommon liberality or obstinacy" for a conqueror to risk losing power by trying to

Figure 1.2. Sir John Barrow, 1st Bt., ca. 1810, attributed to John Jackson, oil on canvas. National Portrait Gallery, London

introduce any significant changes.[30] Henry Hayne, Amherst's private secretary, wrote that a water-powered grindstone the embassy passed on its way south to Canton was "as rude a specimen of Chinese mechanics as one can and will conceive," and was at least two or three decades behind even the "most uncultivated" of the European nations.[31]

This notion of a stagnant China became particularly pronounced in the 1830s, as Britons contrasted the dramatic (though very recent) changes at home with the status quo in China. In September 1834 the *Register* compared the Qing Empire to a "slumbering giant, who might by activity destroy the pigmy beings of the human species, but who is satisfied with possessing the spot where he rests in peace and quietness, and boasting of the strength of his limbs, which by long disuse cannot carry him, so that even children may tease him with impunity."[32] Robert Inglis wrote that China's "moral civilization is nearly the same now as in the time of the Assyrians."[33] Walter Medhurst explained that China had not witnessed the advances in science and the arts that distinguished Europe. "Railways, tunnels, machinery, and all the ramifications and operations of gas and steam, are not to be looked for in China." He could thus declare that China possessed "as much civilization as Turkey now, or England a few centuries ago."[34] In December 1839 the *Press* blamed China's stagnation mainly on the "iron rule of jealous foreign tyrants" who had allowed other nations, "naked barbarians at a time when the Chinese formed already a polished nation, far to outrun them in the race of improvement."[35]

## DESPOTIC CHINA

Even when Britons disagreed about the origins of the Canton System, they were usually convinced the restrictions on foreign trade reflected the wishes of the Qing government rather than of the general population. For Charles Marjoribanks, the mission up the coast in 1832 he had authorized as Select Committee president (but of which the Company's Court of Directors in London had disapproved) before he left Canton, was proof Chinese people everywhere were "most desirous of trade with the English" and "jealous of its being possessed so exclusively by the natives of Canton." The mission had been led by Hugh Hamilton Lindsay ("a most intelligent and enterprising member of the Factory, well acquainted with the Chinese language and character"), accompanied by the Prussian missionary Karl Gützlaff ("a man of very bold and daring character, and admirably conversant with the different dialects of the empire"). Lindsay been received "with great kindness and hospitality" by the people, Marjoribanks claimed, but with "much distrustful jealousy" by local officials. And even they had usually been interested in establishing trade, discouraged only by their fear of angering the emperor should they be discovered.[36] The *Register* argued that the voyage proved "the people of China" were keen to trade with foreigners and would "would gladly receive foreign vessels in their own ports, and thereby avail of the natural advantages which they possess."[37] Lord Napier believed that throughout the empire Chinese people were "most anxious" for British trade and only the "Tartar Government" was opposed.³⁸ The "body of the Chinese Nation is no doubt friendly to us," insisted the *Press* in February 1836. "We promote their own individuals [*sic*] interest, and the Government Officers thwart it."³⁹

Figure 1.3. Charles Albany Marjoribanks, 1835, by and published by Charles Turner, after Andrew Geddes, mezzotint. National Portrait Gallery, London

This "national policy" against foreign trade was possible only because the Qing government was despotic. "The vast empire," Marjoribanks wrote, "is held together by the superincumbent pressure of tyrannic power, acting on the minds of a naturally timid and peaceful people."⁴⁰ Despotism, which, given its popularity by the late nineteenth century in European discourse on China, most Britons would have been familiar with well even before setting foot there, became the explanation for almost everything wrong with China.⁴¹ John Robert Morrison wrote that although the Qing government was often praised and admired, its system of "*strict surveillance* and *universal responsibility*" gave it a stronger character of "military despotism" than any other civil government in the world.[42] According to the surgeon Charles Toogood Downing, despotism had created a police state powerful enough to silence the Chinese city, which at night became "as noiseless as a churchyard, and presents a great contrast to many cities in Europe, where the night-time is the season of jollity and amusement."[43] Despotism was frequently used to explain China's injustice and legal barbarity—especially in the rare cases when foreigners were executed for killing Chinese.[44] John Slade, editor of the *Register*, argued that the laws of China had so little regard for human life that not only were slavery, infanticide, and the sale of children allowed, "the execution of half a score of criminals is announced in the Canton daily paper, in much the same manner as a fashionable arrival or departure is in the Morning Post."[45]

Despotism was the reason for China's lack of cultural, intellectual, and scientific development. As John Davis saw it, "the mind under a despotism has few of those calls for exertion, among the bulk of the people, which in free states give it manly strength and vigour."[46] The blind traveler James Holman, who spent the autumn of 1830 in Macao and Canton, blamed the poor quality of the fine arts in China on the "baneful influence" of despotism. As weak as the artists of Canton were, they were superior to those anywhere else in China because of their exposure to foreign paintings.[47] Some Britons believed even the "arrangement of the Chinese garden around the singular body of the emperor starkly emphasized Asian despotism."[48] Despotism also explained the Chinese adherence to Buddhism and resistance to Christianity. "Three hundred and sixty millions of human beings," bemoaned Walter Medhurst, "huddled together in one country, under the sway of one despotic monarch, influenced by the same delusive philosophy, and bowing down to the same absurd superstition."[49]

Worst of all, Manchu despotism had restricted foreign trade to Canton, depriving China from the benefits free trade would confer and hindering the progress of relations with the Western nations. In May 1828 the *Register* lamented how in an age of "almost universal civilization" the world could be "shut out" from the "vast and fine" commerce that China offered. With its vast, extensive network of harbors, rivers, and canals, China seemed "designed by nature for universal commerce." Yet with the Chinese developing a "growing taste" for European goods, confining foreign trade to one port in the "extreme southern limit of the Empire" both deprived Chinese of foreign goods and made Chinese products too expensive for the foreign market.[50] "The fact is simply this," wrote Charles Marjoribanks, "that foreigners have, for a long succession of years, pursued a system of tame submission to the despotism of China, which, like all other despotisms, trampling upon abject submission, has gone on multiplying its restrictions." Had it not been for the "counteracting resistance" of the East India Company, the British would likely have been driven away from Canton by "the arbitrary exactions and oppressions of the local government."[51]

Although the British also defined themselves against French and Russian despotism, derived supposedly from religion and superstition, Qing despotism became one of the most significant markers for differentiating it from the other great empires—both past and present—thus accounting for the Canton System and its restrictions.[52] John Slade believed the history of the world proved large populations necessarily made governments despotic, resulting in "the utter debasement of the noblest qualities and finest feelings of man." But these effects could sometimes be mitigated by religion. In China, however, where there was no religion "except the worship of sages and heroes, and idols," the only check was the law. To make matters worse, the "stagnant pool" of Chinese life had "poisoned all the springs of human conduct and passions," while the teachings of Confucius had instilled an "almost universal skepticism" among the literati. Slade described the Qing government as "a pure unmixed despotism." Because of the "implicit obedience" demanded to law and regulations, the Chinese had no concept of national equality or reciprocity—evident in how they refused to help foreigners learn their language or study their laws, or to provide advice when they broke Chinese laws.[53]

This fascination with despotism and empires explains why in January 1835 the *Register* dedicated two lengthy articles to comparing the Qing and Roman empires. The basic nature of the two empires had differed greatly. While the Romans' "love of liberty" had made them "masters of the world," Chinese empires had been built on a "general acquiescence in despotism." And while the Roman emperor had been the head of his republic and "the first of a number of free citizens," the emperor of China was the "father of all his subjects" and "heaven's viceregent on earth." Unlike the Roman despot, who at least respected "the will of the people or of his army," the Chinese emperor derived his "sole authority" from "the azure heavens." In the end, however, the Chinese had triumphed. True, the Roman Empire had certainly been in a "more flourishing state" than any Chinese empire, the proof being its "stupendous" monuments, "the traces of which no time could efface." China, however, had only its Great Wall, and "a few pagodas and canals." But while Rome could only boast "the *ruins* of its grandeur," China's large population alone was proof of its "past and present greatness." It was older than the Roman era, its stability "peerless in the pages of history."[54] As the second of the two articles explained, only the Chinese empire had survived. "Hoary-headed, and belonging to an age long gone by, it stands amongst its youthful contemporaries of the west, who have divided the spoils of Rome among themselves."[55]

How had this form of despotism survived, and even thrived, into the Qing era? For Lord Macartney, who spent several days in Canton in December 1793 after his meeting with Qianlong at Chengde, part of the answer lay in the form of the Manchu conquest:

> When the Tartars entered China a century and a half ago, the country had long languished under a weak administration, had been desolated by civil wars and rebellions, and was then disputed by several unworthy competitors. . . . The conquerors, however terrible in arms and ferocious in their manners, were conducted by a leader of a calm judgment as well as of a resolute mind, who tempered the despotism he introduced with so much prudence and policy, that it seemed preferable to the other evils which they had so recently groaned under.

Given all the circumstances, Macartney argued, the Manchus had run China with "wonderful ability and unparalleled success." Yet this could never have been possible had their government not been a despotism.[56]

Macartney had no quarrel with the Chinese being liberated from their despotism. Having spent time in France and the colonial West Indies, what concerned him was the manner and speed this might take:

> A sudden transition from slavery to freedom, from dependence to authority, can seldom be borne with moderation or discretion. Every change in the state of man ought to be gentle and gradual, otherwise it is commonly dangerous to himself, and intolerable to others. A due preparation may be as necessary for liberty as for inoculation of the small-pox which, like liberty, is future health, but without due preparation is almost certain destruction. Thus then the Chinese, if not led to emancipation by degrees, but let loose on a burst of enthusiasm, would probably fall into all the excesses of folly, suffer all the paroxysms of madness, and be found as unfit for the enjoyment of freedom as the French and the negroes.[57]

Emphasizing despotism enabled Britons to convince themselves it was only China's government that was so anti-foreign. Breaking up the Canton System would thus be a double blessing: free trade would follow, and the Chinese people would welcome being released from the grips of Manchu despotism. John Barrow believed the Chinese were "greatly dissatisfied, and not without reason, at the imperious tone now openly assumed by the Tartars."[58] In January 1835, in an article titled "The Civilized World versus China," a contributor named "Delta" condemned the Canton System as a violation of God's law, by which the inhabitants of the world had all been allotted their respective parts "to afford them subsistence and enjoyment." How could China, which occupied a "noticeable portion of the globe," be allowed to separate a tiny population of foreigners from their families and deny them access to "air and healthful exercise"? How had such "base and immoral acts" been tolerated? Not because China was strong, but because Europe had been "*hood-winked.*"[59]

Despotism also enabled Britons to reconcile the unsettling realization that the Chinese who had the most contact with foreigners seemed to be the most recalcitrant. As they would be later in colonial Hong Kong, the British were convinced the Cantonese were more difficult than other Chinese. Barrow noted "the haughty and insolent manner" in which Europeans in Canton were treated. This contempt of foreigners was prevalent not only among the "upper ranks, or men in office," but even among the servants in Canton, who although eager to work for Europeans nevertheless despised them. Barrow recounted how he had once caught his servant "busily employed" in drying tea leaves that had already been used that day for breakfast, and which he now intended to mix with fresh tea leaves and sell. "And is that the way," asked Barrow, "in which you cheat your own countrymen?" No, replied the servant, "my own countrymen are too wise to be so easily cheated, but yours are stupid enough to let us serve you such like tricks." The servant did, however, plead that he had only meant to sell the used tea to the "second sort of Englishmen" in Canton: the Americans.[60]

Henry Hayne of the Amherst embassy wrote that any traveler to Canton witnessed "the national character in its worst guise."[61] Robert Morrison contrasted the Cantonese with the "Chinese colonists" in Southeast Asia and elsewhere, "universally acknowledged to be a superior race of men."[62] According to James Holman, the governor of Guangdong was reported to have once told some mandarins that until he came to Canton he had assumed the customs and habits of its people were the same as in other parts of China; he soon learned otherwise. Holman provided a long and detailed list of the alleged depravity of the people of Canton, and then took the entire empire to task for its poor condition of women, "unprecedented" extent of gambling, frequency of suicide, and cruelty of punishments.[63]

Members of both British embassies to Peking recorded how the contempt for foreigners became worse the closer they got to Canton. "Hitherto," wrote Barrow, the Macartney embassy had received "the greatest respect and civility from all classes of the natives, but now even the peasantry ran out of their houses, as we passed, and bawled after us *Queitze-fan-quei*, which, in their language, are opprobrious and contemptuous expressions, signifying *foreign devils, imps*; epithets that are bestowed by the enlightened Chinese on all foreigners."[64] Hayne observed how when the Amherst embassy was approaching Canton "an immense crowd of people" who came out to watch it pass were "inclined to be very impertinent and soon began to hoot, hiss and laugh at us, as well as to call us Quisi, Devils, Fanqui, Foreign Devils, Hoon-mow, red haired people: These opprobrious terms were new to us, we had rarely or ever heard them in the North." And those were only the ordinary people: the officials in Canton were "haughty, indifferent, and almost disrespectful."[65]

Particularly disquieting was how this behavior appeared to be caused partly by contact with foreigners. Aeneas Anderson, Lord Macartney's valet, regretted how the inhabitants of Canton were "very different in point of honesty, from the people of every other part of China" where the embassy had been. Anderson blamed this local character—"knavish in the extreme"—on Canton being "the only place where there is any communication with the natives of other countries."[66] Charles Downing believed "the language, as well as every thing else, is much depreciated in the neighbourhood of Canton, on account of the great intercourse with foreigners." Even the "poorest and meanest" Chinese could not reconcile himself to being a servant to a foreigner.[67] Walter Medhurst wrote how "passing through the suburbs of Canton, or up and down the river, the cry of 'foreign devil', salutes the ear on every side; even mothers may be seen, teaching their infants to point, and shout the offensive epithet, as the stranger passes by."[68] Nothing was "more common," the *Press* explained in November 1839, than, "when walking through the streets, to see urchins of three or four years old, on see you, cry out 'Fankwei' with all their might, and then run away in great fright at the dreadful apparition."[69] The local English press frequently reported placards with anti-foreign proclamations, sometimes even pasted on the walls of foreign factories.[70]

One way to explain the supposedly poor character of the Cantonese was to blame it on the government. John Davis described the Cantonese as "the very worst specimens of their countrymen," encouraged by local authorities to treat foreigners "as if they were really a degraded order of beings." Davis recalled "an annual edict or proclamation displayed at Canton at the commencement of the commercial season, accusing the foreigners of the most horrible practices, and desiring the people to have as little to say to them as possible." It was "in fact a matter of astonishment that the Chinese people at Canton should be no worse than we find them," given how they were ruled by a government which "openly professes to 'rule barbarians by misrule, like beasts and not like native subjects.'"[71] There were many reasons for the bad feelings toward foreigners, Charles Downing reasoned, including their own conduct. But he blamed the Chinese government for encouraging "these unfriendly notions among the common people, in order to prevent any traitorous coalition being established between them and the foreigners." Explaining why shopkeepers in Canton sometimes treated their foreign customers so rudely, Downing argued it was because they "have to deal besides with a people whom they are taught to despise, and, therefore, cannot consider themselves bound by any ties of honour to behave with justice and propriety."[72]

## THE TARTARS AND THEIR EMPIRE

Who were these "Tartars" who ruled China and how had they become so powerful? Few foreigners in Canton would have ever encountered a Manchu, and not everyone who wrote about China discussed the Manchus and their empire. Robert Morrison, who kept a record of his entire time there, from his arrival in September 1807 to his death in August 1834, rarely discussed the Manchus, whether in his correspondence or in his scholarship on China, even though he had met several on the way to and from Peking on the Amherst embassy. His *View of China* contained a chapter on "the Empire of the Man-Chow Family Which Now Fills the Throne of China," but said little more about the Manchus.[73] Still, many discussions included references to the "Tartars" or "Tatars." The *Chinese Repository*, for example, frequently featured articles and book reviews related to the geography of the Qing Empire and its "colonial possessions."[74]

The only Britons who encountered Manchus on a regular basis were those who went on the two embassies. Lord Macartney observed that although China consisted of two "distinct" nations—the Chinese and the Manchus—they were both subject to the "most absolute tyranny" that could be vested in one ruler. The only distinction was that for the Chinese it was a "foreign tyranny" and for the Manchus a "domestic despotism," even if these "Tartars" derived some consolation by seeing themselves as participants in their emperor's power over the Chinese. Even if the emperor claimed to be impartial between Manchus and Chinese, neither side believed it. The efforts to preserve the Manchu language formed "one unequivocal line of demarcation." Despite being in China for only a short while, Macartney insisted he found "no difficulty" in distinguishing a Manchu from a Chinese, "although their mode of dress and forms of behavior are precisely the same." There was "always something (I know not well how to describe it, *quod sentio tantum*) that indicated the difference in a moment."[75]

Macartney would not have fallen for the "sinicization" theory that dominated the study of Qing history until recently.[76] True, the Manchus had kept Chinese as the language of government; appointed Chinese teachers "of the highest reputation for learning and virtue" to educate their princes, "from whom were to spring the future sovereigns of the empire"; and preserved China's "ancient institutes and laws"—all of which had help reconcile many Chinese to their rule. But from this had emerged a "vulgar mistake" among foreigners that the Manchus had "indiscriminately and sincerely adopted all the maxims, principles, and customs" of the Chinese and that "the two nations were now perfectly amalgamated and incorporated together." Even if the two wore the same dress, it was the *Chinese* who had conformed to

Figure 1.4. George Macartney, 1st Earl Macartney; Sir George Leonard Staunton, 1st Bt., ca. 1785, by Lemuel Francis Abbott, oil on canvas. National Portrait Gallery, London

*Manchu* styles. And even this was only superficial: "the nature and character of each continue unchanged, and their different situations and intrinsic sentiments cannot be concealed under any disguise. Superiority animates the one, depression is felt by the other." European books might speak of them as one nation, but the emperor never lost sight of the distinction that formed the "cradle" of his power. While in Europe a monarch brought in to fill the throne immediately assumed the nationality of his new home—and his descendants continued so with "accelerated velocity"—the situation was different in Asia. "A series of two hundred years, in the succession of eight or ten monarchs, did not change the Mogul into a Hindoo, nor has a century and a half made *Kien-Lung* [Qianlong] a Chinese. He remains at this hour, in all his maxims of policy, as true a Tartar as any of his ancestors." And even if Chinese performed much of the government work, the provincial governors, military commanders, and "great officers of state" were almost all Manchus.[77]

Few were unimpressed by how the Manchus had come to power as, Karl Gützlaff wrote in the *Repository* in 1832, "one petty Tungouse tribe" that first overthrew the Ming and then established its own dynasty.[78] To John Barrow, the Manchu conquest of China had been a "master-piece of policy little to be expected in a tribe of people that had been considered but as half civilized":

> They entered the Chinese dominions as auxiliaries against two rebel chiefs, but soon perceived they might become the principals. Having placed their leader on the vacant throne, instead of setting up for conquerors, they melted at once into the mass of the conquered. They adopted the dress, the manners, and the opinions of the people. In all the civil departments of the state they appointed the ablest Chinese, and all vacancies were filled with Chinese in preference to Tartars. They learned the Chinese language; married into Chinese families; encouraged Chinese superstitions; and, in short, omitted no step that could tend to incorporate them as one nation. Their great object was to strengthen the army with their own countrymen, whilst the Chinese were so satisfied with the change, that they almost doubted whether a change had really taken place.

According to Barrow, the "interrupted succession" of four emperors, all "endowed with excellent understandings, uncommon vigour of mind, and decision of character," had up to now "obviated the danger of such an enormous disproportion between the governors and the governed." Through their "wisdom, prudence, and energy," these four emperors had expanded the Qing Empire to "an extent of which history furnishes no parallel." Like most Western observers in this period, Barrow mocked the weakness of the Qing military. But he marveled at how the "Mantchoo Tartars" employed their troops so differently from European nations. Except for the cavalry stationed on the northern frontier and in the "conquered provinces of Tartary," and the infantry who served as guards in the cities, the rest of the Qing army appeared to be more of a militia that fulfilled a wide assortment of military, civil, and police functions. These troops seemed to live "entirely on the labour of the rest, but contributing something to the common stock."[79]

John Davis acknowledged that the human costs of the Manchu conquest had been "almost beyond belief." But since then, China had "enjoyed a period of general tranquillity scarcely to be equalled even in Chinese annals." The first two emperors had been "extraordinary persons," bringing prosperity to the empire and increasing its population at a rate "absolutely incredible, if measured by European calculations or experience."[80] Even the *Register* was impressed. In March 1835 it explained that "few events" in Chinese history had been as "extraordinary" as the Manchu conquest. China had been defeated by "Tatar hordes," whose "obscure" origins were proof of their "barbarism" and "insignificance" until then. Once they had conquered China, the Manchus ruled with the "greatest wisdom." As a result, China had been revived from its late-Ming decline and even enlarged by the Manchus' "superior skill in governing such a large nation." The Manchus were not known for their courage as the Mongols had been, but they "rose rapidly, and preserved their conquest by a better policy."[81]

Despite their admiration for the Manchus and their early rule, these observers frequently speculated the Qing Dynasty might be approaching its end, even while marveling at its remarkable longevity given the low ratio of Manchu rulers to Chinese subjects—"not much less extraordinary," Davis reckoned, than the British rule over India.[82] Lord Macartney saw signs that not all was well: "The frequent insurrections in the distant provinces are unambiguous oracles of the real sentiments and temper of the people." In China he found the "ground to be hollow under a vast superstructure." The Chinese were beginning to recover from "the blows that had stunned them," to awake from their "political stupor," and to feel their "native energies revive." The slightest conflict might spread the flames of rebellion from "one extremity of China to the other."[83] John Barrow cited reports of a "very serious" rebellion in the western provinces that had spread to Guangdong and was aimed at overthrowing the Manchus. Some forty thousand men had been led by a descendent of the last Ming emperor, emboldened by a prophecy that the Qing Dynasty would be overthrown in 1804.[84] "China is still in a very unsettled state," Robert Morrison reported to the directors of the London Missionary Society in January 1816. "The government seems under the influence of alarm. It supposes enemies where none really exist; and hence it annoys and harasses the people with unnecessary restrictions. Prosecutions and capital punishments are still frequent on account of the late rebellions."[85] Two years later, Morrison wrote that "China remains in the same agitated state as it has been for several years."[86]

The belief that the Qing was beginning to unravel became even more pronounced in the 1830s, partly because foreigners in Canton enjoyed greater access to information about the rest of China. The early issues of the *Repository* paid great attention to a rebellion that had spread through parts of Guangdong, Guangxi, and Hunan. As the paper explained in July 1835, "there never was a period when the extent of its territory was so great as at present. But it has reached its dotage, and every adventurer takes advantage of its helpless state."[87] John Davis argued that the "present Manchow race" had shown "no unequivocal systems of degeneracy." The two greatest Qing emperors, Kangxi and Qianlong, had "sedulously maintained" their Manchu traditions through hunting expeditions beyond the Great Wall. But the Jiaqing and Daoguang emperors had distinguished themselves instead by their "comparative indolence." Consequently, both reigns had resulted in a "mere succession of revolts and troubles." The reign of the current emperor, Daoguang, had been "infested by a continual succession of public calamities" and by "more revolts and insurrections" since the founding of the dynasty.[88]

And they frequently mentioned the Qing government's fear of secret societies. A clear sign of the government's weakness, wrote Davis, was "its extreme dread of numerous associations among the people." The most dreaded of these societies, the "*San-ho-hoey*, or Triad Society," was devoted to driving out the Manchus. This fear of secret societies explained why the Qing government was so "cruel and unrelenting in punishing their leaders."[89] In August 1836 former *Register* editor Arthur Saunders Keating predicted in the *Repository* that with the "first vigorous and well directed blow from a foreign power," the Qing government would "totter to its base" and the secret societies, "whose object notoriously is the expulsion of the Tartars from the Chinese empire," might soon achieve their goal.[90]

## NOT ENTIRELY UNREASONABLE

That anyone blamed the Manchus for the Canton System and its restrictions should hardly surprise us. What *is* surprising is how often they agreed these restrictions were not entirely unreasonable. In 1813, George Thomas Staunton attributed the system to the "principle of strict subordination and controul [*sic*]" that pervaded "every relation" of life in China. No matter how "despotic and oppressive" this might appear to Westerners, in China it had always been considered "one of the first requisites of a good government, and one of the surest tests of a civilized people." The early, "casual and unconnected" British traders had been "entire strangers to the habits, customs, and language of the natives, as well as irreconcilably different from them, in respect to all their national characteristics." Nothing had made their presence more "odious" than their "apparent disposition and tendency, upon almost all occasions, to a state of anarchy and disorder."[91]

Realizing that traders who came to China were "wholly without any internal government, or system of controul and subordination," Staunton explained, the Qing government had found it necessary to enact "various new regulations and restrictions" for strangers who were neither "sufficiently powerful and united to command respect, nor sufficiently guarded and blameless in their general conduct, to overcome prejudices and conciliate esteem." Instead of prohibiting foreign trade, the government had determined to prevent "every hazard of ill consequence" by adopting and enforcing the "most jealous and vexatious precautions." Rather than being able to participate "in any thing like a free trade and intercourse with the natives generally," foreigners were "totally forbidden" to live in Canton beyond the trading season and confined "strictly" to a tiny section in the suburbs of the city of Canton.[92]

Henry Ellis of the Amherst embassy argued that the foreign relations of China were probably "more confined than those of any other country of the same extent to be met with in the history of the world." But this policy of discouraging foreign trade was not as unreasonable as it might appear. In an empire held together by the pressure of a "moral similarity" that flattened both the "better energies" and the "evil passions" of people to a level of "unnatural uniformity," it was only natural the government would be suspicious of any "improvement or vitiation" that unlimited contact with other nations might bring. And given how China was self-sufficient, it had no "adequate motive" for encouraging foreign relations based on trade. The government had thus chosen to draw "a line of moral, as well as territorial demarcation," between its own subjects and those of other nations. This also explained why the Qing government restricted commerce between China and Russia to a form of "limited barter" on the Sino-Russian frontiers.[93]

At least in the early 1820s, Robert Morrison had believed there was "every probability" the Chinese might concede if the European merchants insisted on having their families with them at Canton.[94] In May 1834, however, after some twenty-five years in China, he explained to his son that its massive population "fully" justified the Qing government's policy against letting foreigners bring their families to Canton. "Why should they allow foreign families to increase their population; when the native is overabundant."[95] John Davis argued that the Manchus restricted foreign trade to Canton "with such obstinacy to a point so unsuited to its extension" for two reasons: "to remove the danger of external involvements from the vicinity of the capital" and "to derive the largest possible revenue from internal transit."[96] According to Charles Downing, confining foreigners to this tiny section was designed to prevent them from settling in China while treating Canton as "a kind of counting-house" and then retiring to their own country. This explained why the Qing authorities kept so close a watch on the foreigners and forbade them to bring their families to Canton, "so that their thoughts may be constantly directed to the time when they shall leave in order to join them."[97]

In February 1838 the *Canton Press* reasoned that the "extreme reluctance" of the Chinese to allow foreigners into China arose partly from their "peculiar manners and the pride which a long course of prosperity has engendered," and partly from their government, "which being in the hands, not of the children of soil, but of foreign conquerors . . . dread every collision with foreign nations as threatening the subversion of their power." The Chinese realized that with increased contact with foreigners, many of their "most cherished" institutions would be "shaken." Their tradition of isolation had made them "incapable of appreciating any but their own laws, institutions, and manners." Even if they could be persuaded to appreciate the progress the West had made in politics and "all arts of civilized life," they might not be ready for "western improvements" to be "thrust upon them." They would be like that famous prisoner in the Bastille, who after being incarcerated for so long, returned voluntarily after the French Revolution. "Thus will it be with the Chinese, unless they are brought to associate with other nations by imperceptible degrees, so as not too grossly to shock the prejudices and habits which thousands of years have rendered dear to them."[98]

They also realized the Qing government's concerns about foreign trade were driven by the rise of British power elsewhere in Asia. As the *Press* explained, the government was aware of the "rapid strides" the British were making in India, "so as even already to press upon the frontiers of the Empire." Considering how well the Qing's foreign policy had preserved its territory, especially compared with "the fate of so many Indian monarchies, now totally annihilated and merged in the British empire," it was hardly surprising the Qing court was so determined not to "deviate from a line of policy which has been hitherto so eminently successful."[99]

In his public letter to Charles Grant, Charles Marjoribanks argued that given the "course and character" of China's contact with foreign nations, it was hard not to understand the government's "extreme jealousy." The Qing ministers at Peking were "well aware" of the scale of Britain's possessions in India. "In our war with Nepaul, we were treading on the very confines of China. During the Burmese campaign, on our advance to Ummerapoora, we were knocking at the very gates of the Chinese empire." In these recent campaigns, both Nepal and Burma had requested help from the Qing emperor, thereby fueling his suspicion of the British. The solution to allaying this jealousy and apprehension was to improve trading relations with China, though not through submission. "You must, in short, satisfy the Chinese government that you possess a giant's strength; that you are aware of its excellence, but have no inclination to exercise it in a tyrannous disposition."[100]

Walter Medhurst agreed that the Qing authorities' secretiveness verged on paranoia. "They are afraid of every petty horde on their borders, and suspect every foreign nation of having designs on their country. They anticipate nothing but disaster from the reciprocation of kind offices, between their own countrymen and strangers . . . they have, therefore, resolved to keep to themselves as much as possible." Although the Manchus had once retained a "few foreign literati" (Catholic missionaries) in Peking for their skills in astronomy and mathematics, they had since stopped employing foreigners "in order that they may keep native information from leaking out, and foreign opinions from creeping in." But Medhurst disagreed that the Qing government's restrictions were irrational:

They see the rapid strides which Europeans are making towards conquest and power, in the eastern world; and how the English, in particular, from the establishment of a factory, have proceeded to the erection of a battery; and then sending out their armies, have subdued whole kingdoms to their sway; till they number a hundred millions among their subjects, whom they keep in awe by a few thousand European troops. The Chinese, seeing this, could not but be alarmed for their safety, and the integrity of their empire.[101]

Even James Matheson, one of the most vocal critics of the Canton System, saw a certain logic in its evolution, arguing that the restrictions had more to do with greed than with arrogance or fear. Explaining Britain's "unfortunate position" in China, in 1836 Matheson wrote in a lengthy pamphlet how the difficulties the early English traders had faced in opening trade with China was the fault of "rival Europeans"—specifically the "treacherous" (and, of course, Catholic) Portuguese—rather than hostility toward foreigners by the Chinese. The "wily" Chinese had soon learned to appreciate the value of a trade that drew so many Europeans, willing to pay the "costly bribes" the Portuguese had grown used to offering. As commercial rivalry increased among the Europeans, the Qing government discovered that a system of restrictions was the "readiest engine" to continue this trade. The distance from Peking enabled the Canton authorities to "indulge their rapacity" to an extent "never contemplated or sanctioned" by the imperial court. By prohibiting locals from teaching Europeans their language, they were able to eliminate any checks on their abuses and to misrepresent these foreigners to the emperor "without the smallest chance of being contradicted." Gradually they were able to obtain his majesty's sanction of the most "ingeniously" planned system of "oppression and abuse."[102]

## THEMSELVES TO BLAME

It was easy, of course, to blame this sad state of affairs on China's lack of information about the outside world. In an article in December 1839 on why the Qing government was "a total stranger to foreign politics," the *Press* declared there was not a "single native" in Canton with a solid knowledge of foreign countries:

> The linguists and pilots have some smattering, and Howkwa [the senior hong merchant Howqua] may be in possession of a great deal of practical knowledge, but we very much fear, that there is not a single native who is acquainted with the details. But even those who know a little are men in a humble sphere of life, without any political influence, and despised for having had intercourse with foreigners and knowing more about them than their neighbours. As for the great

men who hold the reins of Government even at Canton, they know less about the English and Americans as we know about the king of Timbuctoo and some other Sambo.[103]

Yet these Britons also sometimes acknowledged that foreigners had done little to endear themselves to the Chinese. The *Press* explained in October 1835 (and then again in January 1838) that because the first European visitors had been "little better than pirates, and the treatment of the Chinese received at their hands must have created a strong prejudice which has not even worn away." Nor had the Jesuit missionaries helped matters, with their "foolish quarrels" and their interference in the "temporal concerns" of the Chinese.[104] In 1836 an author who identified himself only as "A British Resident in China" explained that Chinese foreign policy had not always been so "repulsive and dissocial." True, the government had always been arbitrary and both Chinese and foreigners had been subjected to its "despotic operation." But this "unhappy form" resulted from the "specimens of European character and management" displayed to the Chinese with "such fatal effect" over the sixteenth and seventeenth centuries. Even if the Chinese had come to appreciate British manufactures, these products did little to improve their attitudes toward Britain. The two failed British embassies had even achieved the opposite: the Qing had seen them as "admissions of national inferiority." The solution was not just a show of strength, but a display of "mildness" and "disinterestedness" that would reassure the Chinese the British were no longer to be feared or distrusted.[105]

For Charles Marjoribanks, the foreigners themselves were partly to blame. The "contentions" between the Jesuits and the Dominicans ("a set of infuriated bigots") had led the Qing government "with much reason" to send them home. The earliest European traders to China were often "persons of the most desperate and abandoned character, who committed, and generally with impunity, acts of the most violent description." No wonder the first Chinese impressions of "the European character" were based on "a set of intriguing priests and unprincipled and marauding merchants." The "barbarous and inhuman" massacres of Chinese colonists in Manila by the Spaniards and at Batavia by the Dutch (their entire history in Asia "one of degrading avarice and cruelty") had further diminished Chinese opinion of foreigners. Even if Britain had committed "no such enormities," the Qing government had still triumphed over "European power and dignity." Its emperor had seen the representatives of European kingdoms bear tribute and "grovel in the dust submissively before him," treating their "abject and submissive spirit" with "the contempt and indifference it deserved."[106]

John Davis attributed the Chinese suspicion of foreign traders partly to the conduct of the early European traders—starting with the Portuguese, whose behavior was "not calculated to impress the Chinese with any favourable idea of Europeans." The protracted "contests of mercantile avarice" that followed the arrival of the Dutch, and then the English, had only subjected all Europeans to "a still worse point of view." Consequently, "to this day the character of Europeans is represented as that of a race of men intent alone on the gains of commercial traffic, and regardless altogether of the means of attainment." Alarmed by the "perpetual hostilities" among these "foreign adventurers" and noticing the "close resemblance in their costumes and manners," the Chinese authorities came to view them all with a "degree of jealousy and exclusion" they had not shown toward their predecessors: the "more peaceable and well-ordered Arabs."[107]

Even the British themselves could sometimes be faulted. Several years after the Macartney embassy, secretary George Leonard Staunton wrote that the earliest English traders, arriving as they had during the "weak and unsteady administration of a declining dynasty," had come across to the Chinese as "rash adventurers appearing as if not belonging to any nation." The situation only grew worse as more Englishmen arrived. The unrestrained "passions and caprices" of seamen and "other persons in inferior stations" resulted in "such scenes of excesses and irregularities" that disgusted and offended the Chinese. Even though by the late 1700s the East India Company had been in Canton for more than a century, "not the least approach" had been made to assimilate in terms of "manners, dress, sentiments, or habits." Under such circumstances, it was hardly surprising the Qing had decided to confine foreigners to only one port, and to regulate their conduct, "as if aware of the necessity of preventing the contamination of bad example among their own people."[108]

Robert Morrison pointed out that even though the Chinese were "proud and domineering in an intolerable degree," so too were the British, "who will not admit that Heaven has given anything like 'comfort' to any tribes or nations of human beings out of England."[109] Charles Marjoribanks blamed the Qing policy partly on the early British traders in China ("persons of the most illiterate description") and the home government ("little under the influence of public honour"). Many of the early traders had been little more than pirates, bringing the "British name" into "merited contempt." With the recent "rapid and extraordinary aggrandizement" of Britain's empire in India, this contempt had been transformed into "deep and distrustful apprehension." The Company's Court of Directors had been no better, often giving instructions "of the most discreditable kind" to its agents.[110]

As we shall see in chapter 5, by the mid-1830s it became increasingly common to criticize the British themselves for not being satisfied with the trading conditions at Canton and for breaching Qing regulations. In October

1835, "A Citizen of the World" in the *Press* described his compatriots as "an unruly set":

> We cannot content ourselves with reforming our own institutions, but we must need a touch at all others in China. Although in almost utter ignorance of the character, habits, and genius of the people, we have determined that we ought to regulate the wheels of Government in Canton, instead of contenting ourselves with the goods the Gods provide us . . . all this is bad and ought to be rectified, but is it to be done by fitful acts of outrage and passion, by inconsiderate recklessness, on the one hand; or by endeavouring to render ourselves as disgusting to the feelings of the Chinese on the other as we can? . . . As for Commercial grievances we have none, literally none. Are we not smugglers on a large scale, deceive ourselves as we please, we are smugglers . . . and yet we talk of the Chinese Government as corrupt, aggressive, and unjust. Mr. Editor dost thou remember the story of the Pot and the Kettle?[111]

The *Register* disagreed, supplying an extensive list of legitimate commercial grievances.[112] But according to Medhurst, the British themselves were also to blame by importing so much opium. The Qing government realized opening China to more foreign trade would also mean increasing the amount of opium imported: "by permitting the introduction of these, they lay themselves open to the infection of our intoxicating drugs, and afford an opportunity for the establishment of our colonizing system." Who could fault them for being concerned? "Their policy is for them the wisest that could have been pursued; and if China is closed against us, we may thank ourselves for it."[113]

Even after the end of its monopoly, some continued to blame the current state of affairs on the Company. In August 1836, more than two years after the monopoly was abolished, the *Press*, rarely as critical of the Company and its monopoly as its rival *Register* was, argued that the profits assured by its monopoly explained why the Company had never made the "slightest advance" in improving relations with the local authorities, the imperial government, or the "Chinese in general."[114] Given how much trade had grown in the three years since the monopoly was abolished, the *Press* asked the following month, imagine how much British merchants would have benefited if they had been able to trade freely during those two hundred years of the Company's monopoly. "The ports of China would long have been on a secure and friendly footing, and Peking would perhaps by this time, be as familiar to tourists as Constantinople or Delhi."[115] Fortunately, the *Press* predicted in February 1838, the free traders were becoming "bolder from success" and would "soon break down many of the barriers which have hitherto stood in the way of unrestricted intercourse."[116]

## HOOD-WINKED

The idea that the Western nations, particularly Britain, had been too compliant with the Qing—or, as "Delta" put it in January 1835, had been "hood-winked" into accepting the restrictions of the Canton System—would become especially pronounced in the years leading up to the Opium War. In the same month "Delta" submitted his piece to the *Register*, a "Constant Reader" of the *Repository* asked whether the "arbitrary measures of a despotic power" that both ran against the "best wishes" of China and violated "natural and rational law" should be allowed to "paralyze" the efforts by foreigners in China to forge an "amicable understanding" between Britain and China. Expressing a sentiment found throughout writings by foreigners in China, he observed that the "darling idea" the Chinese had the right to enforce their own "unnatural system of excluding foreigners" was expressed mainly by those who had never come into contact with them. "They have at the same time forgotten that all those who are intimately acquainted with the Chinese, their language, manners, and government, are without exception at variance with them. How far, therefore, their opinions are to be relied upon, you and your readers must judge for yourselves; but for my own part, since they are based on the phantoms of their own imaginations, and can have no existence except in the Utopia of Du Halde and other Jesuits, I must reject them as unsound."[117]

To be sure, such hostile and aggressive language had begun to appear in the *Register* shortly after its founding in late 1827. And from the mid-1830s on some China hands campaigned and lobbied in Britain for a more aggressive policy. As the *Press* foresaw in January 1838, many of the private traders would become even brasher in circumventing the restrictions against free trade and against importing opium. Yet as we shall see next, even while Britons who visited or lived in Canton offered a range of explanations for the Qing's policies toward foreigners and for the state of Anglo-Chinese affairs, they extended a variety of solutions for improving them.

## NOTES

1. *Canton Register* 2, no. 21 (18 November 1829): 97.
2. Anon., *Facts Relating to Chinese Commerce in a Letter from a British Resident in China to His Friend in England* (London: J. M. Richardson, 1829), 46.
3. *Canton Register* 4, no. 2 (17 January 1831): 8.
4. *Canton Register* 4, no. 16 (15 August 1831): 80–81; original emphasis.
5. "The Ports of China," *Chinese Repository* 1, no. 11 (March 1833): 456–57. On the Qing name for the Kirghiz, who had been involved in the unrest of the 1820s and 1830s with Khoqand and the Khojas, see Joseph Fletcher, "Ch'ing Inner Asia

c. 1800," in *The Cambridge History of China*, vol. 10, *Late Ch'ing, 1800–1911*, part 1, ed. John K. Fairbank (Cambridge: Cambridge University Press, 1978), 64. Thanks to Matthew Mosca for suggesting that the *Repository* translators may have mistaken "Burut" for the Buryat Mongols, who would not have been anywhere near Kashgar.

6. "Notices of Modern China: Introductory Remarks on the Characteristics, the Present Condition, and Policy, of the Nation," *Chinese Repository* 4, no. 1 (May 1835): 19–20.

7. Frank Trentmann, *Free Trade Nation: Commerce, Consumption, and Civil Society in Modern Britain* (Oxford: Oxford University Press, 2008); Yukihasa Kumagai, *Breaking into the Monopoly: Provincial Merchants and Manufacturers' Campaigns for Access to the Asian Market, 1790–1833* (Leiden, NL: Brill, 2013).

8. Morrison to directors, 2 April 1815, CWM (Church World Missions), South China Incoming Correspondence, Box 1, Folder 4, Jacket B, Archives and Special Collections, School of Oriental and African Studies Library (SOAS).

9. *Canton Register* 1, no. 9 (26 February 1828): 36.

10. "Right of Petition," *Canton Register* 8, no. 2 (13 January 1835): 6–7.

11. *Canton Register* 3, no. 16 (18 August 1830): 67.

12. Napier to Grey, 21 August 1834, reprinted in Great Britain, Foreign Office, *Correspondence Relating to China. Presented to Both Houses of Parliament, by Command of Her Majesty* (London: T. R. Harrison), 1840), 6–27.

13. John Francis Davis, *The Chinese: A General Description of That Empire and Its Inhabitants* (London: Charles Knight, 1836), vol. 2, 55.

14. "British and Chinese Relations," *Canton Press* 3, no. 21 (27 January 1838): n.p.

15. Charles Marjoribanks, *Letter to the Right Hon. Charles Grant, President of the Board of Control: On the Present State of British Intercourse with China* (London: J. Hatchard, 1833), 5.

16. "Remains of Foreigners at Honam Opposite Canton," *Canton Press* 2, no. 6 (15 October 1836): n.p.

17. "Laws of the Chinese Empire, in Relation to Foreigners," *Canton Register* 6, nos. 15/16 (24 October 1833): 90–91.

18. "Early Foreign Intercourse with China," *Chinese Repository* 3, no. 3 (July 1834): 115.

19. Davis, *Chinese*, vol. 1, 19–20, 24.

20. "The Ports of China," *Chinese Repository* 1, no. 11 (March 1833): 456–57; original emphasis.

21. "Free Trade with China," *Chinese Repository* 2, no. 8 (December 1833): 373.

22. Napier to Grey, 21 August 1834, FO 17/12/10–11, The National Archives of the UK (TNA); also in *Correspondence Relating to China*, 27.

23. "Foreign Relations of the Chinese Empire," *Canton Register* 8, no. 3 (20 January 1835): 11.

24. Walter Henry Medhurst, *China: Its State and Prospects, with Special Reference to the Spread of the Gospel; Containing Allusions to the Antiquity, Extent, Population, Civilization, Literature, and Religion of the Chinese* (London: J. Snow, 1838), 19.

25. "Notices of Modern China," 19–20.

26. See, for example, Raymond Dawson, *The Chinese Chameleon: An Analysis of European Conceptions of Chinese Civilization* (Oxford: Oxford University Press, 1967), chap. 4; Colin Mackerras, *Western Images of China* (New York: Oxford University Press, 1989), chap. 4; and D. E. Mungello, *The Great Encounter of China and the West, 1500–1800* (Lanham, MD: Rowman & Littlefield, 1999), chap. 5.

27. Li Chen, *Chinese Law in Imperial Eyes: Sovereignty, Justice, and Transcultural Politics* (New York: Columbia University Press, 2016), 104.

28. Robert Morrison, *A View of China, for Philological Purposes: Containing a Sketch of Chinese Chronology, Geography, Government, Religion & Customs* (Macao: Printed at the Honorable East India Company's Press by P. P. Thoms, 1817; London: Black, Parbury, and Allen, 1817), 61.

29. John Barrow, *Travels in China, Containing Descriptions, Observations, and Comparisons, Made and Collected in the Course of a Short Residence at the Imperial Palace of Yuen-Min-Yuen, and on a Subsequent Journey through the Country from Pekin to Canton in Which It Is Attempted to Appreciate the Rank That the Extraordinary Empire May Be Considered to Hold in the Scale of Civilized Nations* (London: Cadell and Davies, 1804), 383–84.

30. Henry Ellis, *Journal of the Proceedings of the Late Embassy to China; Comprising a Correct Narrative of the Public Transactions of the Embassy, of the Voyage to and from China, and of the Journey from the Mouth of the Pei-Ho to the Return to Canton* (London: Printed for J. Murray, 1817), 489–90.

31. 9 December 1816, Henry Hayne Diary, Henry Hayne Papers, David M. Rubenstein Rare Book and Manuscript Library. Staunton had a different impression: describing a large water wheel the embassy passed en route to Canton, he wondered "whether it would be possible for European ingenuity to add any thing to it, or to accomplish the object in view more effectually and with equal economy of labour and materials, in any other manner." George Thomas Staunton, *Notes of Proceedings and Occurrences during the British Embassy to Pekin in 1816* (London: Havant, 1824), 317.

32. "The Chinese Empire," *Canton Register* 7, no. 39 (30 September 1834): 145.

33. "Notices of Modern China," 18–19.

34. Medhurst, *China*, 97–98.

35. "Internal Government of China," *Canton Press* 5, no. 11 (14 December 1839): n.p.

36. Marjoribanks, *Letter to the Right Hon. Charles Grant*, 22–24. On Lindsay, see Robert Bickers, *The Scramble for China: Foreign Devils in the Qing Empire, 1832–1914* (London: Allen Lane, 2011), chap. 2, and "The *Challenger*: Hugh Hamilton Lindsay and the Rise of British Asia, 1832–1865," *Transactions of the Royal Historical Society* 22 (2012): 141–69. On Gützlaff: Jessie Gregory Lutz, *Opening China: Karl A. Gützlaff and Sino-Western Relations, 1822–1852* (Grand Rapids, MI: William B. Eerdmans, 2008); Thoralf Klein, "Biography and the Making of Transnational Imperialism: Karl Gützlaff on the China Coast, 1831–1851," *Journal of Imperial and Commonwealth History* 47, no. 3 (2019): 415–45.

37. "Voyages of Adventure on the Coast of China," *Canton Register* 5, no. 16 (17 October 1832): 114. As Gützlaff himself put it in June 1834, "the fondness for foreigners which the people generally exhibit, though in direct opposition to the exclusive system of their rulers, makes it still more surprising that the government should be able to maintain that system." "Character of Chinese Historical Works," *Chinese Repository* 3, no. 2 (June 1834): 54.

38. Napier to Grey, 21 August 1834, FO 17/12/10–11, TNA; also in *Correspondence Relating to China*, 26.

39. *Canton Press* 1, no. 23 (13 February 1836): 177.

40. Marjoribanks, *Letter to the Right Hon. Charles Grant*, 59.

41. Gregory Blue, "China and Western Social Thought in the Modern Period," in *China and Historical Capitalism: Genealogies of Sinological Knowledge*, ed. Timothy Brook and Gregory Blue (Cambridge: Cambridge University Press, 1999), 75; Ulrike Hillemann, *Asian Empire and British Knowledge: China and the Networks of British Imperial Expansion* (New York: Palgrave Macmillan, 2009), 51.

42. "The Chinese Government and Constitution," *Chinese Repository* 4, no. 1 (May 1835): 11; original emphasis.

43. C. [Charles] Toogood Downing, *The Fan Qui in China in 1836–1837* (London: Henry Colburn, 1838), vol. 2, 244.

44. Li Chen, "Law, Empire, and Historiography of Modern Sino-Western Relations: A Case Study of the *Lady Hughes* Controversy in 1784," *Law and History Review* 27, no. 1 (2009): 36.

45. John Slade, *Notices on the British Trade to the Port of Canton; With Some Translations of Chinese Official Papers Relative to That Trade* (London: Smith Elder, 1830), 53–54.

46. Davis, *Chinese*, vol. 1, 289.

47. James Holman, *Voyage Round the World, Including Travels in Africa, Asia, Australasia, America, etc. etc. from 1827 to 1832* (London: Smith, Elder, 1834), vol. 4, 242. On Holman, see Jason Roberts, *A Sense of the World: How a Blind Man Became History's Greatest Traveler* (New York: Harper Collins, 2006).

48. Elizabeth Hope Chang, *Britain's Chinese Eye: Literature, Empire, and Aesthetics in Nineteenth-Century Britain* (Stanford: Stanford University Press, 2010), 27.

49. Medhurst, *China*, 71. Lord Macartney had held a different view: the "pride of despotism" had made a state religion unnecessary, thereby making it possible for "Lamas and Bonzes, Parsees, Jews and Mahometans" to live together in peace. John Barrow and George Macartney, *Some Account of the Public Life, and a Selection from the Unpublished Writings, of the Earl of Macartney* (London: Cadell and Davies, 1807), vol. 2, 430.

50. *Canton Register* 1, no. 18 (3 May 1828): 71–72.

51. Marjoribanks, *Letter to the Right Hon. Charles Grant*, 5–6.

52. On British attitudes toward the French, see Linda Colley, *Britons: Forging the Nation 1707–1837* (New Haven, CT: Yale University Press, 1992), especially chap. 3.

53. Slade, *Notices on the British Trade*, 43, 45–46, 55.

54. "A Parallel between the Chinese and Roman Empires," *Canton Register* 8, no. 3 (20 January 1835): 11.

55. "A Parallel between the Chinese and Roman Empires," *Canton Register* 8, no. 4 (27 January 1853): 15.

56. Barrow and Macartney, *Some Account of the Public Life*, vol. 2, 442, 447.

57. Barrow and Macartney, *Some Account of the Public Life*, vol. 2, 448.

58. Barrow, *Travels in China*, 416.

59. "The Civilized World versus China," *Canton Register* 8, no. 4 (27 January 1835): 15.

60. Barrow, *Travels in China*, 591–93.

61. Undated entry on Canton and Macao, Hayne Diary, Rubenstein Library.

62. Robert Morrison, *Notices Concerning China, and the Port of Canton, also a Narrative of the Affair of the English Frigate Topaze, 1821–22; with Remarks on Homicides, and an Account of the Fire of Canton* (Malacca: Printed at the Mission Press, 1823), xi.

63. Holman, *Voyage*, 205–7, 209, 216–22, 223–32.

64. Barrow, *Travels in China*, 591–92.

65. 20 and 21 December 1816, Hayne Diary, Rubenstein Library.

66. Aeneas Anderson, *A Narrative of the British Embassy to China in the Years 1792, 1793, and 1794; Containing the Various Circumstances of Embassy the Accounts of Customs and Manners of the Chinese, and a Description of the Country, Towns, Cities, &c. &c.* (London: J. Debrett, 1795), 259–60.

67. Downing, *Fan Qui*, vol. 1, 273, and vol. 2, 99–100.

68. Medhurst, *China*, 287.

69. *Canton Press* 5, no. 8 (23 November 1839): n.p.

70. For example, "Insulting Proclamation Pasted against the Wall of the Foreign Factories," *Canton Register* 3, no. 21 (16 October 1830): 89–90.

71. Davis, *Chinese*, vol. 1, 238.

72. Downing, *Fan Qui*, vol. 2, 33, and vol. 3, 94–95.

73. Morrison, *View of China*, 61–86.

74. For example, the reviews by Morrison's son, John Robert, in *Chinese Repository* 1, no. 2 (June 1832): 33–42; *Chinese Repository* 1, no. 4 (August 1832): 113–22; and *Chinese Repository* 1, no. 5 (September 1832): 170–79.

75. Barrow and Macartney, *Some Account of the Public Life*, vol. 2, 412, 423.

76. Examples of the "new Qing history" that has undermined the sinicization thesis include: Evelyn S. Rawski, "Reenvisioning the Qing: The Significance of the Qing Period in Chinese History," *Journal of Asian Studies* 55, no. 4 (1996): 829–50; Peter C. Perdue, "Comparing Empires: Manchu Colonialism," *International History Review* 20, no. 2 (1998): 255–62; Pamela K. Crossley, *A Translucent Mirror: History and Identity in Qing Imperial Ideology* (Berkeley: University of California Press, 1999); Mark C. Elliott, *The Manchu Way: The Eight Banners and Ethnic Identity in Late Imperial China* (Stanford: Stanford University Press, 2001). Cf. Ping-Ti Ho, "In Defense of Sinicization: A Rebuttal of Evelyn Rawski's 'Reenvisioning the Qing'," *Journal of Asian Studies* 5, no. 1 (1998): 123–55.

77. Barrow and Macartney, *Some Account of the Public Life*, vol. 2, 444–45.

78. "Modern History, from A. D. 1280 Down to the Present Time," *Chinese Repository* 2, no. 3 (July 1835): 118.

79. Barrow, *Travels in China*, 407–8, 412–13.

80. Davis, *Chinese*, vol. 2, 389.

81. "Mantchoo Conquest of China," *Canton Register* 8, no. 9 (3 March 1835): 35.

82. Davis, *Chinese*, vol. 1, 184.

83. Barrow and Macartney, *Some Account of the Public Life*, vol. 2, 445–47.

84. Barrow, *Travels in China*, 416.

85. Morrison to directors, 1 January 1816, CWM, South China Incoming Correspondence, Box 1, Folder 4, Jacket C, SOAS.

86. Morrison to directors, 1 January 1818, CWM, South China Incoming Correspondence, Box 2, Folder 1, Jacket A, SOAS.

87. "Modern History," 128.

88. Davis, *Chinese*, vol. 1, 172–73, 183–84.

89. Davis, *Chinese*, vol. 1, 187, vol. 2, 15.

90. "Military Skill and Power of the Chinese," *Chinese Repository* 5, no. 4 (August 1836): 172.

91. George Thomas Staunton, *Miscellaneous Notices Relating to China and Our Commercial Intercourse with That Country: Including a Few Translations from the Chinese Language*, 2nd ed. (London: John Murray, 1822), 127–29.

92. Staunton, *Miscellaneous Notices Relating to China* 130–31.

93. Ellis, *Journal of the Proceedings*, 434.

94. Morrison, *Notices Concerning China*, iv.

95. 15 May 1834, MS5829/135/1, Archives and Manuscripts, Wellcome Library.

96. Davis, *Chinese*, vol. 2, 424–25.

97. Downing, *Fan Qui*, vol. 1, 298–99. Amasa Delano, an American naval captain and Revolutionary War veteran who made three voyages to China in the late 1790s, made a similar observation in *A Narrative of Voyages and Travels in the Northern and Southern Hemispheres, Comprising Three Voyages around the World* (Boston: E. G. House, 1817), 541.

98. "British and Chinese Intercourse," *Canton Press* 3, no. 24 (17 February 1838): n.p.

99. "British and Chinese Intercourse," n.p. On Qing views of India, see Matthew M. Mosca, *From Frontier Policy to Foreign Policy: The Question of India and the Transformation of Geopolitics in Qing China* (Stanford: Stanford University Press, 2013).

100. Marjoribanks, *Letter to the Right Hon. Charles Grant*, 56–57.

101. Medhurst, *China*, 135–36, 498–99.

102. James Matheson, *The Present Position and Prospects of the British Trade with China: Together with an Outline of Some Leading Occurrences in Its Past History* (London: Smith, Elder, 1836), 81, 84.

103. *Canton Press* 5, no. 11 (14 December 1839): n.p.

104. *Canton Press* 1, no. 5 (10 October 1835): 35; "British and Chinese Relations," *Canton Press* 3, no. 21 (27 January 1838): n.p.

105. A Resident in China, *British Intercourse with Eastern Asia* (London: Edward Suter, 1836), 15–17.

106. Marjoribanks, *Letter to the Right Hon. Charles Grant*, 3, 28–30. On the massacres in Batavia and Manila, see: Lynn Pan, *Sons of the Yellow Emperor: A History of the Chinese Diaspora* (New York: Kodansha, 1994), 32–37; Leonard Blussé, *Visible Cities: Canton, Nagasaki, and Batavia and the Coming of the Americans* (Cambridge, MA: Harvard University Press, 2008), 41; Philip A. Kuhn, *Chinese among Others: Emigration in Modern Times* (Lanham, MD: Rowman & Littlefield, 2008), 62–63.

107. Davis, *Chinese*, vol. 1, 20–21, 100, 111.

108. George [Leonard] Staunton, *An Authentic Account of an Embassy from the King of Great Britain to the Emperor of China: Including Cursory Observations Made, and Information Obtained, in Travelling through That Ancient Empire and a Small Part of Chinese Tartary* (London: G. Nicol, 1797), vol. 1, 11–12, 14–15.

109. Morrison, *Notices Concerning China*, v.

110. Marjoribanks, *Letter to the Right Hon. Charles Grant*, 2–4.

111. *Canton Press* 1, no. 7 (24 October 1835): 50.

112. *Canton Register* 8, no. 43 (27 October 1835): 171–72.

113. Medhurst, *China*, 136.

114. *Canton Press* 1, no. 49 (13 August 1836): 387.

115. *Canton Press* 1, no. 52 (3 September 1836): 412.

116. "British and Chinese Relations," *Canton Press* 3, no. 21 (27 January 1838): n.p.

117. "Intercourse with the Chinese," *Chinese Repository* 3, no. 9 (January 1835): 395. Jean-Baptiste Du Halde, a French Jesuit, was the author of a massive work published in French in 1736 and translated into English two years later as *The General History of China*.

*Chapter Two*

# The Crying Abuses
## *Solutions*

In early December 1834, more than eighty British subjects in Canton (almost the entire community) petitioned King William IV to dispatch an expedition to avenge the abuse Lord Napier had suffered two months earlier at the hands of the Guangdong authorities. The new commissioners appointed to superintend British affairs after Napier's untimely death were not only unrecognized by the "constituted authorities" of China, they were also forbidden to appeal directly to the imperial government in Peking and even to reside in their new jurisdiction. The "most unsafest of all courses" would be "quiet submission to insult": had Lord Napier's mission been "properly sustained by an armed force," the British in Canton would not be in their current "degraded and insecure position."

It was time to send a minister, accompanied by "a sufficient maritime force," to demand "ample reparation" for the "insult" and "humiliating conduct" that had aggravated Napier's illness and death, and for the "arrogant and degrading language used towards your Majesty and our country." If the Qing government refused to comply, the British could easily cut off the "greater part" of China's external and internal commerce, intercepting revenues on their way to Peking and "taking possession of all the armed vessels of the country." Such actions would show the "power and spirit of Great Britain to resent insult" and to "speedily induce" the Qing to submit to "just and reasonable terms." Far from leading to all-out war, this would be "the surest course for avoiding the danger of such a collision."

The petitioners believed they alone understood the solution to Britain's problems in China. Any future minister to China must be instructed to "put himself in communication" with the British merchants in Canton, "qualified as they must be in a certain degree by their experience and observation" to recommend the necessary course of action and help him understand the many trading benefits currently being "curtailed" or even "lost." The petitioners also absolved themselves of any responsibility for the "disabilities and restrictions" affecting British trade in China, blaming it instead on the "long acquiescence in the arrogant assumption of supremacy over the monarchs and people of other countries, claimed by the Emperor of China for himself and his subjects." They reminded their king that previous attempts at negotiation had not only failed but were even partly to blame for the current state of affairs.

Prompted by their understanding of Lord Amherst's behavior in 1816, even considering the possibility of kowtowing to the Jiaqing Emperor, they urged King William not to allow any future minister to "swerve in the smallest degree from a direct course of calm and dispassionate, but determined maintenance of the true rank of your Majesty's empire in the scale of nations." Any deviation from such a "just position" would lead to even "worse consequences" than if the British merchants in Canton were left to conduct their own affairs with the local authorities, "each as he best may." Equally importantly, any future minister must not be allowed even to "set foot on the shores of China, until ample assurance is afforded of a reception and treatment suitable to the dignity of a minister of your Majesty, and the honor of an empire that acknowledges no superior on earth."[1]

Even after the Napier fiasco of 1834, however, there was never any consensus. As the *Canton Register* explained in late September 1836, even Britons who had spent many years in China and were "equally capable of forming a judgment" held "widely different if not diametrically opposite sentiments" on the matter.[2] And even the *Register* itself could be inconsistent, occasionally challenging publications by writers it generally supported. In its review of James Matheson's 1836 pamphlet calling for a more aggressive policy, the paper asked whether, even if Matheson's sentiments reflected those of many Britons in Canton, such measures might not lead to war. True, the Chinese had given great cause for offense. They had called foreigners "barbarians" and prevented them from going where they pleased. They had spoken disrespectfully of the king of England. But was this a "good and substantial reason" to send a fleet on a five-month voyage simply to "teach insolent men better manners"?[3]

## VISITORS WEIGH IN

Even visitors often offered suggestions, to the point where practically every Briton who wrote about his time in China seems to have had his own remedy. Lord Macartney is known for describing the Qing Empire as "an old crazy first-rate man of war" that would not sink immediately but instead drift as a wreck and be "dashed to pieces on the shore." Yet his prediction that the disintegration of the empire might occur even without a conflict with Britain—through the "common course of things without any quarrel or interference on our part"—has overshadowed how many possibilities he considered for improving Britain's position in Canton. Ideally, and with "proper management," the British could shape the China trade ("as we seem to have done the trade every where else") to fit their own needs. But this would require more "skill, caution, temper, and perseverance" than could be expected. Still, if the Qing were to halt trade, it would be easy enough to retaliate by severing their coastal trade and communications between north and south, and by fomenting trouble elsewhere:

> We might probably be able from Bengal to excite the most serious disturbances on their Thibet frontier, by means of their neighbors there, who appear to require only a little encouragament [*sic*] and assistance to begin. The Coreans, if they once saw ships in the Yellow Sea acting as enemies to China, might be induced to attempt the recovery of their independence. The thread of connexion between this empire and Formosa [Taiwan] is so slender, that it must soon break of itself; but a breath of foreign interference would instantly snap it asunder.

Macartney envisioned minimal resistance to such a move. The Portuguese ("dead in this part of the world, although their ghost still appears at Macao") would cause little trouble. Both "useless" and "disgraceful" to them, Macao could be taken easily—either by "fair terms" or with a small force from India; any "compensation and irregularity" could be settled easily afterward. Alternatively, if the British formed a settlement on a nearby island such as Lantao, Macao would quickly "crumble to nothing." Once the forts at the Bocca Tigris (Humen) were destroyed, the British would control the river. The entire trade of Canton and its surroundings would be "annihilated in a season," and the millions of Chinese who depended on it would be "almost instantly reduced to hunger and insurrection." They would "overrun" the country as beggars and robbers, taking with them "misery and rebellion." Russia would then seize the opportunity to re-establish its power along the Amur River.[4]

How might a "serious quarrel" with China affect Britain and its empire? The slightest interruption of the China trade, Macartney continued, would harm British settlements in India, which depended on their exports of opium and cotton. For Britain itself, the effect would be "immediate and heavy." Wool manufacturing would "feel such a sudden convulsion, as scarcely any vigilance and vigor in government could for a long time remedy or alleviate." The British would also lose their burgeoning exports to China of metals, manufactured goods, and clocks and watches "and similar articles of ingenious mechanism." They would be deprived not only of raw silk but also of an "absolute necessary of life": tea. The disintegration of the Qing Empire ("no very improbable event") would cause a "complete subversion" of trade across the globe. With China's ports opened, foreign "adventurers" would search "every channel, creek, and cranny" of China for markets. The result would be "much rivalry and disorder," though mighty Britain, thanks to "the weight of her riches" and "the genius of her people," would benefit the most from such a revolution and outshine all rivals.[5]

Macartney was no warmonger, though. He argued strongly against any "offensive measures" or "hostile conduct" while a "ray of hope" remained for "gentle ones." He dismissed the idea of acquiring territory on the Chinese continent as "too wild to be seriously mentioned"—especially if the British could get what they needed though better trading conditions. The best solution would be to have a king's minister, or a Company's with a king's commission (as had been done in Lisbon and St. Petersburg), resident throughout the year in Canton but completely unconnected with trade. Macartney was convinced his embassy had exposed the Qing court to so many Britons, whose "brilliant appearance" and "prudent demeanor" had evinced a "most favorable" impression of Britain. He admitted that the administrative system at Canton had been "corrupt and oppressive to a great degree" and the British traders there had suffered. But he cautioned against exaggerating this suffering, especially considering the "vast difference" between Asian and European manners "and that our customs appear as strange and unaccountable to them as theirs can possibly do to us." Unable to understand the mutual advantages that derived, the rulers of China were naturally "astonished" to learn of the "unguarded intercourse" among nations in Europe:

> They say to us, why do you visit a country so often, whose laws you dislike and are disposed to disobey? We do not invite you to come among us; but when you do come, we receive you in the manner prescribed by our government, and whilst you behave well, we behave to you accordingly. Respect our hospitality; but do not pretend to regulate or reform it.[6]

Three decades later, James Holman took a harder line. He claimed his lack of sight gave him "a clearer view of the great points, the formations, the resources, the population, the habits and manners" of the places he visited. When Holman, who had failed to reach the Chinese border from Russia on an earlier trip, sailed from Macao in late 1830, he did so without regret, "being eager to escape from the meshes of chicanery and immorality with which the vicinity of Canton abounds." He left China convinced that the British had been far too easy on its government:

They have all the braggart, as well as all the recreant qualities of cowardice in their nature. If we were to make a decided demonstration of hostility, we should speedily obtain all that we require at their hands. A few British men of war would shatter the flimsy armaments of China with as much facility as our presence, even in slight numbers and without power, keeps their vagabond multitudes in check, in the suburbs of Canton.

For Holman, there was no question that foreign trade in China suffered from "every disadvantage" the Chinese government and people's "ignorant pride and vain confidence" could evoke. Their willingness to yield to "every strenuous opposition" to their exclusive policies revealed the weakness of their character, but it also offered "a convincing proof of the prejudicial consequence of too pliant a submission to their jealous regulations."[7]

Figure 2.1. James Holman, ca. 1830s, by Maxim Gauci, printed by Graf & Soret, published by Andrews & Co, lithograph. National Portrait Gallery, London

Nothing in Holman's account suggests any unpleasant personal encounter with Chinese people that would have made him so critical of them. He described a visit with the Company supercargo Hugh Hamilton Lindsay and the botanist William Kerr to the hong merchant Howqua's house and gardens, and one with the chaplain George Harvey Vachell to the home of another merchant. He recorded in great detail a dinner with the Company tea inspectors John Reeves and his son John Russell Reeves (who taught him how to taste tea properly) at the home of another hong merchant. He wrote approvingly of the most prominent Chinese doctor in Canton, who accepted payment only if his patients wished to offer it.[8]

But Holman happened to be in Canton and Macao during a period of "more than ordinary interest and excitement." It coincided with a standoff between the Company and the Canton authorities, for supercargo and former Select Committee president William Baynes had taken his wife from Macao to Canton. Julia Smith Baynes's attendance at a church service in the chapel attached to the Company's factory was "a very agreeable sight to all the English present," offering hope the "barbarous restriction" excluding women would be "ultimately abolished altogether." Holman considered her husband's response to the local authorities a model of English restraint and fortitude: he had shown "firmness and composure of mind" and "utmost calmness and courage." The incident revealed "the situation in which our countrymen are placed in the neighbourhood of Canton, and the constant grievances to which they are subjected." That several other Company men and private traders dared to bring their wives to Canton after the Baynes incident only further proved to Holman that the Chinese were all bluster and both could and needed to be dealt with assertively.[9]

In 1836, G. J. Gordon, who went to Canton from India in 1834 to research tea cultivation, argued that his short time in China enabled him to form a "more impartial judgment" than the private traders who suffered from the "injuries" inflicted by the Canton System. Gordon fully supported the sentiments outlined in the petition of 1834 to King William, which he reprinted in his pamphlet to support his own similar demands for placing British commercial relations with China on a basis "consistent with honour, security, and advantage, national and individual." Given the importance of the China trade to British manufacturing interests, he was surprised and disappointed that the "apathy or indecision" of the British government could allow commercial relations with China to sink to such a "deplorable" state. He exhorted British manufacturers to "unite with one voice to rouse the ministry from the lethargy under which they appear to have slumbered." To make sure his readers understood the extent of "Chinese insolence, rapacity, venality, mendacity, and pusillanimity" that had driven the petitioners, Gordon then spent one hundred pages outlining the history of Anglo-Chinese relations since the 1600s.[10]

## INTIMIDATION OR RESTRAINT?

The most frequently mooted solution was for Britain to assume a more aggressive stance. But even this approach, which involved many different possibilities, was never accepted by all members of the British community in China. And even those who called for a tougher policy toward China often tempered it by urging caution and restraint. One option, the private trader John Slade suggested in 1830, would be to send a fleet of British warships up the Yangzi River, cut off the communications along the Grand Canal, and thus stop the shipping between the northern and southern provinces. It might even be possible "with no very great difficulty" to sever the provinces of Fujian and Guangdong from the rest of the empire.[11]

Slade regretted that because of the "pride and jealousy" of the Qing government, "so large a portion of the human race" should be separated from "the rest of mankind." Still, he warned that protecting trade did not justify interference by the British government or risking war. He considered a war to be "of the most remote probability," finding it hard to imagine how China could ever cause Britain enough offense to justify declaring war. It was "by no means ridiculous" for the Qing to insist on their right to continue their own laws in their own territories and among their own subjects. If those laws were administered "clearly and impartially," there was no reason why foreigners in China should not be governed by them. Slade conceded it would take "an amazing revolution" in "Chinese manners" to save the trade at Canton from its "difficulties and exactions." And he agreed that the Qing government's conduct toward foreigners was neither warranted by China's own laws nor justified by "human feeling." But he reminded his readers that in Canton the Europeans were "suitors"—lured by the silks and teas of China—and it was unreasonable to expect the Qing government to encourage a trade it thought might threaten the "integrity and independence" of its empire.[12]

When the Company threatened to suspend trade in June 1831 during a dispute with local authorities (a move strongly supported by the private traders), "A British Merchant" asserted in the *Register* that the Qing must be taught that Britain would never "consent to purchase Tea at the high price of national disgrace." The sooner a crisis erupted the better, for commerce could not continue in the "present state of uncertainty." Thirty years of attempts at conciliation had become "worn threadbare."[13] In the following issue, however, "An Englishman" maintained that any measures likely to lead to war with China were "altogether unnecessary." Even if the result of a war might be favorable, it would involve "a wide train of consequences" that were "totally remote" from the "simple object" desired: "justice, and toleration and for our commerce."[14] One "Veritas" asked how "A British Merchant" believed the British government could be justified by the opinion of "any civilized community" in using arms to enforce "its own commercial views and regulations in a country where we are permitted to reside for our own convenience and emolument," or how it could tolerate "a system of international commerce conducted on the principles of a smuggling trade."[15]

The *Register* joined the fray with a short article honoring Captain Murray Maxwell, who in 1816 had blasted his way past the forts at the Bocca Tigris to collect Lord Amherst at Whampoa after his failed embassy. "The fact is, Europeans in China will not be treated with respect till they display a higher sense of honor, to preserve which they will both incur risk, and submit to loss."[16] The *Register* found support in another Briton, "Fair Play," who argued it was useless to "sit down quietly and hope for better times." The Chinese were not the only ones who needed to be convinced of the need for change: "The more fully acquainted those at home become with the *real* state of things in this country—the oftener and the stronger this is forced on their attention—the greater is our rational hope of redress." Although "Fair Play" suspected few Britons in Canton would support a war (the "mere display of moral force" being sufficient), he insisted that if the British were to "tamely submit to encroachment and ignominy, it will be in vain to hope for amelioration from the Chinese Government, whose main principle is to degrade us in the eyes of its people."[17]

The calls for a more assertive policy toward China became more vociferous in 1833 with the debates on abolishing the Company's monopoly. Charles Marjoribanks insisted in his open letter to Charles Grant that the best way to deal with China was not a policy of "wretched subserviency" to a "corrupt and despotic" government, but a "strict accordance" with the "sound principles of national honour" the British applied to other nations but for "some ill-defined reason" had never used in China:

> I am well aware there are those who maintain, and who will endeavour to influence your mind upon this subject; that as we have for a long term of years been called dogs at Constantinople, we may as well continue to be called devils at Canton and Pekin; but rest satisfied of one great and practical truth, confirmed by every page of the history of our intercourse with China, that acts of subserviency which have proved injurious to our national character, have invariably proved detrimental to our commercial interests. These are mutually and inseparably associated, they must stand or fall together.

For Marjoribanks, who had been in Canton as a Company writer during the Amherst embassy, the two embassies to Peking had accomplished little "except in increasing our knowledge of the very peculiar character of its people and government, and making a more favourable impression of our own." They proved that in any future negotiations with China, the British should not try to "force indiscriminately" the principles applied to their commercial relations with other countries. The time had come to demand "just and equitable treatment" for British subjects and their property. Commissioners, backed by the British naval squadron in India, should be prepared to occupy one of the islands in the Pearl River. Under such conditions, the British demands would surely be granted quickly. The proposed policy of sending king's commissioners rather than Company representatives would be met with "assumed indifference": the new superintendents would receive no more "regard or attention" than the Company's had. "Do not send our national flag annually to China to be openly insulted by any contemptible minion of its weak and arrogant government. Assume an attitude that you do not blush to own." Unless the new British representatives had enough power, Canton would become "a place of resort for adventurers, bankrupt in fortune and character." Above all, the British must secure a "definite understanding" with the Qing. Until then, their trade with China would be subject to "restrictions, interruptions, and impositions" of the "most vexatious and injurious" kind.[18]

In December 1833, after the news the Company's monopoly would end the following spring had reached Canton, the private trader James Goddard lamented in the *Chinese Repository* how British relations with China had become the "reverse of what takes place in the usual intercourse of nations." Identifying himself simply as "A British Merchant, Formerly of Canton," Goddard ridiculed the notion that sending a superintendent or commissioner would improve Britain's trading position. He doubted that "any honorary appointment could be comprehended by the Chinese." If the Qing government continued to rebuff their demands for better trading conditions, the British might create an embargo on Chinese shipping around Canton or even up the entire coast. They could sever communications by the Grand Canal. They might even land an army of fifteen to twenty thousand men and demand "a substantial commercial treaty under the walls of Peking." The presence of British ships would be "opposed and repulsed" by the Qing government. But the embargo would cut off supplies of fish, rice, and salt, destroy a "large portion" of tribute and revenue, and "carry distress" to the "inmost recesses" of the empire. With the Qing Empire in "so crumbling a state," these ships would be greeted with "joy and satisfaction" by the "great mass" of the Chinese population. Both China and Britain would benefit: China would be liberated from the "barbarous" Manchus, who "despising treaties and the

Great wall," had "seized the destinies" of China and "ruled it with an iron hand"—and had "thrown back ignominy upon ourselves, and disgraced our nation's character."[19]

In February 1834, however, "Another British Merchant" took Goddard to task, insisting that the British had little to offer the Chinese apart from opium. The Chinese were a "happy, thriving, and contented people," even without English products. He agreed that a single gunboat would "make the whole Chinese navy quail," but he cautioned against going beyond "just and honorable measures," reminding him the Qing government was powerful internally because "it pleases and cherishes the mass of the people, and oppresses only the rich, who are always objects of envy to the poor." The government of China had "a firmer hold over the people and more power of effectual control" than either Britain or France, or "any other nation." There was every reason to believe happiness was "more generally diffused" through its massive population. The Qing Empire was larger than all of Europe, enjoyed the "varied productions of every soil and climate," and needed little from other countries. The Chinese, he argued, "can far better do without us, than we without them."[20] The *Register* disagreed, describing "Another British Merchant" as a "discontented, disappointed, individual" rather than "one desirous of the common good."[21]

Convinced that an improvement in Britain's position in China would be good for all the Western nations, many in Canton were curious who the new superintendent would be and how he would behave. When "Delta" offered a detailed list of suggestions for the approaching superintendent in February 1834, the *Register* responded that it would be better to focus on eliminating "local abuses" and opening more ports such as the island of Lintin (Lingding, or Solitary Nail, eighteen miles from Macao and from the Bocca Tigris), rather than trying to persuade the Qing government to alter its regulations for foreign trade.[22] Yet they realized how complicated his situation would be, as the *Register* put it:

> If he yields he loses all his power of doing good in China! If he perseveres, and keeps trade *shut* for six months, he is well abused, and probably recalled! Under that sort of disgrace which attends an unsuccessful mission: these are certainly not very encouraging prospects to induce an opulent and respectable Englishman to leave the quiet of his paternal acres for a wrangle with the wary and cunning Chinese, *or* the more insolent because more mustached Tartar mandarins.[23]

The calls for a more aggressive policy toward China became even louder during the Napier fiasco in the summer of 1834 and the death of Lord Napier that October. A correspondent to the *Register* was concerned that even those who wanted trade to be expanded worried it might lead to rebellion—"the people, in learning the ways of free born men, will be immediately in uproar, bloodshed and rapine will instantly follow." He disagreed:

> Was the country thrown into a state of rebellion when foreigners formerly visited the northern ports, or when the Jesuits spread all over the empire? Has Canton, after having been visited by so many thousand foreigners, been the scene of bloodshed and rebellion? . . . if this never happened within the space of more than a century, during which time many turbulent heads have visited this part of the world, why should then, all at once, the northern ports fall a prey to Jacobinism as soon as British merchants are permitted to visit them?[24]

In September 1834 another anonymous "British Merchant" questioned whether foreigners in Canton should submit to the laws and regulations of China. Was it necessary for buying tea that they should tolerate being called "devils" and "barbarians," under the surveillance of hong merchants and linguists, separated from their wives and families ("putting us on a level with the brute creation"), and allowed to visit the island of Honam only three times per month?[25] The *Register* insisted that in China the British nation had suffered even greater grievances than the "seven great grievances" that had led the Manchus to overthrow the Ming Dynasty. The treatment Napier had received justified a blockade of Canton, supported by a naval force strong enough "to make all foreign flags respect it." The Qing government was "the enemy of the human race," and it was the duty of "all mankind" to "rise up and extirpate their oppressors."[26] "Delta" suggested placing vice-consuls on boats along the coast and in the major rivers, and sending four vessels ("fancy four Gutzlaffs") to different provinces spreading religion and information on European customs and laws. Together, this would, "in one season," help open the "most friendly dealings with millions of Chinese." Experience showed in commercial relations with "all demi-civilized countries," the "natural course of events" was to send a consul or "accredited mercantile adventurer" before rather than after a commercial treaty.[27]

In April 1835, "Enemy to Half-Measures" proposed in the *Register* that the British anchor at Amoy and submit a letter from King William to the Daoguang Emperor demanding reparation for the "insults and injuries" dealt to Lord Napier. If the letter were rejected, the British should "bombard the town till got"; if it were accepted, they should repeat the same strategy at Ningpo, Nanking (Nanjing), and Peking. If the Chinese still refused to sign a treaty on amicable terms, the coastal trade should be "absolutely annihilated" and the British should intercept imperial revenues on their way to Peking.[28]

Still, even after the humiliation and death of Lord Napier, opinions continued to vary. In November 1834, "A Common Place Writer" argued that the "smallest European maritime power" could sever communication between

Formosa and the mainland, enter the Yangzi River, and take control of the Grand Canal, thereby starving the capital and the entire coast. China was no longer a "fairy land": five coastal provinces already depended on British trade, and both land and sea forces were in a "miserable plight." All the better reason to urge "our Celestial friends" to accept a "speedy peace" rather than to "stoop and submit."[29] In an article titled "Barbarism, Civilization," in December the *Register* declared China had no right to "separate itself from the rest of the world, claim submission from its inhabitants, and treat them as conquered barbarians." If all nations followed China's example, "men would then live like the beasts; or be engaged in universal war, against each."[30]

In January 1835 a letter in the *Register* argued that the time had come for some "deliberate and decisive act of interference" by the British government to save relations with China "from the state of degradation into which they have fallen." But a commercial treaty was far from the solution, for it would mean the British would have to comply with China's laws.

> If we were bound by the ties of a commercial treaty with China, it would become the duty of the British consul to caution his countrymen against carrying on the opium trade; against exporting sysee [sic] silver, gold, or other metal; against the contraband trade on the coast; against hiring natives to teach the Chinese language; with a host of other prohibitions, too numerous to be mentioned.

Better simply to stick things out and wait until the Qing were "fully aroused" of their inability to suppress the contraband trade, whereupon they would see the utility of a more open commerce. As British diplomats grew to understand "the Chinese mind" and Qing authorities learned the futility—and the danger—of resisting the British, the problem would resolve itself:

> The irresistible and expansive energy of the free trade will be forcing itself into every nook of the empire; until, at length, the Chinese government, convinced of the impracticability and injustice of attempting to shut out from its people the mighty flood of commercial benefits pouring in upon them, shall concede, with a good grace and of their own free-will, what it might now cost no small expenditure of blood and treasure to extort from them.[31]

The *Register*, which had long supported more direct intervention from the British government, rather than a commercial treaty, agreed. The Chinese were "not yet sufficiently advanced in civilization" for such a treaty, and a "bad treaty" would be "more disadvantageous to our merchants than none at all."[32] Yet even while calling for more intervention from the British government, the *Register* continued to insist that merchants in Canton could handle their own affairs. In April 1835 it argued that the fact that more than 150 British ships had come to China and exported more than 400 million pounds of tea in 1834 "fully proved the ability of British merchants to manage their own business in China without the intervention of an establishment in Leadenhall Street or an *orderly factory* in Canton." Even the "conduct and appearance" of the crews had "put to shame" those of the Company's ships.[33]

With the establishment in September 1835 of the *Canton Press*, the solutions became even more varied. For the *Press*, which frequently stressed its differences with the *Register* on the best way to improve relations with China, the cure was neither aggression nor a commercial treaty but the natural and unrestricted expansion of trade up the China coast. In January 1836, when Qing authorities refused to allow a steamer owned by Jardine, Matheson & Co. to enter the Bocca Tigris, the *Press* suggested that "a rational lesson or two of sound and sober policy" would "bring these *celestials* to become somewhat more *mortal* in their habits and character." But this would be achieved neither by "the remonstrances of a few unaided individuals at the City Gates, nor by any threat of blowing up Canton by pellet guns." Nor would a British superintendent at Canton be of any use. The only solution was a "spirited remonstrance" to the emperor himself at his residence at Peking, led by a British ambassador supported by a naval force.[34] Later that month, the *Press* featured an article accusing the *Register* of representing the "warlike" party.[35]

While the *Register* declared in February 1836 that although China had a "*perfect* right" to enforce its own laws and institutions, it was wrong for "one dominant family and tribe" to be the "sole interpreters" and to require "obedience and respect on the part of the rest of the world," the *Press* continued to insist that commerce, rather than the "manifest injustice of an armed aggression," was the better method for improving relations with China.[36] It disagreed with the *Register* that a commercial treaty would solve the problem. Once trade spread to the point where the government could no longer restrict it, the government would promote the trade it could no longer "effectively destroy."[37] In March 1836 the *Press* criticized an article published the previous month in the *Repository* on the "great desideratum" of obtaining a treaty with China through a display of British naval power. It was "not at all apparent" trying to obtain such a treaty though intimidation would not result in bloodshed. Even worse, the use of force would "throw additional disgrace" on those who advocated it.[38] In April the *Press* disagreed with a correspondent named "Senex," who had suggested that the British station a frigate near the Bocca Tigris as a reminder of the "pride and glory" of Britain.[39] In June it argued that, apart from the temporary stoppage of trade after Lord Napier's arrival, since the end of the Company's monopoly not only had trade increased but also relations with the Chinese had been "fully as cordial if not more so" than ever before.[40]

And when the China Association in London, a group of merchants with interests in China, recommended that an ambassador be sent to Peking and be allowed to perform the kowtow and whatever other ceremonies required, in December 1837 the *Press* demurred: "Great Britain should only treat with China as an equal, and alone in maintaining that position can she ever hope to derive any advantage from Embassies to Peking." Previous embassies from Britain and Europe showed the Chinese would view the ambassador as a mere "tribute bearer come to do homage to their Emperor, and assume the Embassy to be one of mere compliment."[41] "Delta," who had lived in China for eleven years, concurred: "They fancy in England that they *can* and *do* know more of Chinamen than us, resident years and years in it." Even if the chosen ambassador were to be the Duke of Wellington himself, "I would sooner see his head struck off by a sword, than that he should perform the *Ke-Tow* for the *English crown* to China!"[42]

## AT HOME

Back in Britain, private traders such as James Matheson and Hugh Lindsay tried to push opinion toward a more aggressive policy in China. In an open letter of December 1835, Matheson, who had sailed to England that March to champion the cause of the British traders and their petition to King William, warned Lord Palmerston of the "serious apprehensions with which the present extraordinary position of affairs is calculated to inspire those concerned in the trade." It was impossible to limit the "evils" that might accumulate, should the Canton authorities be allowed for another year to "indulge the belief that there is no species of injustice or indignity which they may not practise with impunity, not only towards British merchants, but even towards the representative of our most gracious sovereign."[43]

To make his point, Matheson enclosed a copy of another petition to King William, signed by more than thirty British merchants in Canton. Rather than negotiate at Canton for better trading conditions, the petitioners insisted the British should send a squadron to Amoy with a letter to the emperor, reminding him of the humiliating way Lord Napier had been treated at Canton and hoping to "come to an understanding on this painful subject, as well as on those grievances from which the trade is suffering." As the case of Lord Napier ("His Majesty's Nobleman") showed, any attempt to renew negotiations were "sure to prove fruitless": the local officials there had no authority to deal with foreign powers. British trade with China was already becoming more important by the day and under the "fostering care" of the government would only continue to increase. No other trading relationship required as much "attention and protection" from the British government. China was one of the most important markets for British cotton and woolen textiles and Indian cotton and opium. It provided Britain with raw silk ("the want of which would paralyze a very important and rising branch of our manufactures") and tea ("an article of indispensable consumption"). If the Canton authorities' "unwarranted treatment" of Lord Napier were allowed to pass, without "even a show of remonstrance," the result would be "such a systematic aggravation of existing evils as would lead to constant collisions and interruptions of trade." Ironically, given that the petitioners had earlier blamed the "disabilities and humiliations" experienced in China partly on a "systematic violation of sound policy" by the East India Company, they now pointed out that at least the Company's "united influence and command of capital" had sometimes given it leverage against the Chinese. But with the Company gone and the free traders each pursuing their own "separate and disunited views," they would be no match for the "well-combined machinations" of the Chinese.[44]

Figure 2.2. Nicholas James Sutherland Matheson, 1837, by Henry Cousins, published by and after James Lonsdale, mezzotint. National Portrait Gallery, London

In 1836, Matheson argued in his pamphlet that even if no formal treaty existed between Britain and China, the current policy was a violation of "the principles of justice" and "the law of nations." Particularly vexing was how the Qing government had acknowledged the advantages of foreign trade and allowed it to continue for so long. It was thus "mere trifling" for China now to disregard the law of nations, "on the ground of her having never deigned to recognize it." Among the many examples of the Qing government's "complete recognition" of British trade was its request for "a chief" to be sent out after the end of the Company's monopoly.[45]

Matheson was convinced that Daoguang had neither the desire nor the power to stop trade or drive the British from China—"*if he saw us disposed to offer a serious resistance*." He was far too aware of the corruption, poverty, and "utter imbecility" pervading his empire to provoke a nation as powerful as Britain. In any case, the British traders at Canton had no interest in aggressive measures. They wanted only an end to the "arrogant and offensive" language used by the emperor and his ministers when referring to their king and his subjects; reparations for the insult to Lord Napier and the "national honour"; and freedom from the "intolerable indignities and impositions" from which they had suffered for so long. The Napier fiasco had convinced Matheson that any attempt at negotiations should be avoided and the next British plenipotentiary should have enough power to assert and protect British rights. Most of all, the British must avoid anything that might be construed as "ignominious submission, at the feet of the most insolent, the most ungrateful, the most pusillanimous people on earth."[46]

Hugh Lindsay offered his own remedy for the state of Britain's relations with China in his letter to Palmerston in July 1835, published in March 1836. Like many former Company men, he felt no radical change would have been necessary if the Company's monopoly had been allowed to continue. "Occasional disputes" would have no doubt occurred, but the two sides' commitment to preserving trade would have enabled everything to continue for "an indefinite period" despite the "arrogance" of the Chinese and the "ill-suppressed wrath" of the British residents. In any case, the balance had already been thrown: the Company's monopoly was no more, yet the Cohong's still remained. The "immense interests" the Company had once been able to represent and protect were now no more than "numerous factions without any bond or community of interest."[47]

The "treacherous conduct" of the Canton authorities toward Lord Napier had convinced Lindsay that it would be impossible to send another Briton of "character and talent," forced to yield to the "humiliating concessions of national inferiority" before they would recognize him. Only two options were left: "direct armed interference to demand redress for past injuries, and security for the future"; or a withdrawal of "all political relations"—including all commissioners—from "a country which obstinately refuses to acknowledge such without insult." Lindsay had no interest in Britain taking possession of even the "smallest island" on the Chinese coast; he wanted nothing more than a commercial treaty, "on terms of equality" and granting the British trade to two or more northern ports.[48]

Lindsay's own preference was clear. All that was needed to coerce China and its "countless millions of inhabitants" was a combination of "energetic measures" and "judicious policy." An ambassador from Britain and an admiral from India, in charge of an "amply adequate force" of a dozen or so ships and no more than three thousand men, would be sufficient to demand redress and negotiate a commercial treaty on a "liberal basis." The British would embargo the China coast at the four main ports of Canton, Amoy, Shanghai, and Tientsin (Tianjin). After temporarily commandeering "thousands of native merchant vessels," they would use them to distribute pamphlets (as Lindsay had in 1832, though without much success) reminding civilians that the Qing government—not they—were the targets; that they would be rewarded "punctually and liberally" for supplying provisions; and that, most of all, they too would benefit from a commercial treaty. "By these means confidence would soon be established, and the Chinese would flock to us from all quarters, bringing abundant supplies of every article we might stand in need of." Lindsay had even pinned down the best time for the expedition: after assembling in the Straits of Malacca, the fleet would catch the first monsoon winds up to the China Sea and begin operations by mid-April. The whole thing would be over in less than four months, without causing any "serious inconvenience" to trade. There was no reason to worry about "jealousy" from the French or the Americans, for they would "equally" reap the benefits that would result.[49]

Other China hands, in Canton and in Britain, held different opinions. The *Press* dismissed the grievances which Matheson and Lindsay had complained about in their pamphlets as "more nominal than real." Though "no doubt suffering under severe privation," it argued, "we, in common intercourse with the Chinese suffer none or little of that contumely which are painted in such glaring colors, and that on the contrary our persons are generally respected, and have been protected even where we have been the aggressors."[50] "A Resident in China" wrote that the 1834 petition to King William had to be considered in the circumstance under which the "numerous and highly respectable" signatures had been appended. Buoyed by the advent of free trade and inspired by the "high personal character" of Lord Napier, the majority of the British in Canton had supported his "direct attack" on "the Chinese system." His untimely death had naturally left them disappointed and exasperated. But

"A Resident" cautioned against allowing these feelings to influence British official and public opinion. Given the long history of warfare in Europe up to 1815, why should the British expect the emperor to accept their demands for "free, *unreserved*, and *neighbourly* intercourse"?

> What comparison would the Emperor be likely to draw between that history and the records of his own dynasty? Could he fail to observe, how often *Europe* had been desolated, while *China* has been enjoying uninterrupted peace and security? Would not family pride, and personal distrust, come in as additional arguments for exclusion, while he marked, how many European princes have been driven into exile, since the accession of his line to the throne of China?

Instead of asking their government to take a harder line, the petitioners should urge it to do something to make the Chinese grateful and attract their attention. Rather than use force, which would only hurt the people of China, the British government should adopt a peaceful policy based on "*expediency*, *humility*, and *generosity*." And instead of sending another commissioner like Napier, it should dispatch a consul (allowed to trade, for that was what the Chinese expected) backed by a small naval force with just enough power to protect trade and to "produce a deep moral impression"—"not as a messenger of vengeance, but as a preserver of peace." A tall order indeed, but there was no one better able to "give the blessings of civil and religious liberty to the whole eastern world."[51]

The loudest voice at home against Matheson and Lindsay was of one of Britain's most prominent sinologists. In 1836, George Thomas Staunton (who had not been in China since leaving in January 1817 after the Amherst embassy) wrote that although British trade had recently been in "considerable peril," the crisis now appeared to be over. Despite "the total failure of all the specific measures adopted for its protection," the new system was working well and was likely to continue doing so.

> But we must not urge the machine on too rapidly, so as to put to risk the important advantages which it already confers upon us. The only safe and legitimate basis of commercial intercourse between nations is their *mutual interest*. This object must work its way, though slowly, yet *surely*; whereas schemes, however promising and flattering, which are built upon the dangerous and slippery ground of intimidation, and an appeal to the *fears* instead of the *interests* of independent nations, can only end in *their* alienation and *our* disappointment.

Military force would not only be a "death-blow" to British trade with China; it would also "greatly weaken, if not absolutely annihilate" Britain's "*moral influence*" throughout Asia but particularly upon which its rule of India depended.[52]

Figure 2.3. George Thomas Staunton, 1839, by William Overend Geller, after George Swendale, mezzotint. Wellcome Collection. CC BY 4.0

Staunton disagreed with Lindsay that Britain should try to intimidate China. Blockading China's long coast would be all but impossible: "a more gigantic and portentous scheme of national warfare cannot well be imagined." He also disagreed that, just because some Chinese people up the coast had welcomed visits by British vessels and the opportunity to trade, the British would be able to establish trade there on a regular basis. And even if the general population welcomed trade, could the British convert their entire commerce with China to a "*smuggling trade*"? And if, as Matheson had argued, during the Napier fiasco the Chinese had "abruptly and *ruinously*" suspended trade for more than one month, imagine the consequence of the British suspending it themselves for seven months. Better and more secure trading conditions and access to more ports (as Lindsay had proposed) were certainly desirable.

> But to go to war,—to engage in hostilities for the sake of obtaining such objects,—to endeavor to extort them by force from an independent state, by the terror and sufferings which might arise to the people from our blockades and embargoes, seems to me outrageous, and quite unparalleled in the records of the comparatively civilized warfare of modern days.

Threatening the use of force to demand reparations would not only bring "disgrace and discredit on our flag and name," but would also alienate the British from the Qing government and even from the Chinese people. Appointing another superintendent such as Napier would be "the height of folly." Just as "absurd" would be to continue maintaining an expensive establishment in China, "without any hope of being able to render it efficient for the purposes it was designed to accomplish."[53]

Staunton did, however, agree with Lindsay's second suggestion: to withdraw all British commissioners until something went wrong:

> Here we have, then, on the authority of Mr. Lindsay's knowledge and experience of the Chinese character, a plan, easy and simple, perfectly peaceable as well as legitimate, if not of obtaining all the objects we desire, at least all the objects which the Government of this country contemplated, when they appointed Lord Napier to reside in China as superintendent. Here is, indeed, no appeal which, from all we know of their character, we may expect will be equally effectual—an appeal to their rational self-interest.

For Staunton, the main reason not to make any radical changes was simple: the system worked. At least during his residence in China, British grievances had led to "actual extremities" with the Chinese only once:

> We then certainly struck the British flag, which had been so long accustomed to wave over our establishments, and contemplated the possible necessity of a final abandonment of our position on the Chinese continent; but this was our *ultima ratio*. Not an individual, I believe, at the period—not the highest spirited or the most belligerent of the then British community either in China or India contemplated a resort to *force* in any case, except that of *self-defence*. . . . Schemes of intimidation were never adopted nor even contemplated,—solely because they would have been wholly unjust and indefensible.

In response to Matheson's call for the British government to demand that the emperor stop using such offensive language when referring to foreigners, Staunton argued that the British might as well insist that he "drop the Chinese language forever, and to speak and write in future in English." The spirit of *"supreme and universal dominion"* was so deeply engrained in Chinese official phraseology, hardly a word of it could be retained that "might not be construed into an offence." Although Staunton agreed with Matheson that the prohibition against foreign women visiting Canton was "very hard and very absurd," he pointed out that the Manchus fully understood how the British had also begun their operations at Calcutta with little more than a factory yet ended up with "the conquest of the whole country." It was thus "not quite so unnatural" for them to insist the factories be used solely for their intended purposes, rather than as *"domiciles for our wives and families."*[54]

## IMPROVING THEIR OWN SITUATION

Even when Britons blamed the problems they faced in Canton primarily on the Qing authorities, they often admitted they could do more to improve their own situation. "We, no doubt, labor under many disadvantages here at present," Lord Macartney wrote in his journals, "but some of them we have it in our own power to remove."

> Instead of acting towards the Chinese at Canton in the same manner that we do towards the natives at our factories elsewhere, we seem to have adopted a totally opposite system. We keep aloof from them as much as possible; we wear a dress as different from theirs as can be fashioned; we are quite ignorant of their language (which, I suppose, cannot be a very difficult one; for little George Staunton has long since learned to speak it and write it with great readiness, and from that circumstance has been of infinite use to us on many occasions); we therefore almost entirely depend on the good faith and good nature of the few Chinese whom we employ, and by whom we can be but imperfectly understood in the broken gibberish we talk to them.[55]

Samuel Holmes, Macartney's guard, admitted that the negative views of the British were due to "the irregularities committed by Englishmen at Canton," which had made them "the worst of Europeans." All the more reason for the embassy members to impress the Chinese with "new, just, and more favourable ideas of Englishmen" and to show "even to the lowest officer in the sea or land service, or in the civil line, they are capable of maintaining, by example and by discipline, due order, sobriety, and subordination among their respective inferiors."[56] Were the governments of Europe and America to try as hard to improve their trade with China as they did with other nations, the missionary Robert Morrison argued, the situation could be much better. Appearing to be bent on nothing but profit was as "disreputable" to the Chinese as it was "to all good men."[57]

One way to improve this situation would be by learning Chinese: visitors and longtime residents alike agreed. John Barrow, Macartney's private secretary, conceded the difficulty. Even the Catholic missionaries who had lived in China "for the best part of their lives" in the employment of the Qing government sometimes had trouble composing and translating official documents. But Barrow saw no justification for how, because of its "supposed difficulty," British traders in Canton had "totally neglected the language, as well as every other branch of information respecting the most interesting and extraordinary empire on the face of the globe"—especially in contrast to how Chinese in Canton from the hong merchants down to "even the inferior tradesmen and mechanics" had learned pidgin English. The French, who had already "firmly rooted" themselves in Cochin China, understood the "solid advantages" of learning Chinese and were "at this moment holding out every encouragement to the study of Chinese literature; obviously not without design." Like Macartney, Barrow understood how not learning Chinese put the British at a disadvantage in Canton. Local officials knew they could impose restrictions on British trade "with impunity," as the British could not report such "villainy" to their superiors. But these problems could be solved quite easily if the Company required its writers to learn "five hundred or a thousand" Chinese characters before they could be appointed to China. "If, by neglecting to study the language of the Chinese, we are silly enough to place ourselves and concerns so completely in their power, we are highly deserving of the extortions and impositions so loudly complained of."[58]

In the introduction to his *Chinese Novels* (1822), John Francis Davis lamented how the progress made by Britons in their knowledge of China had been "very inconsiderable." He was "at a loss" to explain the "almost total ignorance" in England before Macartney's embassy of a country with whom the British had traded with for so long, especially compared with the French, who one century earlier had already been conducting their research with "diligence and success." This "singular listlessness" was all the harder to comprehend, given the "extraordinary" nature of the government and the "no less extraordinary" structure of the language. Davis blamed it on the "fancied" or "real" difficulties of learning Chinese, and to the "discouragements" the Chinese had put in its way. Given how at least one side had to understand enough of the other's language for doing business, what gradually emerged was pidgin English—that "base and disgusting jargon" still used in Canton. Most Britons preferred to rely on this "imperfect and confined medium" than to try and learn Chinese. Fortunately, the Macartney embassy, and the published accounts by its members, had stimulated a "general curiosity" in these "singular" people and their country.⁵⁹

Figure 2.4. Sir John Francis Davis, Bart. Arnold Wright and H. A. Cartwright, eds., *Twentieth Century Impressions of Hongkong, Shanghai, and Other Treaty Ports of China: Their History, People, Commerce, Industries, and Resources.* London: Lloyds, 1908

Robert Morrison conceded that the Canton authorities tried to keep foreigners ignorant of their language, literature, and laws, and learning English for the linguists was as difficult as learning Chinese was for the foreigners. And there was little intrinsically of interest in Chinese culture to make a European want to study Chinese. "Abstract Science, or the Fine Arts can learn nothing from China, and perhaps as much is already known, as can be known, to aid the general Philosopher in his reasonings." Still, he hoped a better British acquaintance with the Chinese language might promote a "fuller" and "increasingly cordial understanding" between the two nations.[60] Not understanding Chinese only made the British even more beholden to the local authorities:

> Since foreigners cannot, many of them, write in Chinese; and are not allowed to write to the supreme government, the local officers at Canton, whenever they represent the case of foreigners to Court, put language into their mouths corresponding to these sentiments. Every request made, or demand for justice presented, is converted into a piteous, abject, begging for mercy and compassion to be conferred on poor wretches, who have drifted on great rafts, across an immense ocean, in the hope of being allowed to get the means of existence from the Celestial Emperor's underserved commiseration, &c. Now, when foreigners themselves are supposed to use this language, how can his majesty's ministers advise him to respect such people.

Most importantly, not having a greater knowledge of Chinese also hurt the British in their negotiations with the local authorities during cases of alleged homicides by British seamen. Morrison recommended the establishment of a vice-admiralty court, the head of which would have a few men proficient in Chinese languages and laws.[61]

Although Morrison acknowledged the support from the East India Company's Court of Directors in London for his dictionary and other publications, he regretted they had not provided more language training for their staff in Canton. "The simple recommendation to learn it, which the Court gives to the writers, intended for commercial purposes, does not meet the exigency of the case. The commercial servants have the road to affluence opened to them without knowing a word of Chinese, and they generally despise the recommendation, and ridicule the pursuit." Morrison wanted more than language training. A "mere knowledge" of language was not enough: the Company needed men with an "extensive knowledge" of Chinese law, government, history, and geography. Because of their ignorance, the Company's officers often wrote to the Chinese in a way that only hurt their cause. The Russians, on the other hand, were already training a steady stream of candidates in Chinese language and literature, and even had a college for this purpose. Given that there were already several Britons with a "considerable knowledge" of

Chinese, the only obstacle to producing a cohort proficient in Chinese was the lack of a "well-digested" program of education and support from the Court of Directors or the British government.[62]

Morrison's fellow missionary Walter Henry Medhurst disagreed with the common notion that learning Chinese was "an insuperable difficulty." Through "moderate capacities and due diligence, aided by the increased facilities which now exist," a foreigner could "converse fluently" within two years and 'compose intelligibly' within four." Chinese children learned to speak at the same time British children did. Were Britons to study Chinese with "the simplicity and teachableness of children," they would be "equally successful."[63]

Well into the late 1830s, letters and editorials in the local press complained about the lack of progress in learning Chinese. In March 1828 the *Register* regretted how British merchants had for so long been "generally incapable" of collecting information about "the products and the prices of the interior." They had generally remained "ignorant of the laws and institutions, even in matters affecting human life, except as in interpreted by malicious and timeserving magistrates." Even though Chinese was difficult to learn, that did not sufficiently justify this ignorance. The "true causes" had been "a want of patronage on the part of senior merchants, who often regret too late their own ignorance; and a love of ease too incident to the young and inexperienced."[64] In May 1829 the *Register* rejoiced that the Company's press at Macao would publish Robert Morrison's new Cantonese vocabulary, regretting how "our ignorance of the spoken language of the place" had caused many of the "daily misconceptions" that occurred between foreigners and Chinese, and left "a mistaken as well as unfavorable impression, as to the dispositions and characters of both parties."[65]

In a letter to the *Register* in January 1833, "An Observer" lamented that even though the Company offered a bonus to its employees who studied Chinese, only two Britons in Canton were capable of translating Chinese: Morrison, who translated for the Company, and his son John Robert, who worked for the British private merchants. No one valued the learning of Chinese, even though they all depended on the services of these two translators. "The *profession* of Chinese, in Canton, is somewhat like the profession of medicine in one respect. People in health don't care for the doctor, but the sick apply to him."[66] In December 1834, in the wake of the Napier debacle, the *Register* insisted that the next commissioner to China must "have full powers to encourage the study of the language, and to employ and reward those acquainted with it.[67] What, asked "Philologos" in the *Press* in September 1836, had the British, especially compared with the French, done to promote the study of Chinese? Given that they had "nothing else to do," why not force the

British superintendents at Macao to study Chinese?[68] As the *Register* put it in August 1837, it was as clear as "the noon-day sun" that the more foreigners learned of the Chinese language, the more their "power and respectability" would be increased.

In September 1837, John Robert Morrison wrote that although Britain was "preeminent among the nations" in its commercial and political relations with China, it had "greatly" allowed other nations to surpass it in learning Chinese:

> Russia has her school at Peking, which has as yet, however produced little that the world has been permitted to see. France has her Chinese library, and has long had a professor of the Chinese and Tartar languages. Prussia, that sends a single ship to China once in two years, has her Chinese library and professor. Yea, even Bavaria supports a Chinese professor, at the university of Munich. But the English government has neither of its own accord done anything for Chinese literature, nor has it afforded, even when earnestly applied to the least countenance to the strenuous efforts made by private individuals, to give facilities for acquiring a knowledge of Chinese without the necessity of a distant voyage.

Morrison pointed out how his late father's Chinese library, which he had taken to England in 1824, had been left to languish under the auspices of the London Missionary Society rather than become the foundation of a language school as his father had hoped.[69]

This was about more than language: many Britons in China believed they had weakened their own position by failing to understand—and to convince their countrymen at home and in India—how much the Chinese needed foreign trade. True enough, well into the late 1830s some insisted that, however important the trade at Canton was to foreigners and the Chinese merchants, shopkeepers, and servants involved, it was trifling compared to China's inland trade. John Barrow had written in 1804 that the British needed the Chinese much more than vice versa, especially given that tea, "a century ago a luxury," had become "one of the first necessities of life."[70] Rather than assuming that the monopolistic form of trade in Canton was to blame for the lack of interest in foreign trade, "Another British Merchant" asked in 1834, were it not possible that foreign commerce was "of very little utility or importance to the Chinese nation?" The people of Canton and its neighboring provinces benefited from foreign trade, but the government in Peking derived "little if any advantage" from it.[71] Charles Toogood Downing, the surgeon, wrote that although "a vast number" of Chinese depended "entirely" on the trade at Canton and would be "ruined and driven to desperation" if it were ended, the emperor could afford to be "careless as to whether the foreigners bring their trade to Canton."[72]

Robert Morrison disagreed. Because the local authorities believed the British were dependent on Chinese tea—an impression the British themselves were guilty of fostering—they could afford to stop trade so frequently. And the foreigners were "simple enough" to believe the Chinese when they claimed that they stopped trade because they despised it. In reality, all their "pompous edicts and manifestoes" to the contrary, the Chinese would be "very much disappointed" if the foreigners all withdrew from Canton. The end of trade at Canton would be "a serious inconvenience" for the Qing government:

> The resources of this government are barely sufficient to support its military, naval, and civil establishment; together with the numerous offspring of the original Imperial Clan, and to conduct those public works and charities which must be paid out of the public purse. Some of the provinces, where occasional insurrections occur . . . are not adequate to govern and defend themselves.

Apart from the revenue that that the imperial government derived from the trade at Canton, the patronage that an appointment at Canton carried was highly lucrative. "Almost any office in Canton is considered promotion. It is a standard joke amongst the civilians to use '*promoted*' to Canton, instead of 'appointed'." Morrison insisted that the British could do more to disabuse the Chinese of their conviction that they were nothing more than a "trade-loving, gain-making" lot, and that Britain could not exist without tea.[73]

One of the problems, John Slade argued, was that foreigners did not realize how the Chinese contempt for foreign trade was "all simulation." Although the government was more indifferent than others to foreign trade, it valued this trade much in the way any government did: in terms of how it affected the revenue or demands of the country. "The duties levied on the foreign trade are of too much importance to the imperial treasury to be lightly abandoned; and all the blustering and contempt for trade affected by the government is a farce, ill-got-up, and worse managed." Slade agreed that persuading the Qing government to open another port in Fujian province would help, but it was highly unlikely that the current regime would "court an approximation to Europeans, whose skill and courage must be to it a cause of jealousy and fear." Apart from force, it was difficult to find a "creditable way" for any European government to deal with China. "Embassies are considered as acknowledgments of fealty, and presents are received as tribute."[74]

Hugh Lindsay believed that the British failed to understand the "vast importance" of the coastal trade—"nay, how entirely dependant on it for the very necessaries of life some parts of China are."[75] John Davis argued that the Manchus confined trade with Europe to Canton "with such obstinacy to a point so unsuited to its extension" for two reasons: to "remove the danger of external involvements from the vicinity of the capital" and to "derive the largest possible revenue from internal transit." The Qing authorities imposed a variety of contributions on the hong merchants and farmed out a range of "irregular" charges on foreign trade. And that was only the legal part: the government used the hong merchants "in the manner of a sponge, that, after being allowed to absorb the gains of a licensed monopoly, was made regularly to yield up its contents, by what was very correctly termed 'squeezing.'"[76]

In early 1838 the *Press* devoted a series of five lengthy articles to showing how many Chinese livelihoods depended on the foreign trade, and how local authorities were unlikely to jeopardize such a valuable source of revenue and risk rebellion by halting trade more than occasionally and temporarily.[77] The *Press* also featured a five-part series listing British grievances in China and outlining how to improve Anglo-Chinese relations. With some one million livelihoods depending on foreign trade, both local authorities and the rulers in Peking understood the value of foreign trade only too well to allow any serious interruptions or stoppages. The success of the opium trade in ports along the Chinese coast provided "singular proof" of the "weakness or supineness" of the Qing government to prohibit opium smoking and the opium trade. Once British goods were introduced to the northern ports of China, the Qing government, eager not to be "altogether defrauded of the duties," would be forced to open new ports, and its people would "soon learn to appreciate the advantages of a direct trade."[78]

## SOMEWHERE ELSE

Throughout the early 1800s, British merchants advocated trying to open a second port in China, their choices including Amoy, Shanghai and neighboring Ningpo and Chusan, and Formosa. In 1817, Company tea inspector Samuel Ball wrote that tea was the "only valuable" branch of trade with China and that "scarcely a single article of the Company's imports, except cotton, would ever be brought to China, but for the purchase of tea." Canton was the "most unfavorable" Chinese port for the tea trade while Foochow (Fuzhou), in Fujian province, was the "most favorable." Although the "sudden removal" of a trade of such "great magnitude" would not be easy, it would be less inconvenient and risky than moving to Fujian, where the tea was grown and manufactured, and the native province of most of the merchants who sold it in Canton. Convincing the Chinese that such a change would be mutually beneficial might not even be difficult: "Whatever may have been said of the jealousy and suspicion of these people, it may be doubted whether they are so bigoted to forms as to sacrifice even their smallest interests where a change seems to involve no radical injury to their institutions."[79]

Only in the 1830s, however, did anyone call seriously for an alternative to Canton—a testament, perhaps, to how well the Canton System actually worked. In January 1835 the *Register* explained that although Canton had many natural advantages as an emporium, it also had "great disadvantages." It was as far from the capital at Peking as London was from Constantinople. And less than one-tenth of the foreign exports were from Guangdong province: teas and silks had to travel so far from Fujian, Anhui, and Zhejiang provinces, that by the time they reached Canton their prices were "greatly enhanced"; likewise for foreign imports, "subject to the same tedious conveyance ere they reach the consumers." Imagine how the trade would flourish if allowed to extend beyond Canton.[80] In January 1837 the *Register* suggested several alternatives for placing commercial relations on a more secure footing, "either by purchase or treaty," including Hainan, Formosa, Hong Kong, Chusan, and some other smaller islands.[81]

Some looked farther afield for possibilities. In late 1836 the naturalist and missionary George Tradescant Lay urged Britain to colonize the Bonin Islands, six hundred miles south of Edo (later Tokyo) and an eight-day sail from Canton. The islands might as well be considered to belong to Britain, Lay figured, as Englishmen had lived on one of them for more than ten years. Here, under a "spirited and enlightened" governor, Britons, Americans, and Europeans would enjoy "all the security, and many of the comforts of home, in the very centre of those nations who have hitherto shut their doors against them." The benefits were numerous. The proximity of the islands to China, Formosa, Japan, and the Ryukyus would encourage an "unfettered communication" between foreign and "native" vessels with "equality and mutual respect." Far from the center of the opium trade at Canton, a kind of religious-scientific-commercial utopia would emerge:

> At this place of rendezvous, Chinese, Japanese, Formosans and Lew-chewans [Ryukyuans] would meet and exchange their sentiments, if not by speech at least by writing, which would tend to establish them upon a footing of better understanding with each other, and diffuse a knowledge of the colloquial dialects, peculiar to each nation, among all the rest; while the prospect of advantage, and the comforts of home, would persuade Europeans to come hither to learn the Asiatic languages, that they might act as interpreters, which would enable us to dispense with that mutilated jargon in which all our mercantile transactions are now conducted.

One of the islands would serve as a base for religious and scientific institutions, "where strangers might obtain every kind of instruction, and from whence books might be issued for the improvement of surrounding nations." Foreign merchants would find this "an easy retreat" whenever the governor of Canton decided to stop trade. Under the influences of "religion, science, and the sentiments of political freedom," thousands would learn what it was like to live under the "benign aspect" of "impartial laws" and "religious liberty." Warehouses would provide supplies for repairing and refitting ships from all nations. But none of this could be accomplished without an appeal to the British government, backed by "the concurrent opinions of an enlightened public."[82] Lay's proposal never materialized and seems not to have been discussed widely among the British in Canton. When the *Register* printed excerpts from the proposal in December 1837, it argued that an even more "wise and nobly" move would be to colonize Formosa, in the way the Dutch had Java and the Spanish had Manila. Until this "great project" could be accomplished, however, the paper supported the "immediate colonization" of the Bonin Islands.[83]

One of the only Britons with any significant China experience to suggest withdrawing from Canton altogether was James Brabazon Urmston, chief of the British factory from 1819 to 1826 and a close friend of George Thomas Staunton. In June 1833, just before the decision to abolish the Company's monopoly, Urmston declared in a long pamphlet written from Kent that no one with "any knowledge of China and the circumstances attending our commercial relations with that country" would disagree that Canton was "one of the very worst places" in China that could have been selected as "an emporium for the British trade." It was too far from the areas where British imports were ultimately consumed and from the regions where teas and silks were produced. Homicides committed by foreigners could lead to trade stoppages, as could the rare visits to Canton by Western women (as had occurred in the autumn of 1830) and the occasional attempts to make even minor modifications to the British factory and its grounds.[84]

What, then, would improve Britain's "general relations" with China? Compliance was clearly not the answer, Urmston explained. "Forebearance, conciliation, and indeed submission" to the "capricious insolence" of the Qing authorities had turned out to be the "very worst" policy toward people who "systematically" treated foreigners with "the utmost contumely and hostility." British warships should sail to China whenever necessary and enjoy the "usual rights of hospitality" in terms of anchorage and supplies; nowhere else in the world were British ships denied shelter and access to port. Equally useless as compliance were embassies, both of which had failed, as would be giving the Company's chief at Canton consular powers. A king's consul would never be recognized: like the American consul, he would be "a complete cipher, in his official situation." British authorities under the same flag—one Company chief and one consul—would "be constantly clashing, jealousies would naturally arise, and in all probability they would quarrel." And the Qing would certainly never allow a British resident at Peking.[85]

Urmston also rejected the suggestion of trying to open a second port in China. Because of its "usual jealous policy," the Qing government would see itself less subjected to intrusion by foreigners if it could confine them to one spot. The only reliable solution was a "complete and extensive" change: moving the British trade from the "unnatural and vexatious" restrictions at Canton to somewhere else in China. Not that the Qing would consent readily—at least not by a "mere common-place representation." The British must insist that continuing trade at Canton under the present circumstances was "quite out of the question," but they were eager to remain on good terms somewhere else in China "on fair, just, and honourable terms to both nations." The new port should be a "considerable distance" east of Canton, but even better would be an island on the east coast of China "entirely to ourselves."[86]

The island Urmston proposed was Chusan, in Zhejiang province, which he could not understand why the British had abandoned more than a century earlier. Chusan boasted many advantages, including a good harbor protected from winds, was close to several mainland cities, and provided easy access to Formosa, Japan, the Ryukyus, Korea, and Batavia. Most importantly, it was near the part of China with the "most fertile and productive" and "most flourishing and opulent" provinces and districts, and where the "most extensive" trade and manufacturing occurred. The provinces of Jiangsu and Zhejiang produced the "best and finest" silk in China, and in "vast quantities." This was also the region where most British exports to China were consumed.[87]

Acquiring Chusan would be expensive and require "arduous negociation [*sic*] and discussion." But Urmston was convinced the Qing government would eventually see the wisdom of his proposal. With the foreign traders in a port much closer to the capital in Peking, it could monitor their activities and intervene during disputes between foreigners and Chinese—thus preventing the many "evils and embarrassments" that currently resulted from "the oppressive and arbitrary" policies of the Canton authorities, so far away from the center of imperial power. Even if the Qing government were initially opposed to a British settlement, the local authorities and people there would "rejoice" at being able to participate "fairly and freely" in such a lucrative trade.[88]

Given how much they valued the "importance and regularity" of the trade with Britain, it was impossible to imagine that either the government or the people of the region would offer any "violent objects or hostility." But even if the British had the power to take Chusan "in defiance of the whole force of the Chinese empire," Urmston cautioned against aggression and instead urged conciliation and negotiation. He had recently learned of Lindsay's mission up the coast to learn what commercial advantages might be derived there if the Chinese opened more ports to foreign trade. He appreciated Lindsay's zeal and his knowledge of Chinese. But he doubted Lindsay would find a favorable welcome, insisting any negotiations with the Chinese should be conducted on a more official level.[89]

Urmston was trying to do more than improve British trade with China: he was attempting to secure a new lease on life for the Company. The presence of a "great, long-established, and recognized public body" was of "utmost importance." It had provided the "highest satisfaction" to the Chinese and gained their "unbounded confidence," while the "vast and certain advantages" it had added to the revenues of Britain were "too obvious and notorious" to mention. Recognized and trusted for so long by the Chinese, the Company was the most suitable authority to carry out these negotiations. Its "fine" ships could help move the trade from Canton to Chusan, commanded as they were by "gentlemen of education" and of "the greatest respectability." These "well appointed and disciplined" ships had always proved their worth, not the least by "awing" the Chinese during times of disputes. Having personally relied upon the "cordial, ready, and valuable" support provided by the ships when he was chief of the British factory, Urmston was certain that their captains' "perfect knowledge" of China waters would prove "eminently essential" in carrying out his proposed plan.[90]

Urmston's wish came true, and Chusan eventually became "Britain's first Chinese island."[91] British forces occupied it twice during the Opium War. Even after the war, in accordance with the Treaty of Nanking, they continued to hold the island for payment of the indemnity imposed upon the Qing government. With its "central position, temperate climate, gentle topography and peaceable, industrious population," Chusan seemed to "possess in abundance the materials for a model colony." Many critics contrasted it with Hong Kong, which by the mid-1840s had become known mainly for crime, prostitution, and malaria so prevalent that it was sometimes called "Hong Kong fever." In the end, however, the British occupation of Chusan yielded little. The island failed to become an entrepot, eclipsed by Shanghai. The British had little luck securing reliable collaborators, and missionary endeavors were short-lived. The restoration of the small island to the Qing government both coincided with and influenced souring relations with China, and a "growing disillusionment about what the British thought they could expect of China and its people."[92]

Chusan was restored to Qing rule on 5 June 1846, in accordance with the treaty. John Davis, after more than a decade in England and now back in China as plenipotentiary and governor of Hong Kong, visited to make sure the remaining British traders left the island. Although the Qing government had already paid the final installment of the indemnity in January, Davis hoped to use the island to extract additional concessions from the Qing government. He had been instructed by the Foreign Office to try and retain Chusan as a permanent colony, though he doubted it could ever become a viable trading center and was worried that violating the treaty would send a bad sign to the Chinese. Although an Anglo-French force retook the city of Dinghai in 1860 during the Second Opium War, the brief British occupation of Chusan was all but forgotten.

One man who never forgot was James Urmston. In 1847, writing from the Isle of Wight at a time when the future of colonial Hong Kong looked bleak, he argued that the British could have demanded much more from the Qing than they had. They should have taken Chusan rather than Hong Kong. Although Urmston agreed that the British had no choice but to abide by the treaty and restore Chusan to Qing rule, he remained convinced that "some arrangement" might have been made to retain it "in perpetuity." Hong Kong was "an insignificant barren island which can never prove of the slightest utility of us, beyond a mere garrison, and a harbour for shipping, of which there are many on the coast of China equally eligible and many far superior." Urmston had never understood "on what reasonable grounds we ever in the first instance took possession of, and permanently established ourselves on this barren, out of the way useless rock." Chusan, however, could have become an "invaluable" colony and one of the "most important and desirable naval stations" in Asia. "An extensive, flourishing, and important trade would speedily spring up, benefiting extensively, not merely our own merchants, commerce, and manufactures, but also the immense Chinese commercial community, existing in various ramifications in the vicinity of Chusan, at the numerous large and important ports and cities, placed along the whole Coast of China."[93]

## NOTES

1. FO 17/12/251–53, The National Archives of the UK (TNA); *Chinese Repository* 3, no. 7 (November 1834): 354–60; also in *Canton Register* 7, no. 52 (30 December 1834): 208–9.

2. "Great Britain and China," *Canton Register* 9, no. 39 (27 September 1836): 158–59.

3. *Canton Register* 9, no. 44 (1 November 1836): 181.

4. John Barrow and George Macartney, *Some Account of the Public Life, and a Selection from the Unpublished Writings, of the Earl of Macartney* (London: Cadell and Davies, 1807), vol. 2, 395–96, 398.

5. Barrow and Macartney, *Some Account of the Public Life*, 397–99.

6. Barrow and Macartney, *Some Account of the Public Life*, 399, 400–1, 512–19, 525–26.

7. James Holman, *Voyage Round the World, Including Travels in Africa, Asia, Australasia, America, etc. etc. from 1827 to 1832* (London: Smith, Elder, 1834–1835), vol. 4, 109, 366, 425, 517–18. In his introduction to *The Present Position and Prospects of the British Trade with China: Together with an Outline of Some Leading Occurrences in Its Past History* (London: Smith, Elder, 1836), James Matheson, who according to Holman had a blind uncle and thus showed a "sincerely sympathy" for him (Holman, *Voyage Round the World*, 97), credited his "admirable friend Mr. Holman" for supporting the accuracy of his own observations.

8. Holman, *Voyage Round the World*, vol. 4, 92–94, 139–42, 150–53.

9. Holman, *Voyage Round the World*, vol. 4, 75, 110–11, 176, 234. On the Baynes incident, see also Hosea Ballou Morse, *The Chronicles of the East India Company Trading to China, 1635–1834* (Oxford: Clarendon Press, 1926), vol. 4, 234; Rachel Tamar Van, "The 'Woman Pigeon': Gendered Bonds and Barriers in the Anglo-American Commercial Community in Canton and Macao, 1800-1849," *Pacific Historical Review* 83, no. 4 (2014): 566–71; John M. Carroll, *Canton Days: British Life and Death in China* (Lanham, MD: Rowman & Littlefield, 2020), 97–100.

10. [G. J. Gordon], *Address to the People of Great Britain, Explanatory of Our Commercial Relations with the Empire of China and of the Course of Policy by Which It May Be Rendered an Almost Unbounded Field for British Commerce* (London: Smith, Elder, 1836), 4–5, 12, 13, 120.

11. John Slade, *Notices on the British Trade to the Port of Canton; with Some Translations of Chinese Official Papers Relative to That Trade* (London: Smith Elder, 1830), 72–73.

12. Slade, *Notices on the British Trade to the Port of Canton*, 61, 67, 78, 103–4.

13. *Canton Register* 4, no. 13 (4 July 1831): 62.

14. *Canton Register* 4, no. 14 (15 July 1831): 69.

15. *Canton Register* 4, no. 15 (2 August 1831): 75.

16. *Canton Register* 4, no. 15 (2 August 1831): 76.

17. *Canton Register* 4, no. 16 (15 August 1831): 80–81.

18. Charles Marjoribanks, *Letter to the Right Hon. Charles Grant, President of the Board of Control: On the Present State of British Intercourse with China* (London: J. Hatchard, 1833), 4–5, 32, 50, 53–57, 64–65.

19. "Free Trade with China," *Chinese Repository* 2, no. 8 (December 1833): 355–74.

20. "Free Trade with the Chinese," *Chinese Repository* 2, no. 10 (February 1833): 473–75.

21. "Free Trade with China," *Canton Register* 7, no. 14 (8 April 1834): 53.

22. "Hints for the Approaching Superintendent of British Affairs in China" and "Free Trade with China," *Canton Register* 7, no. 5 (4 February 1834): 19–20.

23. "English Superintendents," *Canton Register* 7, no. 19 (13 May 1834): 73; original emphasis.

24. "Free Trade to All the Ports of the Chinese Empire," *Canton Register* 7, no. 25 (24 June 1834): 100.
25. *Canton Register* 7, no. 35 (2 September 1834): 137–38.
26. *Canton Register* 7, no. 38 (23 September 1834): 151.
27. "Relations with China," *Canton Register* 7, no. 39 (30 September 1834): 155.
28. "What Steps Should the Expected Strength from England Take?" *Canton Register* 8, no. 14 (7 April 1835): 53–54.
29. "On the Recent Discussions, No. 2," *Canton Register* 7, no. 44 (4 November 1834): 174–75.
30. *Canton Register* 7, no. 52 (30 December 1834): 206.
31. "Commercial Treaty with China," *Canton Register* 8, no. 4 (27 January 1835): 14.
32. "Commercial Treaty with China," 14.
33. "Canton," *Canton Register* 8, no. 14 (7 April 1835): 53; original emphasis.
34. *Canton Press* 1, no. 18 (9 January 1835): 137.
35. *Canton Press* 1, no. 20 (23 January 1836): 154–55.
36. *Canton Register* 9, no. 6 (9 February 1836): 24, original emphasis; *Canton Press* 1, no. 22 (6 February 1836): 170.
37. *Canton Press* 1, no. 23 (13 February 1836): 177.
38. *Canton Press* 1, no. 28 (19 March 1836): 221.
39. *Canton Press* 1, no. 33 (23 April 1836): 257.
40. "Free Trade with China," *Canton Press* 1, no. 40 (11 June 1836): 313–14.
41. *Canton Press* 3, no. 12 (25 November 1837): n.p.
42. *Canton Press* 3, no. 13 (2 December 1837): n.p.; original emphasis.
43. *Canton Register* 9, no. 26 (28 June 1836): 103.
44. Copy enclosed in *Canton Register* 9, no. 26 (28 June 1836): 103–4.
45. Matheson, *Present Position and Prospects*, 34, 42–43.
46. Matheson, *Present Position and Prospects*, 61–62, 71–72, 78, 79; original emphasis.
47. Hugh Hamilton Lindsay, *Letter to the Right Honourable Viscount Lord Palmerston on the British Relations with China* (London: Saunders & Otley, 1836), 1–2. The original letter is in Lindsay to Palmerston, 24 July 1835, FO 17/12/354–62, TNA. On Lindsay's own poorly suppressed wrath, see Robert Bickers, "The *Challenger*: Hugh Hamilton Lindsay and the Rise of British Asia, 1832–1865," *Transactions of the Royal Historical Society* 22 (2012): 141–69.
48. Lindsay, *Letter to the Right Honourable Viscount Lord Palmerston*, 3, 4–5, 8.
49. Lindsay, *Letter to the Right Honourable Viscount Lord Palmerston*, 12–18.
50. *Canton Press* 1, no. 49 (13 August 1836): 388.
51. A Resident in China, *British Intercourse with Eastern Asia* (London: Edward Suter, 1836), 8–10, 13–14, 23, 26; original emphasis.
52. George Thomas Staunton, *Remarks on the British Relations with China, and the Proposed Plans for Improving Them* (London: E. Lloyd, 1836), v–vi, 3–4; original emphasis. On Staunton's life in China, see Carroll, *Canton Days*, 64–71.
53. Staunton, *Remarks on the British Relations with China*, 12, 33–35; original emphasis.

54. Staunton, *Remarks on the British Relations with China*, 35–36, 49–50, 57–59; original emphasis.

55. Barrow and Macartney, *Some Account of the Public Life*, vol. 2, 394–95.

56. Samuel Holmes, *The Journal of Mr. Samuel Holmes, Serjeant-Major of the XIth Light Dragoons, during His Attendance, as One of the Guard of Lord Macartney's Embassy to China and Tartary, 1792–3* (London: W. Bulmer, 1798), 108–9.

57. Robert Morrison, *Notices Concerning China, and the Port of Canton, also a Narrative of the Affair of the English Frigate Topaze, 1821–22; With Remarks on Homicides, and an Account of the Fire of Canton* (Malacca: Printed at the Mission Press, 1823), iv.

58. John Barrow, *Travels in China, Containing Descriptions, Observations, and Comparisons, Made and Collected in the Course of a Short Residence at the Imperial Palace of Yuen-Min-Yuen, and on a Subsequent Journey through the Country from Pekin to Canton in Which It Is Attempted to Appreciate the Rank That the Extraordinary Empire May Be Considered to Hold in the Scale of Civilized Nations* (London: Cadell and Davies, 1804), 257, 614–18. On pidgin English, see Carroll, *Canton Days*, 45–49.

59. Davis, *Chinese Novels*, 1–5.

60. Robert Morrison, *A View of China, for Philological Purposes: Containing a Sketch of Chinese Chronology, Geography, Government, Religion & Customs* (Macao: Printed at the Honorable East India Company's Press by P. P. Thoms, 1817; London: Black, Parbury, and Allen, 1817), v.

61. Morrison, *Notices Concerning China*, vii, 83.

62. Morrison, *Notices Concerning China*, 84–85.

63. Medhurst, *China*, 526–27.

64. *Canton Register* 1, no. 11 (15 March 1828): 43.

65. *Canton Register* 2, no. 9 (2 May 1829): 42.

66. *Canton Register* 6, no. 2 (24 January 1833): 9–10; original emphasis.

67. "Free Trade," *Canton Register* 7, no. 52 (30 December 1834): 206.

68. For example, "Sinologues," *Canton Press* 2, no. 3 (24 September 1836): n.p.

69. "Relations of England towards China," *Chinese Repository* 6, no. 5 (September 1837): 246–47. Morrison did, however, note that his father's library had recently been placed in the University College, London, and a professor of Chinese had been appointed.

70. Barrow, *Travels in China*, 400.

71. "Free Trade with the Chinese," 475.

72. C. [Charles] Toogood Downing, *The Fan Qui in China in 1836–1837* (London: Henry Colburn, 1838), vol. 1, 235.

73. Morrison, *Notices Concerning China*, vi–iii, viii, 55; original emphasis.

74. Slade, *Notices on the British Trade*, 60–61, 69–70, 72.

75. Lindsay, *Letter to the Right Honourable Viscount Lord Palmerston*, 15.

76. Davis, *Chinese*, vol. 1, 196; vol. 2, 424–45.

77. "British and Chinese Relations," *Canton Press* 3, no. 20 (20 January 1838): n.p.; *Canton Press* 3, no. 21 (27 January 1838): n.p.; and *Canton Press* 3, no. 22

(3 February 1838): n.p.; "British and Chinese Intercourse," *Canton Press* 3, no. 24 (17 February 1838): n.p.; and *Canton Press* 3, no. 25 (24 February 1838): n.p.

78. "British and Chinese Intercourse," *Canton Press* 3, no. 24 (17 February 1838): n.p.

79. Samuel Ball, *Observations on the Expediency of Opening a Second Port in China* (Macao: Printed at the East India Company's Press, by P. P. Thoms, 1817), 2–3, 23–24, 36.

80. "Free Trade to All the Ports of the Chinese Empire," *Canton Register* 8, no. 2 (13 January 1835): 7–8.

81. "Chinese Islands," *Canton Register* 10, no. 1 (3 January 1837): 3–4; *Canton Register* 10, no. 2 (10 January 1837): 6–7; *Canton Register* 10, no. 3 (17 January 1837): 13–14.

82. G. [George] Tradescant Lay, *Trade with China: A Letter Addressed to the British Public on Some of the Advantages That Would Result from an Occupation of the Bonin Islands* (London: Royston & Brown, 1837), 3–5, 7–8, 10–14. Lay's letter is also in *Chinese Repository* 6, no. 8 (December 837): 381–87.

83. *Canton Register* 10, no. 51 (19 December 1837): 205.

84. James Brabazon Urmston, *Observations on the China Trade: And on the Importance and Advantages of Removing It from Canton, to Some Other Part of the Coast of That Empire* (London: Printed for private circulation only by G. Woodfall, 1834), 5, 23–27, 33.

85. Urmston, *Observations on the China Trade*, 33–37, 41–43.

86. Urmston, *Observations on the China Trade*, 51–52, 54–55.

87. Urmston, *Observations on the China Trade*, 56, 62–71, 78, 81–83.

88. Urmston, *Observations on the China Trade*, 69, 79–80.

89. Urmston, *Observations on the China Trade*, 91–92, 95–97.

90. Urmston, *Observations on the China Trade*, vi–vii, 84, 93–97.

91. Liam D'Arcy–Brown, *Chusan: The Forgotten Story of Britain's First Chinese Island* (Kenilworth, UK: Brandram, 2012).

92. Christopher Munn, "The Chusan Episode: Britain's Occupation of a Chinese Island, 1840–46," *Journal of Imperial and Commonwealth History* 25, no. 1 (1997): 82–83.

93. James Brabazon Urmston, *Chusan and Hong Kong; With Remarks on the Treaty of Peace at Nankin in 1842, and on Our Present Position and Relations with China* (London: James Madden, 1847), 9, 10, 22, 48–50.

*Chapter Three*

# Being There

Understanding China required being there, or so these Britons believed. "Nothing could be more fallacious than to judge of China by any European standard," Lord Macartney wrote at the end of his journals. "My sole view has been to represent things precisely as they impressed me." The observations of the "manners and character" of the Chinese were "chiefly the result of what I saw and heard upon the spot, however imperfectly, not of what I had read in books or been told in Europe." Opinions based solely on the accounts of the early travelers and of the Catholic missionaries were "inadequate and unjust." Although Macartney had read everything about China in all the languages he could understand, as soon as he arrived he began studying "the originals themselves, and lost no opportunity in my power of perusing and considering them." Because contact between Chinese and foreigners was so restricted, his observations could not be taken as anything more than the fruit of his own "researches and reflections."[1]

To George Thomas Staunton, the Macartney embassy (for which he had served as page and unofficial interpreter) marked a new stage in the British understanding of China. It had given a "more accurate and intimate knowledge" of the Qing Empire. For the first time, China had been revealed to Europeans "whose talents and judgment were worthy of their country, and of an enlightened age"—men who could describe the place and its people with "candour and sincerity." Even allowing for the "national prejudices" of its members and for the restrictions placed upon them as they traveled to and from Peking, the embassy had thrown an "entire new light" upon this "extraordinary and interesting empire." Although the embassy's time in China had not been long enough to confirm or disprove many of the details supplied by the missionaries, it had been sufficient to learn that China's alleged superiority in knowledge and virtue—claimed not only by the Chinese themselves but also "too readily" by some European historians—was "in great measure fallacious."[2]

The question of who truly understood China came up again with the Amherst embassy of 1816, particularly whether to perform the kowtow before the Jiaqing Emperor. Three of the East India Company men who had spent time in China—Staunton, John Francis Davis, and Francis Hastings Toone—strongly opposed Lord Amherst's willingness to kowtow and eventually convinced him not to do so.[3] The two embassies also became a matter of disagreement and of expertise. In December 1833 the private trader James Goddard blamed the embassy members for debasing themselves in the eyes of the Chinese by associating with merchants.[4] But in February 1834 "Another British Merchant" insisted that surely such a mix of members of Company men and "high officers of state" must have raised them to their "proper station in the eyes of the Chinese authorities." And while Goddard had blamed the Company for "succumbing to Chinese opinion, as degrading to commercial dignity," this merchant believed that although the embassies had brought little advantage, British commercial interests in China had been "saved from positive evil by this sprinkling of practical and useful men."[5]

As the British community became larger and more settled in the 1820s and 1830s, its members increasingly viewed themselves as the only ones who understood China. Like the "imperial careerers" throughout the British Empire, they often came to see themselves as experts on "natives" and "native affairs."[6] Occasionally we find one appreciating his time there. In July 1831, "Senex" explained in the short-lived *Canton Miscellany* why his "long residence" in China had given him a respect for its "antiquated Customs" that "younger men and passing travellers" could not be expected to feel:

> When I look at Despotic Governments I can draw no distinction between an Eastern and a Western Tyranny in favor of the latter. On the contrary, I conceive the Chinese beat many of our European Governments hollow. . . . Who promoted the happiness of mankind most or stemmed the tide of human misery, the Emperor Kien-lung or the Emperor Napoleon? . . . While Kien-lung was holding the plough in Tartary, the other was driving the ploughshare of destruction through the fairest provinces of Europe.

Like most Britons, "Senex" had arrived in China "positive in the belief, that every thing in my own country was superlative, and resolved to regard every thing in this in the comparative degree." His many years in China had confirmed his sense of cultural and national superiority. But it had also convinced him that comparisons were no longer worth the trouble, and of "the necessity of regarding the Chinese as a race of Exclusives, and of the absurdity of attempting to apply to them those principles which regulate the conduct either of the natives or the Governments of other Countries," and that "vice is not darker nor virtue less transparent in China than in many other Countries."[7]

This was not a typical attitude, however. In the same issue, "Antisinicus" in a poem described "Jealous China" and "Strange Japan" as "but Dead Seas of Man" where "tyrant Custom fetters up the soul, and binds the passions in a cold controul [sic]."[8] Two months later, "Juvenis" insisted that "Senex" had been away from Europe for too long to make a qualified judgment.[9] Another anonymous contributor wrote that although he was "no blind admirer" of the Chinese, he had seen "too much of the dark side of their character" to believe they deserved to be "ranked on a level with any civilized nation whatever." Had "Senex" not become "early discouraged" in his Chinese studies and continued them, he would have concluded otherwise. Had he studied Chinese history, he would have found "a list of Chinese tyrants equalling in atrocity and far surpassing in number, the Monsters who disgraced the Roman purple." And he would have learned that "even the great and amiable" Qianlong had sometimes been a conqueror. Qianlong was "a great Monarch, one of the best in the annals of Chinese history," but he could not be "named in the same page with the Great Napoleon."[10]

In November 1827 the *Canton Register* declared in its first issue that part of its mission would be to reveal the "peculiarities" of the Chinese.[11] An issue several months later included a story about a Manchu military officer who had bought a slave girl he soon discovered was a leper. Although the officer applied to the police for redress, the seller had already absconded. Such "seemingly trivial occurrences" revealed the state of society in this "populous and extraordinary country."[12] Europeans were aware of *Confucian* China, a subsequent issue explained, but the "actual state" of the country could be "correctly" understood only through "facts and proceedings"—of which the *Register* promised to provide.[13] By March, the paper had become even more blunt about its mission to paint a "faithful picture" of China. Though it expressed reservations about accepting articles on the "disgusting depravity" of China, its ultimate goal was the "diffusion of *truth*." Far too much error had already been spread in the world through the "superficial information" disseminated by those who looked only on "the surface of society" and by those who saw men "only in a sort of Holiday dress."[14]

In 1830 the private trader John Slade, who at least then still supported continuing the Company's monopoly, wrote that its officers in Canton offered the "very best evidence" on the state of the China trade. As the only people with access to the records of transactions between Britain and China for two centuries, they were "almost the sole depositaries" of "every important fact" in the history of this trade.[15] In June 1834, Slade, now editor of the *Register*, declared that with the monopoly over, the world now looked to the "free merchants and others" of Canton for "fuller and truer" accounts of China than those transmitted by the "clever Jesuits" and others. "It is on them that the increase, progress, and successful results of the Chinese trade *now* chiefly depend. It is they who can smooth the difficulties that may occur—who can most effectually plead for an advance conciliation in the most attainable manner—who can, in short, unshackle and improve the trade of China itself."[16] Slade would have agreed with a *Register* correspondent who in October 1833 regretted that "so many clever sinalogues" [*sic*]—that is, the Catholic missionaries—who had spent most of their lives in China with "full access to the government archives, and the Emperor himself," had done so little to promote "a free intercourse" between their own nations and the "*exclusive* Chinese."[17]

This chapter examines how these Britons established degrees and hierarchies of "being there" expertise as the foundation of authority for making various arguments, both in China and back in Britain. Not surprisingly given what we have already seen, there were always tensions over whose experience of being there was more authoritative, reliable, or trustworthy. Claims to truth through bearing witness were constructed partly against those of the Jesuits and other Britons. But mere physical experience did not necessarily authorize someone; rather, "fact" became a more complicated economy of truth-value based on a variety of qualifications: length of time spent in China, linguistic proficiency, book-knowledge, and scholarly and commercial networks. This does not mean that experience did not matter, but that it involved many issues ranging from history to political economy, morality, and both British and Chinese commercial policies. Being there was thus both a matter of fact and a rhetorical device. And it was both an actual experience and a trope, for setting the record straight was also a literal activity—through publishing books and pamphlets and through submitting articles and editorials. It was not just about publishing but doing so in a definitive sense.

## CHALLENGING THE JESUITS

Constructing an accurate picture of China often began with questioning the writings of the Jesuit missionaries, even while acknowledging their evangelical efforts and their linguistic abilities. John Barrow wrote that with a few exceptions China remained "unbeaten ground" by British writers. People at home were all too familiar with the "Chinese knavery" practiced at Canton. But they knew almost nothing—at least from the authoritative pen of "an Englishman"—about the "manners, customs, and character of the Chinese nation." The "voluminous communications" of these Catholic missionaries were "by no means satisfactory," and Barrow promised to reveal and explain some of these defects in his own book. Unlike the Jesuits, who had covered China with "tinsel" and "tawdry varnish," he would show "this extraordinary people" in their "proper colours"—not as "their own moral maxims would represent them, but as they really are."[18]

Barrow, less interested in the conversion of the Chinese than in their commercial potential, aimed to provide sufficient information for the reader "to settle, in his own mind, the point of rank which China may be considered to hold in the scale of civilized nations." Early into his book, he explained how the Jesuits' positive impressions of China (and thus those of the Enlightenment philosophes they had influenced) were the ones the Macartney embassy had taken to Peking, only to be disappointed. The Jesuits had exaggerated the level of China's civilization. No one could doubt that China had been "civilized to a certain degree before most of the nations of Europe, not even Greece excepted." But whether it had "continued to improve, so as still to vie with many of the present European states," as the missionaries had claimed, was "not by any means so clear."[19]

This was a fine line to walk. The "vast superstructure of prejudice" in Britain against Catholicism, Catholics, and Catholic states certainly colored many of these writings.[20] Critiquing the European Jesuits was about both religious and national competition. And most Britons were in China in ways qualitatively different from the Jesuits: less immersive, more commercial, and as East India Company (and then government) representatives rather than missionaries. Yet given how much everyone who wrote about China depended on the Jesuits, they could not be dismissed entirely. Far from it, for the British derived much of their knowledge of inland China and the rest of the Qing Empire from the Jesuits—not only from their writings but also from the maps they had produced for the Kangxi Emperor in the early 1700s.[21] Both British embassies relied on Jesuit maps as they headed south to Canton. Thanks to the Jesuits, the British in Canton and at home even had a reasonably good idea of the layout of Peking, shown in maps such as one published in London in 1772.

Barrow never accused the Jesuits of false reporting: it would have been "highly illiberal" to presume such scrupulous and talented men should "studiously sit down to compose fabrications for the mere purpose of deceiving the world." But they might have had their own motives for "setting this wonderful people in the fairest point of view." The more "powerful and magnificent" and the more "learned and refined" they represented China to be, the "greater would be their triumph" if they could make Christianity the "national faith" of China. "Common prudence" may have required them to write favorably of a nation "under whose power and protection they had voluntarily placed

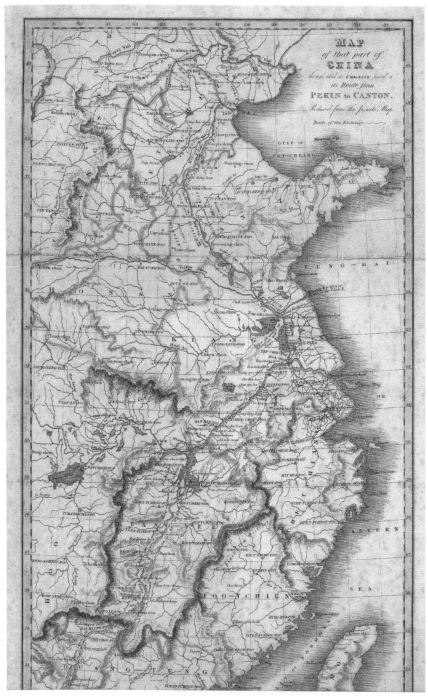

Figure 3.1. *Map of That Part of China through Which the Embassy Passed on Its Route from Pekin to Canton. Reduced from the Jesuits' Map*, ca. 1818. Barry Lawrence Rudman Antique Maps Inc.

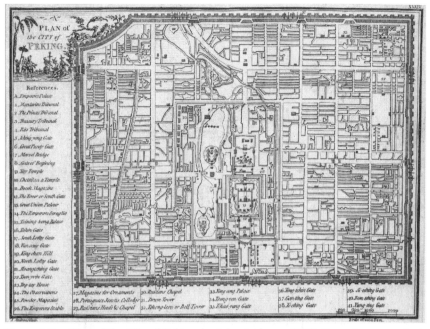

Figure 3.2. *Plan of the City of Peking*, by John Andrews, 1772. Barry Lawrence Rudman Antique Maps Inc.

themselves for life." This tension—between telling the truth but "suppressing some part of it" or telling it in such a way in case it might someday get back to China—explained why the Jesuits often seemed to contradict themselves:

> In the same breath that they extol the wonderful strength of filial piety, they speak of the common practices of exposing infants; the strict morality and ceremonious conduct of the people are followed by a list of the most gross debaucheries; the virtues and the philosophy of the learned are explained by their ignorance and their vices; if in one page they speak of the excessive fertility of the country, and the amazing extension of agriculture, in the next, thousands are seen perishing by want; and whilst they extol with admiration the progress they have made in the arts and sciences, they plainly inform us that without the aid of foreigners they can neither cast, a cannon, nor calculate an eclipse.

Barrow also believed the Jesuits had denied the prevalence of gambling, which he found "so universal" that in "almost every bye-corner" groups could be found "playing at cards or throwing dice." Chinese men might even stake their wives and children "on the hazard of a die." How could the missionaries have failed to realize that two of the favorite and "unmanly" amusements in China were cock-fighting and quail-fighting? The Chinese had even "extended their enquiries after fighting animals into the insect tribe"—to the point where "the custom of making them devour each other is so common that, during the summer months, scarcely a boy is seen without his cage and his grasshoppers." The Jesuits had also downplayed the severity of flogging with the bamboo. While they had considered it "a gentle correction, exercised by men in power over their inferiors, just as a father would chastise his son," Barrow insisted this "humiliating chastisement, to which all are liable from the prime minister to the peasant," was "too often inflicted in the anger and by the caprice of a man in office, and frequently with circumstances of unwarrantable cruelty and injustice." Most egregiously, the Jesuits had failed to condemn infanticide, a practice (as we shall see in the next chapter) Barrow's five weeks in Peking had convinced him was "not to be surpassed among the most savage nations."[22]

George Thomas Staunton opened his translation of the Qing legal code by explaining that the few Catholic missionaries still remaining in service at Peking, or those operating secretly in the provinces, could hardly be expected to add anything new to the "useful and valuable" information they had already provided. And although the missionaries' many works appeared at first glance to be accurate and comprehensive, a closer look revealed they had been less than "disinterested and impartial observers." Having renounced the world in order to convert the Chinese, it was not surprising they would have been favorably predisposed to them. Their lack of partiality and judgment had cast a "false colouring" on many of their writings, leading to inconsistencies, errors, and misrepresentations. Their efforts to put the Chinese classics in the "most favourable and pleasing light" had sometimes led them to apply too much "European character and style," to the point where the authenticity of their translations was sometimes questioned. They had neglected reliable sources such as the Chinese press, because they failed to support their "highly favourable" image of the government and its people. Staunton meant neither to deny the usefulness of the missionaries' work nor accuse them of "wilful deception or mispresentation"; he simply wanted to caution against "replying implicitly" on their authority and judgment, and to point out the "particular bias" that had colored their writings.[23]

Henry Ellis of the Amherst embassy appreciated the "systematic investigation" the Jesuits had made through their long residence among the Chinese. But their work suffered from its "absurd mixture of miraculous accounts" and "erroneous and exaggerated" conclusions about China's rank in the scale of nations—which they derived from the writings and testimonials of the Chinese themselves—though Ellis attributed this more to credibility than to intentional representation.[24] John Davis explained how the first step in rectifying European ignorance of China had been to purge all the embellishments the Catholic missionaries had "so plentifully" added, and which had "tended rather to mislead, than to inform." It thus fell to the British to give the "first correct account" of a nation, whose people they learned were "neither perfectly wise, nor perfectly virtuous, but who were occasionally reduced to the necessity of *flogging* integrity into their magistrates, and valour into their generals." Still, Davis insisted that even if the "particular situation and prejudices" of the Jesuits had led them to provide information that was sometimes both "scanty and unfaithful," they deserved praise for "being the first who told us any thing on the subject."[25]

## A PECULIAR MONOPOLY

Until the end of the East India Company's monopoly in April 1834, the issue the China hands tried to exert their experience and authority upon the most was one of the key points of tension in Britain's relationship with China: whether the monopoly should be extended.[26] The usual argument was that although wrong in principle, monopoly was necessary in this case. George Leonard Staunton argued that the distinctiveness of the Canton trade made it an exception to Adam Smith's opposition to monopolies. Such a "distant branch of commerce," conducted on such a large scale, had to be "exclusively entrusted" to an organization that could handle large losses and which through its ties to the British government was committed as much to "the public advantage" as to private gain. The "probity, punctuality, and credit" of the Company supercargoes and writers were so well known among the Chinese merchants that "their goods are taken always, as to quantity and quality, for what they are declared in the invoice; and the bales with their mark pass in trade, without examination, throughout the empire." These Company agents were "bred in the habits of method, candour, and punctuality, the characteristics of an honourable merchant, without being led into any of the selfish vices, or low propensities, of which the practice must tend to degrade so useful a profession."[27]

Many Britons in China, especially Company officers, argued that the monopoly worked perfectly well. They had been there and seen it in action (and of course benefited from it). Staunton's son, George Thomas, insisted in 1813 that three features unique to the Canton trade made it necessary to remain as it was: "The peculiar nature and objects of the trade itself; the peculiar character of the Chinese people and government; and lastly, the peculiar measures for promoting the prosperity and security of the trade"—neither of which could be maintained with anything but "a great commercial body" such as the Company. Staunton also opposed appointing a British consul at Canton. No matter how much dignity such a move might bring, it could add "nothing whatever" to the power the Company authorities already enjoyed. They derived their power at Canton entirely from trade, and a consul without any commercial backing would be "little more than a cypher."[28]

For Staunton, the key to the continued success of British trade with China was the continued status of the Company's monopoly. Despite "every dif-

Figure 3.3. George Thomas Staunton, by Martin Archer Shee, oil on canvas. British Embassy, Beijing. The Government Art Collection

ficulty" and the occasional incidences "of the most untoward nature," British trade with China had progressed in "a regular and almost uninterrupted course of improvement" over the past fifty years. The causes of this "progressive amelioration" were obvious. The Chinese realized the thousands of Britons who came each year were "avowedly subject to one head" and almost all of the foreign trade at Canton was under the "vigilant protection" of the sovereign of a "great and powerful nation." And the British had proved themselves "just in their dealings" and "wise and consistent in their proceedings." The "general tenor" of the Company's dealings had not only convinced the Chinese that its "good faith" was "unimpeachable" but caused them to "retract, in favor of the British nation, their generally unfavorable opinion of foreigners." The "credit and character" of the Company and its servants had even produced the unintended result of "sheltering and countenancing" traders of other nations, especially the Americans.[29]

If the current system were preserved, Staunton argued, there would be "no limits" to the improvement and expansion of trade. But if the British were rash enough to "invert this order of things" and "break up that wholesome system of control and subordination" by opening their trade to the "experienced and the inexperienced, the honest and the dishonest, the wary and the unwary," they would most certainly "have the mortification" to see their trade sink into "unprofitableness and insignificance." Far from harming British trade, the "commercial preponderance" the Company enjoyed meant that even the richest Chinese merchants were "unable to contend against us," enabling the Company's servants to regulate prices rather than be captive to the "real state of the internal market of the country" or to the hong merchants.[30]

Staunton then explained that, thanks to its power, the Company was able not only to obtain fair market prices but also to guarantee first access to all Chinese goods sold at Canton. With tea becoming "nearly equivalent to a necessary of life" in Britain and its colonies, "the national interests" required far more from this trade than could be obtained if it were left to private traders. No private traders, with "only a limited and temporary interest" in the tea trade, could ever match the expertise and "more extended experience" of a "public body" such as the Company, which supplied Britain with tea "to the greatest pitch of perfection." Individual speculation could be "hazardous and irregular, and generally ruinous," and would flood the British market with "inferior and objectionable" teas. The benefit to individual traders would be "but small and precarious," while the harm to the Company, the China trade, and "the nation at large" would be "certain" and perhaps even "of serious magnitude."[31]

Rebutting demands for allowing British private traders to trade directly between Canton and Europe and the Americas, Staunton later wrote that everyone who had been in China for more than the six weeks or two months usually required to unload and load a ship was "unanimously adverse." Most of these men had been affiliated with the Company. But even one private British trader who had managed to remain in Canton "under the protection of a foreign flag" (by serving as a consul) opposed opening the trade, just as some of the "leading advocates" for ending the monopoly were former Company men. The opinions in favor of opening the trade were mainly "theoretical and speculative," while those against it were mainly "practical, and grounded on a considerable degree of local knowledge and experience."[32]

In March 1829 an anonymous British merchant in Canton explained in a long letter published in London that although he was opposed to the "spirit of monopolies" in principle, the trade with China was "decidedly" an example of where an exception was necessary. Those at home who criticized the monopoly were either "wilfully blind to, or experimentally ignorant of," its scale and complexity. If these critics tried to learn the causes for its existence and longevity, they would find it "peculiarly adapted" to the China trade, which was so unique it required a system of its own. With "every branch" of foreign trade in Canton dominated by a handful of hong merchants, who functioned as a monopoly more "confined and coercive" than any in the world, the "absolute command of great capital and credit" was "imperatively required." A situation "totally at variance" with that in other countries required an equally anomalous solution. "No principle of free trade can reach it." Fortunately, the Company's huge capital, the management and discipline of its ships, and the scale of its commercial transactions had enabled it exercise "a wholesome control" over both the hong merchants and the local authorities. It was "an indisputable truth" that, without the Company, the "utmost possible confusion" would have resulted. The end of the other European factories at Canton had left their commerce in China "altogether obliterated."[33]

Rather than drive up the price of tea, as critics at home claimed the Company's monopoly and its servants' salaries did, the anonymous merchant insisted that the Company's "influence and power" guaranteed a "tolerably stationary" price for everyone. Without an organization like the Company to maintain the quality and purity of their teas, American and European merchants regularly fell for "inferior bargains." If the monopoly were ended, the tea trade would be "thrown into complete confusion" and with it the "comforts and taste" of the British public. "You, in England, would be reduced to a worse state than that of the Americans, whose best tea is now smuggled into their country from Canada, where our ships carry it, and from whence the Americans are glad to obtain it, as cheaper in price, and better in quality, than what they import in their own ships."[34]

In 1830, Henry Ellis explained how his service in the Company and on the Amherst embassy had enabled him to observe the "practical effects" of the monopoly. Learning that the Company was no longer responsible for the conduct of Britons trading with China would "shake the confidence" of the Chinese, and no consul could ever enjoy "the confidence and influence now attached to the Company's factory." Everything lost by the Company's supercargoes would be used to the advantage of the local authorities and of the hong merchants, "and consequently to the injury of the foreign trade in general." Ellis cited the case of the Americans, whose consul in 1821 had been unable to save the life of an American subject. Francis Terranova, an Italian sailor serving aboard an American ship, had been executed for throwing an earthenware jar at a Chinese boatwoman who then drowned. The "peculiar circumstances" of foreign trade in China had led Ellis to reject "as fallacious" the notion that free trade with China could have the "surprising effects" it had achieved in India.[35]

John Slade praised the "facility and quietness" with which foreign commerce was conducted at Canton. Despite having worked for the private firm of Magniac & Co. and its successor Jardine, Matheson & Co., he insisted that free trade could only be possible with the "total repeal" of the hong monopoly. If the Company's monopoly were ended but the hong monopoly were not, the number of hong merchants would have to be "greatly increased" to meet the demands of the "numerous newcomers." But this would lead to a weaker Cohong and thus greater and "more inquisitorial" surveillance by the local authorities. However wrong a monopoly might be—"on general principles, and more especially so in the present age"—the opponents of the Company were obligated to present a "tolerable case" that free trade would be as profitable as under the current system. In any case, Slade argued, free trade was "a term of some obscurity":

> Where is trade free? Is the trade to Turkey free? Is the wine trade at Oporto free? Does free trade imply a fair, full, unrestricted reciprocity of rights between two nations? If so, where are those two nations which have arrived at this point of knowledge and liberal and confidential communication? It has been said, that the trade to China must be politically free: what is meant by trade being politically free? A freedom from British or from Chinese politics, one or both? A freedom from all fiscal regulations at London and Canton?

Slade concluded that "no free trade can ever hope to attain so commanding a position as that now held by the Honourable Company."[36]

When critics at home argued that America's growing trade with China, free from any charter, proved that monopoly was unnecessary, long-timers pointed out how much of the trade conducted under the American flag was in fact Anglo-American trade, supported by British capital. There was, Staunton insisted, "in reality no similarity" between the two cases. "The English are a great and powerful nation; the Americans, as far as the Chinese are acquainted with them, are the reverse of this, and, indeed, they are as yet scarcely recognised in China as a nation at all." Although the American traders drew "certain advantages" from their neutrality, they benefited mainly from cheaper sailing costs and access to all the major American and European ports, rather than from their neutrality. Furthermore, the Americans were able to purchase their teas with bullion, skins, and sandalwood, "articles which cost them nothing more than the labour of procuring them." Still, they enjoyed few advantages the British did not.[37]

Slade insisted the American trade could never have reached its "climax of prosperity" without the protection extended over all foreign trade in Canton by the "method and magnitude" of the Company's transactions.[38] The anonymous British resident maintained in his letter of 1829 that few of the American merchants in China had made "even a moderate profit" while most of them had "been ruined." New recruits continued to replace "their decayed countrymen," but the bankruptcy of their "parent houses" back home were a "faithful picture" of their unfortunate Chinese speculations. "Nothing, indeed, can be more chimerical, or more dangerous to the latter, than to set up America as a *model* of free trade for our intercourse with Canton; much more prudently may it be regarded as a *beacon* to warn us of the hazard of altering our present course."[39]

And who, many asked, would manage and defend the British community in China if the Company's monopoly were ended, especially during confrontations and disputes—and particularly given how the Americans had been unable to protect themselves against the local government, as seen in the Terranova case? "Even the lower orders of the Chinese," wrote the anonymous merchant, "evinced contempt at the willing blindness and credulity of the employers of the wretched Italian seaman, who, to preserve their own interests, persuaded him to trust himself to the justice of a Chinese tribunal." During cases of accidental death of Chinese by foreigners, the Select Committee had used its "decided exertions" to find the criminal or protect the accused if it believed him to be innocent. Foreign merchants not connected to the Company had never been able to organize themselves well enough against the "arbitrary" measures of the Chinese government. The existing system, with its "regular succession" of Company officers rising "step by step, to rank and responsibility," and becoming "thoroughly conversant" with the "disposition, wiles, proceedings, and views" of the Qing authorities and the hong merchants, produced "that confederacy of well-combined action, supported by capital, which no arts of the natives can effectually combat or neutralize." If the monopoly were ended, "delays, difficulties, complaints, and extortions" would be "endless and incalculable. There will be no one to whom the aggrieved free trader can appeal for redress."[40]

Then there was the problem of having so many additional British seamen in Canton, Staunton wrote, under "an inferior system of subordination and discipline." Although he doubted the insubordination was as serious as it had been made out to be, "disorders and disturbances" were much more frequent among British seamen than among the Americans. And what if a private British trader, "disgusted with the difficulties and disappointments" he encountered at Canton, should try to open trade farther up the coast or even in the interior? Imagine the "difficulties and embarrassments" this might cause the Company should he be discovered by the Chinese authorities. The danger that would result from opening the trade was "certainly not quite chimerical."[41]

## INTERESTING EVIDENCE

If the China hands agreed that only they were capable of comprehending China, they often disagreed on how to do so. This was as much a matter of difference as a way to highlight the originality and authority of their own contributions. In the introduction to his translation of the Qing legal code, published in 1810, Staunton maintained that the best way to understand China's government and people was through the "interesting evidence" provided in their own "numerous and respectable literary productions." The "best and most authentic" information on any civilized country was to be found in its own works—especially in China, which encouraged literary pursuits and where at least the "rudiments" of literary knowledge were "universally diffused among the natives of every class and denomination." And the most effective way to decipher its government and internal policy was through law. The problem was that this literature was written in the language "least accessible" to foreigners than any "ever invented by man," even if learning it was not impossible.[42] Fortunately, it was one Staunton understood.

Staunton decided to translate the Qing legal code primarily, it has been argued, to "gain epistemic control over the 'inscrutable' Chinese empire" and to untangle the "opaque operation" of Chinese laws regarding foreigners.[43] As he himself put it, many of the problems foreigners faced in China arose from their own "false or imperfect notions of the spirit of their laws."[44] But Staunton was trying to do more than prevent conflict between foreigners and Chinese. His translation aimed to persuade his readers the Chinese indeed had a concept of justice. Unlike accounts such as John Barrow's *Travels in China*, Staunton's introduction showed a "basically sympathetic" view of the

Figure 3.4. Frontispiece, George Thomas Staunton, *Ta Tsing Leu Lee; Being the Fundamental Laws, and a Selection from the Supplementary Statutes, of the Penal Code of China*. London: Cadell and Davies, 1810

Chinese. Likewise, his translation of the code tried to present it as one that was "comprehensible, reasonable, and just."[45]

He was particularly concerned about how Chinese law and punishments had been portrayed in the West, including by his longtime friend and former tutor Barrow, to whom he inscribed his book "in testimony of sincere regard and esteem." In *The Punishments of China* (1801), for example, George Henry Mason had featured twenty-two engravings, with captions in English and French, of various "cruelties" and "barbarous executions" that Staunton insisted were rarely applied. On the contrary, mitigation was so common that, despite its defects and complexity, Chinese people usually referred to the code with "pride and admiration," impressed by its impartiality, consistency, and incorruptibility. Staunton hoped to show in his own translation of an "authentic work" a "just idea" of the "spirit" and the "substance" of the code that had served China's government for so long.[46]

China, Staunton wrote, might not have its own Newton, Locke, or Bacon, or even any "tolerable proficiency" in the sciences. Still, it compared favorably with Europe in the "essential characteristics" of civilization. Even if the virtues of the Chinese were "very inferior" to those of Europeans, they were no worse than those of other non-Christians. And even if the Chinese exhibited some "exceptionable traits" not found in Europe, they also had some "very considerable and positive" moral and political advantages: the "sacred regard" for familial ties; the industry, sobriety, and intelligence of the lower classes; the "almost total" lack of feudal rights and privileges; the equal distribution of land; and the "natural incapacity and indisposition" to carry out "ambitious projects and foreign conquests." Most importantly, they had a legal code that "if not the most just and equitable" was at least "the most comprehensive, uniform, and suited to the genius of the people for whom it is designed, perhaps of any that ever existed."[47]

But why try so hard in the first place to convince British readers the Chinese had a concept of justice? An ardent supporter of the Company and its monopoly, Staunton was trying to highlight the Company's role in maintaining the jurisdictional status quo in what had become "patently an unstable and hybrid legal environment" in Canton, while overlooking how the British were "eroding and destabilising" the legal order there. With the contraband opium trade conducted by private traders, with the connivance of Company officials and local Qing authorities, the Canton System had become a mixture between "official transactions and a mostly illicit private trade." This ambiguous jurisdictional order, in which the British more or less governed themselves, was a great advantage to the Company, "enabling it to pay lip service to Chinese law while relentlessly probing at its seams in practice." Staunton, this argument goes, presented this order as a weak legal pluralism and as "a natural and inevitable outcome." Given the fragile legal situation in Canton, preserving the Company's status quo was vital for saving Britons from "the wanton depredations of Chinese law." By describing Qing laws as "terrifying in form but mild in practice," he tried to ensure British readers that China was "not too hardline, not fundamentally different, but somewhere reassuringly within the penumbra of the civilisational pale."[48]

Staunton, who had hoped to play an important role in improving Anglo-Chinese relations and even to lead an embassy to Peking, was equally interested in enhancing his own authority and reputation as a sinologist. In August 1807 he explained to his friend and former tutor John Barrow how he had spent much of the summer working on his translation. Instead of translating the entire code, "a task for which I have neither leisure nor perseverance sufficient," he had chosen to select only the laws that were "fixed and original."[49] In a letter to his mother in July 1811, he wrote that Qing officials were usually "too proud and ignorant" to pay any attention to foreigners, "except to give them trouble and inconvenience." The current governor-general, however, remembered Staunton from when he had accompanied his father on the Macartney embassy. As soon as he heard the younger Staunton was in China, he requested to see him and received him with "much cordiality." The governor-general gave him a dinner at his palace with some of the other principal officials; he had even dined with Staunton and several of the Company men at their factory in Macao.[50]

Even before Staunton completed his translation, he had already begun to establish himself as an expert on China. Until the arrival of Robert Morrison in 1807, he was one of the only Britons in Canton since the 1750s to have studied Chinese seriously.[51] In 1805 he helped introduce the smallpox vaccination by translating into Chinese, "with the assistance of a native," a short treatise written by Company surgeon Alexander Pearson.[52] In March 1807 he was busy resolving the *Neptune* affair, an affray between some drunken British sailors and locals in which one Chinese had been killed and several more wounded. The Chinese insisted that the person who dealt the fatal blow be surrendered, and the trade had been suspended.[53]

Staunton's reputation as a sinologist was spreading beyond China. The politician and scholar James Mackintosh, then judge of Bombay, wrote in June 1805 to report that he had established a small society for studying "Oriental matters"; having read about Staunton in Barrow's account, he had taken the liberty of making him a member.[54] Two months later, Mackintosh invited Staunton to write an article on trade between China and Japan and Cochin China, or perhaps on the coasting trade.[55] In August 1806 he asked Staunton to send something on the "Laws, Acts and Manners" of China.[56] Mackintosh importuned again in May 1807, hoping Staunton might be able to gratify his

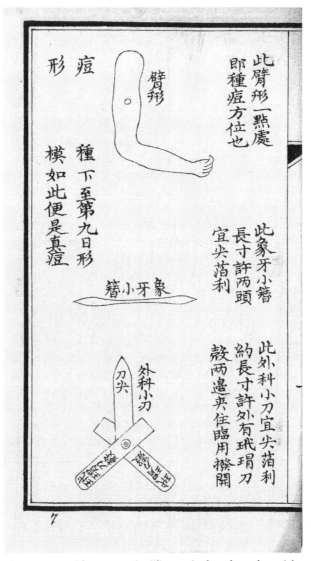

Figure 3.5. Title page, *Yingjiliguo xinchu zhongdou qishu* [An Astonishing Pamphlet on Vaccinations Recently Published in England], second edition. Wellcome Collection. CC BY 4.0

curiosity by writing some articles on the subjects he had mentioned earlier, and particularly "an abridgement of the system of Law which you speak of which will give us more insight into the state of China than all the volumes of the missionaries."[57]

Given Staunton's interest in establishing a "zone of hypothetical equivalence" between the Chinese and English systems and in demonstrating his own authority as a sinologist, it is hardly surprising he stuck to his guns even after returning to England for the last time in January 1817.[58] In his remarks on the Terranova case, he wrote that although it was "quite impossible" to presume Terranova guilty of deliberate murder, it was "altogether" wrong to assume Chinese law made no differentiation in such cases or always demanded blood for blood. The Qing code not only remitted the punishment of accidental death, but also defined such cases with "considerable accuracy." It specified that anyone who killed or wounded another by accident, for example, could atone by paying a fine to the victim's family. Like English law, Chinese law recognized varying degrees of culpable homicide: it reserved beheading for cases of murder but strangulation for manslaughter, and in cases with no "peculiar aggravation" the sentence was usually reduced. Although Terranova's execution had been a violation of Qing law, Staunton argued that it reflected the local government's worries about the foreigners' "insubordinate character" and its eagerness to use any possible opportunity to inflict "salutary fear" upon them.[59]

Staunton's translation may have been of limited influence in persuading British readers that the Chinese had a concept of justice, but it remained the only English translation of the Qing legal code until the late twentieth century.[60] In November 1811 he wrote that he was happy about the "flattering and indulgent manner" in which his translation had been received.[61] He recalled in his memoirs how this "favour and indulgence" had "exceeded my most sanguine expectations."[62] Thanks to Staunton, John Davis wrote, Britain finally had a translation of the Qing legal code, whose author had "an undisputed claim to the honour of being the first Englishman, who ever gave to his country a genuine specimen of the most interesting province of Chinese literature."[63]

## OPINIONS GROUNDED UPON EXPERIENCE

Staunton's linguistic competency and his sense of audience, informed by strategic concerns about Britain's position in China, were a mode of "being there" that was different from the Jesuits and from other Britons. Law became his way of anchoring and displaying expertise. But was a legal code—especially only part of it—any way to understand China? John Slade thought not. Alluding to Staunton's translation, Slade in 1830 asked how any judgment could be made from the "mere perusal" of a code or of institutions "so warped to the will of emperor and his officers." Given how little most people in Britain understood China, it was only common sense to seek this information from "opinions grounded upon experience" and "formed by those who have resided in China, and who have been brought in contact with Chinese"—in other words, men such as Slade himself. His nine years' "RESIDENCE" at Canton enabled him to explain the "sentiments and policy" of the local and imperial governments, popular attitudes toward foreigners, and even the "national character" of the Chinese—"in points of view seldom or never before contemplated by Europeans."[64]

Like Slade's, books and other works on China invariably opened by listing their authors' special credentials.[65] Doing so was a way to gain a competitive authorial edge by distinguishing the terms of one's firsthand experience—from realms of knowledge, expertise, and activity to length of time and residence in China. Even the usually modest Robert Morrison began his *View of China* (1817) by insisting it was "scarcely possible" for someone in Europe to learn Chinese successfully without a Chinese assistant—as he had been able to do in Canton.[66] In *A Chinese Commercial Guide* (1834) his son, John Robert, stressed that, unlike a similar work published two years earlier by the East India Company's press at Macao, his was published in Canton, "near the source of information."[67] James Matheson began his *Present Position and Prospect of the British Trade with China* (1836) by noting how he had spent the past seventeen years in "active commercial pursuits" at Canton. This, along with access to "every source of authentic information," enabled him to present a "faithful and popular" view of British trade with China.[68]

John Davis, convinced that neither the Jesuits nor the new traders who had replaced them as the supposed experts on China had been able to produce objective accounts, opened *The Chinese* (1836) by mentioning his residence of "more than twenty years"—including a journey to Peking with the Amherst embassy and several months as successor to the deceased Lord Napier.[69] His *Sketches of China* (1841) began with a reminder of his "good fortune" to have been "officially attached" to the embassy "under the highest auspices" and of how since the "early age" of eighteen he had devoted himself to learning about this "real 'terra incognita.'"[70] Charles Downing started his book by noting how being a surgeon gave him access to hospitals in Canton and Macao, and "frequently into the most private recesses of the natives." As a medical man, he had been able to "ascertain many things which would otherwise be buried in obscurity," such as the "real state of medicine and surgery in the country" and "the nature of the diseases and accidents to which the Chinese are subject."[71]

Even short-term visitors found ways to distinguish themselves and their accounts. James Johnson, the naval officer, explained in his preface how the descriptions and observations in his book were "copied from *nature*, not from books."[72] James Holman ended his discussion of Chinese culture and society by acknowledging the *Canton Register* and the *Chinese Repository*, both produced by "gentlemen who are practically acquainted with China" and who could be "safely consulted upon all points of interest and importance, in reference to our relations with that Country." But Holman insisted his own account would be different. Although a residence in China, with all its restrictions, might appear "very monotonous," his own efforts to acquire as much information as possible—despite his lack of sight—made his time there "pleasingly diversified" and gave him "peculiar gratification, under the deprivation which I suffer." Holman also highlighted his narrative by explaining how he had been fortunate enough to be "in the midst of the English intercourse with the natives," and to be in Canton during "a period more than ordinary interest and excitement."[73]

Refuting works by others was another way of demonstrating authority. In his *Travels in China*, John Barrow dismissed the account by Lord Macartney's valet, Aeneas Anderson, as "crude notes" made by a "livery servant" and quickly "vamped up by a London bookseller as a speculation that could not fail, so greatly excited was public curiosity at the return of the Embassy." How was anyone to take seriously an author who claimed to have seen growing, on the banks of the Hai River, tea and rice—two crops cultivated no more in north China than they were in England?[74] As we have seen, Staunton introduced his translation of the Qing code by declaring its authenticity and refuting claims by other writers (including Barrow) about the code.

John Davis began his translation of Chinese novels by assessing the strengths and weaknesses of earlier Western works on China. That of Frenchman Joseph de Guignes was "extremely well executed," but little more than a compilation of "all the manuscript dictionaries which he could collect together." A mistake regarding the Qianlong Emperor proved de Guignes was prone to error when "trusted to his own resources." The first part of Robert Morrison's *Dictionary of the Chinese Language* was to be commended for its "earning and industry," though Morrison had used a romanization system that made it difficult for foreigners to pronounce Chinese characters, rather than the older system used by the Jesuits. Davis was less impressed by missionary Joshua Marshman's *Clavis Sinica*, published in Bengal in 1814, which he spent more than thirty pages assessing. Marshman's reliance on ancient texts and his neglect of the modern Chinese had left his work "incomplete." Most importantly, though Davis did not say so explicitly, Marshman had never even been to China.[75]

By the 1830s, the local English-language press regularly featured reviews of books on China. In July 1834 the *Register* described a recent book by Peter Auber as a "mere kernelless shell." Despite his "easy access" to Company records, Auber, secretary to the Court of Directors in London, had produced a "mere compilation of praises" of the Company, "mingled with extracts of letters" from the Court and the consultations of the supercargoes, and "dashed with a soft regret for the good things now lost."[76] In its review of *The Chinese*, the *Register* explained that Davis had written a "very readable" book suitable for readers who had "only *heard* of that vast country." But it was "too favorable" to the Chinese and offered no "general and masterful view" of current state of the free trade: "we can neither discover one word of encouragement nor of advice upon this important subject.[77]

One of the most scathing reviews appeared in September 1838 in the *Repository*, penned by John Robert Morrison. The book in question was Charles Downing's three-volume *Fan Qui in China*. Downing's account had received a generally favorable review in the *Register*, which argued it would be most valued in Britain, "where the field treated is terra incognita to readers, and where a little extravagance is not easily detected."[78] Although Morrison was delighted to see an interest in China within "the bosom of the reading public of the west," he regretted there was "so little in unison with sense, or discernment," as to allow the frequent publication of works such as Downing's. Based downriver at Whampoa, and for only six months at that, Downing had visited Canton occasionally—walking through several streets and visiting the few buildings "worth seeing." He had talked there with a dozen or so foreigners there and in Whampoa with Chinese provisioners, interpreters, and washmen—"persons highly respectable, no doubt, in their way, but hardly well-fitted to communicate information regarding the great empire of which they may have seen, perchance, an area of a dozen miles square."

Downing had then decided to write a book, a task for which he was "wholly incompetent." Although he promised in his title to provide an idea of European life in China, he had instead tried to "beguile" his reader "into a snare," then "drag him along a tedious route" filled with "many wild fancies," and finally "plunge him into the depths of Chinese law, religion, mythology, literature, science, and art, after having first rendered the same turbid by his own splashings therein." Worst of all, Downing had made "a great sacrifice of judgment to vanity" by assuming his months spent mainly at Whampoa enabled him to improve upon the writings of men who had been in China twenty or even forty times longer. And instead of one book on foreign life in China, under "a humble and rather foolish title," he had written three "fashionable-novel-like" volumes of "trivial observation, crude notions, idle fancies, and vain speculations, upon China, its customs, its language, and a numberless host of et-ceteras." A more fitting title would have been: "A Voyage to China, made by a literary body-snatcher, under an attack of scriptital (or scribbling) fever, containing the results of observations personal upon the river of Canton, and observations through the medium of others within the compass of many books."[79]

## THE TERMS CONTROVERSY

The layered competition among different authors explains why debating the true meaning of terms used by the Chinese authorities for describing foreigners also became a way to claim authority and expertise. In his open letter to Lord Palmerston in 1836, former Company supercargo Hugh Hamilton Lindsay lamented how so many people in Britain attached only "small importance" to such an important matter. The "advocates for submission to Chinese arrogance" insisted the word *yi*, which most foreigners in Canton translated as "barbarians" or "devils," meant only "foreigners." Lindsay, however, who on his voyage up the China coast in July 1832 had refused to leave one town until a Qing admiral agreed to delete *yi* from his official correspondence, argued that the Chinese used the term in "the most offensive and insulting" sense—solely to persuade themselves foreigners were morally inferior. The Confucian classics offered ample evidence that *yi* was used to describe those "out of the pale of the Chinese empire, and almost always in a derogatory and contemptuous sense." Showing his knowledge of Chinese history, Lindsay quoted a passage by the Song Dynasty statesman Su Dongpo claiming the *yi* people were like brutes and could not be governed by the same rules as those of China. He urged the British to demand that the Qing officials stop using this and "all other insulting expressions" in future negotiations.[80] James Matheson argued likewise: these "truculent, vain-glorious" people considered "all other inhabitants of the earth" as "BARBARIANS, destitute of all pretensions to civil, political, or moral excellence.[81]

The "super-sign" *yi/barbarian* became one of the most "tragic and costly fabrications in modern diplomatic history." It "flaunted the evidence of the Chinese contempt for foreigners and contradicted the experience of the British elsewhere in their global warfare of sovereign rule."[82] In the years surrounding the Opium War, the British would insist *yi* was deprecating, while Qing officials would argue otherwise. Yet the rhetorical nuances behind various claims of being there reveal the British relationship with China to be more diverse than the usual binary "clash of empires" suggests. Discourses were intertwined: Chinese people could be civilized in literature and art, for example, but "barbaric" in their mode of treating and representing foreigners.[83]

Not all Britons with China experience agreed that *yi* was so offensive and meant "barbarian." Staunton argued that although *yi* was not the "most honorable" term for denoting foreigners, and such insulting terms widened the gap between them and Chinese, it was wrong to assign it a "directly vituperative sense." He preferred to translate the term as "foreigner," and found little merit in Lindsay's quoting of passages from Confucius where the term was used for barbarians. "Now, although the Chinese are certainly not a very *changeable* race, yet to undertake to justify a translation of a word in modern usage by the sense in which it is supposed to have been employed by an author who flourished more than 2000 years ago, is placing rather too great confidence in Chinese immutability." Staunton also dismissed as "nonsensical" the commonly held notion that Qing authorities had referred to Lord Napier as "Barbarian Eye": it was "quite obvious" the term *yimu* meant "Barbarian Head" or "Barbarian Principal Person," not "Barbarian Eye." Although it was "too true" the Chinese had often used "offensive and insulting" terminology when referring to foreigners, translating *yimu* as "Barbarian Eye" was "as false to the letter" as it was "to the spirit of the original."[84]

Peter Perring Thoms, a printer sent by the Company to Macao in 1814 to help produce Robert Morrison's *Dictionary of the Chinese Language*, was even more critical of Lindsay and Matheson. Often dismissed as an amateur sinologist, no doubt because of his working-class background and experience versus that of more privileged men such as Staunton and Davis, Thoms, unlike many of the Company's staff in China, had formed particularly close relationships with literary Chinese, especially his type cutters.[85] In 1818 he translated *The Affectionate Pair*, a collection of forty moral tales, many of them displaying "no small share of ingenuity and talent," and proving, "notwithstanding what has appeared to the contrary in Europe, the Chinese are not destitute of the finer feelings of benevolence, sympathy, and love."[86] In 1824, still in Macao, he published a translation of Chinese courtship poetry, appended somewhat curiously with a detailed list of the revenues of China by province.[87] Thoms, who departed for England in early 1825, did not comment on Lindsay's pamphlet until 1853. But he continued to champion China, its people, and their literature—including by trying to humanize the Chinese through his translations of women's poetry and by submitting translations to the Great Exhibition of 1851.[88]

Here we see, once again, degrees of "being there" expertise. Thoms "neither idolized nor denigrated Chinese culture." But he viewed the Chinese rather than the British as the "truthful and authoritative arbiters of Chinese language and literature." His position later made him "one of the most fervent opponents of armed aggression" in the lead-up to the first and second opium wars.[89] In an 1836 article in the *Monthly Magazine* he took Matheson to task for presenting himself as an expert on China: despite having been there for seventeen years, Matheson had probably "never learnt a single character." Thoms agreed that the Chinese could be "conceited and imbecile." But his own "personal intercourse" had convinced him that *yi*—"as old as almost any word in their language"—was not derogatory. Their official "blustering" notwithstanding, the Chinese often acknowledged Britain's superiority, not only in shipping and commerce, but even as "an intelligent people." Thoms had seen the British referred to in Chinese documents as both *yi* and *yin-ke-le* (English). And given how the British had tolerated the use of *yi* for so many years, why should they now suddenly decide it was offensive?[90]

Thoms added in 1853 that he had hoped in 1836 to use his knowledge of the Chinese language to show there was no reason for foreigners in China "to manifest so much spleen, or rather indignation," at the use of "certain Chinese words" in official documents addressed to foreign merchants at Canton. Many who had read Matheson's pamphlet, including "one gentleman, a long resident in that country, and well acquainted with the Chinese language," agreed that Matheson had not proved the language in such documents was indeed offensive. Confucius, Thoms reminded Lindsay (who had returned to Canton as a private trader after writing his open letter to Palmerston, but then left China forever in 1839), had not been speaking of people in his own time; rather, he was referring to "two distinct tribes or clans of people" who had lived two thousand years earlier. "Mr. L. may speak the Chinese language very well, but, before he again cites quotations from the Four Books of Confucius, he should let them be well embued [sic] with the exhalations of the lamp."[91]

In the decade after the Opium War, Thoms would be seen as out of touch with Chinese affairs. Sinologists and diplomats who believed that *yi* indeed meant "barbarian" became the accepted experts.[92] Yet even the British community in prewar Canton had disagreed about the meaning of *yi*. In August 1837, "Sloth" argued in the *Register* that Lindsay's assertion that *yi* meant "barbarians" because Su Dongpo had used it for the *yi* barbarians of the north, was "quite inadmissible." The "feeling of superiority in the breast of the Chinese" was no more unnatural than among Europeans, Americans, or Russians; *yi* corresponded more closely to "foreigners" or "aliens" than to "barbarians."[93] In the following issue "Lexicon" disagreed: a "learned native" had assured him that the term referred to "those who act without reason" and was most certainly not a positive one. When "Lexicon" asked the *Register* to settle the matter, John Slade, on the authority of a "native teacher," declared that the term could be translated in a variety of ways—from "unpolished" to "uncivilized"—but "in no case" as "barbarian."[94]

When "Lexicon" replied in the next issue that the term meant something worse than "foreign" and foreigners in Canton should not be compared to the "uncivilized and savage tribes" in the interior and frontiers of China, Slade responded with a long discussion of how the term had been used in various

Chinese texts for almost four thousand years. "More than one" Chinese had insisted the term simply meant an outsider who was not a native of China. In any case, the British could never prevent the Chinese from using the term regardless of its meaning. "We are sinking day by day into deeper contempt. Walking is forbidden, our passage boats are stopped, our ships are driven to the offing, boats carrying despatches are seized, hong merchants fail and the foreign merchants are robbed; and all this and more, much more, is borne without any remonstrance." Whether *yi* was an insult or simply a "distinctive term" indicating inferiority, the foreigners were themselves to blame for its continued use. "We are not aware that any general remonstrance has ever been made to the high local officers on the subject. What opinion, then, are those officers to form of all foreigners, when they see them and their national authorities tamely and silently submit to every insult heaped upon them?"[95]

## SETTING THE RECORD STRAIGHT

Britons were not the only foreigners in Canton who tried to claim expertise by refuting the works of others. Partly because of their own uneasy position in China, for example, American missionaries were sometimes critical of writings by other foreigners—even other missionaries. In an October 1832 review in the *Repository* of two earlier European accounts of China, Elijah Coleman Bridgman, who had lived in China for less than three years, explained that even long residence made it "extremely difficult" to form a "correct" knowledge of China. "How difficult then must it be for persons, who have never visited China, nor even come in contact with the Chinese, and who probably have never studied the subject, to dictate what measures ought to be adopted by foreigners, in their intercourse with this people!"[96]

In June 1840, Bridgman described Walter Henry Medhurst's *China: Its State and Prospects* (1838) as "an extempore production" in which "almost every page bears marks of haste." The book had been ranked among the "best modern work on China." But because "perhaps no man living possessed better advantages for giving a correct account of this country," it should have been even better than the others. Based on his own ten years' experience in China, Bridgman argued that Medhurst had judged the Chinese too critically: "Perhaps he has not seen them in so favorable circumstances, as he would have done had he been longer in China." The Chinese people Medhurst had met, mainly in Batavia and along the Chinese coast, might not be "fair representatives of the great mass of the nation." Yet from them he had written of the Chinese "in their collective national character."[97]

Bridgman's countryman and fellow missionary, Samuel Wells Williams, wrote in the *Repository* in June 1839 that every passing traveler seemed to have been "seized with the disease peculiar to such circumstances, and in due time produced a bantling, varying in size from a single duodecimo to a post octavo of three volumes." Williams, who had arrived in China six years earlier, blasted Karl Gützlaff's two-volume *China Opened* for showing "a great lack of research and judgment." As Williams put it, "the materials for the dish may have been good enough originally, but they are served up in so unpalatable a manner, as to disgust the taste, and ill repay the trouble of perusal." Gützlaff was one of the few foreigners fluent in several Chinese dialects and had been able to sail up the China coast. Yet his two volumes, "a little wheat among the chaff," had been written in the "same vague, rambling, helterskelter style, amusing the reader with the appearance of knowledge, but leaving him dissatisfied with the book, and weary of the subject." The book was also full of "unblushing plagiarisms"—including from earlier volumes of the *Repository*. It contained a "good deal of authentic information," but even this was "mixed up with crude theories, careless expressions, and partial mis-statements."[98]

Still, the British tried harder than anyone in Canton to set the record straight, mainly because they had the most at stake. Those who spent time in China often stressed how little the British public knew about it. John McLeod, who joined Lord Amherst's embassy but explored the Yellow Sea and the Ryukyu Islands while the rest of the embassy traveled north to Peking and then down to Canton, wrote that the Chinese had too many misguided admirers. Some blamed their "suspicious meanness, knavery, silly pride, and other ill qualities" on their "depraved mode of government" and its emphasis on "useless forms and ceremonies." If not for these "shackles of the mind," these admirers argued, the Chinese would be a "gay, civil, industrious, and honest people." Another group ("of the true antediluvian school") continued to admire the Chinese solely for their "unvarying habits" and "tenacious adherence" to tradition—venerating them as "living monuments of former times" and "*valuable specimens of the antique.*"[99]

In April 1818, George Thomas Staunton wrote to Robert Morrison that "the whole question" of the Amherst embassy was "passing fact into oblivion in this country" and it was "almost throwing away time" to try and inform the British public about China.[100] Morrison's only furlough in Britain reminded him how little was known about China there. In September 1824 he wrote to the directors of the London Missionary Society that "throughout the land" Britons were ignorant about China.[101] John Slade claimed that their "very great degree of misconception" meant the British public were "most ignorant and therefore the most incompetent to form a correct judgment."[102] In a

Figure 3.6. Charles Gutzlaff [Karl Gützlaff], 1835, by Richard James Lane, after George Chinnery, lithograph. National Portrait Gallery, London

January 1835 article on the foreign relations of China, the *Register* mocked foreigners who, unfamiliar with Chinese history, admired the Chinese for their policy of isolation: "as well might the Chinese congratulate the savages of the Andaman islands or Dajaks [Dayaks] of Borneo, for having been far more successful in this endeavour."[103]

James Matheson reminded his readers in January 1836 how, because of Chinese "exclusivism," contact with foreigners was limited to the "scantiest and most ungracious" form of trade and restricted to the "veriest outposts and confines of the empire." These "extraordinary people" had chosen to "shroud themselves, and all belonging to them, in mystery impenetrable, to monopolize all the advantages of their situation." Whether this exclusivism resulted from conceit or selfishness, or from realizing their "ancient but feeble" political system was of little significance. What mattered was how, confined almost to the "southernmost extremity" of China, fifteen hundred miles from the capital at Peking, foreigners in China were subjected to the "most ignominious *surveillance* and restrictions."[104]

The ignorance of the British public could be forgiven. After all, Slade explained, there was little to interest them in "the exact system of government, the frigid code of morals, the ostentatious theory, and the heartless practice of the duties of life of the Chinese." And given how "fear and avarice" guided their dealings with foreigners, it was neither surprising nor regrettable more was not known about "this insolent nation."[105] Less excusable was how British periodicals seemed to know as little as the public. In January 1835 the *Register* refuted an entry in a commercial dictionary claiming that foreigners in Canton were "at perfect liberty" to deal with any hong merchant and had as wide a choice of trading partners as in Liverpool or New York. "It is of great importance that the real state of the *open market* of Canton should be well known to the world."[106] When a writer in the *Asiatic Journal* criticized the Napier mission later that year, the *Register* accused him of siding with a Chinese governor-general "who knows only the language and laws of his own country; who, if he were summoned to the presence of his emperor, must grovel before him, like a reptile, in the dust." By defending the governor-general (Lu Kun, who had ordered Napier to leave Canton), the writer was condemning Lord Napier—a Scottish peer and a British naval officer "known to his country by his services in every quarter of the globe."[107] And in May 1837 the *Register* chastised London's *Athenaeum* for claiming that the conduct of the British in China had "not been always such as prudence would have dictated" and they seemed to "oscillate between temerity and timidity."[108]

What disturbed Britons in Canton the most was how no one at home—even some former Company men who should have known better—seemed to appreciate the challenges and deprivations they faced. The anonymous merchant from 1829 lamented how the existing state of commercial relations with China were "but little understood" in England. "You, who are not familiar with the politics of China, cannot easily comprehend the variety of open and disguised methods, by which the Officers of Government endeavor to raise a revenue at the expense of the foreign trade." Those "conversant with the subject," on the other hand, understood how the "steady opposition" exhibited by the Company to the "undue exactions" of the Chinese had "infused caution, if not fear," and even helped protect the trade of other countries with China.[109]

In September 1832 the *Register* argued that Staunton, now a member of parliament who saw no need for a radical change in relations with China and supported the renewal of the Company's monopoly, was too soft on the Chinese. Had he forgotten the "shameless effrontery of the mandarins" during the Macartney embassy and how Lord Amherst had been treated during his own embassy? Even worse, in a speech defending the continuation of the Company's monopoly, Charles Forbes, who had been in China forty years earlier, gave a rosy description of trade in Canton the *Register* insisted had never existed, "either then or since, except in his own imagination."[110]

Even the British government could not be counted on. "An Observer" complained in April 1835 that at home the idea of "national honor" in relations with China was "scouted and laughed at." To expect any concern for the British situation in China or the humiliation of Lord Napier and his sovereign was "a mere absurdity."[111] In late October 1835, "A Citizen of the World" wrote in the *Register* that if the government was not willing to protect British trade in China, "those engaged in it must protect themselves as well as they may." If this "shameful desertion" were to be become known by the Chinese authorities, it would be "at the sacrifice of national and individual honour and character."[112] The *Register* in January 1837 lamented how one (unnamed) "petty" island with a "trifling and insecure" commerce had distracted a succession of British cabinets and "aroused all the energies of the people." But China, a "new world" to foreign commerce if opened to free trade, remained a "forgotten or unthought of" country, "lost in the din of party, and abandoned by ignorance and incapacity to the stream of time and chance."[113]

Company servants who returned home in the late 1820s and early 1830s after a long service in China found the lack of understanding and support in Britain particularly galling. James Brabazon Urmston wrote in 1833 that "almost all persons" in Britain ignorant of the "actual state of things" in China believed that foreigners who chose to trade there should be beholden to any regulations the Chinese might apply to them. These Britons failed to understand how neither trade nor "general intercourse" with China was conducted according to the "established and reasonable" regulations governing British trade elsewhere. On the contrary, the laws and regulations for foreign trade at Canton were "altogether vague and undefined," leaving British trade there "all times and seasons" to the "mercy of the caprice and rapacity" of the local authorities and their underlings. Even Robert Morrison, whose "thorough acquaintance" with the "character and disposition" of the Chinese was beyond doubt, and who was "far from being prejudiced against them," had concluded his journal of the Amherst embassy by noting how although the Chinese were not barbarians, they were barbaric in the way they treated foreigners.[114]

Charles Marjoribanks was disappointed by how little Britons understood the Canton System and its "so many multiplied restrictions." The "extremely liberality and generosity" of the hong merchants, for example, had been "most unjustly extolled." True, they were often "scrupulously accurate" in their dealings. But this was a result of the "great liberality and justice" in the transactions of the Company, which had given them a reputation they did not "naturally" possess; otherwise, they were "perhaps the most accomplished liars in the world." Although the hong merchants had been appointed by the Qing government to be responsible for all actions of the foreigners in Canton, they had little control over them. On the contrary, their "very great inadequacy" to handle foreign commerce had enabled so many "outside merchants" to enter the trade—illegally but with the connivance of the local government—thereby driving much of the foreign trade away from Canton to Lintin.[115]

## WAR, HONG KONG, AND BEYOND

The conviction that only those who had been in China could understand what happened there intensified during the Opium War. In a letter of March 1840 to his sister Emma Hislop, Captain Charles Elliot, head of the British forces in China, insisted that people "who breakfast, and sleep at regular hours in London, do not easily understand, that the turn of events amongst the Heathen will not always accommodate itself to *rule,* and men who break rules, are glibly enough set down to be scheming blockheads."[116] In April 1840, John Slade wrote from Macao, where the British had decamped, that it would be impossible for "distant readers" to comprehend the "facts and system" of the opium trade or the policies of the Qing government without reading the four hundred pages of translated (by John Robert Morrison) memorials and edicts in *his* book on the subject. Only through studying such documents would British readers be able to fathom, for example, Commissioner Lin Zexu's "monstrous measures" to suppress the opium trade. Slade urged his "uninformed" readers to take English translations of Chinese edicts and memorials seriously, and not to dismiss them "contemptuously" simply because their style could sometimes be "ridiculously bombastic" and at others "puerile." These documents would prove to Britons who had never been to Canton, studied the "Chinese character and system of government," or familiarized themselves with the "history and manners of that people" through existing books in English or French, that persuading the government or the people of China to "alter their modes of thinking and acting" was much harder than "usually anticipated."[117]

This notion that only those who understood China should be involved in Chinese affairs persisted after the British occupied the island of Hong Kong in January 1841 and began to consolidate their occupation. Lord Palmerston is well known for criticizing Elliot for taking this supposed "barren island, with nary a house upon it." However, many Britons in China also questioned the cession of Hong Kong as yet another example of how Elliot simply did not understand the situation. Two days after the occupation began, the *Press* declared that "for an *independent* British settlement no situation can possibly be more favorably chosen than Hong Kong."[118] And public notices in Hong Kong about the appointment of a chief magistrate and about rules and regulations showed the island would not be abandoned again, as it had been before.[119]

But in February the *Register* predicted that Hong Kong would be "the resort and rendezvous of all the Chinese smugglers, opium-smoking shops and gambling houses will soon spread through its vallies [*sic*] and on the declivities of the hills; to those haunts will flock all the discontested and bad spirits of the empire; the island will be surrounded by *shameens*, and become a Gehenna of the waters."[120] Learning the "wonderful and mortifying" news that the British forces had evacuated Hong Kong after being there for less than a month, the paper wondered how a British possession could be "voluntarily evacuated" by order of the British plenipotentiary. "What opinion can these poor people have of the good faith of England—even of her power, when they see it so miserably misused?"[121]

James Urmston, who, as we saw earlier, continued to maintain that Britain should have taken Chusan rather than Hong Kong, recommended that if Britain ever obtained Chusan "or any other permanent position" in China, whoever was appointed to administer the new acquisition should be "possessed of a knowledge of the character, disposition, and habits of Asiatics." Not everyone sent to China could be expected to understand its "difficult" language. Still, among the "numerous gentlemen" who had been in China, or in India, Penang, Singapore, or Malacca, surely there were some with "a perfect knowledge of the Asiatic character." A "thorough knowledge of Asiatics" and a "perfect knowledge of the Native languages" had enabled "talented gentlemen" to run Britain's other Asian settlements. Henry Pottinger, Elliot's successor, had gone to China in 1841 as plenipotentiary having never been there before and knowing nothing of its language. Thanks, however, to having served in British India, he "thereby at once became thoroughly acquainted with the character and disposition of the Chinese, of all ranks and classes." As a result, Pottinger had been able "the more readily to carry on his negotiations with the public functionaries of the country, to at once detect their sophistry, and defeat their machinations, and to bring his negotiations to a successful termination."[122]

Four years earlier, Charles Elliot had expressed a different opinion. Writing to his sister from his fresh post in the new Republic of Texas (a "den of villains, misery & musquitoes," as he later described it to his youngest son Frederick), Elliot explained how Pottinger was "a very good sort of man." But he was simply not up to the job: he lacked *real* expertise. "He does not understand the business in his hands; and no wonder, for an Indian training is least fitted to give a man the kind of knowledge which is wanted in China. The Chinese are not the Indian people and our position in China has no analogy with our position in India." Neither Pottinger nor the British government understood that methods employed elsewhere in the world would never work in China. And the Treaty of Nanking that Pottinger had helped negotiate showed he simply did not understand China. "Pottinger's arrangement was made to *look well* in England, rather than to *work well* in China. His concern with respect to the detail management of the trade is extremely defective and bald and will lead to mischief. Of that you may be assured."[123]

## NOTES

1. John Barrow and George Macartney, *Some Account of the Public Life, and a Selection from the Unpublished Writings, of the Earl of Macartney* (London: Cadell and Davies, 1807), vol. 2, 409, 411–12.

2. George Thomas Staunton, *Ta Tsing Leu Lee; Being the Fundamental Laws, and a Selection from the Supplementary Statutes, of the Penal Code of China* (London: Cadell and Davies, 1810), viii–ix. These accounts were not accepted uncritically, especially in continental Europe with its anti-British sentiments and rivalries. In 1799, for example, Joseph François Charpentier de Cossigny, an engineer in the French East India Company, published an account of his own visit to China that included negative remarks about George Leonard Staunton's memoirs of the Macartney embassy: *Voyage a Canton, capitale de la province de ce nom, a la Chine; par Gorée, le Cap de Bonne Espérance, et les Isles de France et de la Réunion; suivi d'observations sur le voyage à la Chine, de Lord Macartney et du Citoyen Van-Braam, et d'une esquisse de arts des Indiens et des Chinois* [Voyage to Canton, Capital of the Province of That Name, in China, via Gorée, the Cape of Good Hope, and the Isles of French and Reunion; Followed by Observations on the Voyages to China of Lord Macartney and Van Braam, and a Sketch of Indian and Chinese Arts] (Paris: André, 1799).

3. Hao Gao, "The 'Inner Kowtow Controversy' during the Amherst Embassy to China, 1816–1817," *Diplomacy and Statecraft* 27, no. 4 (2016): 595–614.

4. "Free Trade with China," *Chinese Repository* 2, no. 8 (December 1833): 357–58.

5. "Free Trade with the Chinese," *Chinese Repository* 2, no. 10 (February 1834): 476.

6. David Lambert and Alan Lester, eds., *Colonial Lives across the British Empire: Imperial Careering in the Long Nineteenth Century* (Cambridge: Cambridge University Press, 2006).

7. *Canton Miscellany* 2 (July 1831): 125–29, 132, 135–36.

8. "Jealous China, Strange Japan, They Are But Dead Seas of Man," *Canton Miscellany* 2 (July 1831): 137.

9. *Canton Miscellany* 3 (August 1831): 173.

10. "Observations on the Meaou-tsze Mountaineers," *Canton Miscellany* 3 (August 1831): 201–2.

11. *Canton Register* 1, no. 1 (6 November 1827): 1.

12. *Canton Register* 1, no. 6 (4 February 1828): 22.

13. *Canton Register* 1, no. 7 (11 February 1828): 26; original emphasis.

14. *Canton Register* 1, no. 11 (15 March 1828): 41; original emphasis.

15. John Slade, *Notices on the British Trade to the Port of Canton; with Some Translations of Chinese Official Papers Relative to That Trade* (London: Smith, Elder, 1830), 2–4.

16. "Free Trade," *Canton Register* 7, no. 25 (24 June 1834): 97; original emphasis.

17. "Laws of the Chinese Empire, in Relation to Foreigners," *Canton Register* 6, nos. 15/16 (24 October 1833): 9; original emphasis.

18. John Barrow, *Travels in China, Containing Descriptions, Observations, and Comparisons, Made and Collected in the Course of a Short Residence at the Imperial Palace of Yuen-Min-Yuen, and on a Subsequent Journey through the Country from Pekin to Canton in Which It Is Attempted to Appreciate the Rank That the Extraordinary Empire May Be Considered to Hold in the Scale of Civilized Nations* (London: Cadell and Davies, 1804), 3.

19. Barrow, *Travels in China*, 4, 28–29.

20. Linda Colley, *Britons: Forging the Nation 1707–1837* (New Haven, CT: Yale University Press, 1992), 36.

21. On Jesuit mapmaking in Qing China, see: Laura Hostetler, *Qing Colonial Enterprise: Ethnography and Cartography in Early Modern China* (Chicago: University of Chicago Press, 2001), chap. 2, and "Qing Connections to the Early Modern World: Ethnography and Cartography in Eighteenth-Century China," *Modern Asian Studies* 34, no. 3 (2000): 623–62; and Peter C. Perdue, "Boundaries, Maps, and Movement: Chinese, Russian, and Mongolian Empires in Early Modern Central Eurasia," *International History Review* 20, no. 2 (1988): 263–86, and *China Marches West: The Qing Conquest of Central Eurasia, 1600–1800* (Cambridge, MA: Harvard University Press, 2005), 442–57.

22. Barrow, *Travels in China*, 28, 30–31, 159, 161, 171.

23. Staunton, *Ta Tsing Leu Lee*, iv–vii.

24. Henry Ellis, *Journal of the Proceedings of the Late Embassy to China; Comprising a Correct Narrative of the Public Transactions of the Embassy, of the Voyage to and from China, and of the Journey from the Mouth of the Pei-Ho to the Return to Canton, Interspersed with Observations upon the Face of the Country, the Polity,*

*Moral Character, and Manners of the Chinese Nation* (London: Printed for J. Murray, 1817), 480–81.

25. John Francis Davis, *Chinese Novels Translated from the Originals; to Which Are Added Proverbs and Moral Maxims, Collected from Their Classical Books and Other Sources; the Whole Prefaced by Observations on the Language and Literature of China* (London: J. Murray, 1822), 5–6; original emphasis.

26. On the debates in the 1830s, see Hao Gao, "Understanding the Chinese: British Merchants on the China Trade in the Early 1830s," *Britain and the World* 12, no. 2 (2019): 151–71, and *Creating the Opium War: British Imperial Attitudes towards China, 1792–1840* (Manchester: Manchester University Press, 2020), chap. 3.

27. George [Leonard] Staunton, *An Authentic Account of an Embassy from the King of Great Britain to the Emperor of China; Including Cursory Observations Made, and Information Obtained, in Travelling through That Ancient Empire and a Small Part of Chinese Tartary* (London: G. Nicol, 1797), vol. 3, 366–67, 410.

28. George Thomas Staunton, *Miscellaneous Notices Relating to China and Our Commercial Intercourse with That Country: Including a Few Translations from the Chinese Language*, 2nd ed. (London: John Murray, 1822), 127, 156–57. On defending the monopoly, see Yukihasa Kumagai, *Breaking into the Monopoly: Provincial Merchants and Manufacturers' Campaigns for Access to the Asian Market, 1790–1833* (Leiden, NL: Brill, 2013), chap. 1.

29. Staunton, *Miscellaneous Notices Relating to China*, 136–38, 145–47, 149. Staunton's claim that the Company's monopoly benefited the American merchants was not hyperbole: the American merchant and diplomat Gideon Nye recalled that it "lent more or less protection to all Foreign Trade, at a period else of complete incertitude in the relations with China." Gideon Nye Jr., *Morning of My Life in China: Comprising an Outline of the History of Foreign Intercourse from the Last Year of the Regime of the Honorable East India Company, 1833, to the Imprisonment of the Foreign Community in 1839* (Canton: n.p., 1873), 23–24.

30. Staunton, *Miscellaneous Notices Relating to China*, 151–52, 159–60.

31. Staunton, *Miscellaneous Notices Relating to China*, 170, 177.

32. Staunton, *Miscellaneous Notices Relating to China*, 359–61.

33. Anon, *Facts Relating to Chinese Commerce in a Letter from a British Resident in China to His Friend in England* (London: J.M. Richardson, 1829), 9–12, 20.

34. *Facts Relating to Chinese Commerce*, 9–12, 20, 24, 28, 61.

35. Henry Ellis, *A Series of Letters on the East India Question, Addressed to the Members of the Two Houses of Parliament*, 2nd ed. (London: John Murray, 1830), 1–2, 43, 60. On the Terranova case, see Joseph Benjamin Askew, "Re–visiting New Territory: The Terranova Incident Re-examined," *Asian Studies Review* 28, no. 4 (2004): 351–71.

36. Slade, *Notices on the British Trade*, 26, 31–32, 67–68, 77.

37. Staunton, *Miscellaneous Notices Relating to China*, 177, 182, 187. On the Anglo-American trade, see James R. Fichter, *So Great a Profitt: How the East Indies Trade Transformed Anglo-American Capitalism* (Cambridge, MA: Harvard University Press, 2010).

38. Slade, *Notices on the British Trade*, 32–33, 69.

39. *Facts Relating to Chinese Commerce*, 16–17, 57; original emphasis.

40. *Facts Relating to Chinese Commerce*, 14–15, 57, 61, 64.
41. Staunton, *Miscellaneous Notices Relating to China*, 327–28, 345–46, 350.
42. Staunton, *Ta Tsing Leu Lee*, xi–xiv.
43. Li Chen, *Chinese Law in Imperial Eyes: Sovereignty, Justice, and Transcultural Politics* (New York: Columbia University Press, 2016), 71, 111.
44. Staunton, *Ta Tsing Leu Lee*, xxxiii.
45. James St. André, "'But Do They Have a Notion of Justice?' Staunton's 1810 Translation of the Great Qing Code," *The Translator* 10, no. 1 (2004): 5.
46. Staunton, *Ta Tsing Leu Lee*, xxvi–xxviii.
47. Staunton, *Ta Tsing Leu Lee*, x–xi.
48. S. P. Ong, "Jurisdictional Politics in Canton and the First English Translation of the Qing Penal Code (1810), *Journal of the Royal Asiatic Society of Great Britain & Ireland* 20, no. 2 (2010): 1, 144–45, 164–65.
49. Staunton to Barrow, 25 August 1807, Staunton Papers, David M. Rubenstein Rare Book and Manuscript Library.
50. George Thomas Staunton to Jane Staunton 20 July 1811, Staunton Papers.
51. Susan Reed Stifler, "The Language Students of the East India Company's Canton Factory," *Journal of the North China Branch of the Royal Asiatic Society* 69 (1938): 47–50, 54.
52. George Thomas Staunton, *Memoirs of the Chief Incidents of the Public Life of Sir George Thomas Staunton: One of the King's Commissioners to the Court of Pekin, and afterwards for Some Time Member of Parliament for South Hampshire and for the Borough of Portsmouth* (London: Printed for Private Circulation, 1856), 33. On the treatise, see Angela Ki Che Leung, "The Business of Vaccination in Nineteenth-Century Canton," *Late Imperial China* 29, no. 1 (2008): 5.
53. George Thomas Staunton to Jane Staunton, 22 March 1807, Staunton Papers.
54. Mackintosh to Staunton, 30 June 1805, Staunton Papers. The society Mackintosh mentioned was the Bombay Literary Society. The letters from Mackintosh are also discussed in Chen, *Chinese Law in Imperial Eyes*, 109.
55. Mackintosh to Staunton, 15 August 1805, Staunton Papers.
56. Mackintosh to Staunton, 9 August 1806, Staunton Papers.
57. Mackintosh to Staunton, 7 May 1807, Staunton Papers.
58. Chen, *Chinese Law in Imperial Eyes*, 88.
59. Staunton, *Miscellaneous Notices Relating to China*, 410, 412, 414–15.
60. St. André, "'But Do They Have a Notion of Justice'," 27–28.
61. George Thomas Staunton to Jane Staunton, 15 November 1811, Staunton Papers.
62. Staunton, *Memoirs of the Chief Incidents*, 45.
63. Davis, *Chinese Novels*, 5.
64. Slade, *Notices on the British Trade*, iii–iv, 2–4.
65. James St. André, "Travelling toward True Translation: The First Generation of Sino-English Translators," *The Translator* 12, no. 2 (2006): 195, 197.
66. Robert Morrison, *A View of China, for Philological Purposes: Containing a Sketch of Chinese Chronology, Geography, Government, Religion & Customs* (Macao: Printed at the Honorable East India Company's Press by P. P. Thoms, 1817; London: Black, Parbury, and Allen, 1817), 120.

67. John Robert Morrison, *A Chinese Commercial Guide: Consisting of a Collection of Details Respecting Foreign Trade in China* (Canton: Albion Press, 1834), v.

68. James Matheson, *The Present Position and Prospects of the British Trade with China: Together with an Outline of Some Leading Occurrences in Its Past History* (London: Smith, Elder, 1836), n.p.

69. John Francis Davis, *The Chinese: A General Description of That Empire and Its Inhabitants* (London: Charles Knight, 1836), vol. 1, 1.

70. John Francis Davis, *Sketches of China, Partly during an Inland Journey of Four Months, between Peking, Nanking, and Canton, with Notices and Observations Relative to the Present* (London: Charles Knight, 1841), vol. 1, 5–6.

71. C. [Charles] Toogood Downing, *The Fan Qui in China in 1836–1837* (London: Henry Colburn, 1838), vol. 2, 285.

72. Johnson, *Account*, iii; original emphasis.

73. James Holman, *Voyage Round the World, Including Travels in Africa, Asia, Australasia, America, etc. etc. from 1827 to 1832* (London: Smith, Elder, 1835), vol. 4, 171–72, 176–77, 365.

74. John Barrow, *Travels in China*, 579–80. On Barrow's efforts to rewrite the narrative of the embassy, see Joe Sample, "'The First Appearance of This Celebrated Capital'; or, What Mr. Barrow Saw in the Land of the Chinaman," in *Asian Crossings: Travel Writing on China, Japan and Southeast Asia*, ed. Steve Clark and Paul Smethurst (Hong Kong: Hong Kong University Press, 2008) 31–46.

75. Davis, *Chinese Novels*, 9–10, 21–22, 26–27, 40. On Davis as translator see: James St. André, "The Development of British Sinology and Changes in Translation Practice: The Case of Sir John Francis Davis (1795–1890)," *Translation and Interpreting Studies* 2, no. 2 (2007): 3–42; Lawrence Wang-chi Wong, "'Objects of Curiosity': John Francis Davis as a Translator of Chinese Literature," in *Sinologists and Translators in the Seventeenth to Nineteenth Centuries*, ed. Lawrence Wang-chi Wong and Bernhard Fuehrer (Hong Kong: Research Centre for Translation/The Chinese University Press, 2015), 169–203.

76. *Canton Register* 7, no. 30 (29 July 1834): 119. Peter Auber, *China: An Outline of the Government, Laws, and Policy: and of the British and Foreign Embassies to, and Intercourse with, That Empire* (London: Parbury, Allen, 1834).

77. *Canton Register* 9, no. 45 (8 November 1836): 184–85.

78. *Canton Register* 11, no. 36 (4 September 1838): 144.

79. *Chinese Repository* 7, no. 6 (September 1838): 328–34.

80. Hugh Hamilton Lindsay, *Letter to the Right Honourable Viscount Lord Palmerston on British Relations with China* (London: Saunders and Otley, 1836), 8–10.

81. Matheson, *Present Position and Prospects*, 15.

82. Lydia H. Liu, *The Clash of Empires: The Invention of China in Modern World Making* (Cambridge, MA: Harvard University Press, 2004), 47, 60. See also Dilip K. Basu, "Chinese Xenology and the Opium War: Reflections on Sinocentrism," *Journal of Asian Studies* 73, no. 4 (2014): 927–40; and Song-Chuan Chen, *Merchants of War and Peace: British Knowledge of China in the Making of the Opium War* (Hong Kong: Hong Kong University Press, 2017), chap. 5.

83. Greg M. Thomas, "Evaluating Others: The Mirroring of Chinese Civilisation in Britain," in *Civilisation and Nineteenth-Century Art*, ed. David O'Brien (Manchester: Manchester University Press, 2016), 48–72.

84. George Thomas Staunton, *Remarks on the British Relations with China, and the Proposed Plans for Improving Them*, 2nd ed. (London: E. Lloyd, 1836), 43–44; original emphasis. On the "Barbarian Eye" controversy, see T. H. Barrett, "Hellenic Shadows on the China Coast: Greek Terms for 'Foreigner' and 'Religion' in Early Anglophone Missionary Sinology," *Journal of Translation Studies* (new series) 1, no. 1: 59–84.

85. Patricia Sieber, "Location, Location, Location: Peter Perring Thoms (1790–1855), Cantonese Localism, and the Genesis of Literary Translations from the Chinese," in Wong and Fuehrer, *Sinologists and Translators*, 137–67, and "Universal Brotherhood: Peter Perring Thoms (1790–1855), Artisan Practices, and the Genesis of a Chinacentric Sinology," *Representations* 130, no. 1 (2015): 28–59.

86. P. [Peter] P. [Perring] Thoms, *The Affectionate Pair, or the History of Sung-Kin: A Chinese Tale* (London: Black, Kingsbury, Parbury, and Allen, 1820), iii–iv.

87. P. [Peter] P. [Perring] Thoms, *Chinese Courtship in Verse, to Which Is Added, an Appendix Treating of the Revenue of China, &c., &c.* (Macao: Printed at the Honorable East India Company's Press, Macao, 1824; London: Parbury, Allen, and Kingsbury, 1824).

88. Sieber, "Location, Location, Location," 138, "Universal Brotherhood," 39–47.

89. Sieber, "Location, Location, Location," 131.

90. P. [Peter] P. [Perring] Thoms, "The Present Position and Prospects of Our Trade with China," reprinted in his *The Emperor of China v. the Queen of England: A Refutation of the Arguments Contained in the Seven Official Documents Transmitted by Her Majesty's Government at Hong Kong, Who Maintain That the Documents of the Chinese Government Contain Insulting Language* (London: P. P. Thoms, 1853), 2, 4, 8.

91. Thoms, "An Enquiry into the Import of Sundry Supposed Insulting Terms, Addressed by the Chinese Government to the English Residents in China," in *Emperor of China v. Queen of England*, 1, 14.

92. Basu, "Chinese Xenology," 934–35.

93. *Canton Register* 10, no. 33 (15 August 1837): 136.

94. *Canton Register* 10, no. 34 (22 August 1837): 140–42.

95. *Canton Register* 10, no. 35 (29 August 1837): 144–45.

96. *Chinese Repository* 1, no. 6 (October 1832): 213.

97. *Chinese Repository* 9, no. 2 (June 1840): 74–84.

98. *Chinese Repository* 8, no. 2 (June 1839): 85–86, 92, 97–98. On Bridgman and Williams in Canton, see Kendall A. Johnson, *The New Middle Kingdom: China and the Early American Romance of Free Trade* (Baltimore: Johns Hopkins University Press, 2017), chap. 4.

99. John McLeod, *Narrative of a Voyage in His Majesty's Late Ship Alceste to the Yellow Sea, along the Coast of Corea, and through Its Numerous Hitherto Undiscovered Islands, to the Island of Lewchew; with an Account of Her Shipwreck in the Straits of Gaspar* (London: John Murray, 1817), 159–60; original emphasis.

100. Letter from Staunton, 10 April 1818, in Eliza Morrison, *Memoirs of the Life and Labours of Robert Morrison, Compiled by His Widow, with Critical Notices of His Chinese Works, by Samuel Kidd* (London: Longman, Orme, Brown, Green and Longmans, 1839), vol. 1, 522–23.

101. 7 September 1824, CWM (Council for World Mission)/LMS (London Missionary Society)/16/02/01 South China Incoming Correspondence, Box 2, Folder 2, Jacket D, Archives and Special Collections, School of Oriental and African Studies Library.

102. Slade, *Notices on the British Trade*, 1.

103. "Foreign Relations of the Chinese Empire," *Canton Register* 8, no. 3 (20 January 1835): 11.

104. Matheson, *Present Position and Prospects*, 1–3.

105. Slade, *Notices on the British Trade*, 2, 4.

106. *Canton Register* 8, no. 1 (6 January 1835): 2; original emphasis..

107. *Canton Register* 8, no. 39 (29 September 1835): 154.

108. *Canton Register* 10, no. 19 (9 May 1837): 80.

109. *Facts Relating to Chinese Commerce*, 3, 12–13.

110. *Canton Register* 5, no. 3 (3 September 1832): 90–91.

111. *Canton Register* 8, no. 14 (7 April 1835): 71–72.

112. *Canton Register* 8, no. 43 (27 October 1835): 171–72.

113. "Chinese Islands," *Canton Register* 10, no. 3 (17 January 1837): 14.

114. James Brabazon Urmston, *Observations on the China Trade: And on the Importance and Advantages of Removing It from Canton, to Some Other Part of the Coast of That Empire* (London: Printed for private circulation only by G. Woodfall, 1834), 21–22, 38.

115. Charles Marjoribanks, *Letter to the Right Hon. Charles Grant, President of the Board of Control: On the Present State of British Intercourse with China* (London: J. Hatchard, 1833), 6–8, 15–16, 24.

116. Elliot to Hislop, 23 March 1840, in Susanna Hoe and Derek Roebuck, *The Taking of Hong Kong: Charles and Clara Elliot in China Waters* (Richmond, UK: Curzon, 1999), 118.

117. John Slade, *Narrative of the Late Proceedings and Events in China* (Macao: Canton Register Press, 1839), iii–iv, 79, 103. (Slade's preface was written in April 1840.)

118. *Canton Press* 6, no. 17 (23 January 1841): n.p.

119. *Canton Press* 6, no. 32 (8 May 1841): n.p.

120. "Hong Kong," *Canton Register* 14, no. 8 (23 February 1841): supplement, n.p. Shameen (Shamian) was a small sandbank island in Canton known for gambling and prostitution.

121. "Evacuation of Hongkong," *Canton Register* 14, no. 8 (23 February 1841): supplement, n.p.

122. James Brabazon Urmston, *Chusan and Hong Kong: With Remarks on the Treaty of Peace at Nankin in 1842, and on Our Present Position and Relations with China* (London: James Madden, 1847), 22, 51–54.

123. Elliot to Hislop, 6 September 1843, and to Frederick Elliot, 2 December 1843, in Hoe and Roebuck, *Taking of Hong Kong*, 202, 206; original emphasis.

*Chapter Four*

# Sizing Up China

Most Britons who wrote about China, either while or after spending time there, were interested in opening it to more trade and improving Britain's commercial position. But opening also meant understanding, and three frequent topics of discussion were the size of China's population, the origins of footbinding, and the extent of infanticide. Entangled in various ways, these subjects all involved human bodies and were linked to one of the most popular topics in Western discourse on the Middle Kingdom: "the Chinese character." They were also a way for these Britons to distinguish themselves as experts on the empire and its people. Like the other discussions we have seen, this often meant confirming or debunking works by the Jesuits and by their own countrymen. They also involved Chinese documents and informants, and how much evidence could be obtained from limited sources.

Although they may seem primitive or backward to modern readers, these were often earnest attempts, using the best resources available. They reveal a sophisticated level of interest in China, to open it to more trade—the consumption of Indian opium and British manufactured goods and the continued supply of Chinese tea—but also to understand it. They coincided with an emerging belief in Europe that a nation or culture's level of civilization depended on the status of its women. In December, for example, a correspondent wrote in the *Canton Register* that although in "ancient pagan Rome" a wife was considered a thing, "with the progress of civilization woman also was raised to the laws secured to her." Chinese law, however, considered a wife little more than "a disposable commodity; and by winking at polygamy, lowers female worth considerably." The "punishment of guilt" was much heavier for women, "whilst men act as the uncontrolled umpires of their partners."[1] Estimates of population and depictions of infanticide and footbinding were thus also allegories of British commercial ambitions: projecting different visions of a commercial futurity for China and registering different understandings of commerce and of Chinese women and patriarchy.

## AN IMMENSE AND UNPARALLELED POPULATION

The main reason these Britons were so interested in the size of China's population was commercial. They assumed this huge population, opened to foreign trade beyond Canton, meant an almost unlimited market for imports, and most Chinese people would prefer free trade if only the Qing government would allow it. Explaining the need for another British embassy to Peking, in February 1815 John Barrow, now Secretary to the Admiralty, declared to Lord Buckinghamshire, president of the Board of Control, that the "immense and unparalleled" population of China offered one single, massive market equal to all others the British enjoyed. "The day in which a single pen knife or a pair of scissors the manufacture of England, could be introduced into every family of China, would prove a *white day* in the Calendar of Sheffield and Birmingham."[2]

Britons in Canton often stressed how many Chinese depended on the foreign trade. In January 1838 the *Canton Press* explained that one million livelihoods relied on exports of tea and silk. The best policy for the British was thus to hold their ground and not worry about temporary trade stoppages. Even the Qing government realized halting trade would put it in "great difficulties" and *"the trade has become so necessary to them that the Chinese cannot now do without it."*[3] Given how the "suffering of one of their classes would react upon others," the "whole population" of China's maritime provinces would "be in favor of its preservation nor would they probably quietly submit to its being interrupted."[4]

China's large population presented both obstacles to spreading Christianity and opportunities for missionary work. Imagine the "distressing spectacle" of such "overwhelming numbers" of Chinese "heathen," urged Walter Henry Medhurst in 1838. "One third of the human race, and one half of the heathen world, held by one tie, and bound by one spell; one million of whom are every month dropping into eternity, untaught, unsanctified, and, as far as we know—unsaved." Even if the population increased at only 1 percent per year, this would mean 3,500,000 additional people per year; even according to "the most sanguine calculations, the heathen would multiply faster than they could be brought over to Christianity." Yet China's rapidly expanding population also meant hope: its people were "bursting forth on every side" into the colonies of Southeast Asia, "coming in contact with Christians, and seeking shelter under European governments," where missionaries could work "unimpeded and unprohibited" among them.[5]

Such a large population could also be cause for concern. John Barrow in 1804 predicted a revolution in China would result in "the most horrible consequences." Manchu soldiers would become "tired with slaying," and the millions who escaped execution would die of famine on the "least interruption of the usual pursuits of agriculture."[6] Such concerns continued into the 1830s. Could the empire continue to expand, the *Register* asked in October 1834, without eventually depleting it resources? With a "rising generation" large enough to "frighten the mandarins, who tremble at the prospects before them," this "great mass of man-kind" was approaching a "grand crisis." The only way to avert such a catastrophe was for Chinese "colonists" to expand into Manchuria and into China's western frontiers, perhaps even to the West Coast of America. If China's "so many millions" ever fell into a "state of fermentation," the results would be "awful." And if they refused to "advance with the world," they would "sooner or later fall a sacrifice to their stubbornness."[7] John Francis Davis warned that a "great deal" of "poverty and misery" resulted from how the population was growing faster than it could feed itself. Even if the size of China's population was "a point not so easily to be ascertained," never had there been a people who "held out so many direct encouragements to the growth of population" or completely ignored the type of "prudential restraints" proposed by Thomas Malthus.[8]

They were also interested in how this massive population explained how China functioned, or, more frequently, failed to function as they thought it should. In 1830, John Slade wrote that the "most authentic" information indicated that the seventeen provinces of this "insolent" nation contained 150 million people. This dense population was the root of the empire's many problems. It explained why the Chinese were the most "ignorant and bigoted" of all the "civilized" races—"obstinately tenacious of their own imaginary rights, insultingly regardless of the real rights of others."[9] As we saw in chapter 1, Robert Morrison believed this "overabundant" population justified the Qing government's policy of not allowing foreigners to bring their families to China.[10] The size of the population sometimes revealed the legendary resourcefulness of the Chinese. In yet another article on "the Chinese character," in July 1838 the *Press* wrote how "the people generally are far from idly disposed. The population is so great that the strictest industry, is necessary, to withstand famine."[11]

For some, China's population explained the extent of its poverty. In July 1828 the *Register* declared that Canton probably had more beggars than anywhere else in the world.[12] A correspondent to the *Press* wrote in July 1838 that China's "enormous" population was why "in all haunts and corners hundreds of wretches may be found in a state of absolute starvation or feeding on the most loathsome garbage."[13] John Davis insisted the cases of "extreme poverty and destitution" resulted not from the distribution of wealth, which was perhaps more equal in China than anywhere, but from the unusually large population.[14] Walter Medhurst claimed the "extreme poverty" of the people in south China was "well known" to everyone familiar with the region: Canton was "infested" with beggars.[15] "Beggars swarm," the missionaries Daniel Tyerman and George Bennet wrote during their visit in November 1825.[16]

The size of this population was part of the puzzle of how China had survived for several millennia, supposedly unchanged—a notion that, as we have seen, by the early 1800s became axiomatic in Western discourse on China. Like other foreigners, Britons frequently criticized China's supposed stagnation. But they often marveled at how the Manchus could control China despite being minorities. "He is an absolute monarch," stated the *Register* in April 1828, "over the largest associated population under Heaven. No man on earth has so much power, over so great a number of his fellow-creatures, as the Emperor of China."[17]

In February 1838 the *Press* tried to explain how the Qing government had "with few alterations stood the test of ages." How could such an "immense population" continue to revere its superiors with such "slavish imitation," especially with "neither a military force to keep these masses in awe, nor any other power to control the myriads." The answer could not be in numbers, for the Manchus were only a "handful" compared with the Chinese and had "been long ago enervated and become as weak as the conquered." The only possible conclusion was that the Chinese government was "in unison with the actual state of the nation." This had been achieved not through public opinion ("a thing unknown in China") but rather through careful molding (more effective than the "most persevering efforts" of a "Prussian drill sergeant") by "the plastic hand of Confucius and sundry other sages" as well as "minute and often vexatious laws," which had made the Chinese "what they are now."[18]

Even when Britons complained about the Manchus, they often attributed China's large population to the success of their rule. John Barrow noted that among the many reasons for China's large population was how the "Tartar conquest" had brought a "profound peace" and only "a few Tartar soldiers" had been deployed in the wars and conflicts with India and Russia.[19] "However absurd the pretensions of the Emperor of China may be to universal supremacy," Henry Ellis argued, "it is impossible to travel through his dominions without feeling that he has the finest country within an imperial ring-fence in the world."[20] John Davis cited the "uninterrupted peace" since the "complete establishment of the Manchow dynasty" as one of the reasons for China's large population.[21] Even the *Register*, which rarely had anything positive to say about China, conceded in October 1829 that, if the *Collected Statutes of the Qing Dynasty* (*Daqing huidian*) were correct and China's population had indeed almost doubled since the Qing conquest, it spoke "a great deal in favor of the Tartar Government of China"—though the paper was quick to mention that even with such a large population, emigrating was crime.[22]

For Davis, the reasons for China's massive population were both natural and "political," revealing both the strengths and the weaknesses of China's political and cultural foundations. Its natural advantages had been "improved to the utmost by its industrious inhabitants," while agriculture had been "honoured and encouraged beyond every other pursuit" and labor productivity had been maximized. This resourcefulness and industriousness extended well beyond land: nowhere else in the world was "so much food derived from the waters." The "political causes" that helped "swell the population of China" were "numerous and powerful." One was the form of paternal rights, which made a son, even in such a densely populated country, such an "important acquisition." But even more significant was the "universal system" of maintaining the traditional ideal of having nine generations under one roof. Another political cause was the opposition, "both in law and prejudice," to emigration. Not only was emigrating a crime, but those who returned after making their fortunes overseas also faced the risk of persecution or extortion. If this were not enough to discourage emigration, "the abandonment of his native place, and of the tombs of his ancestors" was "always abhorrent to the mind of a Chinese." As a result, "no persons but the most indigent or desperate ever quit their country."[23]

Getting China's population right—or at least showing they were making a determined effort to do—was also a way of showing they understood China. One reason this was so important was the growing number from the late eighteenth century on of Western works on China, many of them based on speculation and hearsay. "Scarcely any thing," Walter Medhurst wrote, had been "the subject of so much controversy, and at the same time of so much interest, relative to China, as the number of its population. The philosopher, the politician, the merchant, and the Christian are alike concerned to know, how many individuals are congregated together in that immense empire, and what is the rate of increase of its inhabitants." China's large population had led to "numerous hypotheses" among Western demographers and economists who used it to support their own theories about subsistence and famine. But Medhurst had no doubt about who should be believed:

> We have the evidence of men who have long resided in the country, and a variety of estimates taken by the natives themselves, and published by imperial

authority. While the learned of Europe are sitting at home, and calculating what may or may not be, which they decide according to their several hypotheses, and partialities; we have the testimony of eye witnesses and actual residents, as to what really exists. Between these bare supposers and personal enquirers there can be no difficulty in determining on whom most reliance is to be placed.[24]

A seemingly objective and simple question thus opened itself to different methods and motivations for counting. For if they agreed on the need to determine the size of China's population, they rarely concurred on the actual size. Even the population of Canton was difficult to pin down, not the least because foreigners were prohibited from entering the city. John Barrow argued it was difficult to calculate the population of *any* Chinese city, at least by the length of its walls. "Few are without large patches of unoccupied ground within them which, in many instances, far exceeds the quantity of land that is built upon."[25] In 1807, Robert Morrison wrote that a local Chinese merchant had assured him that according to "an accurate census" the city had one million people, "exclusive of women and children."[26] But Daniel Tyerman and George Bennet insisted the "exact population" of Canton could not be ascertained by "any authorized standard of computing."[27]

One obstacle was the large number of people living on the Pearl River. Returning from his embassy to Peking in late December 1793, Lord Macartney found the river "quite covered with boats and vessels of various sorts and sizes; all, even the very smallest, constantly and thickly inhabited."[28] Aeneas Anderson, his valet, felt that the usual estimate of one million within the city, not including the half million in its "large and extensive suburbs," could not possibly include the large population that lived on the river.[29] Henry Hayne, Lord Amherst's personal secretary, believed the large number of boat-dwellers led foreigners to inflate the population of Canton and in turn that of China. "It was the only place we had seen in China where the boats were so numerous as to be anchored in streets or where whole families were residing, as it were in a floating town so described by former writers on China, as it was the case throughout the country. Even taking Canton as the minimum whereas it is the maximum, the account would be most exaggerated."[30] Tyerman and Bennet cited their host, James Brabazon Urmston, who had lived there for twenty years and estimated the population within the walls and in the suburbs to be 500,000, with another 200,000 on the river.[31] John Davis simply noted the "no inconsiderable portion" of the population living on the water.[32]

Another impediment was the reliability of local sources. Robert Morrison obtained much of his news about the China beyond this tiny section of Canton through local helpers and acquaintances. But the flow of information was uneven: the Chinese were "loquacious" when talking and gossiping among themselves, but with foreigners they were "reserved" on "every topic that re-

Figure 4.1. *Junks and Sampans at Canton*, ca. 1780, Chinese artist, gouache. *Photo*: Martyn Gregory Gallery

gards the internal affairs of the Empire." And Morrison sometimes wondered about the reliability of the reports and opinions of his Chinese informants. "A court gazette from Pekin falls into the hands of some," he wrote in January 1808, and they "soon diffuse reports, and as is general, with considerable additions."[33]

These obstacles did not prevent them from making their own estimates. Davis wrote that although the size of the native population had been frequently discussed, so "little authentic information" had ever been found that the question remained "wholly undecided." But Davis assigned little validity to the "sweeping calculations" of one million. "As the whole circuit of the city has been compassed within two hours by persons on foot, it cannot exceed six or seven miles, and, considering that the houses are not more than a single story in height, it seems difficult to imagine how such a monstrous number as a million can be stuffed within its precincts."[34] Charles Toogood Downing, who drew much of his information from Davis, argued otherwise. Based on the "mass of moving human beings in the square before the factories," with "the crowd every moment replaced by herds of others, who seem to have no occupation," he suggested the city's population must be even larger than one million.[35] John Elliot Bingham, lieutenant on HMS *Modeste* during the Opium War, put the population at closer to 800,000.[36]

If even the size of Canton's population was hard to determine, it is hardly surprising there was such disagreement on the population of China. Lord Macartney noted that the figures he had obtained from Catholic missionaries ranged from 200 to no less than 333 million. Having traveled extensively in France and lived there before its revolution ("the late subversion"), he estimated the population of China was at least twice that of France. The "immense numbers" of people he had seen on his embassy were far greater than he had ever imagined.[37] Embassy secretary George Leonard Staunton reckoned that, on average, every square mile in China contained one-third more people than even the most populous country in Europe. His account contained a list, supplied by one of the embassy's handlers, of the population of each province. Although he questioned some of the figures, Staunton remained in awe of this massive population:

> After every reasonable allowance, however, for occasional mistakes, and partial exaggerations in the returns of Chinese population, the ultimate result exhibits to the mind a grand and curious spectacle of so large a proportion of the whole human race, connected together in one great system of polity, submitting quietly, and through so considerable an extent of country, to one great sovereign; and uniform in their laws, their manners, and their language; but differing essentially in each of these respects, from every other portion of mankind; and neither desirous of communicating with, nor forming any designs against, the rest of the world.[38]

No member of the Macartney embassy spent more time and ink trying to show China's population was indeed as large as had been claimed than John Barrow, determined to "set in its true light" a subject "much agitated and generally disbelieved." Through elaborate (and sometimes bizarre) comparisons between city sizes in China and England, the population of China and Holland, and agricultural productivity in China and England and Ireland, Barrow attempted to prove "by facts and analogy" that China was capable of supporting not only more than 330 million people but perhaps even twice that number. Although he conceded Europeans might never be able to determine the exact population of this giant empire, which ranked first "both in extent and population," he claimed to prove it was capable of supporting "this and a much greater population."[39]

The members of the next embassy, as Lord Amherst wrote to the East India Company's Court of Directors in January 1817, enjoyed more freedom to explore the hinterland than "any former Embassy."[40] Arriving during the reign of the Jiaqing Emperor, in the wake of the White Lotus Rebellion and shortly after the suppression of the Eight Trigrams Uprising, they believed China had fallen into decline since the Macartney embassy. Poverty and dilapidation, poor public infrastructure, lack of refinement, unhygienic living conditions, and a weak military—all seemed proof of degeneration.[41] This was particularly evident to Staunton's son, George Thomas, first commissioner and the only member of the embassy to have already been to Peking (as Lord Macartney's page), who commented frequently on these purported signs of Jiaqing's "unprosperous" reign.[42]

Perhaps because they felt China had declined, they were less convinced the population could be as large as had been claimed. True, wrote Staunton, the crowds gathering to view the embassy "seemed to argue a large population." Practically everywhere along the way to Peking, the embassy attracted curious onlookers. Approaching Tientsin, Staunton noted large crowds along the riverbanks. About four miles from the city, more than two thousand people waited in "a most powerful sun" to see the embassy, with a curiosity "which seemed to absorb all their faculties."[43] But no one on the embassy took these crowds seriously as a measurement of China's population.

Henry Ellis was firmly convinced the size of the population had been exaggerated and Chinese cities were no more densely populated than most European capitals. Even though the frequency of the "considerable towns and large villages" the embassy had passed on its way indicated the "comparative population and prosperity" of China, this was partly because the embassy had traveled through the "great line of communication" between the "extreme" provinces of the empire. The "most accurate" Chinese accounts put the population at "considerably" lower than two hundred million, and Ellis saw little reason to doubt they would downplay a figure "so materially connected with their national greatness."[44]

Clarke Abel, the Amherst embassy's chief medical officer and naturalist, wrote that although the cities were "well peopled" and sometimes even "overpeopled," the "intermediate land" rarely seemed to be "fully stocked." He cautioned against making any estimation based on the curious "multitudes" crowding the embassy in the larger towns and cities. Although Abel conceded anyone traveling in a country on a "hurried journey" and under a "suspicious surveillance" could not draw any reliable conclusions, he agreed with Ellis that the "visible" population of China seemed not to be greater than the quality of the land under cultivation.[45]

Though he could not produce any figures to prove it, Walter Medhurst favored the higher estimate. The emphasis placed on agriculture and the honor accorded to it clearly indicated a "dense population," as did the "industry and skill" of the Chinese, "striving to produce as many of the necessaries of life as possible." They "thoroughly" understood the value of rotating and double cropping, and fertilizing with manure: "A stranger is struck with this, on first setting his foot on the shores of China." Equally telling was their resourcefulness and desire to avoid extravagance in their food, dress, and dwellings. The Chinese rarely ate beef, for example, not for religious reasons as in India, but "because oxen are used in husbandry, and they think it a shame, after a poor

Figure 4.2. Clarke Abel, by M. Gauci, after P. W. Wilkin, lithograph. Wellcome Collection. CC BY 4.0

animal has been labouring all his life in their service, to cut him to pieces at last, and then to feed upon his flesh, and make shoes of his hide."[46]

For Medhurst, an even "stronger proof" of China's dense population was the widespread emigration to Southeast Asia—"in spite of restrictions and disabilities," from a land "where learning and civilization reign" to "one where comparative ignorance and barbarity prevail." Why would emigration persist, "unless stern necessity prevailed" and "unless the ever-increasing progeny pressed on the heels of the adult population, and obliged them to seek a precarious subsistence in a less thickly peopled part of the earth?" The

Qing government's willingness since 1825 to bend its "otherwise unalterable" rules by allowing foreign vessels to import rice without having to pay the usual measurement charge and entry fee proved that rice was "greatly needed." If rice had to be imported even in "so fertile a region as China," surely this was further proof that it was "overstocked with inhabitants."[47]

As with the population of Canton, they disagreed about the reliability of the Chinese sources and whether the Qing government had the ability to conduct a proper census. Lord Macartney wrote that although the embassy's chief handler was highly educated and had developed "a strong friendship and affection" for the ambassador, he had "all the vanity of a Chinese": the more impressed he became with the "manifest superiority" of the British, the more inclined he was to exaggerate the population of his country and "other circumstances of national fondness."[48] As the *Register* explained in October 1829, the appropriate section in the *Collected Statutes*, "never intended for the eyes of an European," showed the Qianlong Emperor had preceded Malthus "in his fears of the human." If the *Statutes* were correct, China's population had almost doubled since the Qing conquest in 1644.[49]

In July 1832 the *Register* reported that, according to the latest edition of the *Statutes*, published in 1825, the population of China and its "colonies," based on the 1813 census, was 361,693,879. This would "probably serve to set at rest the numerous speculations concerning the real amount of population in China." Yet even this figure could not be trusted entirely, for the *Register* knew "from several authorities" that people in China were "in the habit of diminishing rather than increasing their numbers, in their reports to Government." Still, as a source published by the Qing regime, "not for the information of curious enquirers, but for the use of its own officers," there was no reason to believe, as some "European speculators" had suggested, the official figure was only half of the true population of China.[50]

Morrison and Medhurst saw little reason to question the dependability of the Chinese sources. In his *View of China*, Morrison explained how in the Qing government "there appears great regularity and system. Every district has its appropriate officer; every street its constable, and every ten houses a tything-man. They have all the requisite means of ascertaining the population with considerable accuracy."[51] However "mendacious" the Chinese usually were, Medhurst argued, they lied only when "interest allures, or when they have no means for ascertaining the truth." Why would they want to publish false figures, especially when they had no idea these sources would ever be made accessible to the outside world and when they had "every possible means" of calculating the size of the population? Given that Europeans accepted "without scruple" other Chinese official figures, why should they not believe Chinese estimates of their own population? "We may make some deductions for the extravagance of eastern nations, and receive with caution the statements of different years, which we can compare together, and endeavour to ascertain the rate of increase; but we are not at liberty to call them liars, till we can prove them to have erred wilfully in this matter."[52]

No one even claimed to be able to determine the population of "Chinese Tartary"—the Qing Empire's northern and western territories—except that it was sparsely populated. As George Leonard Staunton explained, few Chinese ever went beyond Jehol (Rehe), apart from officers sent there on military duty or officials exiled there as punishment. "The Chinese still consider that country as foreign to them."[53] Lord Macartney described the Chinese as being "almost as ignorant of that country as we are. . . . The Chinese talk of Tartary as of a country half as big as the rest of the world besides, but their conceptions of its limits are very dark and confused. There is a wide difference between pretension and possession."[54]

## A HORRID PRACTICE

The enormity of China's population mattered for another reason: for some, it explained the prevalence of infanticide. By the late 1700s and early 1800s, most foreigners in China doubted infanticide could be as extensive as the Catholic missionaries had suggested. Samuel Holmes, Lord Macartney's guard, had been told that "exposing their infants to perish" was "wearing away very fast."[55] Still, they often blamed it on China's massive population. The *Register* observed in May 1829 that unlike India with its "Hindoo Suttee," China was "tolerably free" from "direct cruelty" in its "religious superstitions"—except for its "horrible" infanticide, which in any case was caused not by religious superstition but by "hard-hearted skepticism" and "the visionary dreams of political economy."[56] Walter Medhurst disagreed that infanticide was a systematic attempt to prevent China from becoming overpopulated. But its frequency proved the "great poverty and overwhelming number of the people" and that China was "immensely populous."[57]

Westerners in China, especially missionaries, were often obsessed with determining the extent of infanticide.[58] However, it was only after the Opium War that infanticide—especially of females—became "a totemic cultural marker of China writ large" in Western sources. With unprecedented access to China, in the second part of the nineteenth century writings by missionaries, traders, and diplomats often mentioned infanticide.[59]

What, then, did infanticide mean for Britons who wrote about China before the Opium War and the end of the Canton System? Both travelers and long-time residents discussed the practice, even if they disagreed about its prevalence. Charles Downing mentioned a building in Canton that could accommodate three hundred foundling children who would have otherwise died.[60] The local English-language press often featured translations of imperial edicts against infanticide. Given that infanticide was a mode of harnessing population growth, naturally they idealized their sense of free (or at least less restricted) trade as a better way of regulating population size: a market-based approach rather than through infanticide. Unlike missionaries and other reformers after the Opium War, however, these men wrote about infanticide not to help end it (which in any case they were in no position to do) but to offer a "true" account that was based on refuting the Jesuits and even other Britons.

Members of the two British embassies were well aware of the limitations of their experience in China. Henry Ellis regretted his "personal intercourse with the "higher classes" of Chinese had been so "strictly complimentary and official" and had been conducted through an interpreter. This lack of "actual experience" and "private communication" with Chinese people had left him unable to form a reliable judgment of their "moral qualities"—though he appears to have had little trouble making an unfavorable appraisal nonetheless.[61] Clarke Abel was disappointed his contact with the "higher or better informed classes" had been almost entirely official, with these members of Chinese society "so cased in armour of form that it was impossible to reach their natural character." Nor had he been able to get a good sense of living standards. In the same village where he saw men characterized by "dirt, squalidness, and extreme poverty," in living conditions "more like the dens of beasts than the habitations of men," only moments later he was astonished to encounter three women "not only decently, but handsomely clothed."[62]

Even in the late 1880s, Westerners faced a significant obstacle to gauging the extent of infanticide in China. Because infanticide usually occurred not only within the confines of the home but also within the even less accessible "female sphere of birth," Western men were even less likely than Chinese men ever to see an infant corpse. Any inferences about the extent of infanticide could be drawn only from circumstantial evidence, such as the investigation of infant burial sites, approximations by Chinese informants (both male and female), and Chinese morality books that mentioned infanticide.[63] As with footbinding, all the more notable is how much attention these early Britons paid to infanticide and how hard they tried to understand its causes and determine its extent.

During the Macartney embassy, George Leonard Staunton noted that the practice, usually by exposure, was confined mainly to baby girls and immediately after birth—"before the countenance is animated, or the features formed, to catch the affections rising in the parent's breast."[64] Based on the reports of Catholic missionaries—whose reliability he doubted on most other issues, and whose estimates ranged from ten to thirty thousand—John Barrow estimated nine thousand cases of infanticide per year in the capital, with an equal number for the rest of the empire. He reckoned in Peking alone an average of twenty-four infants were abandoned per day, thrown into a common pit outside the city walls, with some devoured by the loose dogs and swine roaming the streets of the capital. Babies were sometimes thrown into rivers or canals with a gourd tied round their neck to keep their head above water until they either drowned or were rescued by "some humane person." The practice was so common that Barrow claimed to have even seen the body of a dead infant, without any gourd, floating among the boats in the river of Canton, "and the people seemed to take no more notice of it than if it had been the carcass of a dog."[65]

For Barrow, there was little better proof of the "insensible and incompassionate character" of the Chinese than the "horrid practice" of infanticide, "tolerated by custom and encouraged by the government." Still, he tried hard to understand its causes. Some Catholic missionaries had blamed this "unnatural act" on midwives, who strangled the infant at birth but told the mother that her baby had been stillborn. Others had attributed it to the Chinese belief in the migration of souls: parents who feared their children would face a life of poverty thought it better to let them escape to a "more happy asylum." Barrow concluded that infanticide was so prevalent not only because of "extreme poverty and hopeless indigence," but because, as in ancient Greece, it was not prohibited by "positive law." But even he attributed this "unnatural crime" mainly to "extreme poverty and hopeless indigence" and to the frequency of "direful famines" in China—though he wondered how strong could be the "boasted filial affection" of the Chinese for their parents, "when they scruple not to become the murderers of their own children."[66]

As we have seen, the members of the Amherst embassy felt China had declined. Yet they believed the extent of infanticide had been exaggerated. Henry Ellis wrote that China was deteriorating. But he doubted that poverty and "extreme wretchedness" were extensive enough to result in the levels of infanticide that had been claimed.[67] John McLeod also argued that infanticide was less common than Europeans had previously believed, even if the Chinese themselves admitted its prevalence.[68] George Thomas Staunton did not discuss infanticide in his account of the embassy. However, in the introduction to his translation of the Qing code he had argued that infanticide, which had come to be considered by many Europeans as "an indelible stain upon the Chinese character," was practiced only "in the anguish of hopeless poverty" or when birth defects might "render life a painful burden." He contrasted this with the "legalized cruelty and unnatural indifference" of fathers in ancient Rome under similar circumstances.[69]

Like gauging the size of China's population, determining the prevalence of infanticide was also a matter of claiming authority and experience. Clarke Abel explained how the Amherst embassy had not encountered a single case, even though the popular accounts had made him "very watchful for every circumstance" and led him "to look for a lower degree of parental affection in China than in other countries." Abel did not doubt that infanticide was practiced, "especially in time of dreadful scarcity," but he agreed that whenever parents could afford to support their offspring, "there is no country where maternal affection is stronger than in China."[70]

In January 1820 the *Indo-Chinese Gleaner*, published in Malacca by the missionary William Milne (who with Robert Morrison had co-founded the Anglo-Chinese College there) but featuring articles by Britons in Canton and Macao, took Abel to task. He had tried to "wipe from our common nature, the reproach of infanticide" by stating that the members of the embassy had seen nothing during the entire journey between Peking and Canton to confirm proof of this "foul deed" and that he himself had seen parents show their children "much tenderness." Evidence from the testimonies of the "natives themselves," moral tracts exhorting parents not to commit infanticide, and Europeans who had lived in China all proved infanticide existed. By looking only for infants who been exposed publicly, in their travels "post haste" on major roads and rivers, Abel and his fellow travelers had not understood how most infants were "disposed of" not by being exposed publicly but by being drowned indoors in a shallow tub:

> European writers on this subject seem to imagine that the crime is committed by stealth, and that the poor innocents are exposed and left in the streets, or cast into large rivers under cover of darkness, as is sometimes the case with the infants of seduced, or seducing, females in England. This, however, is not the case. Infanticide is not an illegality of which the law takes no notice; or if this seems a solecism, it is an illegality of which the executors of the law take no notice.

Because infanticide was not something the Chinese were proud of, they observed a sort of "decency" in it, never exposing it to foreigners in Canton or to embassy travelers, "before whom they assume the best and most imposing attitude." Not having seen an infant child destroyed was no more proof that infanticide did not exist, than not having seen one born was evidence "against the birth of children in China."[71]

John Davis argued in one of his many discussions of "the Chinese character" that the extent of female infanticide had been "overrated." He allowed that "occasional instances" occurred only in the "chief cities" and most populated areas, "where the difficulty of subsistence takes away all hope from the poorest persons of being able to rear their offspring." Unlike Barrow, Davis believed the incidence had been blown out of proportion in the West "as an argument against the prevalence of parental feeling in China." The "long experience" of Westerners who sailed or rowed daily on the river in Canton confirmed that its "limited existence" had been exaggerated. Even in "very crowded and populous" Canton, which the Chinese themselves considered "the most licentious city in the whole empire," it was rare to see bodies of infants floating in the river. Davis blamed the Western fixation with Chinese infanticide on the Catholic missionaries who, "with all their complete and intimate knowledge of China, had a trick of giving their own colouring to such matters as bore in any way upon the honour and glory of the mission." Not only had these missionaries overstated the prevalence of infanticide, rather than trying to save the children "doomed to be drowned" they had simply baptized them before they died—"a cheap, rapid, and easy work of charity."[72]

Walter Medhurst was interested in infanticide primarily for what it said about China's population, rather than about Chinese values. Its prevalence proved the "great poverty and overwhelming number of the people" and that China was "immensely populous": infanticide was caused by poverty rather than prejudice or "religious considerations." Although Medhurst agreed that infanticide was widespread, he questioned Barrow's estimate of nine thousand cases per year in Peking, and rejected the idea infanticide was part of an attempt keep the empire from becoming overpopulated. Confined "wholly" to females, infanticide was "altogether personal, and not patriotic." Baby girls were "sacrificed to Mammon rather than to Moloch." This explained why infanticide was so much more common in the south, "where the numbers of human beings exceed the powers of the soil to produce sufficient sustenance," and in the capital, "where the myriads of citizens find hardly room to live or to breathe."[73]

Charles Downing recounted a moving story of how a fellow physician on a British ship berthed at Whampoa once discovered a secluded spot where infants were abandoned:

> The surface of the ground was entirely covered with human bones, bleaching in the sun, and a corpse or two was lying there wrapped up in its matted shroud. A little heap in the centre of the enclosure attracted the attention of the foreigner, when he had made his way through the obstructing briers. Judge of his surprise, when on approaching it, he found it to consist of *two infants* placed by the side of each other. One was lying stiff and motionless on the earth, cold and inanimate; the other was above, but almost exhausted. Its feeble breath was scarcely able to give utterance to a low and plaintive moan, whilst its hands were

stretched out from its side, and appeared to be grappling among the whitened bones as if to find a morsel of food.

Determined that this "little innocent" should survive, the physician took it back to his ship and hired a Chinese nursemaid, but it soon died.[74]

But even such heartbreaking accounts were not necessarily accepted uncritically as proof of the prevalence of infanticide. Downing was convinced that the number of children "murdered by their parents" was "very much exaggerated," with infanticide practiced only by the "most indigent of people" and even then only in "times of the greatest calamity." Anyone who visited China could see for himself that "want of affection" was rarely the cause of infanticide, for Chinese mothers showed "as much feeling" for their children as anywhere. Women on the Pearl River often held up their children to foreigners, "expecting you to be as much delighted with them as they are themselves", and nursing their infants "with all the energy of true love."[75] And who in China, asked the *Canton Press* in July 1838, had not noticed the "affectionate and indulgent behaviour" of Chinese parents toward their offspring? Even if infanticide was "too common," it was a result of "utter poverty and destitution."[76]

Infanticide was, of course, not only a "Chinese" practice. In Britain and in continental Europe, state- and church-run agencies were created to deal with the huge numbers of abandoned children. What made the Chinese case so different was not the numbers involved, but that infanticide and abandonment were confined mainly to infant girls.[77] What should impress modern readers is less "the particular cruelty or indifference of late imperial Chinese with regard to their children" than "the immensity of the social problem of unwanted children all over the world."[78] These Britons were well aware that infanticide was not unique to China. In *The Chinese as They Are* (1841) the naturalist and missionary George Tradescant Lay cautioned his readers against making rash judgments: "It would be the part of prudence to speak in a whisper, lest the Chinese should overhear, and ask whether in our own country mothers are not sometimes driven to murder their offspring by an overwhelming dread of shame or the fearful consequences of bastardy?"[79]

## SO EXTRAORDINARY A CUSTOM

What *was* unique to China was footbinding. Almost everyone who wrote about China mentioned it, to the point where by the early 1800s accounts such as John Barrow's hardly needed to introduce the practice and its history. "And yet such introductions did occur and recur, establishing their place not only as descriptive and representational but affective and persuasive."[80]

Writing before the anti-footbinding campaigns in the late nineteenth and early twentieth centuries, these men usually discussed footbinding as something that, however strange or repulsive, needed to be understood on its own terms. Most speculated when and why the custom had begun, observing that all cultures and civilizations had their own "unnatural" practices. Notable in these descriptions are the details, the cultural relativism, and the attempts to figure out how footbinding came about. (Needless to say, given the prohibition against foreign women in Canton, these accounts are all by men. A rare description of footbinding by a Western woman before the Opium War comes from an American, Harriett Low, who in February 1833 saw a "poor creature" in Macao "toddling along on her little feet.")[81]

George Leonard Staunton's "authentic" account of the Macartney embassy included an engraving of a bound foot, based on an "exact model" obtained during the embassy and drawn by the embassy's junior draughtsman, William Alexander.[82] Shortly after arriving in China in September 1807, Robert Morrison wrote that he often saw women "not walking, strictly speaking, but hobbling along the streets."[83] Henry Hayne mentioned bound feet several times in his diary, including how many of the women who stood at their doors to watch the passing embassy "hobbled away on their heals [sic] owing to the detestable custom of crippling their feet." This confirmed that "the accounts of the diminutions of their feet" were "by no means exaggerated." Hayne twice encountered a well-dressed woman riding in a palanquin, her feet "as small as any I had ever seen and neatly dressed in pair of red silk embroidered shoes."[84] Although in South China boatwomen ("generally of doubtful virtue") usually had feet "as nature made them," in the northern and central provinces many women could be seen "hobbling on their heels with cramped feet."[85]

British artists who spent time in China also paid attention to women's feet. Two of the images in *Picturesque Voyage to India; By the Way of China* by Thomas Daniell and his nephew William, who visited Canton in late 1785 or early 1786 en route to Calcutta, featured women with bound feet.[86] William Alexander's *Costume of China* did not contain detailed illustrations of bound feet, but captions to two of the forty-eight drawings discussed the practice. Five of the fifty captions in a later collection of Alexander's drawings also mentioned footbinding.[87] George Chinnery, the best known of the China trade painters, who arrived in Macao in 1825 after working in India for more than twenty years, instead often drew and painted boatwomen with their "natural," unbound feet.[88]

Western authors found it both "natural and easy" to write about Chinese women's hair, dress, and makeup. Footbinding, however, was a particularly difficult topic to discuss.[89] In one of the more farfetched attempts to explain

Figure 4.3. Bound feet and shoes. In George [Leonard] Staunton, *An Authentic Account of an Embassy from the King of Great Britain to the Emperor of China; Including Cursory Observations Made, and Information Obtained, in Travelling through That Ancient Empire and a Small Part of Chinese Tartary*. London: G. Nicol, 1797

Figure 4.4. *A Boatwoman Rowing towards the Shore, Macau*, 1843, George Chinnery, pencil and pen and ink. Photo: Martyn Gregory Gallery

its origins, Daniel Tyerman and George Bennet suggested that this "outrageous fashion" might have been invented by jealous men to keep women from dancing.⁹⁰ Given their limited contact with Chinese society, it is not unusual that most Britons were unable to probe the roots and meanings of footbinding any deeper. They would have had little reason or opportunity to discuss it with the Chinese men they encountered the most often—the hong merchants, compradors, linguists, and servants—let alone with these men's wives, mothers, or daughters, with whom they would have had almost no personal contact. Chinese women were reluctant to talk about footbinding to men, foreign or Chinese.⁹¹

George Lay, whose book included an extended discussion of the practice, marveled at how none of the "multitudes" of Chinese women who sought treatment at the hospitals run by foreigners suffered from ailments caused by footbinding—which might provide a "more intimate acquaintance with the anatomy of this morbid organ, that we might see how nature, under the pressure of so great a calamity, has contrived to maintain the intercourse of the arterial and nervous system, and keep the limb from being materially injured by it." He described a sort of "masonic secrecy" about footbinding—his proof being how a servant, "when her mistress proceeded to unwind the bandages, blushed, and turned her face to the wall."⁹²

In a lecture to the foreign community of Canton in January 1873, the American merchant and diplomat Gideon Nye recalled how not only were foreign women "jealously excluded" from Canton, but how "no Chinese

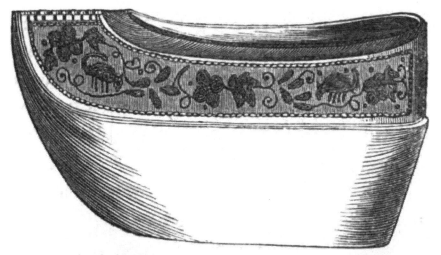

Figure 4.5. Shoe for bound foot. In G. [George] Tradescant Lay, *The Chinese as They Are: Their Moral, Social, and Literary Character*. London: W. Ball, 1841

Lady could even be seen by a Foreigner, except by a stolen glance accidentally and very rarely on the occasion of dining at some Hong Merchant's house, when the natural curiosity of the younger Ladies induced their peering from behind curtains."[93] For Tyerman and Bennet, such a rare occasion occurred in autumn 1825. At a dinner at the home of the merchant Howqua, the meal and entertainment had been of the "most sumptuous kind." But the "greatest rarity" was the sight of their host's new daughter-in-law:

> She stood in a modest and graceful attitude, having her eyes fixed on the floor, though she occasionally raised them, with a glance of timid curiosity, towards the spectators. Her hands, joined together, but folded in her robe, she lifted several times towards her face, and then lowered them very slowly. Her attendants, presuming that the guests would be gratified with a peep at that consummation of Chinese beauty, the lady's feet, raised the hem of the mantle from hers, for a moment or two. They were of the most diminutive kind, and reduced to a mere point at the toe. Her shoes, like the rest of her bridal apparel, were scarlet, embroidered with gold. In justice to the poor creature, during this torturing exhibition (as we imagine it must have been to her), her demeanour was natural and becoming; and once or twice something like half a smile, for an instant, showed that she was not entirely unconscious of the admiration which her appearance excited, nor much displeased by it.[94]

As with the size of China's population and the extent of infanticide, the many obstacles to understanding footbinding did not prevent British observers from trying to learn more about it. Basil Hall of the Amherst embassy wrote how he had learned from an "intelligent" Chinese father that the pain his four daughters' feet suffered while undergoing this "horrid ceremony" and "vile mutilation" was so great he had to leave home for more than a month when the "season of tormenting" began. "He bitterly deplored the total absence of any free will to depart from the established customs of the Empire."[95] George Lay had been informed by the "chief person" at the Buddhist temple on Honam Island that during the binding process his own sister had "suffered much anguish in the sole of the foot, or rather in its lower and more central parts." Recalling a conversation with a Chinese acquaintance, Lay wrote how the man believed that footbinding's only fault lay in how it interfered with a woman's gait. This Lay attributed to the fact that his acquaintance had never seen an unbound female foot. "He was so blessed as not to know the real state of this organ, and therefore his admiration had no alloy."[96]

Why was there so much interest in footbinding? Curiosity, shock, and disgust all played a role. When Clarke Abel encountered three well-dressed women in a village during the Amherst embassy, he studied them and their clothing for some time, until the appearance of soldiers prompted them to "hobble off as fast as their crippled and stunted feet could carry them."[97] Hall recalled how even though the members of the embassy had been prepared for this "peculiar barbarism" by drawings and other descriptions, the "actual sight" of bound feet among some women they encountered on the journey to Peking "caused a feeling of disgust which I shall not attempt to describe."[98] Tyerman and Bennet were "pained" to see the "crippled condition" of upper-class Chinese women whose feet had been "so stunted and cramped in their growth as to be reduced to mere clubs."[99] Lay wrote that he had become used to the sight of small feet on Chinese women—until he had the "misfortune" of seeing one "unmasked."[100]

Footbinding could be a measurement of Chinese values. This engagement, even obsession, with the practice, figured prominently in nineteenth-century Western literature on China and was "intimately connected with an emerging trope in European society: the status of women as a criterion for the status of a civilisation."[101] The caption to the Daniells' illustration of a "lady of quality" explained that in China "women are all reared in ignorance and imbecility."[102] The American missionary Ira Tracy declared in November 1833 that if "a nation's civilization may be estimated by the rank which females hold in society," China was "far from occupying that first place which she so strongly claims."[103] In April 1835, Elijah Coleman Bridgman wrote in the *Chinese Repository* that "national and domestic customs" such as footbinding provided "ample evidence" of the "inefficacy" of Chinese ethical systems. "Not only the minds of the people," Bridgman insisted, "but their bodies also, are distorted and deformed by unnatural usages."[104]

John Barrow began his section on state and society in China (including the "manners, customs, sentiments, and moral character of the people") by pronouncing it an "invariable maxim" that the condition of women in "any nation will furnish a tolerable just criterion of the degree of civilization to which that nation has arrived." He divided nations by how they valued women: those where "the moral and intellectual powers of the mind in the female sex are held in most estimation," governed by laws "best calculated to promote the happiness of the people"; and Asian despotisms where "tyranny, oppression, and slavery are sure to prevail," and where women were "subservient to the sensual gratification, the caprice, and the jealousy of tyrant men." Footbinding was thus only one of many techniques the Chinese had devised to constrain women:

> The Chinese, if possible, have imposed on their women a greater degree of humility and restraint than the Greeks of old, or the Europeans in the dark ages. Not satisfied with the physical deprivation of the use of their limbs, they have contrived, in order to keep them the more confined, to make it a moral crime for a woman to be seen abroad. If they should have occasion to visit a friend or relation, they must be carried in a close sedan chair: to walk would be the

height of vulgarity. Even the country ladies, who may not possess the luxury of a chair, rather than walk, suffer themselves to be sometimes rolled about in a sort of covered wheelbarrow.[105]

Barrow's assertion that the condition of women was a criterion for gauging the degree of a civilization was no doubt related to imagining them as consumers—breaking the bonds of footbinding and saving infants as future consumers for British goods. But not everyone—even on the same embassy—would have agreed with him that the condition of Chinese women was so bad. Aeneas Anderson argued that the Catholic missionaries had exaggerated the "rigid confinement" of Chinese women:

> In different parts of that extensive country, different customs may prevail; and the power of husbands over their wives may be such as to render them matters of their liberty, which they may exercise, with severity, if circumstances should, at any time, suggest the necessity of such a measure, or caprice fancy it: but I do not hesitate to assert, that women, in general, have a reasonable liberty in China; and that there is the same communication and social intercourse with women, which, in Europe, is considered as a principal charm of social life.[106]

Samuel Holmes wrote that in the north the embassy members were greatly surprised by how women "appeared to be under as little restraint here as in England." Although they had been told that it was "very rare" to see a Chinese woman, "not being allowed to leave the house, except in covered chairs or carriages," women could be seen "near every house or village, though not quite in number proportionable to the other sex."[107] Henry Ellis argued after the second embassy that women in China were less degraded than those in Muslim countries, even if they could not inherit land.[108]

They understood, as modern scholars have confirmed, that binding feet had many meanings—to the point where, "there is not one footbinding but many."[109] The members of the Macartney embassy learned from one of their Chinese interpreters that if one of two equally beautiful sisters did not have bound feet but the other did, she would be considered "as in an abject state, unworthy of associating with the rest of the family, and doomed to perpetual obscurity, and the drudgery of servitude."[110] Davis described this "shocking mutilation" of women's feet as the "most unaccountable species" of Chinese taste. But his shock did not stop him from trying to understand its cultural and sociological significance. Like long fingernails that prevented a person from doing manual labor, crippled feet conveyed gentility and helplessness, with the "tottering gait of the poor women, as they hobble along upon the heel of the foot, they compare to the waving of a willow agitated by the breeze."[111]

A two-inch-long foot, explained George Lay, was the "idol of a Chinaman, on which he lavishes the most precious epithets which nature and language can supply." Because footbinding prevented a woman's calf muscles from developing, her leg tapered down to her foot, "without any risings or inflections." Bound feet forced a woman to walk with a "certain degree of curvature" and "never to appear upright," for straight lines and perpendiculars were prohibited by Chinese rules for "regulating the carriage of the body, as well as by the canons of pictorial beauty." This the Chinese regarded as the "perfection of beauty." A "piece of ruined nature," which was rarely even seen by men, was considered "the prime essential of all feminine beauty."[112]

Footbinding symbolized the helplessness of Chinese women. Tyerman and Bennet noted how the "difficulty and misery" of walking were made even worse by the uneven pavements of Canton and Macao, and how "many are obliged to avail themselves of the aid of an umbrella to support their decrepitude as they totter and hobble along."[113] Charles Downing described how seeing an elderly woman walk on bound feet made one think she had lost both legs and was walking on wooden stumps. "You feel a great temptation to go up and offer the old lady the use of your stick to help her along, as she seems in danger of falling every moment. In this tottering manner they proceed, and, if they wish to look behind them, they are obliged to stop and then steady themselves, while they gradually twist the whole body round as far as required."[114]

Yet most observers realized there was more to the picture than helplessness. The caption to "Chinese Lady" in the Daniells' *Picturesque Voyage* explained that Chinese women were less restricted than other Asian women and were able to travel outside the home in palanquins and "saunter in the garden."[115] "It appears very ridiculous to European eyes," Downing wrote, "to see an old lady, verging into dotage, believing all eyes are turned upon her in admiration, because her feet are no larger than those of a child five or six years of age." This "feeble, helpless condition" was "very much admired" by the Chinese, "who delight to see them in danger of falling"—the result being that women made it "one of their principal arts of attraction to endeavour to walk, and thus show their dependent situation." Downing found this very similar to the "affected grace of some of our European damoiselles, who often exaggerate their natural timidity in order to rouse the protecting courage of the lords of the creation."[116] John Davis even argued that footbinding had certain advantages for women: "If the custom was first imposed by the tyranny of the men, the women are fully revenged in the diminution of their charms and domestic usefulness."[117]

They were aware that footbinding was practiced only by Han women, and sometimes not even by them. Lord Macartney reported that "Tartar" women had so far "kept their legs at liberty," even though many husbands wanted to introduce the practice into Manchu families.[118] "The Tartars," wrote Davis, "have had the good sense not to adopt this artificial deformity, and their ladies wear a shoe like that of the men, except that it has a white sole of still greater thickness."[119] Downing explained that footbinding was one of the few Chinese customs that had not been adopted by the Manchu conquerors, "their ladies still wearing their feet as formed by nature."[120] George Leonard Staunton observed that some poor women from mountainous areas did not adopt this "unnatural" custom, but were held in the "utmost" contempt by other Chinese and employed solely in the "most menial domestic offices."[121] The caption to William Alexander's "Boat Girl" in *Picturesque Representations* explained that the feet of such women were "allowed to grow to their full size."[122] Yet they also realized footbinding was not confined to the Chinese upper classes. Davis added that "this odious custom" extended much farther down the social scale than one might expect, especially given its "disabling effect" on women who had to "labour for their subsistence."[123]

Unlike the earlier travelers or the Jesuits, these Britons showed considerable familiarity with both the appearance and the process of footbinding, even though they were sometimes wrong on the details. The most common fallacy was that footbinding began shortly after birth. Aeneas Anderson marveled at how, given that this "extraordinary practice" began in infancy, women could even walk at all. He claimed to have been allowed to measure a young woman's foot, no more than five and a half inches in length.[124] "It is well known," Medhurst wrote, "that the Chinese have a method of binding up the feet of their female offspring, from their earliest infancy."[125] Downing likewise believed footbinding began soon after the birth of a "Chinese maiden of the upper rank."[126]

But even if some were wrong about the timing, they had a much better understanding of the process. As Medhurst explained, this meant compressing the foot and instep with ligatures until the toes gradually bent inward into the sole.[127] John Barrow described how the "distorted and disproportionate member consists of a foot that has been cramped in its growth, to the length of four or five inches, and an ankle that is generally swollen in the same proportion that the foot is diminished."[128] After "years of suffering," Charles Downing explained, "the growth of the part ceases, and the toes become of one piece with the rest of the foot, leaving the lower extremity very similar in appearance to that of a club foot." Downing observed how "when you examine an old Chinese lady, it appears as if that part of the instep near the toes had been cut off, and the rest of the soft parts in the vicinity brought together in a lump, in order to form a good cushion to the stump."[129] George Lay explained how at the age of five "a rich man's daughter has her foot so firmly bound that, in the native phrase, the whole is *killed*." Once "stripped of its gay investments," a bound foot was a "piteous mass of lifeless integument."[130]

They also paid great attention to the shoes and the bandaging, often including illustrations. Barrow wrote how the tiny shoe was "as fine as tinsel and tawdry can make it," while the ankle itself was bandaged with "party-coloured clothes, ornamented with fringe and tassels"; this, he added, the Chinese considered "superlatively beautiful." The fact that the bandages were changed so infrequently, sometimes remaining on the foot until they fell apart, revealed "no very favourable idea" of Chinese standards of cleanliness.[131] This "monstrous fashion," argued Tyerman and Bennet, made Chinese women so "vain" that they tended to "artificially exaggerate" their "deformity" by making the soles of their white, high-heeled shoes "so short that the heel projects two inches backward beyond the shoe, while, forward, the foot terminates in an abrupt stump." To make this "outrage on nature" even "more flagrant," the shoes were "lavishly ornamented."[132] The physician and naturalist George Bennett wrote how shoemakers' shops in the suburbs of Canton were well stocked with shoes, "from those of the small-footed woman decorated in a most tasteful and fanciful manner, to the larger ones of the long-footed race."[133]

Why would such a custom have been instituted in the first place? Lord Macartney noted that one of the embassy's handlers admitted he could not explain the origin of footbinding—except that it was a very old custom that might have resulted from what Macartney called "oriental jealousy" and the desire to keep women at home.[134] It was difficult, George Leonard Staunton explained, to discover why Chinese men had forced this "singular" custom upon women. If they simply wanted to confine women to their homes, they could have done so without "cruelly depriving them of the physical power of motion." No similar practice existed in Turkey or India, where women were even more confined than in China. Such a "preposterous" practice could have been perpetuated only by the "example and persuasion of those who, in their own persons, had submitted to it." No individual woman, even if from the "most exalted rank" as Chinese legend had it, could have forced so many others to inflict such violence upon themselves simply to resemble her. "The emulation of surpassing in any species of beauty, must have animated vast numbers of all ranks, and continued through successive ages, to carry it at last to an excess which defeats, in fact, its intended purpose."[135]

According to Barrow, the origins of footbinding were either "entirely unknown" or explained by "such fabulous absurdities as are too ridiculous to assign for its adoption." The "constant pain and uneasiness" girls suffered while their feet were being bound, until their heels were "entirely obliterated," made it all the stranger such a custom, "so unnatural and strange," could have endured for so long. The silence of the earliest foreign travelers to China on "so extraordinary a custom" meant it must have been adopted within the past few centuries. Although Marco Polo had frequently mentioned the "beauty and dress" of Chinese women, he made no notice of "this singular fashion." Given that the accounts by two Muslim travelers in the ninth century, popularized in Europe in 1733 by the French abbé and orientalist Eusèbe Renaudot, had also paid close attention to the "dress and ornaments" worn by Chinese women, it was hard to imagine they would have overlooked a custom "so singular in its kind as that of maiming the feet," if it had been as common then as it was now. This "monstrous fashion" was usually attributed to the "jealousy" of Chinese men. But Barrow wondered how men could have forced women to "adopt a fashion, which required a voluntary relinquishment of one of the greatest pleasures and blessings of life, the faculty of locomotion; and to contrive to render this fashion so universal that any deviation from it should be considered as disgraceful."[136]

With Robert Morrison and John Davis came better access to Chinese sources. In 1817, Morrison explained matter-of-factly that footbinding was said to have originated during the 900s, when the ruler Li Houzhu ordered his concubine to bind her feet with silk to appear small and in the shape of a new moon.[137] Two decades later, Davis described footbinding as "a custom of whose origin there is no very distinct account, except that it took place about the close of the Tang dynasty, or the end of the ninth century of our era."[138] No doubt drawing from Morrison and Davis, Charles Downing wrote that the origin of the practice was "completely veiled in obscurity," but had arisen toward the end of the Tang Dynasty and had been common among the upper classes ever since.[139]

Still, the old myths and legends sometimes persisted. Conceding the "absence of any information on the subject," Downing ventured that footbinding had been devised to prevent women from interfering in state matters and to "render their fancied incapacity more apparent." It had been introduced when the power in the imperial court of eunuchs and women was at its "greatest heights" and the "ill effects" of their interference in government affairs were "severely felt." The "great efforts" to end their power had "completely succeeded": the eunuchs were "either destroyed or banished from the court, and the ladies disgraced." And if the original purpose of footbinding had been to prohibit women from interfering in state matters, it had succeeded: "The constant personal suffering endured, must necessarily prevent the cultivation of the mind, while the helpless condition of the beauty must render her an object rather of pity than of fear, if she should aim to tread the rugged path of ambition."[140]

Unlike other Chinese practices or customs, in Victorian England "foot-binding as cultural practice evolved quickly into foot-binding as cultural metaphor."[141] For some Britons this was, as George Lay put it, a matter "in which we must ever be at odds with them."[142] In China, the *Canton Register* observed in June 1834, a woman was the "born and appointed slave of man by nature, made such by the same law that gives to the sun its light and to the leopard its spots." Who but the Chinese would "cripple their fair delicate feet?" The "slavish depression" of Chinese women had become "a state to which they submit with resignation if not with content." It was a lesson to foreigners that they were obliged to be "better guardians of the rights and privileges of our fair countrywomen in this recreant land than formerly." Obeying the laws against bringing their women to Canton would only convince the Chinese that the foreigners, too, were "on a level with themselves in our appreciation of females." If bringing their women to Canton would cause the governor of Guangdong to threaten to stop trade (as had occurred in the autumn of 1830 when several Western women had visited from Macao), it was high time to show that "our retaliation will be such that he will always remember Britannia's rod—and find it to be at least as heavy as the Chinese bamboo."[143]

Yet encounters with foreignness can sometimes evoke similarity rather than difference.[144] From the Macartney embassy all the way to the 1830s, most Britons who mentioned footbinding also made comparisons with practices in other cultures—including their own. Lord Macartney wondered why foreigners should be so disgusted or surprised by footbinding, but not by circumcision or the "indecency of castration" long prevalent in Italian opera. It seemed "the whole human species," from the "politest" nations of Europe to the "most barbarous" islanders of the South Seas, was dissatisfied with its natural form. "We find beauty in defects, and we create defects where we do not find them." Having learned from a Catholic missionary at Peking that even a glimpse of a "little fairy foot" was for many Chinese men a "most powerful provocative," Macartney reminded his readers that tight shoes, high heels, and corsets were proof that even Europeans were not "quite free from a little folly of the same kind ourselves" and had little right to ridicule or despise other cultures, "as we can very nearly match them with similar follies and absurdities of our own."[145]

George Leonard Staunton also drew parallels with the corseting of British women, noting that "delicacy of limbs and persons" had always been coveted as much by women as it had been by men.[146] "Few savage tribes," wrote John Barrow, were free from "the unnatural custom of maiming or lopping off some part of the human body" and other supposed "improvements on nature." And even Barrow, who found plenty to condemn in Chinese culture and society, saw no "great reason" to "despise and ridicule the Chinese, or indeed any other nation, merely because they differ from us in the little points of dress and manners."[147]

Even in the 1830s, as attitudes toward the Chinese hardened, Britons continued to make comparisons between footbinding and other "unnatural" practices. John Davis noted the "folly and childishness of a large portion of mankind" to seek distinction even through deformity: "While one race of people crushes the feet of its children, another flattens their heads between two boards." Equally "absurd, and still more mischievous," was the European custom of wearing corsets, which compressed women's waists "until the very ribs have been distorted, and the functions of the vital organs irreparably disordered."[148] Charles Downing conceded that Westerners were "somewhat startled" by such an "odd custom" and could never understand how anyone could find beauty in such a "disgusting spectacle." Still, he considered this form of "curtailing and distorting a part of the human figure" to be "somewhat on a par" with the tattooing and body painting practiced by Pacific islanders. "The same fashion, which leads the people at one end of the world to consider a small waist the height of female elegance, leads those of the other to prize a diminutive foot." It was "entirely a matter of taste." The problem was when such practices went too far, becoming "very unsightly" and "highly injurious to health."[149]

## FOOTBINDING AND THE WAR TO OPEN CHINA

The Opium War provided unprecedented opportunities for Britons to encounter Chinese women and girls with bound feet—talking to them, collecting their shoes as mementoes and souvenirs ("lawful loot," as one former military secretary put it), touching their tiny feet, and even amputating those of deceased females for the purposes of scientific collection, exhibition, and instruction.[150] In August 1840 naval surgeon Edward Cree wrote from Chusan, which the British had recently occupied, that he had seen a woman in a funeral procession who "toddled along very clumsily with her little crippled feet." Two years later, up the Yangzi River near the former capital of Nanking, he noted how the women there were "better looking and fairer" than those at Chusan, while many had "natural sized feet, not crippled."[151] In his report on the Medical Missionary Society's operations at Chusan in 1840–1841, the surgeon William Lockhart mentioned that none of the women who visited the society's hospital had feet "of the natural size." Although some of these feet were less compressed than others, the practice of footbinding was "universal" at Chusan while in Canton and Macao many women left their feet "completely free."[152]

Cree did not revise his journals for binding until 1887, and they were not published until 1981, eighty years after his death. There is little indication

Figure 4.6. William Lockhart, by J. Cochran, after Maull & Polyblank, stipple engraving. Wellcome Collection. CC BY 4.0

that he had any intention of circulating them during his lifetime. And Lockhart's report was aimed primarily at showcasing the work of the Medical Missionary Society and raising money for it. However, other military officers and medical men affiliated with the British expedition during the Opium War published detailed and popular accounts of their time in China.[153] Writing about footbinding became a way to prove not only that they had been in China, but also that they had been able to learn more about this enigmatic land than their predecessors had.

Duncan McPherson, a surgeon attached to the 37th Grenadier Regiment, wrote that "the chief curiosity" to be seen in Macao was "an occasional small-foot woman." His "repeated attempts" to examine a bound foot had all failed. Finally, after being assured he was a doctor and would not divulge what he had seen (exactly which he then did in his book), and after he had slipped her a few dollars, a young woman agreed to let McPherson see her foot. Although at first the "deformed limb" appeared to have been partially amputated, McPherson found upon closer inspection that it had not. "On examining the sole of the foot, I was surprised to see the four small toes bent under and deeply imbedded in the soft substance of the foot, and in a wonderful degree capable of flexion and extension." But the "state of filth" the foot revealed convinced him such feet were rarely exposed, "even for the purpose of cleanliness."[154]

Figure 4.7 Duncan McPherson, Esq., RMD, "In the Costume of a Mandarin." Frontispiece, *The War in China: Narrative of the Chinese Expedition from Its Formation in April, 1840, to the Treaty of Peace in August, 1842*. London: Saunders and Otley, 1843

Captain Arthur Cunynghame, aide-de-camp to Lord Saltoun, commander of the British troops in China, wrote in 1844 that all the women he had encountered possessed the "compressed feet peculiar to the well-born Chinese" and which rarely seemed to be longer than two and a half inches. Had he been "a solitary traveller" in "these distant regions," Cunynghame would have worried that his readers might not believe him. But since the British invasion, "many hundreds" of Europeans had been given "repeated opportunities" to see women with similarly small-sized feet. Displaying his special access to this unique custom, Cunynghame included his own illustration of the skeleton of a bound foot he had taken "from nature"—based on an amputated foot and which would enable his readers to understand how the Chinese produced "what to us appears a most disgusting and hideous deformity, but which, to them, is the *ne plus ultra* of perfection in the female sex."[155]

Cunynghame explained later in his book how he had managed to make the drawing. When a doctor on his ship, "exceedingly anxious" to obtain a specimen of a bound foot, asked for his help in this "laudable desire to forward the ends of science," Cunynghame revealed he had recently seen the fresh corpse of a young woman near where he and his unit had been based. "Having informed him of this, he proceeded to the spot to procure his prize; and very shortly returned with the young lady's pettitoes, wrapped up in his pocket-handkerchief, which some weeks after I saw pickled, after the most approved fashion."[156] Cunynghame's two-volume recollections of his service in China became so popular that they were condensed into a single edition published the following year.[157]

It helped that Britons were now able to move beyond the urban enclaves in Canton and Macao. Indeed, their own freedom of movement enabled them to witness Chinese females on the move. During an encounter with several women, Granville Loch, aide-de-camp to General Hugh Gough during the war, pitied the frightened "poor creatures" as they "hobbled away on their small feet, and in their haste stumbling at every step."[158] John Bingham wrote that during their stay at Chusan he and his colleagues had made frequent visits to the surrounding islands. On one visit they had the opportunity to examine "the far famed little female feet." Bingham was purchasing a pair of satin shoes for bound feet when he and his group were surrounded by a small crowd of curious men, women, and children. When they asked to see the feet of a "really good-looking woman" she refused; a "very pretty interesting girl" was offered up instead. Although the girl was initially "very bashful" and reluctant to expose her "Cinderella-like slipper," she overcame her hesitation when offered a shiny new coin and began removing her bandages and shoe.[159]

What surprised Bingham and his colleagues about the young girl's small foot was not just how "delicately white and clean" it was, but that it appeared

Figure 4.8 Granville Gower Loch, after 1852, by Joseph Brown, after George Richmond, stipple engraving. National Portrait Gallery, London

to have been bound in a fashion different from those in Canton and Macao. Their comprador from Canton was equally surprised, wondering how anyone could walk in a "Chusan shoe" without the high heel common in such shoes from his region. Bingham added that the toes, "doubled under the foot," could be moved only by hand to show that they were "not actually grown into the foot." During another walk, he convinced an older mother of three daughters to sell him the "very pretty pair" of satin shoes she had been wearing. Seeing women with bound feet beyond the confines of the foreign factories at Canton, Bingham had been surprised by how well Chinese women tried to walk on their "tiny *pedestals*." Their gait was similar to "the little mincing walk" of French women, and they could even manage without a walking stick. He recalled how he had often seen them in Macao, "contending against a fresh breeze with a tolerably good-sized umbrella spread."[160]

Even more so than they had at Canton and Macao, British men now realized footbinding was not limited to the upper classes. Having bound feet was a "general characteristic of true Chinese descent," and Bingham reminded his readers that there could not be "a greater mistake" than to assume the practice was confined to "the higher orders," although it was true that they tried harder than the lower classes to make their feet as small as possible. All the women he had seen at Chusan had bound feet. "High and low, rich and poor, all more or less follow the custom; and when you see a large or natural-sized foot, you may depend upon it, the possessor is not of true Chinese blood, but is either of Tartar extraction, or belong to the tribes that live and have their being on the waters."[161]

Greater exposure to more Chinese people did not, however, necessarily mean better or more reliable information about the origins of footbinding or its persistence. "God knows," wondered Granville Loch, "how this barbarous habit of cramping the feet first arose: whether from jealousy on the part of the husbands, or merely a freak of taste, which first became the fashion and then a universal custom, no satisfactory explanation has yet appeared, nor can the Chinese themselves clearly account for its origin."[162] Cunynghame attributed the fact that Chinese women were said to be so "cross-tempered" to how their shoes pinched.[163]

Nor did more exposure necessarily lead to any consensus on the effects of footbinding on female health. Duncan McPherson insisted that the "pain and irritation" caused by the "horrid" process of binding feet, and the lack of exercise it entailed, would "materially injure the general health." The "pallid, sickly look" of some young girls he had met who were undergoing the process "contrasted greatly" with the "healthy, rude appearance" of some poorer Chinese who from an early age had been taught to assist in "all domestic employments."[164]

Loch wrote that binding women's feet was "decidedly prejudicial to the health" and could often even be fatal. As proof he cited the case of a young girl at Chusan who had been treated for "severe hectic fever" by a young British naval surgeon stationed there. When the surgeon removed the girl's bindings to help reduce her fever, he found them covered with ulcers and inflammation. Although he warned the girl's mother that replacing the bandages would kill her, the bandages were on again when he returned. The mother explained that it would be better for her daughter to die than remain unmarried, "and that without improved feet such a calamity would be her inevitable lot." When the surgeon returned again later, he found the house abandoned, with a small coffin left by the door. Inside the coffin lay the body of his young patient. "Being a scientific man, he seized the opportunity of adding the feet to a collection already commenced."[165]

William Lockhart, however, concluded from the large number of female patients of different ages and classes at the Medical Missionary Society's hospital that footbinding did not cause "so much misery as might be expected from the severe treatment to which the feet are subjected in infancy." In the countryside, "strong healthy women" with bound feet could be seen walking "with readiness, and not apparently suffering from any pain in the feet whatever." Some women even walked several miles to the hospital, returning home the same day, "so that locomotion is by no means prevented." Lockhart hoped that a "more intimate acquaintance" with the Chinese would lead to a better understanding of how footbinding affected women's health.[166] McPherson assumed the four small toes bent under and imbedded into the sole would become anchylosed ("or a bony union formed"). Examining a skeleton foot, however, he found the bones "all separate, but displaced." He was impressed by, "when properly bandaged and shod," the young woman he had met "hobbled up and down her stair with apparent ease."[167]

As with so many of the observers we have met, many Britons who wrote about bound feet during the Opium War saw it as another example of the demeaned status of women in China. Yet even then most took a relativist approach. Lockhart cautioned against judging the Chinese: "torturing as this treatment of the feet would appear to be, and unsightly as are its consequences, it is perhaps on the whole not more injurious to health and comfort, than are the practices inflicted by fashion on the female sex in western nations."[168] It would be as difficult to explain the origin of this "barbarous practice," reasoned McPherson, "as for that of squeezing the waists of English women out of all natural shape by stays, or flattening the heads amongst the natives on the Columbia."[169] Cunynghame drew even more explicit comparisons between footbinding and corseting:

> We must, however, be cautious ere we criticise too freely the apparent follies and inconsistencies of our neighbours, lest they retort our sneers upon ourselves, which with some show of reason they might perhaps do, in the case of some of the tight-laced ladies of London and Paris, much more injury accruing from the compression applied to this vital part of the body, the waist, than confining the extremities, where the injury can be but local; and I trust I shall not be excluded from all the circles of the fair sex in my own country if I pronounce the opinion, that as much deformity is sometimes produced by unnatural attempts to counterfeit the shape of the wasp, as by endeavours to imitate the beautiful and agile foot of the lively fawn.[170]

Loch admitted that he and many of his colleagues had become so accustomed to seeing small feet that a Chinese woman would "appear to want some peculiar grace without the deformity of the crippled feet,—so much does custom guide and regulate what is commonly called taste." He realized:

> How true it is that a fashion, however absurd in itself, when once generally adopted, must be followed by the most sedate and sapient, or they lose the semblance of wisdom and appear ridiculous. It is therefore not surprising that the Chinese consider us in the latter light, as all our habits, manners, forms, customs, appearances, and dress are so diametrically opposite to theirs.[171]

Given the long sweep of Anglo-Chinese encounters, why does it matter what Britons thought about China's population or about infanticide and footbinding? The usual picture of the Western presence in China is a linear one, becoming more and more "progressive" or "humanitarian"—missionaries becoming less critical of Chinese religion, women missionaries seeing their Chinese converts as "sisters," and Chinese reformers trying to end footbinding and "liberate" women. In the late 1800s, for example, Western women travelers to China and reformers such as Alicia Little would both orientalize and embrace Chinese women as sisters, their bound feet causing "curiosity and fascination, but primarily repulsion."[172]

Contrary to common assumptions, some Britons viewed China, its people, and their civilization *less* critically during this period than after the Opium War and the opening of the treaty ports. In the second part of the nineteenth century, Britons and other Westerners stressed the difference between China and the West, and the superiority of the West, through practices such as infanticide and footbinding; underlying any assessment about the prevalence of infanticide was "an implicit judgment about the barbarity or humanity of Chinese civilization as a whole, as compared to Western society."[173] In the period we have seen, infanticide, but especially footbinding, were just as often signs of similarity as they were of difference. Finally, even the Opium War cannot be seen simply as a *military* conflict. It extended the reach of British contact with China—geographically, physically, and humanly.

## NOTES

1. "Spirit of the Chinese Laws," *Canton Register* 7, no. 51 (23 December 1834): 202–3.

2. Barrow to Buckinghamshire, 14 February 1815, IOR/G/12/196, India Office Records and Private Papers, British Library; original emphasis. Also in IOR/G/12/197, British Library.

3. "British and Chinese Relations," *Canton Press* 3, no. 20 (20 January 1838): n.p; original emphasis.

4. "British and Chinese Relations," *Canton Press* 3, no. 21 (27 January 1838): n.p.

5. Walter Henry Medhurst, *China: Its State and Prospects, with Special Reference to the Spread of the Gospel; Containing Allusions to the Antiquity, Extent, Population, Civilization, Literature, and Religion of the Chinese* (London: J. Snow, 1838), 71–72, 74–75, 80.

6. John Barrow, *Travels in China, Containing Descriptions, Observations, and Comparisons, Made and Collected in the Course of a Short Residence at the Imperial Palace of Yuen-Min-Yuen, and on a Subsequent Journey through the Country from Pekin to Canton in Which It Is Attempted to Appreciate the Rank That the Extraordi-

nary Empire May Be Considered to Hold in the Scale of Civilized Nations (London: Cadell and Davies, 1804), 397.

7. "Population of China," *Canton Register* 7, no. 40 (7 October 1834): 160.

8. John Francis Davis, *The Chinese: A General Description of That Empire and Its Inhabitants* (London: Charles Knight, 1836), vol. 2, 383–84.

9. John Slade, *Notices on the British Trade to the Port of Canton; with Some Translations of Chinese Official Papers Relative to That Trade* (London: Smith Elder, 1830), 2–4.

10. 15 May 1834, MS5829/135/1, Archives and Manuscripts, Wellcome Library.

11. "The Character of the Chinese," *Canton Press* 3, no. 45 (14 July 1838): n.p.

12. *Canton Register* 1, no. 29 (26 July 1828): 114.

13. "The Poor Laws in China," *Canton Press* 3, no. 47 (28 July 1838): n.p.

14. Davis, *Chinese*, vol. 1, 243.

15. Medhurst, *China*, 39–40.

16. Daniel Tyerman and George Bennet, *Journal of Voyages and Travels by the Rev. Daniel Tyerman and George Bennet, Esq. Deputed from the London Missionary Society, to Visit Their Various Stations in the South Sea Islands, China, India, & C., between the Years 1821 and 1829*, compiled by James Montgomery (London: F. Westley and A. H. Davis, 1831), vol. 2, 253.

17. *Canton Register* 1, no. 14 (5 April 1828): 55.

18. "Remarks upon the Chinese Government," *Canton Press* 3.25 (24 February 1838): n.p.

19. Barrow, *Travels in China*, 587.

20. Henry Ellis, *Journal of the Proceedings of the Late Embassy to China; Comprising a Correct Narrative of the Public Transactions of the Embassy, of the Voyage to and from China, and of the Journey from the Mouth of the Pei-Ho to the Return to Canton, Interspersed with Observations upon the Face of the Country, the Polity, Moral Character, and Manners of the Chinese Nation* (London: Printed for J. Murray, 1817), 323.

21. Davis, *Chinese*, vol. 2, 388.

22. "Population," *Canton Register* 2, no. 18 (3 October 1829): 85.

23. Davis, *Chinese*, vol. 2, 384, 386–88.

24. Medhurst, *China*, 22–23, 48.

25. Barrow, *Travels in China*, 500.

26. 26 November 1807, Council for World Mission (CWM)/South China Journals (SCJ), 1807–1842, Folder 4, Archives and Special Collections, School of Oriental and African Studies Library (SOAS).

27. Tyerman and Bennet, *Journal of Voyages*, vol. 2, 254.

28. John Barrow and George Macartney, *Some Account of the Public Life, and a Selection from the Unpublished Writings, of the Earl of Macartney*, vol. 2 (London: T. Cadell and W. Davies, 1807), 391.

29. Aeneas Anderson, *A Narrative of the British Embassy to China in the Years 1792, 1793, and 1794; Containing the Various Circumstances of Embassy the Accounts of Customs and Manners of the Chinese, and a Description of the Country, Towns, Cities, &c. &c.* (London: J. Debrett, 1795), 257.

30. Undated entry on Canton and Macao, 130, Henry Hayne Diary, Henry Hayne Papers, David M. Rubenstein Rare Book and Manuscript Library.

31. Tyerman and Bennet, *Journal of Voyages and Travels*, vol. 2, 254.

32. Davis, *Chinese*, vol. 2, 26–27.

33. 1 January 1808, CWM/SCJ, Folder 5, SOAS.

34. Davis, *Chinese*, vol. 2, 26–27.

35. C. [Charles] Toogood Downing, *The Fan Qui in China in 1836–1837* (London: Henry Colburn, 1838), vol. 2, 1–2.

36. John Elliot Bingham, *Narrative of the Expedition to China from the Commencement of the War to Its Termination in 1842: Sketches of the Manners and Customs of That Singular and Hitherto Almost Unknown Country* (London: Henry Colburn, 1842), vol. 2, 259.

37. Barrow and Macartney, *Some Account of the Public Life*, vol. 2, 460.

38. George [Leonard] Staunton, *An Authentic Account of an Embassy from the King of Great Britain to the Emperor of China: Including Cursory Observations Made, and Information Obtained, in Travelling through That Ancient Empire and a Small Part of Chinese Tartary* (London: G. Nicol, 1797), vol. 3, 388–90.

39. Barrow, *Travels in China*, 2, 577–83.

40. Amherst to chairman and deputy chairman of Court of Directors, 4 January 1817, IOR/G/12/197, British Library. Also in IOR/G/12/198, British Library. Amherst expressed similar sentiments later: Amherst to Canning, 3 March 1817, Batavia, IOR/G/12/198, British Library.

41. On the embassy members' descriptions of decline, see Hao Gao, "The Amherst Embassy and British Discoveries in China," *History* 99, no. 337 (2014): 568–87. For a more positive view of the Jiaqing period, see Wensheng Wang, *White Lotus Rebels and South China Pirates: Crisis and Reform in the Qing Empire* (Cambridge, MA: Harvard University Press, 2014).

42. George Thomas Staunton, *Notes of Proceedings and Occurrences during the British Embassy to Pekin in 1816* (London: Havant, 1824), 205.

43. Staunton, *Notes of Proceedings and Occurrences*, 40–41, 69.

44. Ellis, *Journal of the Proceedings*, 46, 431–32, 491.

45. Clarke Abel, *Narrative of a Journey in the Interior of China, and of a Voyage to and from That Country, in the Year 1816 and 1817: Containing an Account of the Most Interesting Transactions of Lord Amherst's Embassy to the Court of Pekin, and Observations on the Countries Which It Visited* (London: Orme and Brown, 1818), 204–5; Ellis, *Journal of the Proceedings*, 264–65.

46. Medhurst, *China*, 32–33, 36–37.

47. Medhurst, *China*, 42.

48. Barrow and Macartney, *Some Account of the Public Life*, vol. 2, 461.

49. "Population," 85.

50. "Statement of the Population of China and Its Colonies," *Canton Register* 5, no. 9 (2 July 1832): 64.

51. Robert Morrison, *A View of China, for Philological Purposes: Containing a Sketch of Chinese Chronology, Geography, Government, Religion & Customs* (Ma-

cao: Printed at the Honorable East India Company's Press by P. P. Thoms, 1817; London: Black, Parbury, and Allen, 1817), 62.

52. Medhurst, *China*, 50.

53. Staunton, *Authentic Account of an Embassy*, vol. 3, 390.

54. Barrow and Macartney, *Some Account of the Public Life*, vol. 2, 462–63.

55. Samuel Holmes, *The Journal of Mr. Samuel Holmes, Serjeant-Major of the XIth Light Dragoons, during His Attendance, as One of the Guard of Lord Macartney's Embassy to China and Tartary, 1792–3* (London: W. Bulmer, 1798), 131.

56. "Cruel Superstitions of a Physical Nature," *Canton Register* 2, no. 9 (2 May 1829): 45.

57. Medhurst, *China*, 46–47.

58. Raymond Dawson, *The Chinese Chameleon: An Analysis of European Conceptions of Chinese Civilization* (Oxford: Oxford University Press, 1967), 150.

59. Michelle T. King, *Between Birth and Death: Female Infanticide in Nineteenth-Century China* (Stanford: Stanford University Press, 2014), 8.

60. Downing, *Fan Qui*, vol. 2, 240–41.

61. Ellis, *Journal of the Proceedings*, 197–98, 439.

62. Abel, *Narrative of a Journey*, 87–88, 232.

63. King, *Between Birth and Death*, 79.

64. Staunton, *Authentic Account of an Embassy*, vol. 2, 336.

65. Barrow, *Travels in China*, 169–71. Less dramatic forms of abandonment were more common: infants were often placed in baskets, hung in trees where dogs and pigs could not reach them, in the hope that they might be rescued and raised; some were left on stone baby towers provided by Buddhist nunneries. See D. E. Mungello, *Drowning Girls in China: Female Infanticide since 1650* (Lanham, MD: Rowman & Littlefield, 2008), 10.

66. Barrow, *Travels in China*, 167–68, 172–75.

67. Ellis, *Journal of the Proceedings*, 431.

68. John McLeod, *Narrative of a Voyage in His Majesty's Late Ship Alceste to the Yellow Sea, along the Coast of Corea, and through Its Numerous Hitherto Undiscovered Islands, to the Island of Lewchew* (London: John Murray, 1817), 147–48.

69. Staunton, *Ta Tsing Leu Lee*, x–xi.

70. Abel, *Narrative of a Journey*, 233–35.

71. "Infanticide in China," *Indo-Chinese Gleaner* 11 (1820): 225–28.

72. Davis, *Chinese*, vol. 1, 246–47, vol. 2, 28–20.

73. Medhurst, *China*, 43–47.

74. Downing, *Fan Qui*, vol. 3, 263–66; original emphasis.

75. Downing, *Fan Qui*, vol. 3, 266–67.

76. "The Character of the Chinese," *Canton Press* 3, no. 45 (14 July 1838): n.p.

77. Mungello, *Drowning Girls in China*, 3–4.

78. King, *Between Birth and Death*, 7.

79. G. [George] Tradescant Lay, *The Chinese as They Are: Their Moral, Social, and Literary Character* (London: W. Ball, 1841), 46.

80. Elizabeth Chang, "Binding and Unbinding Chinese Feet in the Mid-Century Victorian Press," in *Writing China: Essays on the Amherst Embassy (1816) and*

*Sino-British Cultural Relations*, ed. Peter J. Kitson and Robert Markley (Cambridge: D. S. Brewer, 2016), 139.

81. Harriett Low Hillard, *Lights and Shadows of a Macao Life: The Journal of Harriett Low, Travelling Spinster*, ed. Nan P. Hodges and Arthur W. Hummel (Woodinville, WA: The History Bank, 2002), 509.

82. Staunton, *Authentic Account of an Embassy*, vol. 1, 423; also in vol. 2, 46.

83. 19 September 1807, CWM South China Journals, Folder 3, SOAS.

84. 11 August, September 5, 16 and 17 December 1816, Hayne Diary, Rubenstein Library.

85. Undated entry on Canton and Macao, Hayne Diary, 131, Rubenstein Library.

86. Thomas Daniell and William Daniell, *A Picturesque Voyage to India; By the Way of China* (London: Longman, Hurst, Rees, and Orme, 1810).

87. William Alexander, *The Costume of China: Illustrated in Forty-Eight Coloured Engravings* (London: William Miller, 1805), and *Picturesque Representations of the Dress and Manners of the Chinese, Illustrated in Fifty Coloured Engravings, with Descriptions* (London: John Murray, 1814). On Alexander see: Harriet Crawley, "Alexander's Views of China," *Arts of Asia* 9, no. 5 (1979): 62–73; Susan Legouix, *Image of China: William Alexander* (London: Jupiter Books, 1980); and Frances Wood, "Closely Observed China: From William Alexander's Sketches to His Published Work," *British Library Journal* 24, no. 1 (1998): 98–121.

88. On Chinnery, see Patrick Conner, *George Chinnery, 1774–1852, Artist of India and the China Coast* (Woodbridge, UK: Antique Collectors' Club, 1993), and "George Chinnery and His Contemporaries on the China Coast," *Arts of Asia* 23, no. 3 (1993): 66–81.

89. Patricia Ebrey, "Gender and Sinology: Shifting Western Interpretations of Footbinding, 1300–1890," *Late Imperial China* 20, no. 2 (1999): 11, 25–26.

90. Tyerman and Bennet, *Journal of Voyages and Travels*, vol. 2, 267.

91. Ebrey, "Gender and Sinology," 26.

92. Lay, *The Chinese as They Are*, 30–31.

93. Gideon Nye Jr., *The Morning of My Life in China: Comprising an Outline of the History of Foreign Intercourse from the Last Year of the Regime of the Honorable East India Company, 1833, to the Imprisonment of the Foreign Community in 1839* (Canton: n. p., 1873), 70.

94. Tyerman and Bennet, *Journal of Voyages and Travels*, vol. 2, 264.

95. Basil Hall, *Voyage to Loo-Choo, and Other Places in the Eastern Seas, in the Year 1816: Including an Account of Captain Maxwell's Attack on the Batteries at Canton; and Notes of an Interview with Buonaparte at St. Helena, in August 1817* (Edinburgh: A. Constable, 1826), 53–54.

96. Lay, *The Chinese as They Are*, 29–31.

97. Abel, *Narrative of a Journey*, 87–88.

98. Hall, *Voyage to Loo-Choo*, 53.

99. Tyerman and Bennet, *Journal of Voyages and Travels*, vol. 2, 245–46.

100. Lay, *The Chinese as They Are*, 31.

101. Antonia Finnane, *Changing Clothes in China: Fashion, History, Nation* (New York: Columbia University Press, 2008), 29.

102. Daniell and Daniell, *Picturesque Voyage*, n.p.

103. "Remarks, Concerning the Condition of Females in China," *Chinese Repository* 2, no. 7 (November 1833): 13.

104. "Small Feet of the Chinese Females," *Chinese Repository* 3, no. 12 (April 1835): 537.

105. Barrow, *Travels in China*, 138–41.

106. Anderson, *Narrative of the British Embassy*, 261.

107. Holmes, *Journal of Mr. Samuel Holmes*, 130.

108. Ellis, *Journal of the Proceedings*, 486.

109. Dorothy Ko, *Cinderella's Sisters: A Revisionist History of Footbinding* (Berkeley: University of California Press, 2005), 2.

110. Staunton, *Authentic Account of an Embassy*, vol. 1, 423–24; also in vol. 2, 46–47.

111. Davis, *Chinese*, vol. 1, 252–53.

112. Lay, *The Chinese as They Are*, 30–32.

113. Tyerman and Bennet, *Journal of Voyages and Travels*, vol. 2, 246.

114. Downing, *Fan Qui*, vol. 2, 41–42.

115. Daniell and Daniell, *Picturesque Voyage*, n.p.

116. Downing, *Fan Qui*, vol. 2, 41–42.

117. Davis, *Chinese*, vol. 1, 253.

118. Barrow and Macartney, *Some Account of the Public Life*, vol. 2, 426.

119. Davis, *Chinese*, vol. 1, 253.

120. Downing, *Fan Qui*, vol. 2, 45.

121. Staunton, *Authentic Account of an Embassy*, vol. 1, 423; also in vol. 2, 46.

122. Alexander, *Picturesque Representations*, n.p.

123. Davis, *Chinese*, vol. 1, 253.

124. Anderson, *Narrative of the British Embassy*, 72, 255.

125. Medhurst, *China*, 441.

126. Downing, *Fan Qui*, vol. 2, 43.

127. Medhurst, *China*, 441.

128. Barrow, *Travels in China*, 73.

129. Downing, *Fan Qui*, vol. 2, 43–44.

130. Lay, *The Chinese as They Are*, 29, 31; original emphasis.

131. Barrow, *Travels in China*, 73, 76.

132. Tyerman and Bennet, *Journal of Voyages and Travels*, vol. 2, 246.

133. George Bennett, *Wanderings in New South Wales, Batavia, Pedir Coast, Singapore, and China. Being the Journal of a Naturalist in Those Countries, during 1832, 1833, and 1834* (London: Richard Bentley, 1834), vol. 2, 94.

134. Barrow and Macartney, *Some Account of the Public Life*, vol. 2, 426.

135. Staunton, *Authentic Account of an Embassy*, vol. 1, 424–25; also in vol. 2, 47–48.

136. Barrow, *Travels in China*, 73–76. Marco Polo's failure to mention footbinding has led some scholars to doubt whether he ever went to China. See, most notably,

Frances Wood, *Did Marco Polo Go to China?* (London: Secker and Warburg, 1995), 72–75. C.f. Stephen G. Haw, *Marco Polo's China: A Venetian in the Realm of Kublai Khan* (London: Routledge, 2006), 55–56.

137. Morrison, *View of China*, 28.

138. Davis, *Chinese*, vol. 1, 252–53.

139. Downing, *Fan Qui*, vol. 2, 44.

140. Downing, *Fan Qui*, vol. 2, 45. Downing may have derived this from the account by Captain Amasa Delano, who recalled how he had been "told by the Chinese" that footbinding began as a punishment for women who had tried to interfere in state affairs, but had since become a "mark of honour" restricted to women "of pure Chinese blood." Amasa Delano, *A Narrative of Voyages and Travels in the Northern and Southern Hemispheres, Comprising Three Voyages around the World* (Boston: E. G. House, 1818), 541.

141. Chang, "Binding and Unbinding," 139.

142. Lay, *The Chinese as They Are*, 29.

143. "Condition and Treatment of Females in China: Right of Residence of Foreign Ladies with Their Husbands and Fathers in Canton, or Elsewhere," *Canton Register* 7, no. 24 (17 June 1834): 93–95.

144. See, for example, Nicholas Thomas, *Colonialism's Culture: Anthropology, Travel and Government* (Princeton: Princeton University Press, 1994), 51–54.

145. Barrow and Macartney, *Some Account of the Public Life*, vol. 2, 426–29.

146. Staunton, *Authentic Account of an Embassy*, vol. 1, 425; also in vol. 2, 48.

147. Barrow, *Travels in China*, 73–74.

148. Davis, *Chinese*, vol. 1, 253–54.

149. Downing, *Fan* Qui, vol. 2, 42–44.

150. Robert Jocelyn, *Six Months with the Chinese Expedition: Leaves from a Soldier's Note-Book* (London: John Murray, 1841), 61.

151. 15 August 1842, CRJ/5, and 23 July 1842, CRJ/8, National Maritime Museum. Thanks to Gary Luk for sharing his copies of these entries, which can also be found in Edward H. Cree, *The Cree Journals: The Voyage of Edward H. Cree, Surgeon R.N., as Related in His Private Journals, 1837–1856*, ed. Michael Levien (Exeter, UK: Webb and Bower, 1981), 62, 106.

152. William Lockhart, "Report of the Medical Missionary Society's Operations at Chusan in 1840–41," *Chinese Repository* 10, no. 8 (August 1841): 462. A slightly modified version of this report appears in Lockhart's *The Medical Missionary in China: A Narrative of Twenty Years' Experience* (London: Hurst and Blackett, 1861), 337.

153. James Hayes, "'That Singular and Hitherto Almost Unknown Country': Opinions on China, the Chinese, and the 'Opium War' among British Naval and Military Officers Who Served during Hostilities There," *Journal of the Royal Asiatic Society Hong Kong Branch* 39 (1999): 211–33.

154. Duncan McPherson, *Two Years in China: Narrative of the Chinese Expedition, from Its Formation in April, 1840, to the Treaty of Peace in August, 1842* (London: Saunders and Otley, 1842), 40, 42–43.

155. Arthur Cunynghame, *An Aide-De-Camp's Recollections of Service in China: A Residence in Hong-Kong: and Visits to Other Islands in the Chinese Seas* (London: Saunders and Otley, 1844), vol. 1, 110–11.

156. Cunynghame, *An Aide-De-Camp's Recollections of Service in China*, vol. 1, 174–75.

157. Arthur Cunynghame, *The Opium War: Being Recollections of Service in China* (Philadelphia: G. B. Zieber, 1845).

158. Granville G. Loch, *The Closing Events of the Campaign in China: The Operations in the Yang-Tze-Kiang and Treaty of Nanking* (London: J. Murray, 1843), 89.

159. Bingham, *Narrative of the Expedition*, vol. 2, 16–18.

160. Bingham, *Narrative of the Expedition*, vol. 2, 19, 23–24

161. Bingham, *Narrative of the Expedition*, vol. 2, 19–20.

162. Loch, *Closing Events of the Campaign*, 89, 92–93.

163. Cunynghame, *An Aide-De-Camp's Recollections*, vol. 1, 176.

164. McPherson, *Two Years in China*, 44–45.

165. Loch, *Closing Events of the Campaign*, 91–92.

166. Lockhart, "Report of the Medical Missionary Society's Operations," 462.

167. McPherson, *Two Year in China*, 44.

168. Lockhart, "Report of the Medical Missionary Society's Operations," 462, and *Medical Missionary in China*, 337.

169. McPherson, *Two Years in China*, 45.

170. Cunynghame, *An Aide-De-Camp's Recollections*, vol. 1, 111.

171. Loch, *Closing Events of the Campaign*, 89–90.

172. Julia Kuehn, "Knowing Bodies, Knowing Self: The Western Woman Traveller's Encounter with Chinese Women, Bound Feet and the Half-Caste Child, 1880–1920," *Studies in Travel Writing* 12, no. 3 (2008): 267, 282. See also Susan Schoenbauer Thurin, *Victorian Travelers and the Opening of China, 1842–1907* (Athens: Ohio University Press, 1999), chap. 6; Mrs. Archibald [Alicia Ellen Neve] Little, *Intimate China: The Chinese as I Have Seen Them* (London: Hutchinson, 1899), chaps. 6 and 7.

173. King, *Between Birth and Death*, 8.

*Chapter Five*

# The Opium Debates

On 17 March 1839, Lin Zexu ordered all foreigners in Canton to surrender "every particle" of opium they owned or held, and to sign a bond—on penalty of death—promising they would never again import the drug. They were given three days to comply. "A great excitement prevailed among the foreign community," the *Canton Press* reported. It was now clear that Lin fully intended to suppress the opium trade. He had threatened to execute several hong merchants if the foreigners refused to give up all their opium, forced the foreign merchants to sign a bond promising not to sell opium any longer, and required those who did not traffic to identify those who did. He had also summoned to an interrogation Lancelot Dent, head of one of the two most powerful British firms in China. Dent had refused, but his house was being guarded to prevent him from escaping. No foreign boats were allowed to leave Canton.[1] At a meeting of the Canton Chamber of Commerce on 21 March, the members agreed to surrender one thousand chests of opium, which according to James Matheson had satisfied the hong merchants.[2] On 27 March, Charles Elliot, plenipotentiary and superintendent of British trade in China, held himself responsible, on behalf of Her Majesty's government, for each chest of British-owned opium that was surrendered.[3]

Lin, appointed commissioner for frontier defense in December 1838 and entrusted with eradicating opium, had been given no specific instructions for how to do so apart from combining "leniency and rigor." But he was convinced that moral righteousness and decisive action would impress both the British and Chinese opium dealers.[4] Although Elliot personally opposed the opium trade, on 6 April he wrote to Lord Palmerston that this "rash man is hastening on in a career of violence, which will react upon this empire in a terrible manner."[5] Six days later, he issued another public notice, reminding those who had not yet sworn never to sell opium to realize that "the liberties and possibly the lives of the whole foreign community now shut up at Canton hang upon their present forbearance." Any seizure of opium could "immediately afford a pretext for their continued imprisonment."[6]

The process was taking much longer than expected, however. On 1 May, Matheson relayed to William Jardine in London the "astounding intelligence" that Elliot and all foreign merchants had been placed in "durance" since 22 March in order to "extort" them to surrender the opium.[7] Twelve days later, Matheson wrote that most Britons and other foreigners were making plans to leave for Macao.[8] Elliot issued at least one more public notice, reminding British subjects that according to Qing law anyone importing opium could be executed.[9] Finally, on 22 May, he again ordered the British traders to surrender their opium and prepare to quit Canton; the British Crown could not be responsible for the safety of anyone who remained. Three days later, Elliot had left with sixteen Britons previously held hostage by the local authorities. All remaining British subjects had already departed or were preparing to do so within a few days.[10]

By late May, more than twenty thousand chests of opium had finally been surrendered. As the *Canton Register* put it, the "grave of £2,500,000 of British government property" had been dug. After much speculation about how this would be carried out, on 17 June the opium was destroyed in the presence of Elijah Coleman Bridgman, the American ardently anti-opium merchant Charles W. King, and King's wife.[11] No sooner had the news of the surrender and destruction of the opium reached England in autumn 1839, than the various East India and China associations and the merchants of London, Manchester, Leeds, Liverpool, Blackburn, and Bristol all urged Palmerston to retaliate and compensate the China traders for their losses. They reminded him that although the Qing government had every right to ban opium, it had not only known about the opium trade but even sanctioned it for many decades.[12]

No commodity has ever been associated with a particular country or culture as opium has been with China. And no nation has ever been stigmatized as much as Britain for importing opium to China, as if the trade and the war it caused were somehow a well-hatched conspiracy to create a giant nation of addicts.[13] Opium was probably the world's largest commodity of the time, and China is estimated by the end of the nineteenth century to have consumed 95 percent of the world's supply.[14] The drug became inextricably linked with the "opening" of China and seen by many twentieth-century historians as the chief source of their nation's problems. Although the number of actual addicts was small relative to the empire's immense population, as with bound feet, the "opium sot" became a classic image of China and its people.[15]

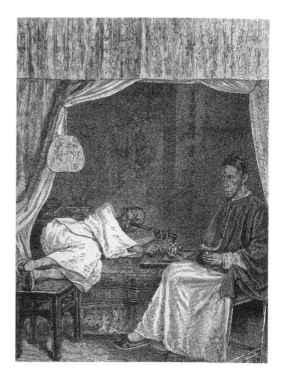

Figure 5.1. *Chinese Opium Smokers*, late nineteenth century, wood engraving. Wellcome Collection. CC BY 4.0

Figure 5.2. *Chinese Opium-Smokers*, late nineteenth century, wood engraving. Wellcome Collection. CC BY 4.0

Neither the Opium War nor the opium trade, however, was a clash of cultures. The British declared war on China not only to avenge Lin's destruction of the opium, but also to maintain national honor and credibility, particularly since they had recently faced crises in Argentina and Mexico and now found themselves confronted with a Russian push in Central Asia that threatened the security of India. Defending Britain's national honor and dignity was all the more important because Palmerston was desperate to preserve prime minister Lord Melbourne's precarious Whig government by avoiding a collision with the Conservatives, who hoped to use the China crisis to drive apart the Whigs and the Radicals, who supported a more assertive policy toward China.[16]

On the Chinese side, recent studies have revealed sophisticated debates within the Qing government about whether opium should be legalized or prohibited; debunked the conventional image of opium turning China into a nation of addicts; and shown how opium served a variety of medical and social purposes.[17] They have also exposed how important Chinese participation was for the opium trade: "Foreign smugglers only delivered opium to Canton; it needed the Chinese themselves to transport and distribute it to the inland areas."[18] Nor was opium a foreign-relations concern confined to China's southeast coast. It became "an empirewide crisis that spread among an ethnically diverse populace and created regionally and culturally distinct problems of control for the Qing state."[19]

This chapter examines the debates about opium among those who were most responsible for importing it: British private merchants. These debates reflected a range of opinions and attitudes, not only about China's right to prohibit opium and Britain's to import it, but also about the nature of the British presence in China. Many merchants agreed that the Qing government was fully justified in prohibiting the opium trade. Some were convinced that the Chinese themselves had caused the demand for opium, while others argued that its traffic threatened Britain's legitimate commerce with China. In the face of growing skepticism about the opium trade, both in Britain and even by Britons in India where the opium was produced, these debates also enabled Britons in China once again to present themselves as the only ones who truly understood the Middle Kingdom. Similar to how, in what has been called "the inner Opium War," networks of Qing scholars and officials debated how to cope with the opium trade and the British threat, Britons in Canton disagreed—with each other and with both official and popular opinion at home—on how to respond to the Qing government's efforts to curb the opium trade.[20] They also waged their own campaign to obtain compensation from the British government for the surrendered opium.

## OPIUM MANIA

Opium had not always figured prominently in British writings on China: the entire arrangement of the trade was based on the knowledge that the drug was contraband. According to Hosea Ballou Morse, who worked for the Chinese Imperial Maritime Customs Service from 1874 to 1908, since 1733, when the East India Company was granted its own monopoly in eastern India, it had avoided "even the appearance of any connexion" with the sale of opium in China. It forbade the carriage of opium "even in the smallest quantity" on its own ships. Instead, the Company subcontracted the shipping to private "country" traders. Nevertheless, because of the importance of the trade to the revenue of British India, the Company was deeply interested in the volume of opium sales. The Select Committee in Canton regularly submitted to the government of India detailed reports of a traffic that remained "shrouded in mystery."[21]

The first extensive Company correspondence on opium did not develop until the early 1780s.[22] The Canton consultation files for March 1782 to January 1783, for example, include detailed instructions on transporting opium from India to China, the risks involved in this new venture, which routes to take and which colors to fly, and warnings not to communicate with passing vessels or even enter a ship as being laden with opium.[23] When William Milburn, who had made seven voyages for the Company to China and the East Indies, wrote his book *Oriental Commerce* in 1813, he listed the value of opium and cotton imports from India to Canton but said little more about the opium.[24]

Accounts by Britons who visited or lived in China, however, invariably mentioned opium. John Barrow wrote in 1804 that "great quantities of this intoxicating drug are smuggled into the country, notwithstanding all the precautions taken by the government to prohibit the importation of it." Even the governor of Guangdong, Barrow insisted (though without saying how he knew), "very composedly takes his daily dose of opium."[25] Given the huge expansion of the opium trade in the late 1700s and early 1800s, it would have been hard by then for anyone to miss it: while some two hundred chests had entered China in 1729, the number doubled by 1789—the increase overwhelmingly after 1773, when the Company started to subcontract the shipping of opium to China through the country traders.[26]

Still, as late as the 1820s, the Company continued to write about opium with great caution. A secret letter of January 1827 from the Select Committee to the Court of Directors in London included a thorough discussion of opium: the ease of selling it and the connivance at every stage, how it was consumed, and how the trade was likely to increase to "an unlimited extent." The letter explained how although it had previously been considered "impolitic" for the Committee to be "officially furnished" with returns from the opium, the drug had become "much too prevailing a vice" in China to be prohibited there, as long as foreign ships were permitted to visit China.[27]

Perhaps nowhere did the foreign opium traders' shrewd resourcefulness, the local demand for opium, and the Qing government's inability (and, often, unwillingness) to curb the opium trade converge more clearly than in the explosive growth of opium—and of the foreign trade in general—from the island of Lintin. After 1821, when Canton authorities drove the opium trade from Whampoa, private traders shifted the depot for opium distribution from Macao to the small islands of Hong Kong, Cumsingmoon (Jinxingmen), and, mainly, Lintin. Fleets of fast opium clippers shipped the drug from Calcutta, where hulks anchored off Lintin received it. From there the opium was transported and distributed by Chinese smugglers. Robert Morrison wrote in February 1822 that with so many ships at Lintin, the local population had increased to around two thousand. The island was attracting migrants from the mountainous border region between Guangdong and Fujian.[28]

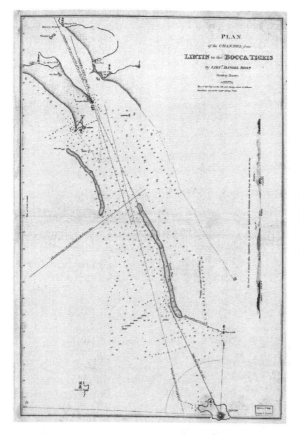

Figure 5.3. *Plan of the Channel from Lintin to the Bocca Tigris*, ca. 1810, by Daniel Ross. Library of Congress Geography and Map Division

Lintin eventually handled even more foreign goods than Canton and Whampoa. The Select Committee's secret letter in January 1827 to the Court of Directors noted that the local authorities had stopped putting up any "material interference" with the opium ships there.[29] In 1833, Charles Marjoribanks wrote in his open letter to Charles Grant that the trade at Lintin was "greatly more extensive" than that at Whampoa. "From twenty to forty ships now regularly rendezvous at Lintin, and the adjacent islands, where an illicit trade is carried on, not only in opium, but in goods of every description."[30]

Figure 5.4. *The Opium Ships at Lintin in China*, 1838, by Edward Duncan, after William Huggins, aquatint. Hong Kong Maritime Museum. Copyrights by Hong Kong Maritime Museum

As the Canton opium market gradually became saturated, traders looked eagerly up the coast for new markets, taking over and expanding the illegal trade already initiated in the 1820s by Chinese merchants, often in collusion with local officials. Jardine and Matheson, the largest of the country traders, fitted a second fleet of armed clippers that loaded at Lintin and then sold the opium farther up the coast. This coastal trade became even larger than the one at Lintin and was impossible to suppress, for the Qing had no deep-sea navy and the southeast coast was so long and dotted with so many inlets. "Let us cherish our Lintin trade," declared the *Register* in February 1834, "and endeavour to multiply *Lintins* along the whole extent of the Chinese coast."[31]

The result of this expansion in opium trading and consumption was obvious. "Smoking houses, abound in Canton," wrote James Holman the traveler, "and in every town and village in the empire." The use of opium had become "so universal" among the Chinese that the "daily fulminations" against it had "not the slightest effect in decreasing the prevalence of so general a habit." Holman recounted how he and several other curious visitors to Canton tried smoking opium in pipes prepared by William Jardine's comprador. "I found two pipes quite sufficient to make my head ache; but this was the only effect it produced on me, for it did not give the least agreeable sensation, either at the time I was smoking, or subsequently, and I was glad to seek relief in a cup of tea."[32]

That some of these writings were by physicians or naturalists lent a degree of authority. Clarke Abel of the Amherst embassy explained that opium was smoked in "all parts of the empire" and the Chinese considered it "one of the greatest luxuries."[33] In 1834, George Bennett provided a detailed account of how this "extensive and lucrative" trade was carried out—from how the opium was unloaded off British ships onto armed smuggling boats, to how the chests were opened and the opium balls or cakes wrapped in small bags easier to smuggle, and to how the opium was finally refined by boiling.[34] Charles Toogood Downing wrote that an "immense quantity" of opium was consumed each year. Males and females of all ranks—even officials and soldiers—smoked opium. The importation of opium was one of the "most reasonable" causes of the Chinese dislike for foreigners. And it was "undoubtedly" one of the "most important" reasons for the state of the current relationship between China and the foreign nations. As long as the opium trade continued, it was "hopeless" to expect the Daoguang Emperor to agree to an "amicable alliance" with Britain. "He would hardly enter into a more friendly intercourse with those whom he considers plotting with the scum of the people to defy the laws of the land, and corrupting his subjects."[35]

Especially after the decision in 1833 to abolish the Company's monopoly the next year, even former Company officers discussed the opium trade more or less openly, revealing not only the use of the drug but also its function in the country trade. Printed for private distribution, James Brabazon Urmston's *Observations on the China Trade* (1833) was aimed not at the opium trade per se, but at explaining why Britain's "valuable and very important" China trade should be removed from Canton to Chusan. He described how the opium trade, although contraband, was of "considerable importance" to Britain because so much of the revenue from its sale at Bengal went to the government of India. The trade could be defended neither on moral nor political grounds, but only on commercial ones, "because of the extraordinary system of it on the part of the Chinese." The importation of the drug was "connived at by every authority in the empire, from the emperor downwards." The opium trade in China was, "in fact, a perfect anomaly."[36]

In the same year, Charles Marjoribanks urged Charles Grant to limit the amount of opium produced in British India. The trade in this "pernicious poison" hurt the impression of "the foreign character" in "the minds of all intelligent Chinese."

> You are well aware of the extent to which this deleterious drug is now introduced into that country. To any friend to humanity it is a painful subject of contemplation, that we should continue to pour this black and envenomed poison into the sources of human happiness and well-being. The misery and demoralization which it creates are almost beyond belief; but we console ourselves with the reflection, that if we did not poison the Chinese at this round rate, somebody else would, and the trade proceeds with no other consideration from all parties engaged in it, than how much profit may be made by it.

Opium, Marjoribanks explained, was smoked mainly by those in "the higher ranks of life." Almost all "persons of wealth" were addicted, "while Chinese political and moral philosophy is satisfied by anathematizing it as a fiendish invention of the foreigner." The large number of opium ships at Lintin made it impossible for the "imbecile" Qing government to suppress the illicit trade there. Marjoribanks could not imagine a system "so perfectly and thoroughly contemptible." Anyone who had witnessed the "frightful ravages and demoralizing effects" of opium in China, could not but "feel deeply upon this subject."[37]

Two of Britain's greatest sinologists, both former Company men, also discussed opium. In 1836, George Thomas Staunton wrote that it was "hardly possible to conceive a greater moral and physical injury" than that inflicted upon the Chinese by the opium imported by the British. "By the ample supply which we thus administer to their inflamed passions, of this tempting but deleterious drug, the health, the morals, and the honest industry of the people are undermined (as far as its consumption extends) in a way that no Christian moralist and philanthropist can contemplate without pain." Unfortunately, Staunton added, the production of opium was so important for the economy and revenue of India, there was probably no point in complaining about it.[38] John Francis Davis noted how the value of this "pernicious drug" was greater than that of all other English imports combined and formed an important part of the revenue of British India.[39]

Missionaries sometimes wrote about opium, especially how it impeded their evangelical work. Walter Henry Medhurst explained in 1838 that opium was "regularly introduced" and "openly sold" throughout China. "Notwithstanding the prohibition, opium shops are as plentiful in some towns of China, as gin shops are in England. . . . Into these shops, all classes of persons continually flock, from the pampered official to the abject menial." The emperors of China had thus "wisely and patriotically" tried to stop the "onward march" of this "threatened evil." Realizing the futility of asking the foreign community of Canton to abandon the opium trade or of expecting the Chinese government to suppress it, Medhurst called upon the Company to "greatly diminish" the trade by discontinuing the cultivation of opium in India. If the British could end the slave trade, surely they could do the same for the opium.[40]

At least in this period, however, missionaries never led any concerted campaign against opium. Most were too dependent on opium traders to be openly critical. No missionary collaborated with foreign opium traders as actively as Karl Gützlaff, nicknamed "the Apostle of China" for distributing Christian tracts from Jardine and Matheson's opium clippers.[41] Still, they all relied on the opium trade in one way or another. Although Robert Morrison privately disapproved of its trade, he rarely mentioned opium in his published works or in his private letters and journals (many of which were sent back to Britain on opium ships). One of the few times he did so was when describing the *Topaze* affair of December 1821, where two villagers on Lintin were killed in a skirmish with British sailors from the frigate *Topaze*. But even here Morrison was concerned less about opium and smuggling than about the affrays that sometimes broke out between Chinese and foreigners, and in particular the Chinese policy of requiring a life for a life in the case of homicide.[42]

Nor did the missionaries agree on the seriousness of the opium problem or how to end it. Opium, declared George Tradescant Lay in 1837, "when taken as a luxury, destroys every sinew of the body, and enervates the mind, and renders the person using it a fit companion only for the lost of the human race."[43] In August 1838, Lay included in his long list of "means of doing good in China" the "non-participation in the sale of opium," which by the "perverseness of men" through misuse had degenerated from a "valuable drug" into a "bane which destroys both body and soul." To profit "by another's downfall" was un-Christian. The opium trade was a "blot upon the fair character of commerce, whose end from the very first was to make men social, wise, and happy." Free trade led to civilization and often to Christianity, while the opium trade encouraged corruption and rendered foreigners "contemptible in the eyes of the Chinese."[44]

The *Register* later claimed that while Lay was in Canton he had been "an uncompromising opponent to the opium trade."[45] But Lay discussed opium less in terms of morality or health than in economics. Writing during the

Opium War, he argued that opium had nothing to do with the Qing government's decision to "throw down the gauntlet with Britain, and hurl defiance in her teeth." For it was "these very Tartar authorities" who had been the "chief promoters" of the opium trade and had derived "large profits" from it. Lay considered the negative effects of smoking opium a symptom rather than cause of China's predicament. One of the main reasons for the rise in opium consumption was the Qing government's prohibitory edicts, "for the inhibition gives a charm to enjoyment, and the seller and the custom-house officer a triple interest in the sale." The Qing authorities had pursued a policy as "wicked" in theory as it had been in been in practice." Lay's remedies for China's "opium mania" show that opium was never his primary concern: he was calling the Qing government to task for instrumentalizing opium in its polices of governance. Once trade became free, China's "general constitution" would become strong enough to "overcome any disease that may have seized upon one of her members." Likewise, "many evils" would "correct" themselves—"if the priest and the magistrate will but leave them alone."[46]

## OPIUM IN THE PRESS

The most heated discussions and debates about the opium trade occurred within Canton, in its three main English-language periodicals: the *Canton Register*, *Canton Press*, and *Chinese Repository*. By exposing the "evils" of the Canton System through the local English-language press, these publications helped shape popular images of China and influence both public opinion and policymaking in London. But the press also subjected the opium trade to unwanted scrutiny in Britain. Even some of the most vocal supporters of a more aggressive policy toward China realized that deliberations about opium in Canton would attract unwanted attention. After "A British Merchant" argued in the *Register* in May 1831 that the British government needed to teach the Chinese that Britain would never agree to buy tea "at the high price of national disgrace," a reader who called himself "Veritas" warned British merchants not to "obtrude" the matter of opium on "a thinking public." Nowhere in the world, he declared, "is the character of a smuggler held up to admiration; still less when he is the purveyor of moral degradation and disease." Westerners in China would never be treated with respect until they learned to "display a higher sense of honor."[47]

At least in the early years the *Register* tried to be impartial, but it drew attention to opium almost from its inception. In its fifth issue, in January 1828 (now edited by James Matheson and Robert Morrison), the paper announced that to help its readers "in forming their opinions regarding the Prospects of the Opium market" for the next trading season, it would provide "very full details" of the consumption and supply compared with the preceding season. The figures showed an "extraordinary" increase in the amount of opium consumed over the previous nine months, "and still more in the value obtained for it."[48] Several weeks later, the *Register* explained that although the opium trade was a "moral question" of which "different persons form different opinions," and although the Chinese government considered opium to be "pernicious" and thus prohibited the trade, the facts proved "how weak human laws are against human passions." After listing the cases for and against opium, the paper insisted it would not take a side.[49] Most of the *Register* articles on opium over the next year were of a descriptive nature, rarely making any judgment. An article in May 1828 described opium as a "poison which has flowed through the Empire for many years," but which was both tolerated by local authorities and profitable to them.[50] The following August, the *Register* wondered how so much opium could be consumed in China, noting that 14,000 chests had been imported into Canton that year alone.[51]

Under the new editorship of Arthur Saunders Keating, who had old ties to Jardine and Matheson, in 1830 the *Register* became more defensive of the opium trade. In December 1832 it featured a report on the specially designed (and armed) "fast crab" smuggling boats that were being built at Lintin. Moving the drug between there and Canton had become so "admirably managed" that vessels were rarely interfered with. The opium boats passed before the factories in broad daylight. Sometimes the opium was even transported by the same boats sent down to stop the smugglers. This situation was unlikely to change, "so long as the *free traders* can afford to pay the mandarin so much better for not fighting than the government will for doing his duty."[52]

Commenting on Governor-General Li Hongbin's proclamation against the importation of "opium dirt," in March 1832 the *Register* pointed out that opium was neither a "luxury of recent introduction into China, nor has the taste for it been created by foreigners." The Chinese smoked their opium much like the Europeans drank their port or madeira:

> The fact is that the Chinese are, in all matters of luxury, a highly refined people—they neither drink the Opium in a liquid state, as the debauchees of some countries—nor swallow it crude, as the Turks, Indians and Malays (and who ever heard of a Chinese running *a-muk*?). Before the Opium is deemed fit for use, it is free from all but the pure substance—it loses all unpleasant flavor, and becomes grateful and even aromatic.

Were there a commercial treaty between Britain and China banning the importation of "the forbidden juice," those who broke the law would indeed not be entitled to protection from the British government. But this was not the case. Although the Qing government had a "moral right" to ban "an article of *universal* luxury," it was clear the Chinese "must have and will have the Drug" and if the Europeans and Americans did not provide it someone else would. The opium trade suited everyone involved: "The only people who seem dissatisfied, with this useful and pleasant state of things, are those who volunteer an opinion on a subject in which they are no way interested, at, and which . . . they do not, in the least, understand." With Indian opium for Chinese tea, "one drug thus balances the other." Contrary to the impression of British publications and even some speakers in the House of Commons, the merchants in Canton were not seeking any intervention from the British government to protect the opium trade. "No assertion can be more thoroughly untrue. We have never heard a demand for such privileges even hinted at."[53]

The *Repository* also frequently drew attention to opium. In its maiden issue, published in May 1832, the paper reported that two hundred of the Qing soldiers sent to suppress a rebellion in Guangdong, Guangxi, and Hunan were addicted to opium and had to be sent back.[54] In August it mentioned a rumor that the son of the governor of Guangdong had taken some opium with him to give the "great men about the court" in Peking.[55] When listing the imports to Canton that year, editor Elijah Bridgman included opium from British India and from Turkey (imported by American merchants). He also noted that "nearly the whole" of the opium trade was now conducted at and around Lintin, where vessels found a "safe and convenient anchorage."[56] In December 1833 the merchant James Goddard observed how the illicit opium trade was "so interwoven with our financial system in India as well as with our commerce, that it is not inferior in importance to the revenue obtained from tea at home."[57]

With this kind of coverage, it is hardly surprising that, by the time the *Press* came into being in 1835, the extent of the opium trade in China was already known to many in Britain. In the same year Robert Philip, a clergyman and supporter of the London Missionary Society's overseas endeavors, published an open letter to the philanthropist and abolitionist James Cropper of Liverpool—*No Opium! Or, Commerce and Christianity, Working Together for Good in China*, which he described as "the first public call for the Abolition of the Opium Trade."[58]

Meanwhile, Charles Elliot was regularly sending dispatches to Lord Palmerston, enclosing edicts from the provincial authorities railing against the opium trade. Two such edicts in autumn 1836 ordered eight British merchants (including Jardine and Dent) suspected of trading opium to leave Canton within two weeks, though Elliot doubted the order would be enforced.[59] And in 1836 the anonymous "Resident in China" argued from London that this "lamentable traffic" threw "such deep discredit, and such suspicion" on

British trade with China, that it "gives a color of benevolence to the Chinese edicts, which restrict and brand us."⁶⁰

Even after the Qing authorities began to crack down on opium smoking in 1837, the local press continued to list opium imports and prices. The committee of the recently established Canton Chamber of Commerce ruled on commercial disputes involving opium, decisions included in its annual reports and published in the local press.⁶¹ In January 1837 the *Repository* announced a £100 prize for the best essay on the opium trade, "showing its effects on the commercial, political, and moral interests of the nations and individuals connected therewith, and pointing out the course they ought to pursue in regard to it."⁶² To prove that his paper was open to all views, three months later Bridgman provided a purely descriptive account of the opium trade.⁶³ As of December 1839, however, no submissions either for or against the trade had been deemed worthy enough of the prize. The deadline had been extended, and former Lord Chancellor Henry Brougham, chairman of the Society for the Diffusion of Useful Knowledge in Britain, would head the prize committee.⁶⁴

## THE ISSUES

The debates among the British in China centered on several interrelated issues. One was the physiological effects of opium: how much harm, if any, the drug caused smokers. Although he would later change his tune, John Slade argued in 1830 that the Qing government had "a just cause" for prohibiting the importation of a product that was "destructive to the energies and health of its subjects."⁶⁵ Even if opium was readily available in England and used for a wide range of medicinal purposes, British physicians were often critical of its use for recreational purposes. Charles Downing wrote that "the great bulk" of the medical profession had determined that it was "much deleterious" than liquor or tobacco. Although a few "favoured individuals" could smoke opium without "paying dearly for their folly," most became "victims to misery and disease." While at least an alcoholic might have temporary remissions, for the opium-smoker it was "one continued state of excitement, without the slightest intermission."⁶⁶

In August 1838, "S.S.S." explained in the *Press* how a Chinese friend had described for him the ruinous effects of opium. And a friend more familiar with the Chinese had informed him that he had never met a single Chinese person who would "advance one plea" for opium. In the "narrow circle" of foreigners in Canton, each knew of "some half a dozen at least" Chinese people "whom the drug has brought to an untimely end." Even if foreigners and their "Chinese informants" were mistaken about the extent of the injury inflicted by the opium trade, it was "unquestionably true" that most Chinese believed foreigners were the "immediate instrument of the harm." Worst of all, this "poison" was being sold by Christians. "The very arms that should be stretched out to rescue, are dealing around a thousand deaths."[67]

Others were less convinced. "However injurious a profuse use of this narcotic may be, to the constitution of the smoker," declared the *Register* in April 1828, "still its demoralizing effects, which are witnessed in the Opium gambling-houses at Singapore, and other Eastern places, is unknown in China."[68] In January 1832, "Anti Humbug" insisted in the *Register* that the British government received far more revenue from the sale of "poisons in the shape of ardent spirits" than from opium, and that opium was far less "offensive to third parties" than "blue ruin."[69] In March 1836 an editorial in the *Register* doubted that moderate use of opium was any more injurious than that of spirits and wine.[70] And even when Britons believed opium was harmful, they sometimes argued it was less so in China than elsewhere. In May 1840, "Medicus" cited in the *Press* a range of European medical opinions since the 1600s—surely sufficient to prove the "deleterious influence of opium upon the human constitution." Still, he argued, in China the mortality rate appeared not to be so "great and rapid" as these opinions would suggest: a "very moderate allowance" seemed to be compatible with "a long enjoyment of tolerable health."[71]

For most traders, selling opium made perfect sense. They were providing a commodity that the Chinese had already used widely and which had many benefits, even if it could sometimes be harmful. Opium was "a commercial panacea that opened a Chinese market that had stubbornly remained closed until seduced by opium."[72] British medical theory did not accept the principle that a person could become addicted to a cure. In the age before aspirin, opium was the most commonly used analgesic. Jardine and Matheson had learned of its therapeutic properties while studying medicine in Edinburgh. They arrived in China when the stunning boom in opium sales was the "single most dramatic feature" of a "sweeping reconfiguration" of the China trade. Jardine was well aware that the emperor's edicts prohibiting the sale of opium were driven by the debilitating effects of addiction. However, he insisted that drug abuse was the fault of the buyer, not the seller.[73]

In the first of a series of heated exchanges with the anti-opium American merchant David Washington Cincinnatus Olyphant (the major benefactor of the *Repository*), in August 1838 the *Register* argued that even if opium had "prejudicial effects" on its users, it was far less harmful than liquor. "If the proscription of Opium is to be followed by a corresponding increase in the manufacture of *shuy-hing* [Shaoxing wine], or the introduction of some of the refined luxuries of Europe, we say leave us the Opium Pipe, and spare us the disgusting scenes of a Gin Palace." The only people who could end the opium trade were the Chinese themselves; until then, any efforts by the foreign community in Canton to "break the spell" would be "powerless."[74] The next month the *Register* added that the steady expansion of the opium trade was made possible not only by the "*tacit compliance*" of the local authorities but also by their "*encouragement*." The "cowardly and tyrannical" prohibitions were an "utter disgrace" to Chinese law: "too corrupt or too dastardly, or both" to stop smuggling, the government had instead chosen to "seize, brand, torture, and murder its own subjects for indulging in a mere luxury at the worst."[75] In October the paper carried an article from a British magazine on how opium had helped improve the health of the famed abolitionist William Wilberforce and of the surgeon and poet George Crabbe.[76]

"Delta," a British subject and self-confessed opium-seller, explained in April 1840 that although he did not smoke opium ("I prefer Claret and Madeira"), were he to give up wine for a stimulant he would choose opium over porter, gin, or tobacco. Not only was the abuse of opium less offensive than that of wine, opium had the "unrivalled advantage" for the poor because "a smaller value of money applied to excitation goes a greater length and has more force than in any other known stimulant." He sold opium because it was profitable and not prohibited under any British law, and because those he observed using it and purchasing it from him were "strictly honest in their dealings, and their course of transactions far more orderly than in any other men using excitable food."[77]

The *Press* failed to find "Delta's" argument "at all convincing." It was the law of China, not of Britain, that mattered. Even if the evils of using opium had been "painted with much exaggeration," habitual users became "physically and moral debased" and many premature deaths were caused "solely" by the "immoderate" use of opium.[78] When "Delta" wrote one week later, asking why the opium trade should suddenly be considered immoral and illegal, given how neither Chinese nor foreigners had said anything about it for forty years, the *Press* replied that the Chinese had the right to enact and enforce their own laws, and the benefits of opium were "much outweighed by its attendant evils." Even if the moderate use of opium provided only a "sensual and idle gratification," habit gradually degenerated into necessity, until the user finally became "so thoroughly a slave to that taste as to live solely for it, and to become careless of every duty of life, to the utter ruin of his character and health."[79]

In any case, the physiological effects of opium smoking comprised only a small portion of the debates in Canton. Far more important were matters of legalization, prohibition, and smuggling. Very few foreigners took seriously the emperor's edicts prohibiting opium. The trade had been tolerated for so long and the Qing government simply appeared too weak to restrict it. "The truth," wrote Charles Marjoribanks, "is that the edicts of the emperor fulminated from Pekin, are often issued without any expectation, and sometimes without even any wish, that they should be obeyed." Like the legal trade, the opium trade was riddled with corruption. Marjoribanks claimed there was not a single foreign merchant in Canton, "however respectable," who did not pay bribes to customs officers to evade government duties.[80] James Urmston wrote that the "importation and introduction" of opium was "connived at by every authority in the empire, from the emperor downwards."[81] Walter Medhurst regretted how the imperial government was "absolutely powerless" in preventing the introduction and trafficking of opium. It was a "well-known circumstance" that even the governor-general received "a very respectable consideration, for winking at these illicit transactions."[82]

The *Register* insisted in February 1838 that the fact that opium was imported with the "full knowledge" of government officers at all levels was "too notorious to require any elucidation." Recent transactions had been "so glaring" that it was impossible to doubt the sincerity of either the local or the imperial government to deal "an entire and final stop" to the opium trade.[83] George Lay recalled watching a well-armed smuggling boat in the harbor of Hong Kong transfer a huge cargo of opium from an American ship, "under the auspices of the government flag." Opium schooners passed government cruisers near the Bocca Tigris forts "without let of hindrance," discharging their cargo as close as possible to Canton "in the full light of day."[84]

Many insisted the prohibitions themselves were to blame for China's ills. In November 1839 the *Press* charged that Lin Zexu was playing "a desperate game" and too many lives were at stake. His sincerity in ending the opium trade was "worthy of the highest praise," but the means were "execrable."[85] In early December the *Press* wrote that Lin's "indiscriminating measures" against the opium trade had hurt the legal trade, which explained the rise in robbery on the river and in Macao.[86] By the end of the year, the "distress" among the Chinese population was "extreme" and "a general gloom" had spread.[87] "Delta" argued in his piece of April 1840 that the greatest evil arose not from smoking opium but from the Chinese laws against it, which made smoking a solitary practice instead of a social one. "*Legalize it, and both these evils are abolished!*"[88]

Even some of the few merchants in Canton who did not sell opium thought it should be legal. "Britannicus" wrote in the *Press* that although he had always refused to participate in the opium trade, "according to the Law of our Land it must still continue a *legal* trade until condemned by express act of parliament."[89] The *Press* disagreed. Even if opium was too "deeply rooted" in China to be suppressed, legalization would not help. Consider the licensed opium shops in British settlements in Southeast Asia: "A sad sight it was to see those intoxicated wretches in an outward state of torpor, incapable apparently of any bodily exertion, each smoking his pipe in *solitude*, busy only apparently with the images conjured up in his own brain by the Opium fumes, and unconscious or careless of anything passing around him."[90]

They were also aware of the debates about legalization within the Qing court. Memorials and edicts were translated frequently, often in their entirety. In July 1836 the *Press* and the *Repository* published a translation of senior official Xu Naiji's memorial on why opium should be legalized to enable regulation and taxation.[91] Charles Elliot described this "State Paper" in a dispatch to the Foreign Office as a "public confession" that "the Chinese cannot do without our opium" and that the Qing government was too "false and feeble" to suppress the trade.[92] So sure were many foreigners that the trade would be legalized, they were surprised by the emperor's edict of July 24 that opium would remain illegal—though for some reason this news did not reach Canton until the first week of October and came as such a surprise that the *Press* issued a special edition.[93] As late as October, Elliot wrote that the British in Canton expected soon to receive "the final orders" from Peking for the legalization of opium.[94]

In January 1837 the *Repository* published translations of memorials from Chinese officials opposed to legalizing the opium trade.[95] When forwarding translations of the memorials for and against legalization to Palmerston in February 1837, Elliot still predicted opium would eventually be legalized.[96] (Not everyone agreed: that October, James Matheson wrote to Captain Alexander Grant in London that legalization was "no longer thought of" and the government was now "making a strong effort for the entire suppression.")[97] In January 1839 the *Press* published a translation of Zhili governor-general Qishan's memorial to the emperor, recommending that he temporarily end foreign intercourse with China "in order to stop the deluge of opium poison that is now over flowing the country."[98]

But just who were the smugglers—the British who shipped the drug from India, the Chinese who delivered it, or both? When Elliot in December 1838 warned captains of British vessels engaged in opium smuggling to leave the area, the *Press* supported him. Opium smuggling at Whampoa and Canton had "already exposed our community to great risk." If allowed to continue, it would not only embarrass the foreign merchants but endanger the hong merchants, linguists, "and other natives who are altogether innocent."[99] When the *Register* criticized Elliot's warning notice, the *Press* fired back that because of the smuggling "every Chinese connected with us is placed in daily jeopardy of his life and fortune." Even the "innocent domestics" of a

British merchant had been arrested and jailed. A riot had broken out, and the "'entire" foreign trade at Canton had been closed for more than three weeks. "Thus the most important trade in the world is stopped and imperilled."[100] When foreigners expressed outrage in early 1839 after learning that convicted dealers and smokers would be executed in front of the factories, a resident who signed himself simply as "P" pointed out that "the executions at which we take such umbrage are but the result of *our own acts*." The faster the foreigners abandoned the opium trade, "the fewer executions may they be obliged to witness at their doors."[101]

Many traders prided themselves on selling only the best quality opium, bristling at the term "smuggler." Jardine, who with Matheson had pioneered the "coasting trade" (peddling opium directly along the coast), asserted it was the East India Company and the Chinese, not the private traders, who were smugglers. At his farewell dinner in January 1839, the largest and grandest the foreign community had ever witnessed, he declared:

> I hold, gentlemen, the society of Canton high; it holds a high place, in my opinion, even among the merchants of the east; yet also I know that this community has often heretofore and lately been accused of being a set of smugglers: this I distinctly deny; we are not smugglers, gentlemen! It is the Chinese government, it is the Chinese officers who smuggle, and who connive at and encourage smuggling, not we; and then look at the E. I. Company: why the father of all smuggling and smugglers is the E. I. Company.[102]

Yet only one year earlier Jardine had described the practice whereby British, European, and Parsi traders had started to replace the Chinese "smugglers"—and deliver opium directly to Whampoa themselves—as "disgusting."[103]

## JAMES INNES

No Briton in China participated as actively in the opium debates as the feisty Scottish trader James Innes, who would brook no criticism of opium. After the *Repository* in November 1836 reprinted a pamphlet against opium by Archdeacon Thomas Dealtry of Calcutta, Innes slammed the clergyman for attacking a product that enabled the government of India to pay his "and such like" salaries. The British government had closed its eyes to the opium trade for the past twenty years, just as the Church of England had. Opium was "a useful soother, a *harmless* luxury, and a precious medicine, *except to those who abuse it*." Both "experience and observation" showed that millions of Chinese smoked opium as "a rational and sociable article of luxury and hospitality," while the number of "*victimized smokers*" paled when compared with the "many sober and well regulated families that present a pipe of opium to a distant neighbor visiting them, as yeomen in England thirty years since did a bottle of wine." If opium were proven to be more harmful than Innes believed, then by all means stop the trade:

> But do not stop; carry through the principle. . . . Depopulate the Rhine. Lay the vineyards of fair France waste! Abolish tobacco in Virginia, and in Manila! Prohibit the growth of barley in Norfolk: because a few deluded reprobates attend the gin palaces in England, and smoke all day long in China and elsewhere. When the public are prepared for this equal measure, I shall not petition for the white poppy of India being made an exception.

And which would the archdeacon prefer: force the trade into "the hands of desperadoes, pirates, and marauders" or keep it within "a body of capitalists, not participating certainly in what they carry, but in fact supplying an important branch of the Indian revenue safely and peaceably"?[104]

Innes's hyperbole cut against the factional grain of the opium trade. When "Another Reader" dismissed his comparison of opium to wine as "mere 'fudge'" and accused him of trying to defend "what is, in itself, manifestly indefensible," Innes replied that although he was open to all opinions, he would not argue with men who, "like the Archdeacon, first assume that opium merchants are disseminating poison, and on that assumption proceed to abuse and condemn them in this world and the next." Far from being "solely poison," opium, used in moderation, was "a healthful and exhilarating luxury, given by a beneficent Deity for man's use and enjoyment."[105]

And when in April 1837 Arthur Keating questioned the logic of an opium dealer being able to judge the morality of the trade, Innes (who had once agreed to serve as Keating's second in a proposed but subsequently aborted duel with the American editor William Wightman Wood), now mocked him: "He seems to fancy himself on a bench of justice, with a big wig on his head, and me pleading as a criminal." Eleven years earlier, Innes had encountered a comprador managing one of the "best filled and most used treasuries" in Canton and producing "clear and satisfactory accounts" for his employer. The comprador had smoked opium daily for seven years and in 1836 retired to his native district in "perfect health" and with "a large fortune."[106] Keating responded by describing an imaginary trial and by ridiculing Innes for trying to beautify the picture of an opium smuggler, "on his high trotting horse, armed to the teeth, ready for all comers, and jogging along with two chests of opium," into that of a "genteel" merchant, "at his desk, his pen behind his ear, folding up opium orders."[107]

If any single person did more to inflame tensions between the Chinese and the foreigners, it was neither Lin Zexu nor Charles Elliot but James Innes. In

Figure 5.5. James Innes, by Lamqua or studio, oil on canvas. *Photo*: Martyn Gregory Gallery

early December 1838 the American merchant Robert Bennet Forbes wrote to his wife, Rose, in Boston that the foreign community had been "thrown into a state of excitement" after a shipment of opium Innes was trying to smuggle into Canton had been seized. The scene was almost comical: Innes had hired Chinese porters to transport the opium in silver specie boxes—in broad daylight—and had bribed the local mandarin; government troops, who became suspicious when they saw one porter carrying two boxes when normally one box required two men, "pounced upon them and made a seizure of 12 boxes."

Under torture, or so Forbes surmised, the porters had claimed that the opium came from an American ship rather than implicate Innes.[108]

Forbes had no sympathy for Innes—"a madman and I should not care if he were caught and hanged." But he understood all too well how much trouble such incidents could cause: "The Chinese in all these cases let the foreigners alone, stop the trade and squeeze the Hong Merchants of large sums and then all goes on again as before—they never attempt to touch us." Several days later, the hong merchants had withdrawn their threat of demolishing Innes's house, though they still insisted that he leave Canton. Forbes had seen Howqua, who looked "ten years older being very much harassed by this affair."[109]

When Howqua ordered that Innes's factory be broken into and searched, threatening to tear down his house, Innes declared he would hold him and the Cohong liable for any property lost or destroyed. Hugh Hamilton Lindsay, chairman of the Chamber of Commerce, had to remind the hong merchants that even though the chamber disapproved of such acts, because Innes was not a member it had no control over his actions and was in any case "purely a commercial body."[110] On December 16 the hong merchants complained to the chamber that, in light of the Innes affair, Governor-General Deng Tingzhen had condemned them to wear the cangue as a warning to others. Only after their "most earnest entreaties" were they "spared the degradation." All factory tenants were to sign a bond promising not to smuggle opium; anyone caught doing so would be sent away.[111]

Elliot now warned Innes of the "very disastrous consequences" his actions might produce, imploring him to extricate himself from a "very unsuitable position." Innes reluctantly agreed, providing that the two Chinese porters would be "safe and free from torture, and the trade no longer obstructed on my account."[112] At a meeting of all foreign residents in Canton on December 17, Elliot cautioned that the illicit opium trade on the river posed "disastrous consequences" for "innocent men" and "every native" connected to foreigners, as well as "distressing degradation of the foreign character." In a public notice the following day, he ordered all British subjects "either habitually or occasionally engaged" in the illicit opium trade to withdraw beyond the Bocca Tigris.[113]

The Innes fiasco showed how volatile the opium situation had become—and how the British authorities neither could control him nor had any rights in the matter.[114] As Elliot explained to Lord Palmerston in early January 1839, the senior hong merchants had complained "in bitter terms" about the "cruel and ruinous consequences" caused by the illicit traffic in opium carried in small craft up the river from Whampoa. "Till the other day," he wrote, "I believe there was no part of the world where the foreigner felt his life and property more secure than here in Canton." But the riots that erupted after the

Innes incident had convinced him otherwise. "For a space of near two hours the foreign factories were within the power of an immense and excited mob, the gate of one of them was absolutely battered in, and a pistol was fired out, probably without ball, or over the heads of the people, for at least it is certain that nobody fell."[115]

Fortunately, Innes finally confessed that the opium was indeed his and had come from his boat, not from the American ship, and absolved the two Chinese porters from all willful participation in the offense; they had been ignorant of the true content of the boxes. Following the riots in front of the factories, he agreed to leave Canton for Macao. Not only was the trade reopened, but Elliot was able also to open a direct communication with Governor-General Deng. "It is," he wrote to Palmerston, "the first permanent intercourse of the kind which has never existed between this ancient Empire and the Western world."[116]

But Innes remained impenitent. In May 1839 he insisted in a letter to Elliot that his departure for Macao had not been "an expiation of any supposed offence on my part," and demanded that Elliot retract the charge that he had "designedly added to the miseries" of the British in Canton.[117] When the Qing authorities learned that Innes was also involved in opium-smuggling in Macao, they demanded that Elliot seize him and "with severity expel him hence to his own country."[118] And when Elliot asked the governor of Macao to deport him, in June 1839 Innes sent a petition to Queen Victoria explaining that during his thirteen years in China he, like at least 90 percent of the British subjects in China, had traded "considerably" in opium, not only selling the drug to licensed hong merchants but even delivering it to the boats of the governor-general and other officials. Elliot, instead of considering the sworn evidence of "credible witnesses," had tried to punish a loyal British subject "on the notoriously false evidence of Chinese! and the tattle of women! and on the gossip of men all unsworn!" Innes had thus been forced to abandon his house in Macao and to "wander without shelter" in "a very distant and most unhospitable country," in poor health and unable to carry on his business.[119]

In October 1840, Innes learned that Elliot had asked Lord Palmerston for permission to arrest him in Macao if he continued to defy the Chinese authorities. He placed a notice in the *Press* and *Register* declaring that Elliot had no right to arrest him and that the leader of any party—"if possible, Capt. Elliot himself"—sent to apprehend him would be shot "through the head, or heart, by a well practised rifle, and then the party allowed to perform their lawless duty."[120] But his antics impressed at least one member of the local British community: in November 1840 an anonymous letter (signed only with a triangle) to the *Register* blasted Elliot for forcing the "humane" governor of Macao to banish Innes.[121]

## SETTING THE RECORD STRAIGHT, AGAIN

There was yet another issue, perhaps the most important one of all. Britons in Canton became increasingly concerned that neither official nor public opinion at home—or sometimes even in India, where the opium was cultivated—supported them or understood the situation in China. They felt ignored, sometimes even betrayed, by their own government and misunderstood by their compatriots. Both of these sentiments and frustrations could be magnified or intensified after certain incidents.

Sometimes this simply required setting the record straight or offering a different opinion. When the *Bombay Gazette* suggested that Qing officials might convince the imperial court to add a clause making opium legal with a moderate duty, the *Press* responded in May 1838 that even if Britain and China completed a commercial treaty, the number of edicts revealed how the Qing government would never tolerate the opium trade. And if British merchants stopped importing opium, the Americans and other traders would do it instead.[122] More often than not, it meant showing how only those with real China experience were qualified to judge the situation. In June 1838 the *Register* reprinted an article from the *Friend of India* on Chinese efforts to curb the opium trade. The *Friend* had described the complexities of the opium trade as being "so strange and anomalous as to stagger belief."

> We see on the one hand the civilized, the enlightened, the Christian Government of Britain in the East, straining every nerve to increase the cultivation of Opium in India, for the express purpose of drugging the Chinese Empire. On the other hand, we see the half civilized Government of China directing all its efforts to the exclusion of an article which cannot fail to sap the foundation of all social, political and manly virtue in its subjects.

The *Register* responded that the opium trade had continued despite the Qing government's alleged efforts. Everyone knew the trade was too lucrative to be stopped. And opium was not only a "poison" as critics so often claimed; it was also used as medicine: "If it sometimes destroys it also sometimes saves life."[123] After the *New York Evening Star* carried an article on the "dreadful effects" of opium and the British determination to violate the "enlightened" mandates of the Daoguang Emperor, in March 1839 the *Press* published a long piece on the history of opium and its trade in China. It did so for the benefit of "distant readers" who might be "too easily led astray" by the coverage in the British and North American newspapers, "which is likely to prejudice the public mind more against the Opium trade than it deserves."[124]

These efforts to set the record straight became even more intense after the surrender and destruction of the opium. Almost immediately after the foreigners had given up their opium, the debates took a different direction, turning to why the British government ought to compensate them for their losses. Historians who have seen Elliot's order to surrender the opium as a clever ruse to push Britain into war with China have overlooked how much prodding and assuring it took for him to convince his countrymen to do so, not to mention how long it took to be compensated. In June 1842 the *Press* lamented that, more than three years after Lin had destroyed their opium, nothing had been done to compensate the owners.[125] Some Parsi merchants were not compensated until almost twenty years later, and even then only for part of the value of the opium they had surrendered. At least two Parsis committed suicide because of their losses.[126]

In May 1839, as Elliot was issuing his public notices ordering all British subjects to surrender their opium, James Matheson sent his nephew Alexander home to help promote their company's cause.[127] Meanwhile, a group of British subjects in Canton wrote to Palmerston to protest the Qing government's "recent acts of aggression" and "acts of violence"—including the stoppage of the "whole legal trade" of Canton, the "forcible detention" of all foreigners there, and the "open and undisguised" threat of execution. This was no longer simply a matter of why the Qing government should suddenly decide to enforce its prohibition against opium; it was also an attempt to show that the British government had sanctioned, "implied, if not openly expressed," the opium trade. No penalties had ever been enforced for importing opium, and the House of Commons had always recognized the "peculiar character" of the trade and its importance for the revenues of British India. Criticism of Elliot suddenly (and temporarily) abated. His "deep sense of public spirit" had driven him, "at no inconsiderable risk, to endeavor to rescue British life and property from a position of fearful jeopardy." The petitioners now implored Palmerston to fulfill Elliot's guarantee of compensation. British commerce could never be carried on safely, let alone flourish, "where our persons and property are alike at the mercy of a capricious and corrupt government."[128]

Especially after the destruction of the opium, the local press paid close attention to the debates in Britain and India regarding the opium and China crises. It realized opinion in Britain was not necessarily supportive. In December 1839 the *Register* wrote that the news from home was not good: it had been nine months since the foreigners had surrendered their opium, yet prime minister Lord Melbourne had said nothing about compensation. His silence seemed "absurd" and was a "culpable neglect" of "a most important question" that affected not only the China trade but also what "the natives of India" would think of the "thorough good faith of the British government." The *Register* hoped that when the surrender of the opium was discussed in

Parliament, "the stability of our Indian empire,—being an empire of opinion only—may not be forgotten."[129]

In an April 1840 article titled "Justice to the China Merchants," the *Register* stressed how the opium had been purchased by merchants from the East India Company, "a branch of the British government." And even if it had been imported against Qing law, the evasion of this law had been "countenanced and encouraged" by the British government.[130] That June, the *Press* and the *Register* both published accounts from British newspapers on the formation of a society in London opposing the opium trade, which its members believed prevented the spread of Christianity in China and impeded the growth of legitimate trade.[131] The following month the *Register* published an article titled "Fallacies of the Opium Question," in which it dismissed the *Asiatic Journal* as "another defender of the Chinese and the E. I. company's monopoly of the manufacture of opium—*acquitting them of all participation in the opium trade!*"[132]

The *Repository* was hardly making matters any better. In May 1839, with a crisis looming, Elijah Bridgman warned "our friends and readers in distant parts" to be careful in condemning those involved in the opium trade and in offering their own suggestions for how to end it. Although Bridgman claimed to single out Britain only because it stood "first and almost alone in the production of opium," he argued that the negative effects of opium were "much greater" than that of liquor. Smuggling opium was the "fruitful source of evils, destroying life, property, and morals."[133] In December, Bridgman reported that the consumption and traffic of opium had risen "with most extraordinary rapidity, and have led to—or at least hastened on—events of the most fearful nature."[134] In January 1840 he wrote that only a few foreigners in Canton still supported the use of opium or its traffic. "Many, even of those engaged in the trade, do not hesitate to declare that it is an evil—and a great evil."[135]

The other two presses were thus eager to publicize any opinion in Britain and India supporting the private traders. In July 1839 the *Register* published a memorial from a group of British merchants at Bombay reminding the Privy Council that the opium trade had been "encouraged and promoted" by the Indian government with the "express sanction and authority" of the British government and parliament, "with the full knowledge" it was "contraband and illegal." This had been a source of "immense profit" to the Indian government, and mainly through the opium trade had the British merchants been able to purchase "so readily and extensively" the tea imported into England, which in turn provided the British government with "very important revenue."[136] In January 1840 the *Press* published an August 1839 article from the *Atlas* explaining the need for a hard line against China. The British should send "a few frigates" up the river to demand compensation for "every article" that had been taken away. "All the armies which the emperor could bring into the field would not stand for a quarter of an hour against the crews of a couple of English frigates."[137]

Also in January 1840, the *Press* published a lengthy letter of August 1839 from "One Long Resident in China," now living in London, to John Horsley Palmer, former governor of the Bank of England. Noting how much agitation there was in Britain and America against the opium trade, with presses even offering prizes for the best essays against it, he explained that from his own experience of "Chinese habits," as a "national vice" he preferred opium to any "ardent spirit." A "happy thing" it would be if the British chose to use opium over spirits. While the European "spirit-drinking debauchee" was a "violent, often a furious madman" who committed crimes of all degrees of heinousness," the Chinese "opium debauchee" was only a "dreaming, quiet, and useless member of society." The author had known many Chinese who smoked opium "without feeling the slightest injury" and who were "moderate men, like our gentlemanly wine-drinkers." Importing opium was illegal, but so were living year-round in Canton, learning the language, and employing Chinese servants. "Shall we condemn every one who has been by the peculiarly undefined state of international commerce compelled to such breaches?" Trading in opium was "as little sinful" as dealing in any another stimulant.[138]

In March 1840 the *Register* reprinted articles from Indian newspapers arguing that since the governments of Britain and India had been involved all along in the opium trade, steps had to be taken to compensate and protect the British merchants.[139] Later that April, the *Register* published a November 1839 circular by the Bombay Chamber of Commerce on the situation in China and the importance of the China trade for India and Britain. It also included a piece by "A Voice from the East," in Bombay, pointing out that "the great mass" of the opium surrendered had not been in Chinese waters and was therefore not contraband. As Elliot had demanded its surrender, it was "neither seized, nor physically nor legally seizable" by the Qing government.[140] In July 1840 the *Register* published a petition to the House of Commons from Indian opium traders seeking compensation for their lost revenue.[141] Even when opinion outside China supported compensation, the situation sometimes still needed to be clarified. After a judge in Madras argued in July 1839 that the destruction of the opium had been a violation of international law, the *Register* insisted in January 1840 that international law meant a system of rights "utterly known" to the government of China.[142]

The other part of the strategy was refuting criticism in Britain and India. In 1839 the Rev. Algernon Sydney Thelwall of the Trinitarian Bible Society in

London published *The Iniquities of the Opium Trade with China*, explaining the effects of opium when taken as a stimulant, how it was imported by the British to China, and the extent of its use there. Supported by translations of "authentic" Chinese edicts and memorials from the *Repository*, materials from India, and extracts from books by John Davis and Walter Medhurst, Thelwall concluded that the opium trade "brought the greatest dishonour upon the British flag" and "grossly dishonoured" the "name and profession" of Christianity. Even more embarrassing for the British merchants in Canton, Thelwall condemned the opium trade as a *"system of determined smuggling."*[143]

In November 1839 both the *Press* and the *Register* refuted Thelwall's tract. The *Press* agreed with much of what he wrote, but then observed that this information came mainly from the *Repository* and from translated reports by Chinese officials. Only recently had the Qing government taken steps to suppress opium. Before then, the "whole" of the opium trade had been conducted "not only with the connivance of the local Government, but under its own immediate protection." Government boats received the drug from foreign ships and delivered it to Chinese vessels. With fixed fees and duties, the trade had been carried out with "as much safety and regularity as any other recognized." Given how the opium trade had enjoyed the protection of the Qing government for more than fifty years, why should foreigners now believe it was suddenly sincere about ending it? Contrary to what Thelwall had claimed, the British were not the only ones who imported the drug. Nor was opium to blame for the lack of progress of Christianity. Foreigners had faced the same prohibitions long before the opium trade: witness how hard the "indefatigable" Catholic missionaries had been struggling in China.[144]

The *Register* used the occasion to rebut both Thelwall and Walter Medhurst. Even the "oldest and best informed" foreign residents in China could not support Thelwall's claim that the evil done by smoking opium as a "mere luxury" was greater than the good done by taking it for medicinal purposes. And there was no evidence for Medhurst's claim that China's population growth had decreased from 3 percent per year to 1 percent since the opium trade began. The *Register* also disagreed that the opium trade prevented free trade with China: trade with the West had been confined to Canton in 1717 by the Kangxi Emperor and then in 1757 by Qianlong—"before the English had any transactions in the opium trade."[145]

After reprinting an article from the *Times* of London on the "iniquities" of the opium trade, in October 1839 the *Register* promised it would publish its own article on the iniquities of trade in other stimulants such as tea, wine, and gin.[146] In January 1840 the paper declared that the author of an article in London's *Weekly Chronicle* showed "so much ignorance of the real state and conduct of that trade, that we consider it undeserving of serious refutation."

The *Register* advised the writer to "revert to something that he does understand and not to China, and the opium trade, of which he knows nothing."[147] In August the *Press* wrote that even though opium was a "nauseous" drug, not all of the "differences" with China, let alone the war, had been caused by the opium trade. The war had indeed accelerated the "rupture" between Britain and China. But so "many other causes" had "long existed" that war was inevitable.[148]

## OPIUM AND WAR

The opium crisis led to war, inevitable or not. But there was never one voice or opinion on opium. Almost all foreigners in Canton wanted to see China opened to more trade. But even those who sold the drug sometimes disagreed on how this should happen. Discussions about opium were never simply about opium: they were also about the nature of the British presence in China. Once the opium had been surrendered and destroyed, opium became a unifying force. But the situation had not always been so cut and dry. And these discussions and debates were not necessarily dominated by prominent figures such as James Matheson and William Jardine (who left Canton for England in January 1839 before the opium crisis blew truly up). Not everyone who sold or debated opium was as eccentric or controversial as James Innes, but this was still a matter of personalities, with different views and opinions. Opium was always subject to rethinking—from how it was to be imported, or smuggled, to what effects it had on users, and to how it affected Anglo-Chinese relations.

These discussions continued into the Opium War, often intertwined with those about how the British should seek retribution from China and how the war should be fought. In December 1839, "Ramrod" wrote from Urmston Bay (Tung-koo), a small inlet southeast of Lintin where some of the foreign traders had taken refuge, that no one in the past six months had been able to offer a good solution to the problem. No one understood the importance of the China trade—"the *best* trade that ever Great Britain possessed"—and how, with the exception of another war with France or America, "no greater calamity" could hit Britain than a prolonged stoppage of trade with China. Rejecting the idea that the Chinese were a "nation of cowards," he nonetheless insisted Britain had an "undoubted right and title" to demand redress from them. Once the sword was drawn, it should not be returned to its scabbard until the British had drawn "ample satisfaction."[149]

Throughout the Opium War, some Britons in China remained concerned about the unpopularity of their cause in India and at home. When in March

1840 the *Times* published an article critical of the war with China ("follies and offences crammed into one spot, and into a single year, enough to cover with humiliation the proudest empire, and to make her name a laughing stock") and the "unprincipled adventurers" who had caused it, the *Register* offered a list of responses to the "ignorance" of the London press.[150] On 26 May, the first anniversary of the day when Elliot and the sixteen proscribed merchants left Canton, the *Register* included a report from a physician in Calcutta on the medical benefits of opium, which made it even more useful than quinine for the "dangerous Bengal remittent fevers so fatal and so difficult to manage."[151]

In late February 1841 the *Friend of India* argued that although the limited treaty giving the British the island of Hong Kong suggested to the "whole civilized world" that a "mighty expedition" had "ended in smoke," the confiscation of opium in 1839 had been legal according to both the "international law of Europe" and the "peculiars law of China," regardless of how "violent and illegal might have been the mode of effecting it."[152] In a long letter to Jardine in August, Matheson predicted that, even with Charles Elliot out of the picture and Henry Pottinger now in charge of the British expeditionary force, there would be very little chance of a peace for nearly one year. The only reason Matheson had been willing to accept "almost any sort of settlement" was the unpopularity of the traders' cause in Britain and the smallness of the expeditionary force and the "inefficiency" of its commanders. He also hoped such a paltry settlement might offer a "better *Casus Belly*" [sic] on some future occasion," though it would be "infinitely better" if Pottinger could preclude this by making a "*good* settlement."[153]

As it did with footbinding, the war offered firsthand opportunities for British soldiers and doctors to observe the consumption and effects of opium in China. Military secretary Robert Jocelyn wrote that "not even the most strenuous partisans" could deny the demoralizing impact of the drug.[154] The surgeon Duncan McPherson, one of the few foreigners in China who wrote about his own experience with smoking opium, found himself "not at all surprised at the great partiality and craving appetite always present with those who are long accustomed to its use." He contrasted the effects of the drug on an occasional user and a regular one:

> The spirits are renovated, and melancholy is dissipated; the most delightful sensations and the happiest inspirations are present when only partaken to a limited extent, and to those not long accustomed to its use. If persevered in, these pleasing feelings vanish, all control of the will, the functions of sensation and volition, as well as reason, are suspended, vertigo, coma, irregular muscular contractions, and sometimes temporary delirium, supervene.

Given the popular belief that opium was so harmful, McPherson expected the Chinese to be a "shrivelled, and emaciated, and idiotic race." But the opposite appeared to be true: "We find them to be a powerful, muscular, and athletic people, and the lower orders more intelligent, and far superior in mental acquirements, to those of corresponding rank in our own country." He noted how opium had recently been used "with considerable success" in Bengal as a substitute for quinine, adding that while many of the British troops in Hong Kong had suffered from fevers, "comparatively fewer" of the Chinese had suffered, "though exposed to the same exciting causes." This suggested that "the habitual use of opium is not so injurious as is commonly supposed; its effects, certainly, are not so disgusting to the beholder as that of the sottish, slaving drunkard." When used in moderation, the drug could help treat any disease. Unfortunately, it was often abused, "like many others of the choicest gifts of Providence."[155]

Despite the many different opinions about opium and the best course of action to take against China, one view rarely wavered: opium was too deeply embedded in Chinese life to be eradicated. Keith Stewart Mackenzie, military secretary to Commodore Gordon Bremer, recalled how during an excursion into the interior of Hong Kong, a village elder had invited Mackenzie and the other officers to sit down in his house, "an invitation I accepted with pleasure." Minutes later, the elder offered Mackenzie a pipe of opium, "with all the paraphernalia belonging to it," which he declined. It was "but one instance out of many" Mackenzie had experienced, "of the partiality of the Chinese for the drug." The "well known venality" of the local officials was so intense that Mackenzie claimed he had never entered one's house without finding opium. This, he explained, revealed the misbelief among some Britons that opium smoking was "not universal" or "connived at by government officers." To talk of the Qing government suppressing opium smoking, "or even wishing to do so," was "about as absurd as to attempt to stop beer drinking in the United Kingdom."[156]

## NOTES

1. *Canton Press* 4, no. 29 (23 March 1839): n.p.

2. Matheson to Jardine, 1 May 1839, MS JM C5/4, Jardine Matheson Archive (JMA). Also in Alain Le Pichon, ed., *China Trade and Empire: Jardine, Matheson & Co. and the Origins of British Rule in Hong Kong, 1827–1843* (Oxford: Published for the British Academy by Oxford University Press, 2006), 358.

3. *Canton Press* 4, no. 30 (30 March 1839): n.p.

4. Frederic Wakeman Jr., "The Canton Trade and the Opium War," in *The Cambridge History of China*, vol. 10, *Late Ch'ing, 1800–1911*, part 1, ed. John K. Fairbank

(Cambridge: Cambridge University Press, 1978), 184–85. See also Hsin-pao Chang, *Commissioner Lin and the Opium War* (Cambridge, MA: Harvard University Press, 1964), chap. 5, and Harry G. Gelber, *Opium, Soldiers and Evangelicals: Britain's 1840–42 War with China, and Its Aftermath* (Basingstoke, UK: Palgrave Macmillan, 2004), chap. 4.

5. Elliot to Palmerston, 6 April 1839, in Great Britain, Foreign Office, *Correspondence Relating to China, Presented to Both Houses of Parliament, by Command of Her Majesty* (London: T. R. Harrison, 1840), 385.

6. *Canton Press* 4, no. 32 (13 April 1839): n.p.

7. Matheson to Jardine, 1 May 1839, MS JM C5/4, JMA. Also in Le Pichon, *China Trade and Empire*, 357–58, 366.

8. Matheson to Jardine, 13 May 1839, MS JM C5/4, JMA.

9. *Canton Press* 4, no. 37 (18 May 1839): n.p.

10. *Canton Press* 4, no. 38 (25 May 1839): n.p.

11. *Canton Register* 12, no. 23 (4 June 1839): 104, and *Canton Register* 12, no. 29 (16 July 1839): 127–29; *Canton Press* 4, no. 42 (20 July 1839): n.p.

12. Great Britain, Foreign Office, *Memorials Addressed to Her Majesty's Government, by British Merchants Interested in the Trade with China. Presented to Both Houses of Parliament by Command of Her Majesty* (London: T. R. Harrison, 1840), 1–23.

13. In any case, the strategy was related more to currency than fostering addiction. The country trade was built up to circumvent the Canton System's silver requirements, enabled by bills-of-exchange that kept British silver in England. The subsequent drain of silver from China upset its bimetallic currency policy.

14. Carl Trocki, *Opium, Empire, and the Global Political Economy: A Study of the Asian Opium Trade, 1750–1950* (London: Routledge, 1999), 126.

15. In *Material Culture in Europe and China* (London: Macmillan, 1997), 234–38, S.A.M. Adshead estimates there were twelve million regular users in China in the nineteenth century, far from an epidemic. Similarly, in *Narcotic Culture: A History of Drugs in China* (Chicago: University of Chicago Press, 2004), 1, Frank Dikötter, Lars Laamann, and Zhou Xun question the conventional narrative of opium rendering "China into a nation of hopeless addicts, smoking themselves to death while their civilisation descended into chaos." Richard Newman argues that the physiological dangers of opium consumption in Qing China were "greatly exaggerated" then and have been accepted uncritically as evidence of the "social damage done by British imperialism." Richard K. Newman, "Opium Smoking in Late Imperial China," *Modern Asian Studies* 29, no. 4 (1995): 766. See also Jonathan Spence, "Opium Smoking in Ch'ing China," in *Conflict and Control in Late Imperial China*, ed. Frederic Wakeman Jr. and Carolyn Grant (Berkeley: University of California Press, 1975), 143–73.

16. Glenn Melancon, "Honour in Opium? The British Declaration of War on China, 1835–1840," *International History Review* 21, no. 4 (1999): 854–74, and *Britain's China Policy and the Opium Crisis: Balancing Drugs, Violence and National Honour, 1833–1840* (Aldershot, UK: Ashgate, 2003).

17. For example, Keith McMahon, *The Fall of the God of Money: Opium Smoking in Nineteenth-Century China* (Lanham, MD: Rowman & Littlefield, 2002);

Man-houng Lin, *China Upside Down: Currency, Society, and Ideologies, 1808–1856* (Cambridge, MA: Harvard University Asia Center, 2006), chap. 2.

18. Yangwen Zheng, *The Social Life of Opium in China* (Cambridge: Cambridge University Press, 2005), 67.

19. David A. Bello, *Opium and the Limits of Empire: Drug Prohibition in the Chinese Interior, 1729–1850* (Cambridge, MA: Harvard University Asia Center, 2005), 1.

20. James M. Polachek, *The Inner Opium War* (Cambridge, MA: Harvard University Press, 1992).

21. Hosea Ballou Morse, *The Chronicles of the East India Company Trading to China, 1635–1834* (Oxford: Clarendon Press, 1926), vol. 4, 151, 326–27.

22. According to Morse, the first Company reference to actual dealings in opium at Canton was in May 1780. Morse, *Chronicles of the East India Company*, vol. 2, 51.

23. IOR/G/12/76, India Office Records and Private Papers, British Library.

24. William Milburn, *Oriental Commerce; Containing a Geographical Description of the Principal Places in the East Indies, China, and Japan* (London: Black, Parry, 1813), vol. 2, 483.

25. John Barrow, *Travels in China, Containing Descriptions, Observations, and Comparisons, Made and Collected in the Course of a Short Residence at the Imperial Palace of Yuen-Min-Yuen, and on a Subsequent Journey through the Country from Pekin to Canton in Which It is Attempted to Appreciate the Rank That the Extraordinary Empire May Be Considered to Hold in the Scale of Civilized Nations* (London: Cadell and Davies, 1804), 152.

26. Figures from Timothy Brook and Bob Tadashi Wakabayashi, "Opium's History in China," in *Opium Regimes: China, Britain, and Japan, 1839–1952*, ed. Timothy Brook and Bob Tadashi Wakabayashi (Berkeley: University of California Press, 2000), 6.

27. Fraser, Plowden, and Millett to Court of Directors, 28 January 1827, IOR G/12/286, British Library.

28. Robert Morrison, *Notices Concerning China, and the Port of Canton, also a Narrative of the Affair of the English Frigate Topaze, 1821–22; with Remarks on Homicides, and an Account of the Fire of Canton* (Malacca: Printed at the Mission Press, 1823), 50.

29. Fraser, Plowden, and Millett, Canton, to Court of Directors.

30. Charles Marjoribanks, *Letter to the Right Hon. Charles Grant, President of the Board of Control: On the Present State of British Intercourse with China* (London: J. Hatchard, 1833), 20, 22.

31. "Free Trade with China," *Canton Register* 7, no. 5 (2 February 1834): 19; original emphasis.

32. James Holman, *Voyage Round the World, Including Travels in Africa, Asia, Australasia, America, etc. etc. from 1827 to 1832* (London: Smith, Elder, 1834), vol., 4, 93, 254, 256.

33. Clarke Abel, *Narrative of a Journey in the Interior of China, and of a Voyage to and from That Country, in the Year 1816 and 1817: Containing an Account of the Most Interesting Transactions of Lord Amherst's Embassy to the Court of Pekin, and*

*Observations on the Countries Which It Visited* (London: Orme and Brown, 1818), 215.

34. George Bennett, *Wanderings in New South Wales, Batavia, Pedir Coast, Singapore, and China. Being the Journal of a Naturalist in Those Countries, during 1832, 1833, and 1834* (London: Richard Bentley, 1834), vol. 2, 23–25.

35. C. [Charles] Toogood Downing, *The Fan Qui in China in 1836–1837* (London: Henry Colburn, 1838), vol. 1, 48–49, and vol. 3, 169, 175–76, 182, 192–93.

36. James Brabazon Urmston, *Observations on the China Trade: And on the Importance and Advantages of Removing It from Canton, to Some Other Part of the Coast of That Empire* (London: Printed for private circulation only by G. Woodfall, 1834), iii–iv, 84, 86–87.

37. Marjoribanks, *Letter to the Right Hon. Charles Grant*, 16–20.

38. George Thomas Staunton, *Remarks on the British Relations with China, and the Proposed Plans for Improving Them*, 2nd ed. (London: E. Lloyd, 1836), 69.

39. John Francis Davis, *The Chinese: A General Description of That Empire and Its Inhabitants* (London: Charles Knight, 1836), vol. 2, 432, 436.

40. Walter Henry Medhurst, *China: Its State and Prospects, with Special Reference to the Spread of the Gospel; Containing Allusions to the Antiquity, Extent, Population, Civilization, Literature, and Religion of the Chinese* (London: J. Snow, 1838), 85, 87, 92, 93–94.

41. Jessie Gregory Lutz, *Opening China: Karl A. Gützlaff and Sino-Western Relations, 1822–1852* (Grand Rapids, MI: William B. Eerdmans, 2008), especially 68, 78–79; and Karl F. A. Gützlaff, *Journal of Three Voyages along the Coast of China in 1831, 1832, & 1833, with Notices of Siam, Corea, and the Loo-Choo Islands* (London: Frederick Westley and A. H. Davis, 1834).

42. Robert Morrison, *Notices Concerning China*, 67.

43. G. [George] Tradescant Lay, *Trade with China: A Letter Addressed to the British Public on Some of the Advantages That Would Result from an Occupation of the Bonin Islands* (London: Royston and Brown, 1837), 9–10.

44. "Means of Doing Good in China," *Chinese Repository* 7, no. 4 (August 1838): 193–97.

45. *Canton Register* 14, no. 26 (29 June 1841): supplement, n.p.

46. G. [George] Tradescant Lay, *The Chinese as They Are: Their Moral, Social, and Literary Character* (London: W. Ball, 1841), 3–4, 8, 12.

47. *Canton Register* 4, no. 13 (4 July 1831): 62, and *Canton Register* 4, no. 15 (2 August 1831): 75.

48. *Canton Register* 1, no. 5 (15 January 1828): 17.

49. *Canton Register* 1, no. 7 (11 February 1828): 27.

50. *Canton Register* 1, no. 18 (3 May 1828): 72.

51. *Canton Register* 1, no. 33 (23 August 1828): 134.

52. *Canton Register* 5, no. 20 (20 December 1832): 141–42; original emphasis.

53. *Canton Register* 5, no. 6 (17 March 1832): 33.

54. *Chinese Repository* 1, no. 1 (May 1832): 31.

55. *Chinese Repository* 1, no. 4 (August 1832): 159.

56. "Description of the City of Canton," *Chinese Repository* 2, no. 7 (November 1833): 299–301.

57. "Free Trade with China," *Chinese Repository* 2, no. 8 (December 1833): 363.

58. Robert Philip, *No Opium! Or, Commerce and Christianity, Working Together for Good in China: A Letter to James Cropper, Esq., of Liverpool* (London: Ward, 1835).

59. Edicts from heads of provincial government, 23 November 1836 and 13 December 1836, enclosed in Elliot to Palmerston, 7 February 1837, in *Correspondence Relating to China*, 183–87.

60. A Resident in China, *British Intercourse with Eastern Asia* (London: Edward Suter, 1836), 30.

61. For example: "First Annual Report of the General Committee of the Canton Chamber of Commerce," *Chinese Repository* 6, no. 7 (November 1837): 331–32; "Second Annual Report of the Committee of the Canton General Chamber of Commerce," *Chinese Repository* 7, no. 7 (November 1838): 388.

62. "Premium for an Essay on the Opium Trade," *Chinese Repository* 5, no. 9 (January 1837): 413.

63. *Chinese Repository* 5, no. 12 (April 1837): 546–53.

64. "Premium of One Hundred Pounds Sterling, for an Essay on the Opium Trade," *Chinese Repository* 8, no. 8 (December 1839): 425–26.

65. John Slade, *Notices on the British Trade to the Port of Canton; with Some Translations of Chinese Official Papers Relative to That Trade* (London: Smith Elder, 1830), 65–66.

66. Downing, *Fan Qui*, vol. 3, 171, 178, 181.

67. *Canton Press* 3, no. 51 (25 August 1838): n.p.

68. *Canton Register* 1, no. 15 (12 April 1828): 57.

69. *Canton Register* 5, no. 1 (2 January 1832): 4.

70. *Canton Register* 9, no. 9 (1 March 1836): 34; original emphasis.

71. *Canton Press* 5, no. 34 (23 May 1840): n.p.

72. McMahon, *God of Money*, 4.

73. Richard J. Grace, *Opium and Empire: The Lives and Careers of William Jardine and James Matheson* (Montreal: McGill–Queen's University Press, 2014), 85, 340–42.

74. *Canton Register* 11, no. 35 (28 August 1838): 142

75. *Canton Register* 11, no. 39 (25 September 1838): 157–58.

76. "Opium: Its Beneficial Effects on Mr. Wilberforce and Mr. Crabbe," *Canton Register* 11, no. 44 (30 October 1838): 176..

77. "The Confessions of an Opium-Seller in China—a British Subject," *Canton Press* 5, no. 28 (11 April 1840): n.p.

78. *Canton Press* 5, no. 28 (11 April 1840): n.p.

79. *Canton Press* 5, no. 29 (18 April 1840): n.p.

80. Marjoribanks, *Letter to the Right Hon. Charles Grant*, 6.

81. Urmston, *Observations on the China Trade*, 87.

82. Medhurst, *China*, 88.

83. "The Future," *Canton Register* 11, no. 6 (6 February 1838): 24.

84. Lay, *The Chinese as They Are*, 10.
85. *Canton Press* 5, no. 7 (16 November 1839): n.p.
86. *Canton Press* 5, no. 10 (7 December 1839): n.p.
87. "Local News," *Canton Press* 5, no. 17 (25 January 1840).
88. "Confessions of an Opium-Seller in China," n.p; original emphasis.
89. *Canton Press* 5, no. 26 (28 March 1840): n.p.; original emphasis.
90. *Canton Press* 5, no. 28 (11 April 1840): n.p.; original emphasis.
91. *Canton Press* 1, no. 44 (9 July 1836): 345–47; *Chinese Repository* 5, no. 3 (July 1836): 138–44. The translated memorial can be found in Alan Baumler, ed., *Modern China and Opium: A Reader* (Ann Arbor: University of Michigan Press, 2001), 6–11.
92. Elliot to Foreign Office, 27 July 1836, in *Correspondence Relating to China*, 138.
93. *Canton Press* 2, no. 5 (8 October 1836): n.p.
94. Elliot to Foreign Office, 10 October 1836, in *Correspondence Relating to China*, 138.
95. *Chinese Repository* 5, no. 9 (January 1837): 390–405.
96. Elliot to Palmerston, 2 February 1837, in *Correspondence Relating to China*, 153.
97. Matheson to Grant, 20 October 1837, in Le Pichon, *China Trade and Empire*, 31.
98. *Canton Press* 4, no. 20 (19 January 1839): n.p.
99. *Canton Press* 4, no. 16 (22 December 1838): n.p.
100. *Canton Press* 4, no. 17 (29 December 1838): n.p.
101. *Canton Press* 4, no. 26 (2 March 1839): n.p.; original emphasis.
102. *Canton Register* 12, no. 5 (29 January 1839): n.p. It was not only the foreigners who blamed the Chinese for smuggling: Governor-General Ruan Yuan (who, at least according to British sources, like other higher-level provincial officials was not involved in opium smuggling) also accused the hong merchants of aiding the foreigners by providing them with the means for distributing opium. Betty Peh-T'i Wei, *Ruan Yuan, 1794–1849: The Life and Work of a Major Scholar Official in Nineteenth Century China before the Opium War* (Hong Kong: Hong Kong University Press, 2006), 156–57.
103. Le Pichon, *China Trade and Empire*, 325, note 11. On the Parsis, see Jesse Palsetia, "The Parsis of India and the Opium Trade in China," *Contemporary Drug Problems* 35 (2008): 647–78.
104. *Chinese Repository* 5, no. 8 (December 1836): 367–70; original emphasis. On Innes, see John M. Carroll, *Canton Days: British Life and Death in China* (Lanham, MD: Rowman & Littlefield, 2020), 1–2, 61–64.
105. "Another Reader": *Chinese Repository* 5, no. 9 (January 1837): 407–12; Innes: *Chinese Repository* 5, no. 11 (March 1837): 524–27. .
106. Keating: *Chinese Repository* 5, no. 12 (April 1837): 560–71; Innes: *Chinese Repository* 6, no. 1 (May 1837): 40–44.
107. *Chinese Repository* 6, no. 2 (June 1837): 92–96.

108. Robert Bennet Forbes, *Letters from China: The Canton-Boston Correspondence of Robert Bennet Forbes, 1838–1840*, ed. Sarah Forbes Hughes (Mystic, CT: Mystic Seaport Museum, 1996), 73.

109. Forbes, *Letters from China*, 74–75; original emphasis.

110. *Canton Press* 4, no. 14 (8 December 1838): n.p., *Canton Register* 11, no. 50 (11 December 1838): 101–2; Innes to Howqua, 6 December 1838, enclosed in Elliot to Palmerston, 2 January 1839, in *Correspondence Relating to China*, 330–31.

111. "Stoppage of the Trade," *Canton Press* 4, no. 15 (15 December 1838): n.p.; "Letter from the Hong Merchants," *Canton Press* 4, no. 16 (22 December 1838): n.p.

112. Elliot to Innes, 11 December 1838; Innes to Elliot, 13 December 1838; both enclosed in Elliot to Palmerston, 2 January 1839, in *Correspondence Relating to China*, 331.

113. Observations by Elliot at general meeting, 17 December 1838; Public notice, 18 December 1838; both enclosed in Elliot to Palmerston, 2 January 1839, in *Correspondence Relating to China*, 332–33.

114. On managing British subjects in China, see Robert Bickers, "Legal Fiction: Extraterritoriality as an Instrument of British Power in China in the 'Long Nineteenth Century,'" in *Empire in Asia: A New Global History*, vol. 2, ed. Donna Brunero and Brian P. Farrell (London: Bloomsbury Academic, 2018), 53–80.

115. Elliot to Palmerston, 2 January 1839, in *Correspondence Relating to China*, 327.

116. Elliot to Palmerston, 2 January 1839, in *Correspondence Relating to China*, 329.

117. Innes to Elliot, 17 May 1839, enclosed in Elliot to Palmerston, 14 June 1839, in *Correspondence Relating to China*, 422.

118. Prefect of Canton to Elliot, enclosed in Elliot to Palmerstone, 18 May 1839, in *Correspondence Relating to China*, 412–13.

119. 8 June 1839, enclosed in Innes to Elliot, 12 June 1839, in *Correspondence Relating to China*, 426–27.

120. *Canton Press* 6, no. 5 (31 October 1840), n.p., and *Canton Register* 13, no. 43 (27 October 1840): 224; also quoted in Lindsay Ride and May Ride, *An East India Company Cemetery: Protestant Burials in Macao*, ed. Bernard Mellor (Hong Kong: Hong Kong University Press, 1996), 224.

121. "Captain Charles Elliot's Illegal Acts," *Canton Register* 13, no. 48 (1 December 1840): 257.

122. *Canton Press* 3, no. 37 (19 May 1838): n.p.

123. "Opium," *Canton Register* 11, no. 24 (12 June 1838): 95–97.

124. *Canton Press* 4, no. 27 (9 March 1839): n.p.

125. *Canton Press* 7, no. 36 (4 June 1842): n.p.

126. Madhavi Thampi, "Parsis in the China Trade," *Revista de Cultura/Review of Culture*, international edition, 10 (2004): 22. Approximately one quarter of the chests surrendered were owned by Parsi merchants.

127. Matheson to Jardine, 1 May 1839, MS JM C 5/4, JMA. Also in Le Pichon, *China Trade and Empire*, 369.

220    Chapter Five

128. *Canton Press* 4, no. 38 (25 May 1839): n.p; *Canton Register* 12, no. 22 (28 May 1839): 101; *Chinese Repository* 8, no. 1 (May 1839): 32–35; also enclosed in Elliot to Palmerston, 29 May 1839, in *Correspondence Relating to China*, 418–20.

129. *Canton Register* 12, no. 51 (24 December 1839): 217.

130. "Justice to the China Merchants," *Canton Register* 13, no. 14 (7 April 1840): 71–72.

131. *Canton Press* 5, no. 37 (13 June 1840): n.p; *Canton Register* 13, no. 26 (30 June 1840): 126.

132. "Fallacies of the Opium Question," *Canton Register* 13, no. 30 (28 July 1840): 150; original emphasis.

133. "Remarks on the Present Crisis in the Opium Traffic," *Chinese Repository* 8, no. 1 (May 1839): 3, 6–8.

134. "Premium of One Hundred Pounds Sterling, for an Essay on the Opium Trade," *Chinese Repository* 8, no. 8 (December 1839): 425–26.

135. "Prospects and Probable Consequences of War between the Governments of China and Great Britain," *Chinese Repository* 8, no. 9 (January 1840): 444.

136. *Canton Register* 12, no. 30 (23 July 1839): 130.

137. *Canton Press* 5, no. 15 (11 January 1840): n.p.

138. *Canton Press* 5, no. 16 (18 January 1840): n.p.

139. *Canton Register* 13, no. 11 (17 March 1840): 55–56.

140. *Canton Register* 13, no. 16 (21 April 1840): 75–78.

141. *Canton Register* 13, no. 29 (21 July 1840): 144.

142. *Canton Register* 13, no. 4 (28 January 1840): 18.

143. A. [Algernon] S. [Sydney] Thelwall, *The Iniquities of the Opium Trade with China; Being a Development of the Main Causes Which Exclude the Merchants of Great Britain from the Advantages of an Unrestricted Commercial Intercourse with That Vast Empire* (London: W.H. Allen, 1839), 2, 61, 173; original emphasis.

144. *Canton Press* 5, no. 7 (16 November 1839): n.p.

145. *Canton Register* 12, no. 48 (26 November 1839): 197.

146. *Canton Register* 12, no. 44 (29 October 1839): 176.

147. *Canton Register* 13, no. 3 (21 January 1840): 14.

148. *Canton Press* 5, no. 44 (1 August 1840): n.p.

149. *Canton Press* 5, no. 11 (14 December 1839): n.p; original emphasis.

150. *Canton Register* 13, no. 25 (23 June 1840): 115.

151. *Canton Register* 13, no. 21 (26 May 1840): 101–2.

152. *Friend of India*, 25 February 1841, reprinted in *Canton Press* 6, no. 37 (12 June 1841): n.p.

153. Matheson to Jardine, 23 August 1841, MS JM C5/7, JMA; original emphasis. Also in Le Pichon, *China Trade and Empire*, 499.

154. Robert Jocelyn, *Six Months with the Chinese Expedition: Leaves from a Soldier's Note-Book* (London: John Murray, 1841), 5.

155. Duncan McPherson, *Two Years in China: Narrative of the Chinese Expedition, from Its Formation in April, 1840, to the Treaty of Peace in August, 1842* (London: Saunders and Otley, 1842), 245–49.

156. Keith Stewart Mackenzie, *Narrative of the Second Campaign in China* (London: Richard Bentley, 1842), 163–64.

*Epilogue*

# China Freed

Many of the men in this book hoped a more aggressive policy would encourage the Qing government to relax its restrictions on foreign trade. Some wished the Western nations, especially the British, would help end the Canton System and usher in an era of freer trade. Still others supported preemptive policies that might prevent war. In August 1836, Arthur Saunders Keating insisted in the *Chinese Repository* that although "as a principle" he was opposed to war and had "no wish to see its horrors brought here by any of the civilized nations of the western world," it was the "moral duty" of one of the foreign countries coming into increased contact with China to sign a commercial treaty before "quarrels of a murderous nature spring out of misunderstandings." The United States had already sent envoys to Cochin China and Siam, and Keating hoped a similar "experiment" might be tried at Peking. The "evil day" of conflict could be delayed. But "come, at length, it must; if a treaty of commerce be not effected, by which the subjects of both the native and foreign powers may at once be protected and controlled." Keating believed a "proper interference" would prevent "the catastrophe which may else be drawn on the Chinese empire by the arrogance of its rulers."[1]

Even if force was occasionally advocated, there was rarely any consensus. Some of these accounts were attempts to reduce, rather than promote, the likelihood of war. In the last page of his lengthy record of his time in China, Charles Toogood Downing explained that although "seen in their very worst phase up the Canton river, the stranger cannot help thinking highly of the Chinese." With "kindly feelings" toward the "blackhaired race," he "most heartily" wished they would acquiesce to "a friendly commercial treaty" before "their weak and defenceless condition may tempt some of the bolder nations of the west to resort to unpleasant expedients—the *ultima ratio regum*."[2]

Citing the Chinese proverb about a man at the bottom of a well, who judges others without forming a "thorough acquaintance with them," Walter Henry Medhurst wrote that "the Chinese have been at the bottom of the well, with regard to foreigners." But he also insisted that "we are not unfrequently at the bottom of the well, with regard to them." Medhurst aimed to "bring each party to the brink, and exhibit them to each other."[3]

And come to the brink they eventually would. The result, however, would be the Opium War and then the Treaty of Nanking, the first of twenty-odd "unequal treaties" imposed on China over the next ninety years. This one required China to pay a huge indemnity (twenty-one million silver dollars, over three years). It ended the system that since the mid-1700s had restricted Western trade to Canton, opened four more ports to foreign trade, and granted the right to appoint British consuls at all five ports. And it ceded to Britain "in perpetuity" Hong Kong (regrettably for James Brabazon Urmston, not Chusan). A minor conflict in the history of the British Empire, the Opium War is still seen by many Chinese people as a watershed—the beginning of "modern" China. Even after almost two centuries, both the war and the treaty are often raised as examples of foreign aggression and Chinese victimhood, especially when critics in Britain and other Western nations comment on human rights or other controversial matters.[4]

None of this, however, should suggest the war was inevitable, or that all Britons who visited or lived in China were interested only in opening it by force or in expanding the opium trade. The war was a break with previous British policy, not a continuation of it, and the opium crisis was the trigger rather than the cause.[5] Lord Palmerston's decision to send an expedition to China was based on several factors; making a nation of opium addicts was not one of them. As we have seen, from the Macartney embassy in the 1790s all the way to the Opium War, the solutions for improving Britain's footing in China were as diverse as the explanations for why the Qing government had confined trade with the West to Canton.

To be sure, by the time war came, many Britons in China had lost patience with peaceful methods and were ready to see their objective met through force. In June 1840, with almost everyone now waiting out the war in Macao, an anonymous writer in the *Canton Register* opposed the rumored appointment of George Thomas Staunton as the next superintendent of trade. "Sir George the negotiator" was a man of those East India Company days, when "tea was every *thing*, national honour *nothing*." His appointment (which never occurred and may never have even been considered) would lead only to "deception, humbug, and future danger from the Chinese; and so, after all our sufferings, another disgraceful cloud over our country, which few alive

Figure E.1. Henry John Temple, 3rd Viscount Palmerston, 1840, by John Samuelson Templeton, after Sir William Charles Ross, printed by M & N Hanhart, published by Thomas McLean, lithograph. National Portrait Gallery, London

will live to see the sun shine through." The solution was not negotiations: it was "long 32 pounders."[6]

Not everyone, however, favored such a combative approach. In November, five months after the expeditionary force had reached Canton from Singapore, "A British Subject" argued in the *Register* that although many foreigners suspected the Qing commanders were trying to buy time to build up their defenses, there was still good reason to believe Daoguang wanted to prevent more bloodshed:

> To wish for war, general and determined hostilities, which would result in so much misery and bloodshed, is not right in my view till all of the means fail. Besides this, would it expedite the business? Is our exchequer prepared for such an event? And what would be the end at last? The general trade would be recommenced, but surely not under very favourable auspices, after myriads of families had been ruined, inland commerce destroyed, cities ransacked and burnt, and

perhaps the energies of the country for a time annihilated, and its resources impoverished.... Let us then hope, that in spite of all our fears and predictions, that China may yet be opened to an unrestricted intercourse with foreign and Christian nations, and *that* without the necessity of war.[7]

They also disagreed on how easy China might be to defeat. Some believed the Qing would be powerless against the British or other foreign powers. Charles Downing described the "art of war in the Celestial Empire" as "probably at as low an ebb as it possibly can be." The navy was "even more contemptible" than the army, "the whole fleet of men-of-war having been known to fly before a single, unarmed, foreign merchantman." Cannon were poorly made, with gunpowder so weak "the cannon-balls appear often to fall out of the mouths of the guns."[8] Others were less sure. "We should be sorry to underrate the power of our opponents," an anonymous merchant "long established in business in China" wrote to the *Times* in September 1839. Even though China was the "greatest monarchy in the world," it was less powerful than "third rate" states in the West. Its people were unused to war, its soldiers poorly equipped for a "long and hazardous campaign." Still, he warned, "the Celestial Government is a mighty Colossus capable of the most powerful exertions for a short season, in time of need backed by the hordes of Mongolians, and able to march any number of soldiers in the field, if there is money sufficient to pay them."[9]

Even after the hostilities in early November 1839 following Charles Elliot's order to blockade the Pearl River, opinions varied. The *Canton Press* argued that the Qing could never protect a coast almost two thousand miles long. The historical record showed China was not "impregnable": even the Japanese had been able to attack in the fifteenth and sixteenth centuries. The *Press* implored Lin Zexu and his colleagues to "repent of their former misdeeds and retrace their steps to the ancient policy of the country, that has kept it safe since times immemorial." Too many lives were at stake, and the Qing soldiers had already begun to "grumble at the hardships to which they are exposed."[10]

Two years later, the *Press* noted how the Qing forces were putting up a more effective resistance than anyone had anticipated. But had the British pursued the war as effectively as they could have? Unless more troops were sent by the early part of the next year, "we may expect that year also to pass over as the present has, nearly done, viz without approaching to the attainment of the objects contemplated by the Expedition."[11] John Francis Davis, now back in Britain, found the "moral power and influence" of the Qing Empire over its neighbors a "standing miracle," given the "real weakness and inefficiency of its military institutions." He saw "every reason" to believe

China was "as weak and unwarlike" as when the Manchus conquered it three hundred years earlier.[12]

One of the few points of agreement was that the expedition needed better leadership. In November 1840 a merchant critical of Elliot's plans to negotiate with the Qing authorities wrote in the *Register* that the British had done "nothing whatever to exhibit our power." Instead, they had suffered and submitted to "new outrages."[13] The "great delay" in settling relations with China, the *Register* explained one week later, had been "a matter of surprise and disappointment to all men" and had "tended much to break down commercial confidence all over the eastern world."[14] "One of the People" wrote that Elliot seemed to have forgotten "there is still in China a British mercantile community." There had been no word from him since the arrival of his "ill-fated" expedition. "We are without any information as to what has been or is intended to be done." The *Register* concurred: the "whole proceedings" had been "quite incomprehensible."[15]

Patience wore even thinner into the next year. In its account of the previous year's events, the *Press* observed in January 1841 that "every reader must be struck by the want of energy and decision that has marked the conduct of the Expedition."[16] "War," one merchant wrote the same month, "is a serious business, not a child's plaything: its horrors are not to be trifled with. . . . Is it *decent* that Great Britain should be bargaining for her rights like a petty trader with his wares?"[17] A reader submitted an open letter to Elliot insisting "the best service you can now perform is to leave us."[18] In an even more critical letter three weeks later, the same reader now signed himself as "Petreius"—after the celebrated Roman soldier during the Cimbrian War who killed his own tribune because he had "hesitated to attack the enemy." The Qing had ceded Chusan and Chuenpe (Chuanbi, a small island near the Bocca Tigris), but what had the British gained?[19]

In February the *Press* hoped the negotiations would be broken off soon, as the conditions obtained from the Qing were not as good as they could be.[20] The *Register* regretted the British had not won more than a "paltry indemnity" and the tiny island of Hong Kong. Why had Elliot taken Hong Kong, when the Qing authorities were reported to be willing to offer one or even more ports on the northeast coast? Throughout the negotiations, the British had paid too much deference to the "most assuming and insolent government in the world" and too much veneration for the emperor, "already more than sufficiently inflated by the adoration that is paid to him by his own subjects."[21]

By mid-March, James Matheson wrote to William Jardine in London, the fighting had resumed and Elliot's blockade was hurting the trade. "Canton is almost abandoned by its inhabitants, and all valuable property removed in consequence of the approach of our forces, and how or when this state of chaos is to end it is impossible to hazard a conjecture."[22] When Elliot tried to reopen the trade later that month, Matheson wrote how the sense of "personal security" and "security of property" necessary for conducting trade was still lacking and was "not in the power of man" to instill. "It is the result of *circumstances* and not to be done by 100,000 victorious bayonets."[23] The *Press* noted it had been more than nine months since the expedition began. But where were the results? Elliot could have taken Canton, but in his "singular moderation" had instead agreed to let foreign ships trade at Whampoa. "Are we already becoming such good friends of the Chinese, that means of annoying their government are no longer to be resorted to?" From the day the expedition arrived, "no regular plan" had been followed: "The intentions of one day have given place to new resolves on the next, and the Chinese were sufficiently astute to take measure of the Plenipotentiary's capabilities, and to counteract his timid and vacillating policy."[24]

Even when the *Press* in early May 1841 expressed pleasant surprise that the temporary trade agreement Elliot brokered had worked "so uninterruptedly" for one month, it explained that there was every reason not to be optimistic.[25] The *Register* warned readers not to be too sanguine about the resumption of trade at Canton until "the establishment of political & unrestricted commercial relations with the whole empire." And the "unaccountable delays" in Elliot's movements, and his many tactical mistakes, might impede this. There was still no indemnity, "reparation for insults and injuries," or "certain security that persons and property in future trading with China shall we [*sic*] protected from insult or injury, and that their trade and commerce *be maintained on a proper footing*. . . . It must be apparent to all Chinese statesmen that in England's case, the national honour and interests have been sacrificed to personal vanity and individual profit."[26] "Are we at war with the Chinese or not," asked the *Press* in early October 1841.[27]

Serious criticism came also from India and England. In late January 1841 a group of British merchants in Bombay petitioned the House of Lords with the usual list of grievances. It had been nearly two years since the opium crisis began, and "by the latest intelligence its speedy re-establishment on a firm, stable, and honorable footing, continues uncertain."[28] Even if no more could have been expected from Elliot, "who has long ago proved to the satisfaction of every body his utter incompetence for the task which he has undertaken," claimed the *Englishman* in February, "a great deal more was expected by the British nation from an expedition quite strong enough to have enforced any demand, reasonable or unreasonable, and certainly amply sufficient to have obtained such a settlement as was required, which would have been as advantageous to the Chinese as to ourselves." There was only one consolation: "A fresh rupture must soon take place, arising out of the smuggling trade, when it may be hoped that some wiser man than Capt. Elliot may be found to bring matters to a settlement."[29]

In April the *Friend of India* criticized the way the British commanders, especially Elliot, had handled matters and the "disgraceful" peace they had made.[30] In a letter originally printed in the *Sun* and subsequently reprinted in the *Register*, a Briton who had once lived in India complained to Palmerston that based on his "tolerable insight into the Chinese character," Britain's "whole course of dealing with "this race of ignorant men, who really are, for the most part, in a state of semi-barbarism," had been "impolitic and vain." The appointment of Napier had been misguided, but that of Elliot was even worse. From the moment he had arrived at Canton, there had been "a sort of Chinese incubus on his mind, cramping his energies, enfeebling his motions," and "paralyzing his whole powers of thought and action." He had shown "such pusillanimous forbearance, that the Chinese themselves must have been at once both gratified and astonished." Elliot had "forfeited, by his weak and vacillating conduct, the confidence of all." He should be "instantly recalled" and replaced by "a negotiator of known talent."[31]

Some now even argued that Lord Napier would have been better. The *Atlas* asked why the British were settling for Hong Kong and why the recent expedition to Chusan, which cost so many British lives, had ever been mounted. "NAPIER would have been the man for this expedition. A man who would have written out his terms and kept his rockets flying till they were granted should have been the leader of this squadron."[32] A subsequent *Atlas* article described Elliot as the "most imbecile and wrong-minded creature that ever cursed the service of a country." So far, the history of the war had been "more like an extravagant tale of an army of heroes controlled by a council of idiots than like a detail of real facts occurring in the present day."[33]

Downriver at Hong Kong, some worried that Elliot's low esteem among the British merchants might jeopardize the long-term prospects of the new acquisition. Matheson, who earlier had supported Elliot's restraint and had witnessed the Union Flag being raised there on 26 January 1841, wrote in August to Jardine (who was less convinced of the value of Hong Kong) in London that "I fear Elliot's unpopularity will in some degree descend on his pet child, Hong Kong." Matheson urged Jardine to use his influence in London to retain the island, or at least "some place near this river, where alone the English are known and multitudes of natives are ready to become our subjects and trade with us." But he still preferred Hong Kong, which once developed and settled, "could hardly fail to become a considerable emporium."[34] Part of the reason for Matheson's concern was pragmatic: in early July he had reported to Jardine that their firm's building at Hong Kong was "going on apace" and they had eight thousand bales of cotton stored there.[35]

The *Press* and the *Register* also wavered and bickered as they had for so long—now about the potential of Hong Kong. In January 1841 the *Press* proclaimed that "for an *independent* British settlement no situation can possibly be more favorably chosen than Hong Kong."[36] But when the *Calcutta Courier* praised Elliot and referred to the British traders in China as "grumblers," the *Register* in April dismissed the cession of Hong Kong as "indeed, nothing!"[37] And was the British government even committed to retaining the island? In August the *Press* argued that it was "extremely hazardous" for any British subjects to "spend much money upon such buildings at Hongkong from which Island the British protection may be withdrawn at any moment."[38] In November the *Register* announced that a medical committee had declared Hong Kong "a place utterly unfit for the residence of English troops."[39] Although the paper had to retract these comments in the following issue after learning the troops had been unable to land there because of a lack of barracks, not because of the "general unhealthiness" of the island, it added that according to rumor public money was being spent on making roads "instead of erecting shelter for the men who are to fight our battles in this country."[40]

Even after the British had occupied Hong Kong for one full year, there was little agreement on its potential. By January 1842 the *Register* had changed its tune, observing that the number of new buildings was rising and that "the greatest perseverance and industry prevail in the erection of godowns and wharves"—though it then observed how many "daring and successful" robberies had been committed.[41] The *Press* took a similar approach, noting how "great activity" was taking place and houses and warehouses were "springing up in all directions," though also commenting on the crime.[42] A *Press* contributor complained that the island still lacked public buildings: "No forum, circus, agora, theatre; and worse than all, no Temple of religious Worship"; fortunately, the Chinese merchants had "evinced much good taste" in their private buildings.[43] In February an "Idler in Hong Kong" wrote that only the "most egregious ignorance" of the "true principles of political economy" and "modern colonization" could prevent Hong Kong from becoming a self-sustaining colony and "one of the most important commercial entrepots in the east." Yet in the same issue the *Press* editors, having recently made a special expedition there, argued that although the island had many trading advantages, it also had numerous drawbacks, among them the hot summers and cold winters.[44]

In a lengthy comparison with Singapore, in May 1842 the *Press* concluded that "spots better qualified" for a town could have been than the present site at Hong Kong. Kowloon, across the harbor, for example, offered better weather with its southernly winds and a "fine level space" for a town.[45] The fact that all public works were being discontinued almost proved that the British government had never intended to occupy the island permanently and make it a commercial center; "and if so will be a severe disappointment to many who have already invested large sums of money in building there."[46] When a contributor to the *Press* warned in June against settling in Hong Kong, another replied that the island was more likely to become "a place possessing a thriving trade" than "a receptacle for all the scoundrels of the immediate neighbourhood."[47] After the *Register* suggested Hong Kong would become the "future capital of Anglo-China," the *Press* doubted whether the British government was committed to retaining the island, cautioning the *Register* against trying to "puff Hongkong into greater importance than it deserves."[48]

Figure E.2. *Harbour of Hong Kong.* In Thomas Allom, *China, in a Series of Views, Displaying the Scenery, Architecture, and Social Habits, of That Ancient Empire.* London: Fisher, Son, & Co., 1843

Navy men who visited Hong Kong during the war also had their doubts. Keith Stewart Mackenzie found the inhabitants "industrious and obliging": they seemed to have been "very peaceably disposed" and had not shown "any marked approbation or disapprobation" of their new rulers. But he saw little of worth in Hong Kong apart from its proximity to Canton and the "extensive quarries of granite with which the island abounds." Kowloon would have been "a far more preferable and eligible site." Most of the new "native" subjects were only provisioners and laborers who had followed the British from Canton, and few Chinese or British merchants were living there. Nevertheless, "extensive improvements" were underway and the inhabitants seemed "fully alive to the benefits of our rule." Should the British decide to retain Hong Kong, many Chinese "of wealth and respectability" would "eagerly embrace" the protection of British rule. Before long, the inhabitants would be "enrolled among the peaceable and loyal subjects of our Gracious Queen."[49]

Throughout the Opium War, some China Britons remained uncomfortable about how it was being fought. "We ought not to aim at the legs, but at the heart," the *Press* explained in August 1841. But it also reminded readers that "England can have no ambitious views upon territorial possessions and aggrandizement. It cannot desire the humiliation of China, nor be stimulated by revenge to goad it into concession."[50] "War is already bad enough," wrote "Stickler for National Rights" the following month, "but when waged against millions of innocent lives, it becomes horrible." It was therefore crucial to "punish" only those who took up arms against the British, and "never to be hard upon the innocent":

> Neutralize the efforts of the natives, shew them their true interests, treat them as you would the Chinese immigrants at Singapore, promise them protection and keep your word, and you may rest assured, that victory will be easy and the settlement of affairs speedy. If the brunt of the war is to fall upon the nation, let us beware, lest we become the extortioners, but let us be kind, generous and steady in our behavior, and soon we shall bless the hour in which we took this resolution.[51]

In late June 1842, as the war drew to a close, "Expedit" wrote in the *Register* that the opium trade put the British in an embarrassing situation. To make matters worse, some ships' captains had gone ashore in the Pearl River to an islet known to the foreigners as Dane's Island where, "without meeting with either insult of molestation, but merely out of wantonness," they had hauled an image out of a temple and smashed it to pieces by rolling it down a steep hill. Imagine, "Expedit" asked, if the British did such a thing in India, or foreigners in England. Even the often-bellicose *Register* agreed, and on both counts: "The conduct of the captains of vessels in entering a pagan temple, and destroying the images, deserves the severest reprehension, and can only arise from utter ignorance of the decencies of life and total recklessness."[52]

Both residents and visitors realized that preserving the peace after the war would be no easy task. "No sensible or humane person can desire another contest with the Chinese," an anonymous field officer wrote in 1843, "yet great skill and judgment will be required to avert the evil." It would be as necessary to protect the Chinese from "the violence of European adventurers, as the Europeans from the insults of the Chinese." The British must allay Chinese fears of any territorial aggrandizement. And if they interfered in the internal affairs of China, other European nations would do the same: "Wars, not confined to Asia, will be the too probable consequences."[53]

Their different and sometimes conflicting opinions notwithstanding, most agreed on two points: ordinary Chinese people would support the end of the Canton System and its restrictions, even by war, and an opened China would offer unlimited markets. "The Government of China is purposely absurd," explained George Tradescant Lay in 1841, before being appointed interpreter to the British expedition later that year, "but the people are reasonable in their views and conceptions." The Opium War was a chance not only to open China but perhaps even to install a new leadership, liberating the country from years of oppressive isolationism and creating countless new opportunities for commerce and evangelism. Once the "natives" realized China's government had changed, they would "rank with the most quiet, most happy, and best conducted subjects of the British empire." The "records of many rebellions" showed that China's "industrious and thriving people" were desperate for "a few draughts of freedom." Freed from the "Tartar yoke" and ruled by a "native prince," China would be opened to "all the fair appulses of commerce, religion, and science."[54]

Imagine the possibilities of unrestricted trade with the whole of China, the *Register* asked its readers in May 1841, even while reminding them not to be too optimistic about the resumption of trade at Canton until the British had secured "the establishment of political and unrestricted commercial relations" with the entire Qing Empire. "Let the English manufacturers contemplate the demand of nearly 400,000,000 customers, whose temperament fits them to be the most desirable as well as the most numerous customers in the world." A liberated China would matter even more to Britain in the nineteenth century than the discovery of the Americas had to Europe in the fifteenth. The "new world" had been "thinly peopled by savages and half-civilized communities." But in "*China freed*" the British would "*discover* 400,000,000 of the most ancient, the most industrious the most self-enjoying race in the world, without prejudice of religion or caste; the various climatics requiring clothing of all descriptions, from the warm and costly fur to the finest cambric." With the "two Americas" trying their best "to impede and to destroy" the demand for British manufactured goods, a freed China would be "a new world to England."[55]

Yet China freed never became as free or as new as the *Register* predicted. Even with Hong Kong a colony and four more ports open to foreign trade,

Canton remained the most important commercial and missionary center for another decade. Until the Treaty of Tientsin in 1858 during the Second Opium War, ratified two years later by the Convention of Peking, Westerners were limited to living and working in the treaty ports. Walter Medhurst wrote in 1850 that the only way a foreigner could travel in the interior was to dress and "pass" as a Chinese, which he had done in 1845 and then published his account in more than six hundred pages.[56] As in Canton, missionaries made few converts despite the efforts of Hudson Taylor, the legendary founder of the China Inland Mission, and Timothy Richard, better known as an organizer of relief efforts in Shandong and Shanxi and as an advocate of national reform.[57] The pioneering evangelist Griffith John, who went in 1861 with the London Missionary Society, blamed China's leaders for its many problems and believed that most Chinese people desired to be rid of their Manchu overlords. In 1877 he described China as "*dead—terribly* dead."[58]

As it had before the Opium War, the British community in China continued to produce prominent sinologists, interpreters and translators, and educators. One of George Lay's three sons, Horatio Nelson Lay, who studied Chinese under Karl Gützlaff, became acting British vice-consul in Shanghai and helped establish the Chinese Maritime Customs Service. He served as interpreter to Lord Elgin during the second war and played an important role in coercing the Qing delegation to accept the terms of the Treaty of Tientsin, partly by revealing from captured documents that the Qing's chief negotiator, Qiying, had referred to the British as "barbarians."[59] James Legge, who worked first in Malacca and then in Hong Kong, found more success in sinology than in evangelism.[60] Robert Hart revolutionized the Customs Service, which became not only Britain's "imperial cornerstone" in China but "an international civil service" and a massive knowledge-generating enterprise that published books, guides, translations, statistics, reports, charts, scientific data, and more.[61] The diplomat Thomas Francis Wade devised a system of transliterating Mandarin and in 1888 became the first professor of Chinese at Cambridge.[62] Herbert Allen Giles, also a sinologist and diplomat, popularized Chinese literature and culture for Western audiences, refined Wade's transliteration system and in 1897 succeeded him at Cambridge.[63] John Fryer helped introduce Western scientific works to China through his translations, later becoming a professor at the University of California at Berkeley.[64]

Still, British interests in China remained primarily economic. Yet even though the British controlled the largest share of its foreign trade for many decades, China never became the El Dorado many had hoped for.[65] Although by the late 1800s foreigners were more or less free to live and trade beyond the treaty ports, many became frustrated with existing institutional frameworks. They always had some sort of Chinese authority to deal with, even if it was often "formally reduced, even ceded" in treaty ports, concessions, and spheres of influence.[66] As they had in Canton, they continued to complain about the Chinese government and its restrictions, often using the local English press to draw attention to their plight. As in Canton, Britons in Shanghai and other treaty ports often faced an apathetic public and a critical press at home.[67] They frequently felt misunderstood by their compatriots, ignored and sometimes even betrayed by their own government.

Walter Henry Medhurst knew this all too well. Not the missionary, who died in London in 1857 after some forty years in Asia, but his son of the same name. Born in Batavia and like his father a talented linguist, the younger Medhurst had served as an interpreter during the Opium War and with the British consular service in several treaty ports, eventually in Shanghai. In 1868 he led an expedition to demand reparations after a missionary station in the city of Yangzhou was attacked. While in London in 1872 he wrote *The Foreigner in Far Cathay*, arguing that foreigners in China, whether merchants, missionaries, or consuls, had been misunderstood at home— usually seen in a light "by no means complimentary to the persons concerned." Though "numerous bulky volumes" had been written about China and its people, and communication with the West now "vastly extended," Medhurst was astonished by "how vague, and in some cases how erroneous," the prevalent notions remained of China and its relations with Britain.[68] Like so many of the China hands we have met, he aimed to set the record straight.

It was bad enough that the typical image of a "Chinaman" was a "quaint but stolid besotted creature, who smokes opium perpetually, and drowns his daughters as fast as they appear, whose everyday food consists of puppies, kittens, rats, and such like garbage; whose notions of honor, honesty, and courage, are of the loosest; and to whom cruelty is a pastime." Even worse was how little was known about the British and other foreign communities in China:

> The merchants are set down as adventurers, with whom smuggling is a habit, men of few scruples, violent, and ever ready to plunge the mother-country into war to serve their personal ends. Missionaries are characterized as indiscreet, officious, over-zealous, and peculiarly partial to appeals to the persuasive powers of the "inevitable gunboat;" whilst consuls and naval commanders are regarded as much too apt to abet both classes of residents, instead of restraining them within legitimate limits.

No one at home seemed to understand how the foreign presence was "on the whole humanizing and improving the Chinese." Or how Shanghai was on its way to becoming the "healthiest and most agreeable residence in the East," thanks neither to the British government nor to the local Chinese authorities but to "the perseverance and enterprise, individual and general, of the foreign settlers themselves." Medhurst promised to present foreigners in China "somewhat more worthily than they have had credit for"—and to prove that, "with a few drawbacks of character," the Chinese had "many interesting and even commendable traits."[69]

Unlike his father, who had partly blamed the British, especially the opium traders, for the state of Anglo–Chinese relations in the late 1830s, the junior Medhurst wished the British had pushed even harder during the two opium wars. Charles Elliot should have occupied Canton instead of just attacking it. Henry Pottinger should have headed for Peking at the "moment of triumph" instead of withdrawing to Canton. And Lord Elgin should have occupied more of Peking during the second war. Whereas the missionary had urged mutual restraint and understanding, his consul son believed the British should have dealt "the earliest blows" much, much earlier—when the Qing was still "comparatively strong"; when its court had not "succumbed to the influences of luxury and vice"; when corruption had not yet "wholly demoralized the administrative departments"; and when the empire still had "many master minds" who had not "lost the traditions of the vigorous and patriotic rule which had marked the reigns of the earlier Emperors of this dynasty, and the more complete contact with foreign progress and civilization."[70]

Medhurst rejected the "condemnatory tone" the British press had taken toward the foreign presence in China. Merchants had become so associated with the opium trade, and "the alleged obtrusion of it upon the Chinese by force," that they had almost become synonymous with adventurers and smugglers, vilified as "rapacious" and "aggressive." He urged his readers to dismiss the misconception that opium was "smuggled into, or forced upon, the country" or that "any moral turpitude of necessity attaches to the man who deals in the drug." Even back in the days when the Qing government strictly prohibited the opium traffic, it was tolerated by both local authorities in Canton and higher officials in Peking. The "indignation and patriotism" of "the famous Commissioner Lin" had created the impression, "which has since taken so strong a hold on the public mind," that the Opium War had been waged with the "unrighteous object" of forcing opium upon China. But the British demand for compensation for "the property arbitrarily seized" was "but one out of several grounds of complaint which then called for redress." In any case, importing opium had since been legalized by treaty, and the drug was now so "extensively" cultivated "upon their own soil" to reduce the demand for the Indian-grown product.[71]

It was also a mistake to assume, as the American press so often did, that only British firms imported opium. True, the British controlled the largest share, but they also dominated every other part of China's foreign trade. Nor in China did selling opium mean "any more demoralization of character" than selling beer, wine, or liquor did in Britain. On the contrary, anyone who knew anything of the "leading merchants in China" would have learned from *experience* that "in intelligence, integrity, worth, and liberality, they come behind none of the so-called merchant princes of Great Britain." Medhurst found it "almost an impertinence" even to try and dispute the unsavory features often attributed to them. His only criticism was that they rarely bothered even to learn spoken Chinese, which required little more than "an average intellect and a moderate share of determination" and would free them from "the domination of roguish brokers and compradores" and open the door to a "more extended acquaintance and friendly intercourse to the mutual advantage of both parties." There was "perhaps no country in the world" where British merchants were "so lamentably ignorant of the customs and resources of the locality" as they were in China—all because they did not understand the language.[72]

He had no more sympathy for those who, "for want of consideration or from mere prejudice," thought poorly of the work and character of missionaries (though he wished they could have left their denominational differences at home and not called attention to their influence by building "pretentious" foreign-style churches).[73] But it was the British consuls whose reputation he was most concerned about salvaging. Reminiscent of Staunton defending the Company's monopoly and the integrity of its officers, he noted the recent tendency in Britain to characterize China consuls "as officious, as aggressive, as fond of indulging a little brief authority, and as being too ready to claim naval assistance in the adjustment of questions." These were nothing but "the random verdicts of individuals who do not know our Consuls, and are simply ignorant of the difficulties by which they are beset." No one at home realized how hard these consuls had it: hounded by their countrymen to secure even more treaty privileges, yet confronted by the Qing authorities "in a spirit which goes far towards neutralizing their efforts to carry out that treaty on principles of justice to both parties."[74]

Medhurst did not flaunt his credentials as so many of the writers we have met did. But he nevertheless found ways throughout his book to demonstrate his expertise and authority. He was careful to distinguish his views from those of travelers, including by revealing his great familiarity with the customs, languages, practices, and "the character" of the Chinese. He blamed the unfounded impression, for example, of "a nation of infanticides" on "the stories which cursory visitors, even observing travellers, are apt to bring home." Such people invariably mentioned the "baby towers" where infants were left to die, "suspicious little bundles" floating in ponds and canals, carts said to be used to collect abandoned children, and miniature coffins placed throughout fields. Had they understood the language and been able to probe deeper, they would have realized how "the relics seen" were also sometimes used for deceased children. Although infanticide was practiced to an "infamous extent" in some towns and districts, it was much less common in others; Medhurst reckoned it occurred no more frequently than in European cities, "and then only with the object of concealing another act of frailty." The Chinese showed "a marked attachment" for their offspring, and one could barely set foot in a city or town without realizing that all those stories about infanticide had been exaggerated. "At every few steps in a Chinese street may be encountered a delighted father, or a decrepit grandame, proudly fondling a chubby child, dressed in all the colors of the rainbow, and loaded with as many amulets, charms, and ornaments as it can well can."[75]

Given Medhurst's claim about the "humanizing" effect of the foreign presence and the "many interesting and even commendable traits" of the Chinese, it may seem puzzling how pessimistic he became toward the end of his book about China and its relations with Britain and the other foreign nations. Any moral influence foreigners had been able to exert by their "mere presence" was "simply *nil*." Chinese people had not been improved by increased contact with foreigners or by adopting their ideas and habits, while the few Westernized Chinese that Medhurst had encountered were, with "very rare exceptions, most insufferable creatures." Nor had the introduction of Western technology made much difference in attitudes toward foreigners. He noted, for example, how even passengers who benefited from traveling in Western vessels (including "some of the largest and finest river steamers that the Americans can build") continued to use "barbarian" and "foreign devil" when conversing among themselves. And although many less knowledgeable observers had claimed, "from high places and in authoritative style," that the Chinese desired progress and better relations with the West—a feeling often endorsed by British and American newspapers—Medhurst insisted that anyone able "to live amongst the people, to converse with the mandarins, and to study the numerous memorials addressed to the throne by leading statesmen" knew better. Many merchants would of course prefer to see foreign relations expanded. But "the ruling powers deprecate progress for its own sake even at the slowest rate of advance, whilst the mass of the people are altogether indifferent to the subject."[76]

China, Medhurst concluded, was by no means ready for an "instantaneous reception" of the "highly advanced condition of civilization to which we and other Western peoples have become accustomed." More "shocks and awakenings" through conflicts with foreign powers would be necessary, for the Qing government was still too "wrapped up in notions of its strength and self-importance" to appreciate the need to change its foreign policy. It could not keep "shilly-shallying indefinitely, one moment solemnly accepting international obligations, and another moment covertly receding from them."[77]

What, then, *was* China ready for? Medhurst's pessimism becomes less surprising (and less pessimistic) when we consider how, like so many of the men in this book—including "Ramrod" with that proposal in October 1839 for occupying several islands—he was offering his plan for how relations with China ought to be handled. It was based not on the impressions and opinions of others, but on his own firsthand experience and expertise. The thirty years since the Opium War, which happened to coincide with Medhurst's own time in China, had shown how readily Chinese merchants would join commercial ventures initiated by foreign capitalists. By gradually introducing the railway, steamship, and telegraph, foreign merchants would find "abundant opportunities" to benefit from the Chinese love of trade. The treaties must be promulgated and made law across the empire, ensuring that officials and ordinary people alike would see their government was sincere in "admitting foreigners to friendly relations on terms of entire equality" and would "readily do their part in making friendly advances." Enforcing the treaty stipulations must be "firm and uncompromising," guaranteeing that foreigners in China enjoyed every right they were "reasonably entitled to." In other words:

> Let the commercial enterprise of the people be taken advantage of to introduce the thin end of the wedge of progress wherever and whenever the opportunity offers itself; let knowledge be sown broad-cast throughout the land by means of suitable and instructive publications in the native language; and let foreign powers combine to treat China justly, and at the same time see to it that she acts as justly by them.

Were this all done properly, Medhurst declared, it would not be long before "a regeneration ensues, which shall at once satisfy the longings of the diplomatist, the merchant, and the missionary."[78]

## NOTES

1. "Military Skill and Power of the Chinese," *Chinese Repository* 5, no. 4 (August 1836): 177; original emphasis.

2. C. [Charles] Toogood Downing, *The Fan Qui in China in 1836–1837* (London: Henry Colburn, 1838), vol. 3, 326–27.

3. Walter Henry Medhurst, *China: Its State and Prospects, with Special Reference to the Spread of the Gospel; Containing Allusions to the Antiquity, Extent, Population, Civilization, Literature, and Religion of the Chinese* (London: J. Snow, 1838), 98–99.

4. Julia Lovell, *The Opium War: Drugs, Dreams and the Making of China* (London: Picador, 2011); Stephen R. Platt, *Imperial Twilight: The Opium War and the End of China's Last Golden Age* (New York: Knopf, 2018), xxi–ii.

5. Song-Chuan Chen, *Merchants of War and Peace: British Knowledge of China in the Making of the Opium War* (Hong Kong: Hong Kong University Press, 2017), 6.

6. *Canton Register* 13, no. 29 (21 July 1840), supplement, n.p.; original emphasis.

7. *Canton Register* 13, no. 47 (24 November 1840): 250; original emphasis.

8. Downing, *Fan Qui*, vol. 3, 324–25.

9. *Times* (London), 11 September 1839, reprinted in *Canton Press* 5, no. 16 (18 January 1840): n.p.

10. *Canton Press* 5, no. 7 (16 November 1839): n.p.

11. *Canton Press* 7, no. 6 (6 November 1841): n.p.

12. John Francis Davis, *Sketches of China, Partly during an Inland Journey of Four Months, between Peking, Nanking, and Canton, with Notices and Observations Relative to the Present* (London: Charles Knight, 1841), vol. 2, 229, 239.

13. *Canton Register* 13, no. 44 (3 November 1840): 231.

14. *Canton Register* 13, no. 45 (10 November 1840): 239.

15. *Canton Register* 13, no. 47 (24 November 1840): 250; original emphasis.

16. "The Bygone Year," *Canton Press* 6, no. 14 (2 January 1841): n.p.

17. *Canton Register* 14, no. 3 (19 January 1841): 10; original emphasis.

18. *Canton Press* 6, no. 14 (2 January 1841): n.p.

19. *Canton Press* 6, no. 17 (23 January 1841): n.p.

20. *Canton Press* 6, no. 19 (6 February 1841): n.p.

21. *Canton Register* 14, no. 7 (16 February 1841): 31–32, and extra, n.p.

22. Matheson to Jardine, 19 March 1841, MS JM C5/6, Jardine Matheson Archive (JMA).

23. Matheson to Jardine, 28 March 1841, MS JM C5/6, JMA; original emphasis.

24. *Canton Press* 6, no. 26 (27 March 1841): n.p.

25. *Canton Press* 6, no. 31 (1 May 1841): n.p.

26. *Canton Register* 14, no. 18 (4 May 1841): 107; original emphasis.

27. *Canton Press* 7, no. 2 (9 October 1841): n.p.

28. *Bombay Times*, 30 January 1841, reprinted in *Canton Press* 6, no. 30 (24 April 1841): n.p.

29. *Englishman*, 17 February 1841, reprinted in "Chinese Affairs," *Canton Press* 6, no. 30 (24 April 1841): n.p.

30. *Friend of India*, 15 April 1841, reprinted in *Canton Register* 14, no. 25 (22 June 1841): 155.

31. *Canton Register* 14, no. 30 (27 July 1841): 195–supplement, n.p.

32. *Atlas*, 10 April 1841, reprinted in *Canton Press* 6, no. 43 (24 July 1841): n.p.

33. "Heroism Neutralized by Folly," *Canton Register* 15, no. 12 (22 March 1842): 60. Originally in *Atlas*, 9 October 1841.

34. Matheson to Jardine, 23 August 1841, MS JM C 5/7, JMA. Also in Alain Le Pichon, ed., *China Trade and Empire: Jardine, Matheson & Co. and the Origins of British Rule in Hong Kong, 1827–1843* (Oxford: Published for the British Academy by Oxford University Press, 2006), 497.

35. Matheson to Jardine, 3 July 1841, MS JM C5/7, JMA.
36. *Canton Press* 6, no. 17 (23 January 1841): n.p; original emphasis.
37. *Canton Register* 14, no. 17 (27 April 1841): supplement, n.p.; original emphasis.
38. "Regulations of the Port of Hongkong," *Canton Press* 6, no. 47 (21 August 1841): n.p.
39. *Canton Register* 14, no. 46 (16 November 1841): supplement, n.p.
40. *Canton Register* 14, no. 47 (23 November 1841): 292. One week later, the *Register* published a letter from the commander of British troops at Hong Kong, who insisted that the report of the island's unhealthiness had been false and that no medical committee had even been formed. *Canton Register* 14, no. 48 (30 November 1841): supplement, n.p.
41. *Canton Register* 15, no. 3 (18 January 1842): 13.
42. *Canton Press* 7, no. 20 (12 February 1842): n.p.
43. *Canton Press* 7, no. 21 (19 February 1842): n.p.
44. "Hong Kong," *Canton Press* 7, no. 22 (26 February 1842): n.p. On the uncertainty of early colonial Hong Kong see: Christopher Munn, *Anglo-China: Chinese People and British Rule in Hong Kong, 1841–1880* (Richmond, UK: Curzon, 2001); John M. Carroll, *Edge of Empires: Chinese Elites and British Colonials in Hong Kong* (Cambridge, MA: Harvard University Press, 2005), chap. 2.
45. "Singapore and Hongkong," *Canton Press* 7, no. 32 (7 May 1842): n.p.
46. "Hong Kong," *Canton Press* 7, no. 34 (21 May 1842): n.p.
47. *Canton Press* 7, no. 40 (2 July 1842): n.p.
48. *Canton Press* 7, no. 40 (2 July 1842): n.p.
49. Keith Stewart Mackenzie, *Narrative of the Second Campaign in China* (London: Richard Bentley, 1842), 160, 164–66.
50. "Present and Future," *Canton Press* 6, no. 47 (21 August 1841): n.p.
51. *Canton Press* 6, no. 49 (4 September 1841): n.p.
52. *Canton Register* 15, no. 27 (5 July 1842): supplement.
53. Anon., *The Last Year in China, to the Peace of Nanking: As Sketched in Letters to His Friends, by a Field Officer, Actively Employed in That Country. With a Few Concluding Remarks on Our Past and Future Policy in China* (London: Longman, Brown, Green, and Longmans, 1843), 193–94.
54. G. [George] Tradescant Lay, *The Chinese as They Are: Their Moral, Social, and Literary Character* (London: W. Ball, 1841), vi–vii, 7.
55. *Canton Register* 14, no. 18 (4 May 1841): 107, supplement, n.p.; original emphasis.
56. Walter Henry Medhurst, *A Glance of the Interior of China Obtained during a Journey to the Silk and Green Tea Countries* (London: J. Snow, 1850). On Medhurst's "passing," see Elizabeth H. Chang, "Converting Chinese Eyes: Rev. W. H. Medhurst, 'Passing,' and the Victorian Vision of China," in *A Century of Travels in China: Critical Essays on Travel Writing from the 1840s to the 1940s*, ed. Douglas Kerr and Julia Kuehn (Hong Kong: Hong Kong University Press, 2007), 27–38.
57. John Charles Pollock, *Hudson Taylor and Maria: Pioneers in China* (London: Hodder and Stoughton, 1962); Paul Richard Bohr, *Famine in China and the Missionary: Timothy Richard as Relief Administrator and Advocate of National Reform,*

*1876–1884* (Cambridge, MA: Harvard University East Asian Research Center, 1972); Lauren F. Pfister, "Rethinking Mission in China: James Hudson Taylor and Timothy Richard," in *The Imperial Horizons of British Protestant Missions, 1880–1914*, ed. Andrew Porter (Grand Rapids, MI: William B. Eerdmans, 2003), 183–212.

58. *Records of the General Conference of the Protestant Missionaries of China Held at Shanghai, May 10–24, 1877* (Shanghai: American Presbyterian Mission Press, 1878), 33; original emphasis.

59. Jack J. Gerson, *Horatio Nelson Lay and Sino-British Relations, 1854–1864* (Cambridge, MA: Harvard University Press, 1972); Jonathan Spence, *To Change China: Western Advisers in China* (New York: Little, Brown, 1969), chap. 4. Four generations of Lays lived and worked in China, three of them (including Lay's two other sons) in the Maritime Customs.

60. Norman J. Girardot, *The Victorian Translation of China: James Legge's Oriental Pilgrimage* (Berkeley: University of California Press, 2003); Lauren F. Pfister, *Striving for "the Whole Duty of Man": James Legge and the Scottish Protestant Encounter with China* (New York: Peter Lang, 2004).

61. Spence, *To Change China*, chap. 4; Donna Brunero, *Britain's Imperial Cornerstone in China: The Chinese Maritime Customs Service, 1854–1949* (London: Routledge, 2006); Robert Bickers, *The Scramble for China: Foreign Devils in the Qing Empire, 1832–1914* (London: Allen Lane, 2011), especially chap. 7; Catherine Ladds, *Empire Careers: Working for the Chinese Customs Service, 1854-1949* (Manchester: Manchester University Press, 2013).

62. James C. Cooley Jr., *T. F. Wade in China: Pioneer in Global Diplomacy, 1842–1882* (Leiden: Brill, 1981).

63. Philip R. Marshall, "H. A. Giles and E. H. Parker: Clio's English Servants in Late Nineteenth-Century China," *The Historian* 46 (1984): 520–38.

64. Adrian A. Bennett, *John Fryer: The Introduction of Western Science and Technology into Nineteenth-Century China* (Cambridge, MA: Harvard University Press, 1967); Spence, *To Change China*, chap. 5.

65. Jürgen Osterhammel, "Britain and China, 1842–1914," in *The Nineteenth Century*, vol. 3 of *The Oxford History of the British Empire*, ed. Andrew Porter (Oxford: Oxford University Press, 1999), 161.

66. Albert Feuerwerker, "The Foreign Presence in China," in *The Cambridge History of China*, vol. 12, *Republican China*, part 1, ed. John K. Fairbank (Cambridge: Cambridge University Press, 1983), 128.

67. Robert Bickers, *Britain in China: Community, Culture and Colonialism 1900–1949* (Manchester: Manchester University Press, 1999), and "Shanghailanders: The Formation and Identity of the British Settler Community in Shanghai, 1837–1937," *Past and Present* 159 (1998): 161–212.

68. Walter Henry Medhurst, *The Foreigner in Far Cathay* (London: Edward Stanford, 1872), 1, 2.

69. Medhurst, *Foreigner in Far Cathay*, 2–4, 14. Eight years earlier, Medhurst had written that in Shanghai "foreigners are everything"—"the depository and source of all wealth, influence, and power": "Reminiscences of the Opening of Shanghae to Foreign Trade," *Chinese and Japanese Repository* 15 (12 October 1864): 87.

70. Medhurst, *Foreigner in Far Cathay*, 8–11.
71. Medhurst, *Foreigner in Far Cathay*, 18–20.
72. Medhurst, *Foreigner in Far Cathay*, 20–21, 30; original emphasis.
73. Medhurst, *Foreigner in Far Cathay*, 31, 39–40. On the criticism of missionaries that Medhurst was trying to refute, see Bickers, *Scramble for China*, 240–41.
74. Medhurst, *Foreigner in Far Cathay*, 52–53.
75. Medhurst, *Foreigner in Far Cathay*, 89–91.
76. Medhurst, *Foreigner in Far Cathay*, 176, 179–81, original emphasis.
77. Medhurst, *Foreigner in Far Cathay*, 183–84.
78. Medhurst, *Foreigner in Far Cathay*, 185, 189, 190.

# Bibliography

## ARCHIVES AND MANUSCRIPTS

**India Office Records and Private Papers, British Library, London**
IOR (India Office Records) G/12 (China Factory Records ca.1695–1858).

**Archives and Special Collections, School of Oriental and African Studies Library, University of London**
CWM (Council for World Mission/London Missionary Society)/16/02/01 South China Incoming Correspondence, ca. 1803–1927.
CWM South China Journals, 1807–1842.

**Archives and Manuscripts, Wellcome Library, London**
MS 5829: Letters to John Robert Morrison from Robert Morrison.

**Jardine Matheson Archive, Cambridge University Library**
MS JM/C (Out-Correspondence) 5 (Private letters from James Matheson).

**The National Archives of the UK, Kew**
FO 17 (Foreign Office: Political and Other Departments: General Correspondence before 1906, China).

**Caird Library and Archives, National Maritime Museum, Greenwich, London**
CRJ (Edward Hodges Cree).

**David M. Rubenstein Rare Book and Manuscript Library, Duke University, Durham, North Carolina (accessed through Adam Matthew Digital, "China: Trade, Politics and Culture, 1793–1980)"**
Henry Hayne Diary, 1816–1817, Henry Hayne Papers, 1797–1828.
George Thomas Staunton Papers, 1743–1885.

## PUBLISHED WORKS

Abel, Clarke. *Narrative of a Journey in the Interior of China, and of a Voyage to and from That Country, in the Years 1816 and 1817; Containing an Account of the Most Interesting Transactions of Lord Amherst's Embassy to the Court of Pekin, and Observations on the Countries Which It Visited.* London: Orme and Brown, 1818.

Adshead, S. A. M. *Material Culture in Europe and China.* London: Macmillan, 1997.

Alexander, William. *The Costume of China: Illustrated in Forty-Eight Coloured Engravings.* London: William Miller, 1805.

Anderson, Aeneas. *A Narrative of the British Embassy to China in the Years 1792, 1793, and 1794; Containing the Various Circumstances of the Embassy, with Accounts of Customs and Manners of the Chinese, and a Description of the Country, Towns, Cities, &c. &c.* London: J. Debrett, 1795.

Anon. *Facts Relating to Chinese Commerce in a Letter from a British Resident in China to His Friend in England.* London: J. M. Richardson, 1829.

Anon. *An Intercepted Letter from J– T–, Esq. Writer at Canton, to His Friend in Dublin, Ireland.* 3rd edition. Dublin: N. M. Mahon, 1804.

Anon. *The Last Year in China, to the Peace of Nanking: As Sketched in Letters to His Friends, by a Field Officer, Actively Employed in That Country. With a Few Concluding Remarks on Our Past and Future Policy in China.* London: Longman, Brown, Green, and Longmans, 1843.

Askew, Joseph Benjamin. "Re-visiting New Territory: The Terranova Incident Re-examined." *Asian Studies Review* 28, no. 4 (2004): 351–71.

Auber, Peter. *China: An Outline of the Government, Laws, and Policy: and of the British and Foreign Embassies to, and Intercourse with, That Empire.* London: Parbury, Allen, 1834.

Ball, Samuel. *Observations on the Expediency of Opening a Second Port in China.* Macao: Printed at the East India Company's Press, by P. P. Thoms, 1817.

Barrett, T. H. "Hellenic Shadows on the China Coast: Greek Terms for 'Foreigner' and 'Religion' in Early Anglophone Missionary Sinology." *Journal of Translation Studies* (new series) 1, no. 1: 59–84.

Barrett, T. H. *Singular Listlessness: A Short History of Chinese Books and British Scholars.* London: Wellsweep Press, 1989.

Barrow, John. *Travels in China, Containing Descriptions, Observations, and Comparisons, Made and Collected in the Course of a Short Residence at the Imperial Palace of Yuen-Min-Yuen, and on a Subsequent Journey through the Country from Pekin to Canton in Which It Is Attempted to Appreciate the Rank That the Extraordinary Empire May Be Considered to Hold in the Scale of Civilized Nations.* London: Cadell and Davies, 1804.

Barrow, John, and George Macartney. *Some Account of the Public Life, and a Selection from the Unpublished Writings, of the Earl of Macartney.* Vol 2. London: Cadell and Davies, 1807.

Basu, Dilip K. "Chinese Xenology and the Opium War: Reflections on Sinocentrism." *Journal of Asian Studies* 73, no. 4 (2014): 927–40.

Baumler, Alan, ed. *Modern China and Opium: A Reader*. Ann Arbor: University of Michigan Press, 2001.

Bello, David A. *Opium and the Limits of Empire: Drug Prohibition in the Chinese Interior, 1729–1850*. Cambridge, MA: Harvard University Asia Center, 2005.

Bennett, Adrian A. *John Fryer: The Introduction of Western Science and Technology into Nineteenth-Century China* Cambridge, MA: Harvard University Press, 1967.

Bennett, George. *Wanderings in New South Wales, Batavia, Pedir Coast, Singapore, and China. Being the Journal of a Naturalist in Those Countries, during 1832, 1833, and 1834*. Vol. 2. London: Richard Bentley, 1834.

Bickers, Robert. *Britain in China: Community, Culture, and Colonialism 1900–1949*. Manchester: Manchester University Press, 1999.

Bickers, Robert. "The *Challenger*: Hugh Hamilton Lindsay and the Rise of British Asia, 1832–1865." *Transactions of the Royal Historical Society* 22 (2012): 141–69.

Bickers, Robert. "Legal Fiction: Extraterritoriality as an Instrument of British Power in China in the 'Long Nineteenth Century.'" In *Empire in Asia: A New Global History*, vol. 2, edited by Donna Brunero and Brian P. Farrell, 53–80. London: Bloomsbury Academic, 2018.

Bickers, Robert. "Revisiting the Chinese Maritime Customs Service." *Journal of Imperial and Commonwealth History* 36, no. 6 (2008): 221–26.

Bickers, Robert, ed. *Ritual and Diplomacy: The Macartney Mission to China, 1792–1794*. London: British Association for Chinese Studies and Wellsweep Press, 1993.

Bickers, Robert. *The Scramble for China: Foreign Devils in the Qing Empire, 1832–1914*. London: Allen Lane, 2011.

Bickers, Robert. "Shanghailanders: The Formation and Identity of the British Settler Community in Shanghai, 1837–1937." *Past and Present* 159 (1988): 161–212.

Bingham, John Elliot. *Narrative of the Expedition to China from the Commencement of the War to Its Termination in 1842: Sketches of the Manners and Customs of That Singular and Hitherto Almost Unknown Country*. Vol. 2. London: Henry Colburn, 1842.

Blue, Gregory. "China and Western Social Thought in the Modern Period." In *China and Historical Capitalism: Genealogies of Sinological Knowledge*, edited by Timothy Brook and Gregory Blue, 57–109. Cambridge: Cambridge University Press, 1999.

Blussé, Leonard. *Visible Cities: Canton, Nagasaki, and Batavia and the Coming of the Americans*. Cambridge, MA: Harvard University Press, 2008.

Bohr, Paul Richard. *Famine in China and the Missionary: Timothy Richard as Relief Administrator and Advocate of National Reform, 1876–1884*. Cambridge, MA: Harvard University East Asian Research Center, 1972.

Brook, Timothy, and Bob Tadashi Wakabayashi. "Opium's History in China." In *Opium Regimes: China, Britain, and Japan, 1839–1952*, edited by Timothy Brook and Bob Tadashi Wakabayashi, 1–27. Berkeley: University of California Press, 2000.

Brunero, Donna. *Britain's Imperial Cornerstone in China: The Chinese Maritime Customs Service, 1854–1949*. London: Routledge, 2006.

Carroll, John M. "The Amherst Embassy to China: A Whimper and a Bang." *Journal of Imperial and Commonwealth History* 48, no. 1 (2020): 15–38.

Carroll, John M. *Canton Days: British Life and Death in China*. Lanham, MD: Rowman & Littlefield, 2020.

Carroll, John M. "The Canton System: Conflict and Accommodation in the Contact Zone." *Journal of the Hong Kong Branch of the Royal Asiatic Society* 50 (2010): 51–66.

Carroll, John M. *Edge of Empires: Chinese Elites and British Colonials in Hong Kong*. Cambridge, MA: Harvard University Press, 2005.

Carroll, John M. "Sorting Out China: British Accounts from Pre-Opium War Canton." In *The Cultural Construction of the British World*, edited by Barry Crosbie and Mark Hampton, 126–44. Manchester: Manchester University Press, 2016.

Carroll, John M. "'The Usual Intercourse of Nations': The British in Pre-Opium War Canton." In *Britain and China: Empire, Finance and War, 1840–1970*, edited by Robert Bickers and Jon Howlett, 22–40. Abingdon, UK: Routledge, 2015.

Chang, Elizabeth. "Binding and Unbinding Chinese Feet in the Mid-Century Victorian Press." In *Writing China: Essays on the Amherst Embassy (1816) and Sino-British Cultural Relations*, edited by Peter J. Kitson and Robert Markley, 132–51. Cambridge: D. S. Brewer, 2016.

Chang, Elizabeth Hope. *Britain's Chinese Eye: Literature, Empire, and Aesthetics in Nineteenth-Century Britain*. Stanford: Stanford University Press, 2010.

Chang, Elizabeth H. "Converting Chinese Eyes: Rev. W. H. Medhurst, 'Passing,' and the Victorian Vision of China." In *A Century of Travels in China: Critical Essays on Travel Writing from the 1840s to the 1940s*, edited by Douglas Kerr and Julia Kuehn, 27–38. Hong Kong: Hong Kong University Press, 2007.

Chang, Hsin-pao. *Commissioner Lin and the Opium War*. Cambridge, MA: Harvard University Press, 1964.

Chen, Li. *Chinese Law in Imperial Eyes: Sovereignty, Justice, and Transcultural Politics*. New York: Columbia University Press, 2016.

Chen, Li. "Law, Empire, and Historiography of Modern Sino-Western Relations: A Case Study of the *Lady Hughes* Controversy in 1784." *Law and History Review* 27, no. 1 (2009): 1–53.

Chen, Song-Chuan. "The British Maritime Public Sphere in Canton, 1827–1839." PhD dissertation, University of Cambridge, 2008.

Chen, Song-Chuan. *Merchants of War and Peace: British Knowledge of China in the Making of the Opium War*. Hong Kong: Hong Kong University Press, 2017.

Clarke, Prescott. "The Development of the English Language Press on the China Coast, 1827–1881." MA dissertation, University of London, 1961.

Clifford, Nicholas. *"A Truthful Impression of the Country": British and American Travel Writing in China, 1880–1949*. Ann Arbor: University of Michigan Press, 2001.

Colley, Linda. *Britons: Forging the Nation 1707–1837*. New Haven, CT: Yale University Press, 1992.

Conner, Patrick. *George Chinnery, 1774–1852, Artist of India and the China Coast*. Woodbridge, UK: Antique Collectors' Club, 1993.

Conner, Patrick. "George Chinnery and His Contemporaries on the China Coast." *Arts of Asia* 23, no. 3 (1993): 66–81.
Cooley, James C. Jr. *T. F. Wade in China: Pioneer in Global Diplomacy, 1842–1882.* Leiden, NL: Brill, 1981.
Crawley, Harriet. "Alexander's Views of China." *Arts of Asia* 9, no. 5 (1979): 62–73.
Cree, Edward H. *The Cree Journals: The Voyage of Edward H. Cree, Surgeon R.N., as Related in His Private Journals, 1837–1856.* Edited by Michael Levien. Exeter, UK: Webb and Bower, 1981.
Crossley, Pamela K. *A Translucent Mirror: History and Identity in Qing Imperial Ideology.* Berkeley: University of California Press, 1999.
Cunynghame, Arthur. *An Aide-De-Camp's Recollections of Service in China: A Residence in Hong-Kong: and Visits to Other Islands in the Chinese Seas.* Vol. 1. London: Saunders and Otley, 1844.
Cunynghame, Arthur. *The Opium War: Being Recollections of Service in China.* Philadelphia: G. B. Zieber, 1845.
Daniell, Thomas, and William Daniell. *A Picturesque Voyage to India; by the Way of China.* London: Longman, Hurst, Rees, and Orme, 1810.
D'Arcy-Brown, Liam. *Chusan: The Forgotten Story of Britain's First Chinese Island.* Kenilworth, UK: Brandram, 2012.
Daunton, Martin, and Rick Halpern, eds. *Empire and Others: British Encounters with Indigenous Peoples, 1600–1850.* London: University College of London Press, 1999.
Davis, John Francis. *The Chinese: A General Description of That Empire and Its Inhabitants.* 2 vols. London: Charles Knight, 1836.
Davis, John Francis. *Chinese Novels Translated from the Originals; to Which Are Added Proverbs and Moral Maxims, Collected from Their Classical Books and Other Sources; the Whole Prefaced by Observations on the Language and Literature of China.* London: J. Murray, 1822.
Davis, John Francis. *Sketches of China, Partly during an Inland Journey of Four Months, between Peking, Nanking, and Canton, with Notices and Observations Relative to the Present.* 2 vols. London: Charles Knight, 1841.
Dawson, Raymond. *The Chinese Chameleon: An Analysis of European Conceptions of Chinese Civilization.* Oxford: Oxford University Press, 1967.
Delano, Amasa. *A Narrative of Voyages and Travels in the Northern and Southern Hemispheres, Comprising Three Voyages around the World.* Boston: E. G. House, 1818.
Dikötter, Frank, Lars Laamann, and Zhou Xun. *Narcotic Culture: A History of Drugs in China.* Chicago: University of Chicago Press, 2004.
Downing, C. [Charles] Toogood. *The Fan Qui in China in 1836–1837.* 3 vols. London: Henry Colburn, 1838.
Ebrey, Patricia. "Gender and Sinology: Shifting Western Interpretations of Footbinding, 1300–1890." *Late Imperial China* 20, no. 2 (1999): 1–34.
Elliott, Mark C. *The Manchu Way: The Eight Banners and Ethnic Identity in Late Imperial China.* Stanford: Stanford University Press, 2001.

Ellis, Henry. *Journal of the Proceedings of the Late Embassy to China; Comprising a Correct Narrative of the Public Transactions of the Embassy, of the Voyage to and from China, and of the Journey from the Mouth of the Pei-Ho to the Return to Canton.* London: Printed for J. Murray, 1817.

Ellis, Henry. *A Series of Letters on the East India Question, Addressed to the Members of the Two Houses of Parliament.* 2nd ed. London: John Murray, 1830.

Fan, Fa-ti. *British Naturalists in Qing China: Science, Empire, and Cultural Encounter.* Cambridge, MA: Harvard University Press, 2004.

Fay, Peter Ward. *The Opium War 1840–1842: Barbarians in the Celestial Empire in the Early Part of the Nineteenth Century and the War by Which They Forced Her Gates Ajar.* Chapel Hill: University of North Carolina Press, 1975.

Feuerwerker, Albert. "The Foreign Presence in China." In *The Cambridge History of China*, vol. 12, *Republican China*, part 1, edited by John K. Fairbank, 128–207. (Cambridge: Cambridge University Press, 1983).

Fichter, James R. *So Great a Profitt: How the East Indies Trade Transformed Anglo-American Capitalism.* Cambridge, MA: Harvard University Press, 2010.

Finnane, Antonia. *Changing Clothes in China: Fashion, History, Nation.* New York: Columbia University Press, 2008.

Fletcher, Joseph. "Ch'ing Inner Asia c. 1800." In *The Cambridge History of China*, vol. 10, *Late Ch'ing, 1800–1911*, part 1, edited by John K. Fairbank, 35–106. Cambridge: Cambridge University Press, 1978.

Forbes, Robert Bennet. *Letters from China: The Canton-Boston Correspondence of Robert Bennet Forbes, 1838–1840.* Edited by Sarah Forbes Hughes. Mystic, CT: Mystic Seaport Museum, 1996.

Gao, Hao. "The Amherst Embassy and British Discoveries in China." *History* 99, no. 337 (2014): 568–87.

Gao, Hao. *Creating the Opium War: British Imperial Attitudes towards China, 1792–1840.* Manchester: Manchester University Press, 2020.

Gao, Hao. "Going to War against the Middle Kingdom? Continuity and Change in British Attitudes towards Qing China." *Journal of Imperial and Commonwealth History* 45, no. 2 (2017): 210–31.

Gao, Hao. "The 'Inner Kowtow Controversy' during the Amherst Embassy to China, 1816–1817." *Diplomacy and Statecraft* 27, no. 4 (2016): 595–614.

Gao, Hao. "Prelude to the Opium War? British Reactions to the 'Napier Fizzle' and Attitudes towards China in the Mid Eighteen-Thirties." *Historical Research* 87, no. 237 (2014): 491–509.

Gao, Hao. "Understanding the Chinese: British Merchants on the China Trade in the Early 1830s." *Britain and the World* 12, no. 2 (2019): 151–71.

Gelber, Harry G. *Opium, Soldiers and Evangelicals: Britain's 1840–42 War with China, and Its Aftermath.* Basingstoke, UK: Palgrave Macmillan, 2004.

Gerson, Jack J. *Horatio Nelson Lay and Sino-British Relations, 1854–1864.* Cambridge, MA: Harvard University Press, 1972.

Girardot, Norman J. *The Victorian Translation of China: James Legge's Oriental Pilgrimage.* Berkeley: University of California Press, 2003.

Goddard, James. *Remarks on the Late Lord Napier's Mission to Canton; in Reference to the Present State of Our Relations with China*. London: Printed for private circulation, 1836.

[Gordon, G. J.] *Address to the People of Great Britain, Explanatory of Our Commercial Relations with the Empire of China and of the Course of Policy by Which It May Be Rendered an Almost Unbounded Field for British Commerce*. London: Smith, Elder, 1836.

Grace, Richard J. *Opium and Empire: The Lives and Careers of William Jardine and James Matheson*. Montreal: McGill-Queen's University Press, 2014.

Great Britain, Foreign Office. *Correspondence Relating to China, Presented to Both Houses of Parliament, By Command of Her Majesty, 1840*. London: T. R. Harrison, 1840.

Great Britain, Foreign Office. *Memorials Addressed to Her Majesty's Government, by British Merchants Interested in the Trade with China. Presented to Both Houses of Parliament by Command of Her* Majesty. London: Printed by T. R. Harrison, 1840.

Gu Changsheng. *Cong Malisun dao Situ Leideng: Laihua xinjiao chuanjiaoshi pingzhuan* [From Robert Morrison to Leighton Stuart: Critical Biographies of Christian Missionaries to China]. Shanghai: Shanghai renmin chubanshe, 1985.

Gützlaff, Karl F. A. *Journal of Three Voyages along the Coast of China in 1831, 1832, and 1833, with Notices of Siam, Corea, and the Loo-choo Islands*. London: F. Westley and A. H. Davis, 1834.

Hall, Basil. *Voyage to Loo-Choo, and Other Places in the Eastern Seas, in the Year 1816; Including an Account of Captain Maxwell's Attack on the Batteries at Canton; and Notes of an Interview with Buonaparte at St. Helena, in August 1817*. Edinburgh: A. Constable, 1826.

Harrison, Henrietta. "Chinese and British Diplomatic Gifts in the Macartney Embassy of 1833." *English Historical Review* 133, no. 560 (2018): 65–97.

Haw, Stephen G. *Marco Polo's China: A Venetian in the Realm of Kublai Khan*. London: Routledge, 2006.

Hayes, James. "'That Singular and Hitherto Almost Unknown Country': Opinions on China, the Chinese, and the 'Opium War' among British Naval and Military Officers Who Served during Hostilities There." *Journal of the Royal Asiatic Society Hong Kong Branch* 39 (1999): 211–33.

Hevia, James L. *Cherishing Men from Afar: Qing Guest Ritual and the Macartney Mission of 1793*. Durham, NC: Duke University Press, 1995.

Hillard, Harriett Low. *Lights and Shadows of a Macao Life: The Journal of Harriett Low, Travelling Spinster*, edited by Nan P. Hodges and Arthur W. Hummel. Woodinville, WA: The History Bank, 2002,

Hillemann, Ulrike. *Asian Empire and British Knowledge: China and the Networks of British Imperial Expansion*. New York: Palgrave Macmillan, 2009.

Ho, Ping-Ti. "In Defense of Sinicization: A Rebuttal of Evelyn Rawski's 'Reenvisioning the Qing'." *Journal of Asian Studies* 5, no. 1 (1998): 123–55.

Hoe, Susanna, and Derek Roebuck. *The Taking of Hong Kong: Charles and Clara Elliot in China Waters*. Richmond, UK: Curzon, 1999.

Holman, James. *Voyage Round the World, Including Travels in Africa, Asia, Australasia, America, etc. etc. from 1827 to 1832.* Vol. 4. London: Smith, Elder, 1834–1835.

Holmes, Samuel. *The Journal of Mr. Samuel Holmes, Serjeant-Major of the XIth Light Dragoons, during His Attendance, as One of the Guard of Lord Macartney's Embassy to China and Tartary, 1792–3.* London: W. Bulmer, 1798.

Hostetler, Laura. *Qing Colonial Enterprise: Ethnography and Cartography in Early Modern China.* Chicago: University of Chicago Press, 2001.

Hostetler, Laura. "Qing Connections to the Early Modern World: Ethnography and Cartography in Eighteenth-Century China." *Modern Asian Studies* 34, no. 3 (2000): 623–62.

Hunter, William C. *Bits of Old China.* London: Kegan Paul, Trench, 1885.

Jocelyn, Robert. *Six Months with the Chinese Expedition: Leaves from a Soldier's Note-Book.* London: John Murray, 1841.

Johnson, James. *An Account of a Voyage to India, China, &c. in His Majesty's Ship Caroline, Performed in the Years 1803–4–5, Interspersed with Descriptive Sketches and Cursory Remarks.* London: J. G. Barnard, 1806.

Johnson, Kendall A. "Extraterritorial Publication and American Missionary Authority about the 'Opium War': Contesting the Eloquence and Reciprocity of John Quincy Adams's 'Lecture on the War with China.'" *Literature & History* 29, no. 1 (2020): 37–59.

Johnson, Kendall A. *The New Middle Kingdom: China and the Early American Romance of Free Trade.* Baltimore: Johns Hopkins University Press, 2017.

King, Frank H. H., ed., and Prescott Clarke. *A Research Guide to China-Coast Newspapers, 1822–1911.* Cambridge, MA: East Asian Research Center, Harvard University, 1965.

King, Michelle T. *Between Birth and Death: Female Infanticide in Nineteenth-Century China.* Stanford: Stanford University Press, 2014.

Kitson, Peter J. "The 'Catastrophe of This New Chinese Mission': The Amherst Embassy to China of 1816." In *Early Encounters between East Asia and Europe: Telling Failures*, edited by Ralf Hertel and Michael Keevak, 67–83. Abingdon, UK: Routledge, 2017.

Kitson, Peter J. "The Dark Gift: John Francis Davis, Thomas De Quincey and the Amherst Embassy to China of 1816.'" In *Writing China: Essays on the Amherst Embassy (1816) and Sino-British Cultural Relations*, edited by Peter J. Kitson and Robert Markley, 56–82. Cambridge: D. S. Brewer, 2016.

Kitson, Peter J. *Forging Romantic China: Sino–British Cultural Exchange 1760–1840.* Cambridge: Cambridge University Press, 2013.

Klein, Thoralf. "Biography and the Making of Transnational Imperialism: Karl Gützlaff on the China Coast, 1831–1851." *Journal of Imperial and Commonwealth History* 47, no. 3 (2019): 415–45.

Ko, Dorothy. *Cinderella's Sisters: A Revisionist History of Footbinding.* Berkeley: University of California Press, 2005.

Kuehn, Julia. "Knowing Bodies, Knowing Self: The Western Woman Traveller's Encounter with Chinese Women, Bound Feet and the Half-Caste Child, 1880–1920." *Studies in Travel Writing* 12, no. 3 (2008): 265–90.

Kuhn, Philip A. *Chinese among Others: Emigration in Modern Times*. Lanham, MD: Rowman & Littlefield, 2008.

Kumagai, Yukihasa. *Breaking into the Monopoly: Provincial Merchants and Manufacturers' Campaigns for Access to the Asian Market, 1790–1833*. Leiden, NL: Brill, 2013.

Ladds, Catherine. *Empire Careers: Working for the Chinese Customs Service, 1854–1949*. Manchester: Manchester University Press, 2013.

Lambert, David, and Alan Lester, eds. *Colonial Lives across the British Empire: Imperial Careering in the Long Nineteenth Century*. Cambridge: Cambridge University Press, 2006.

Lay, G. [George] Tradescant. *The Chinese as They Are: Their Moral, Social, and Literary Character*. London: W. Ball, 1841.

Lay, George Tradescant. *Trade with China: A Letter Addressed to the British Public on Some of the Advantages That Would Result from an Occupation of the Bonin Islands*. London: Royston and Brown, 1837.

Legouix, Susan. *Image of China: William Alexander*. London: Jupiter Books, 1980.

Le Pichon, Alain, ed. *China Trade and Empire: Jardine, Matheson & Co. and the Origins of British Rule in Hong Kong, 1827–1843*. Oxford: Published for the British Academy by Oxford University Press, 2006.

Leonard, Jane Kate. "W. H. Medhurst: Rewriting the Missionary Message." In *Christianity in China: Early Protestant Writings*, edited by Suzanne Wilson Barnett and John King Fairbank, 107–19. Cambridge, MA: Harvard University Press, 1985.

Lester, Alan. "British Settler Discourse and the Circuits of Empire." *History Workshop Journal* 54 (2002): 24–48.

Leung, Angela Ki Che. "The Business of Vaccination in Nineteenth-Century Canton." *Late Imperial China* 29, no. 1 (2008): 7–39.

Levine, Philippa. "Naked Natives and Noble Savages." In *The Cultural Construction of the British World*, edited by Barry Crosbie and Mark Hampton, 126–44. Manchester: Manchester University Press, 2016.

Li Guorong, Qin Bo, and Li Bing, eds. *Diguo shanghang: Guangzhou shisanhang* [Imperial Trading Houses: Guangzhou's Thirteen Hongs]. Beijing: Jiuzhou chubanshe, 2007.

Lin, Man-houng. *China Upside Down: Currency, Society, and Ideologies, 1808–1856*. Cambridge, MA: Harvard University Asia Center, 2006.

Lindsay, Hugh Hamilton. *Letter to the Right Honourable Viscount Lord Palmerston on the British Relations with China*. London: Saunders and Otley, 1836.

Little, Mrs. Archibald [Alicia Ellen Neve]. *Intimate China: The Chinese as I Have Seen Them*. London: Hutchinson, 1899.

Liu, Lydia H. *The Clash of Empires: The Invention of China in Modern World Making*. Cambridge, MA: Harvard University Press, 2004.

Loch, Granville G. *The Closing Events of the Campaign in China: The Operations in the Yang-Tze-Kiang and Treaty of Nanking*. London: J. Murray, 1843.

Lockhart, William. *The Medical Missionary in China: A Narrative of Twenty Years' Experience*. London: Hurst and Blackett, 1861.

Lovell, Julia. *The Opium War: Drugs, Dreams and the Making of China*. London: Picador, 2011.

Lutz, Jessie Gregory. *Opening China: Karl A. Gützlaff and Sino–Western Relations, 1822–1852*. Grand Rapids, MI: William B. Eerdmans, 2008.

Mackenzie, Keith Stewart. *Narrative of the Second Campaign in China*. London: Richard Bentley, 1842.

Mackerras, Colin. *Western Images of China*. New York: Oxford University Press, 1989.

McLeod, John. *Narrative of a Voyage in His Majesty's Late Ship Alceste, to the Yellow Sea, along the Coast of Corea, and through Its Numerous Hitherto Undiscovered Islands, to the Island of Lewchew; with an Account of Her Shipwreck in the Straits of Gaspar*. London: John Murray, 1817.

McMahon, Keith. *The Fall of the God of Money: Opium Smoking in Nineteenth-Century China*. Lanham, MD: Rowman & Littlefield, 2002.

McPherson, Duncan. *Two Years in China: Narrative of the Chinese Expedition, from Its Formation in April, 1840, to the Treaty of Peace in August, 1842*. London: Saunders and Otley, 1842.

Malcolm, Elizabeth L. "The *Chinese Repository* and Western Literature on China 1800 to 1850." *Modern Asian Studies* 7, no. 2 (1973): 165–78.

Marjoribanks, Charles. *Letter to the Right Hon. Charles Grant, President of the Board of Control: On the Present State of British Intercourse with China*. London: J. Hatchard, 1833.

Marshall, Philip R. "H. A. Giles and E. H. Parker: Clio's English Servants in Late Nineteenth-Century China." *The Historian* 46 (1984): 520–38.

Matheson, James. *The Present Position and Prospects of the British Trade with China: Together with an Outline of Some Leading Occurrences in Its Past History*. London: Smith, Elder, 1836.

Medhurst, Walter Henry. *China: Its State and Prospects, with Special Reference to the Spread of the Gospel; Containing Allusions to the Antiquity, Extent, Population, Civilization, Literature, and Religion of the Chinese*. London: J. Snow, 1838.

Medhurst, Walter Henry. *The Foreigner in Far Cathay*. London: Edward Stanford, 1872.

Medhurst, Walter Henry. *A Glance of the Interior of China Obtained during a Journey to the Silk and Green Tea Countries*. London: J. Snow, 1850.

Medhurst, Walter Henry. "Reminiscences of the Opening of Shanghae to Foreign Trade." *Chinese and Japanese Repository* 15 (12 October 1864): 79–88.

Melancon, Glenn. *Britain's China Policy and the Opium Crisis: Balancing Drugs, Violence and National Honour, 1833–1840*. Aldershot, UK: Ashgate, 2003.

Melancon, Glenn. "Honour in Opium? The British Declaration of War on China, 1835–1840." *International History Review* 21, no. 4 (1999): 854–74.

Melancon, Glenn. "Peaceful Intentions: The First British Trade Commission in China, 1833–5." *Historical Research* 72, no. 180 (2000): 33–74.

Milburn, William. *Oriental Commerce: Containing a Geographical Description of the Principal Places in the East Indies, China, and Japan*. Vol 2. London: Black, Parry, 1813.

Min, Eun Kyung. "Narrating the Far East: Commercial Civility and Ceremony in the Amherst Embassy to China (1816–1817)." In *Interpreting Colonialism*, edited by Byron R. Wells and Philip Steward, 160–80. Oxford: Voltaire Foundation, 2004.

Morrison, Eliza. *Memoirs of the Life and Labours of Robert Morrison, Compiled by His Widow, with Critical Notices of His Chinese Works, by Samuel Kidd*. 2 vols. London: Longman, Orme, Brown, Green and Longmans, 1839.

Morrison, John Robert. *A Chinese Commercial Guide: Consisting of a Collection of Details Respecting Foreign Trade in China*. Canton: Albion Press, 1834.

Morrison, Robert. *Notices Concerning China, and the Port of Canton, Also a Narrative of the Affair of the English Frigate Topaze, 1821–22; with Remarks on Homicides, and an Account of the Fire of Canton*. Malacca: Printed at the Mission Press, 1823.

Morrison, Robert. *A View of China, for Philological Purposes: Containing a Sketch of Chinese Chronology, Geography, Government, Religion & Customs*. Macao: Printed at the Honorable East India Company's Press by P. P. Thoms, 1817; London: Black, Parbury, and Allen, 1817.

Morse, Hosea Ballou. *The Chronicles of the East India Company Trading to China, 1635–1834*. Vol. 4. Oxford: Clarendon Press, 1926.

Mosca, Matthew M. *From Frontier Policy to Foreign Policy: The Question of India and the Transformation of Geopolitics in Qing China*. Stanford: Stanford University Press, 2013.

Mungello, D. E. *Drowning Girls in China: Female Infanticide since 1650*. Lanham, MD: Rowman & Littlefield, 2008.

Mungello, D. E. *The Great Encounter of China and the West, 1500–1800*. Lanham, MD: Rowman & Littlefield, 1999.

Munn, Christopher. *Anglo-China: Chinese People and British Rule in Hong Kong, 1841–1880*. Richmond, UK: Curzon, 2001.

Munn, Christopher. "The Chusan Episode: Britain's Occupation of a Chinese Island, 1840–46." *Journal of Imperial and Commonwealth History* 25, no. 1 (1997): 82–112.

Murray, Alexander. *Doings in China: Being the Personal Narrative of an Officer Engaged in the Late Chinese Expedition, from the Recapture of Chusan in 1841, to the Peace of Nankin in 1842*. London: Richard Bentley, 1843.

Napier, Priscilla. *Barbarian Eye: Lord Napier in China, 1834, Prelude to Hong Kong*. London: Washington Brassey's, 1995.

Newman, Richard K. "Opium Smoking in Late Imperial China." *Modern Asian Studies* 29, no. 4 (1995): 765–94.

Nye, Gideon Jr. *The Morning of My Life in China: Comprising an Outline of the History of Foreign Intercourse from the Last Year of the Regime of the Honorable East India Company, 1833, to the Imprisonment of the Foreign Community in 1839*. Canton: n.p., 1873.

Ong, S. P. "Jurisdictional Politics in Canton and the First English Translation of the Qing Penal Code (1810). *Journal of the Royal Asiatic Society of Great Britain & Ireland* 20, no. 2 (2010): 141–65.

Osterhammel, Jürgen. "Britain and China, 1842–1914." In *The Nineteenth Century*, vol. 3 of *The Oxford History of the British Empire*, edited by Andrew Porter, 149–69. Oxford: Oxford University Press, 1999.

Palsetia, Jesse S. "The Parsis of India and the Opium Trade in China." *Contemporary Drug Problems* 35 (2008): 647–78.

Pan, Lynn. *Sons of the Yellow Emperor: A History of the Chinese Diaspora*. New York: Kodansha, 1994.

Perdue, Peter C. "Boundaries, Maps, and Movement: Chinese, Russian, and Mongolian Empires in Early Modern Central Eurasia." *International History Review* 20, no. 2 (1988): 263–86.

Perdue, Peter C. *China Marches West: The Qing Conquest of Central Eurasia, 1600–1800*. Cambridge, MA: Harvard University Press, 2005.

Perdue, Peter C. "Comparing Empires: Manchu Colonialism." *International History Review* 20, no. 2 (1998): 255–62.

Pfister, Lauren F. "Rethinking Mission in China: James Hudson Taylor and Timothy Richard." In *The Imperial Horizons of British Protestant Missions, 1880–1914*, edited by Andrew Porter, 183–212. Grand Rapids, MI: William B. Eerdmans, 2003.

Pfister, Lauren F. *Striving for "the Whole Duty of Man": James Legge and the Scottish Protestant Encounter with China*. New York: Peter Lang, 2004.

Philip, Robert. *No Opium! Or, Commerce and Christianity, Working Together for Good in China: A Letter to James Cropper, Esq., of Liverpool*. London: Ward, 1835.

Platt, Stephen R. *Imperial Twilight: The Opium War and the End of China's Last Golden Age*. New York: Knopf, 2018.

Polachek, James M. *The Inner Opium War*. Cambridge, MA: Harvard University Press, 1992.

Pollock, John Charles. *Hudson Taylor and Maria: Pioneers in China*. London: Hodder and Stoughton, 1962.

Porter, David. *The Chinese Taste in Eighteenth-Century England*. Cambridge: Cambridge University Press, 2010.

Rawski, Evelyn S. "Reenvisioning the Qing: The Significance of the Qing Period in Chinese History." *Journal of Asian Studies* 55, no. 4 (1996): 829–50.

*Records of the General Conference of the Protestant Missionaries of China Held at Shanghai, May 10–24, 1877*. Shanghai: American Presbyterian Mission Press, 1878.

A Resident in China. *British Intercourse with Eastern Asia*. London: Edward Suter, 1836.

A Resident in China [Hugh Hamilton Lindsay]. *Remarks on Occurrences in China, since the Opium Seizure in March 1839 to the Latest Date*. London: Sherwood, Gilbert, and Piper, 1840.

Ride, Lindsay, and May Ride. *An East India Company Cemetery: Protestant Burials in Macao*. Edited by Bernard Mellor. Hong Kong: Hong Kong University Press, 1996.

Roberts, Jason. *A Sense of the World: How a Blind Man Became History's Greatest Traveler*. New York: Harper Collins, 2006.

Rubinstein, Murray. "The Wars They Wanted: American Missionaries' Use of *The Chinese Repository* before the Opium War." *American Neptune* 48 (1988): 271–82.

St. André, James. "'But Do They Have a Notion of Justice?' Staunton's 1810 Translation of the Great Qing Code." *The Translator* 10, no. 1 (2004): 1–31.

St. André, James. "The Development of British Sinology and Changes in Translation Practice: The Case of Sir John Francis Davis (1795–1890)." *Translation and Interpreting Studies* 2, no. 2 (2007): 3–42.

St. André, James. *Translating China as Cross-Identity Performance*. Honolulu: University of Hawai'i Press, 2018.

St. André, James. "Travelling toward True Translation: The First Generation of Sino-English Translators." *The Translator* 12, no. 2 (2006): 189–210.

Sample, Joe. "'The First Appearance of This Celebrated Capital'; or, What Mr. Barrow Saw in the Land of the Chinaman." In *Asian Crossings: Travel Writing on China, Japan and Southeast Asia*, edited by Steve Clark and Paul Smethurst, 31–46. Hong Kong: Hong Kong University Press, 2008.

Sieber, Patricia. "Location, Location, Location: Peter Perring Thoms (1790–1855), Cantonese Localism, and the Genesis of Literary Translations from the Chinese." In *Sinologists and Translators in the Seventeenth to Nineteenth Centuries*, edited by Lawrence Wang-chi Wong and Bernhard Fuehrer, 137–67. Hong Kong: Research Centre for Translation/The Chinese University Press, 2015.

Sieber, Patricia. "Universal Brotherhood: Peter Perring Thoms (1790–1855), Artisan Practices, and the Genesis of a Chinacentric Sinology." *Representations* 130, no. 1 (2015): 28–59.

Slade, John. *Narrative of the Late Proceedings and Events in China*. China: Canton Register Press, 1839.

Slade, John. *Notices on the British Trade to the Port of Canton; with Some Translations of Chinese Official Papers Relative to That Trade*. London: Smith, Elder, 1830.

Spence, Jonathan. "Opium Smoking in Ch'ing China." In *Conflict and Control in Late Imperial China*, edited by Frederic Wakeman Jr. and Carolyn Grant, 143–73. Berkeley: University of California Press, 1975.

Spence, Jonathan. *To Change China: Western Advisors in China, 1620–1960*. New York: Little, Brown, 1969.

Staunton, George [Leonard]. *An Authentic Account of an Embassy from the King of Great Britain to the Emperor of China; Including Cursory Observations Made, and Information Obtained, in Travelling through That Ancient Empire and a Small Part of Chinese Tartary*. 3 vols. London: G. Nicol, 1797.

Staunton, George Thomas. *Memoirs of the Chief Incidents of the Public Life of Sir George Thomas Staunton: One of the King's Commissioners to the Court of Pekin,* and *Afterwards for Some Time Member of Parliament for South Hampshire and for the Borough of Portsmouth*. London: Printed for Private Circulation, 1856.

Staunton, George Thomas. *Miscellaneous Notices Relating to China and Our Commercial Intercourse with That Country: Including a Few Translations from the Chinese Language*. 2nd ed. London: John Murray, 1822.

Staunton, George Thomas. *Notes of Proceedings and Occurrences during the British Embassy to Pekin in 1816*. London: Havant, 1824.

Staunton, George Thomas. *Remarks on the British Relations with China, and the Proposed Plans for Improving Them*. London: E. Lloyd, 1836.

Staunton, George Thomas. *Ta Tsing Leu Lee; Being the Fundamental Laws, and a Selection from the Supplementary Statutes, of the Penal Code of China*. London: Cadell and Davies, 1810.

Stifler, Susan Reed. "The Language Students of the East India Company's Canton Factory." *Journal of the North China Branch of the Royal Asiatic Society* 69 (1938): 46–82.

Tan Yuanheng. *Guangzhou shisanhang: Ming-Qing 300 nian jiannan quzhe de waimao zhi lu* [The Thirteen Hongs of Guangzhou: The Ming-Qing's 300-Year-Long Difficult and Winding Road of Foreign Trade]. Guangzhou: Guangdong jingji chubanshe, 2015.

Thampi, Madhavi. "Parsis in the China Trade." *Revista de Cultura/Review of Culture* (international edition) 10 (2004): 16–25.

Thelwall, A. [Algernon] S. [Sydney]. *The Iniquities of the Opium Trade with China; Being a Development of the Main Causes Which Exclude the Merchants of Great Britain from the Advantages of an Unrestricted Commercial Intercourse with That Vast Empire. With Extracts from Authentic Documents*. London: W. H. Allen, 1839.

Thomas, Greg M. "Evaluating Others: The Mirroring of Chinese Civilisation in Britain." In *Civilisation and Nineteenth-Century Art*, edited by David O'Brien, 48–72. Manchester: Manchester University Press, 2016.

Thomas, Nicholas. *Colonialism's Culture: Anthropology, Travel and Government*. Princeton: Princeton University Press, 1994.

Thoms, P. [Peter] P. [Perring]. *The Affectionate Pair, or The History of Sung-Kin: A Chinese Tale*. London: Black, Kingsbury, Parbury, and Allen, 1820.

Thoms, P. [Peter] P. [Perring]. *Chinese Courtship in Verse, to Which Is Added, an Appendix Treating of the Revenue of China, &c., &c*. London: Parbury, Allen, and Kingsbury; printed at the Honorable East India Company's Press, Macao, 1824.

Thoms, P. [Peter] P. [Perring]. *The Emperor of China v. the Queen of England: A Refutation of the Arguments Contained in the Seven Official Documents Transmitted by Her Majesty's Government at Hong Kong, Who Maintain That the Documents of the Chinese Government Contain Insulting Language*. London: P. P. Thoms, 1853.

Thurin, Susan Schoenbauer. *Victorian Travelers and the Opening of China, 1842–1907*. Athens: Ohio University Press, 1999.

Trentmann, Frank. *Free Trade Nation: Commerce, Consumption, and Civil Society in Modern Britain*. Oxford: Oxford University Press, 2008.

Trocki, Carl. *Opium, Empire, and the Global Political Economy: A Study of the Asian Opium Trade, 1750–1950*. London: Routledge, 1999.

Tyerman, Daniel, and George Bennet. *Journal of Voyages and Travels by the Rev. Daniel Tyerman and George Bennet, Esq. Deputed from the London Missionary Society, to Visit Their Various Stations in the South Sea Islands, China, India, &C., between the Years 1821 and 1829*. Compiled by James Montgomery. Vol 2. London: F. Westley and A. H. Davis, 1831.

Urmston, James Brabazon. *Chusan and Hong Kong: With Remarks on the Treaty of Peace at Nankin in 1842, and on Our Present Position and Relations with China*. London: James Madden, 1847.

Urmston, James Brabazon. *Observations on the China Trade: And on the Importance and Advantages of Removing It from Canton, to Some Other Part of the Coast of That Empire*. London: Printed for private circulation only by G. Woodfall, 1834.

Van, Rachel Tamar. "The 'Woman Pigeon': Gendered Bonds and Barriers in the Anglo-American Commercial Community in Canton and Macao, 1800–1849." *Pacific Historical Review* 83, no. 4 (2014): 561–91.

Van Dyke, Paul A. *The Canton Trade: Life and Enterprise on the China Coast, 1700–1845*. Hong Kong: Hong Kong University Press, 2005.

Wagner, Tamara S. "Sketching China and the Self-Portrait of a Post-Romantic Traveler: John Francis Davis's Rewriting of China in the 1840s." In *A Century of Travels in China: Critical Essays on Travel Writing from the 1840s to the 1940s*, edited by Douglas Kerr and Julia Kuehn, 13–26. Hong Kong: Hong Kong University Press, 2007.

Wakeman, Frederic Jr. "The Canton Trade and the Opium War." In *The Cambridge History of China*, vol. 10, *Late Ch'ing, 1800–1911*, part 1, edited by John K. Fairbank, 161–212. Cambridge: Cambridge University Press, 1978.

Wang, Gungwu. *Anglo-Chinese Encounters since 1800: War, Trade, Science and Governance*. Cambridge: Cambridge University Press, 2003.

Wang, Wensheng. *White Lotus Rebels and South China Pirates: Crisis and Reform in the Qing Empire*. Cambridge, MA: Harvard University Press, 2014.

Wei, Betty Peh-T'i. *Ruan Yuan, 1794–1849: The Life and Work of a Major Scholar Official in Nineteenth Century China before the Opium War*. Hong Kong: Hong Kong University Press, 2006.

Wong, Lawrence Wang-chi. "'Objects of Curiosity': John Francis Davis as a Translator of Chinese Literature." In *Sinologists and Translators in the Seventeenth to Nineteenth Centuries*, edited by Lawrence Wang-chi Wong and Bernhard Fuehrer, 169–203. Hong Kong: Research Centre for Translation/The Chinese University Press, 2015.

Wood, Frances. "Closely Observed China: From William Alexander's Sketches to His Published Work." *British Library Journal* 24, no. 1 (1998): 98–121.

Wood, Frances. *Did Marco Polo Go to China?* London: Secker and Warburg, 1995.

Ye, Xiaoqing. "Ascendant Peace in the Four Seas: Tributary Drama and the Macartney Mission of 1793." *Late Imperial China* 26, no. 2 (2005): 89–113.

Zhang Wenqin. *Guangdong shisanhang yu zaoqi Zhongxi guanxi* [The Thirteen Hongs of Canton and Early Sino-Western Relations]. Guangzhou: Guangdong jingji chubanshe, 2009.

Zheng, Yangwen. *The Social Life of Opium in China*. Cambridge: Cambridge University Press, 2005.

# Index

Page references for illustrations and maps are italicized.

Abel, Clarke, 8, *148*, 151; on Buddhism, 15; on Chinese medicine, 13–14; on footbinding, 159; on infanticide, 153; on opium, 15, 190; on population, 147

Alexander, William, 156, 163

Americans, 2, 40, 77, 89, 113, 195, 206; benefit from Company's monopoly, 109, 110, 111, 112, 134n29; missionaries, 125

Amherst, Lord, 62, 68, 69, 100, 129, 146

Amherst embassy, 8–9, 16, 29, 42, 111, 119, 126; in Canton, 13–14; on character of Canton people, 40–41; on footbinding, 159; on infanticide, 152–53; and kowtow controversy, 100; on Qing decline, 146–47

Amoy (Xiamen), 30, 71, 74, 77, 88

Anderson, Aeneas, 8, 18, 120; on character of Canton people, 41; on footbinding, 163; on population of Canton, 144; on women, 161

Anglo-Chinese College (at Malacca), 153

Auber, Peter, 120–21

Ball, Samuel, 88–89

Barrow, John, 8, *34*, 115, 116; on character of Canton people, 40; on China as market, 140; compares Qing and Russian empires, 33; criticizes Anderson, 120; on despotism, 39; on footbinding, 155, 163, 164, 165, 166; on infanticide, 151–52; on Jesuits, 102–6; on learning Chinese, 82, 86; on Manchu conquest, 43–44, 142; on opium, 15, 187; on population, 144, 146; on Qing military, 44; on rebellion, 45, 141; on women, 160–61

Batavia, 9, 50, 91, 125, 233

Baynes, Julia Smith, 66

Baynes, William, 66

Bennet, George, 10; on beggars, 142; on footbinding, 158, 159, 160, 162, 164; on population, 144

Bennett, George, 10, 164, 190

Bingham, John Elliot, 10, 145, 170–72

Bocca Tigris (Humen), 63, 68, 73, *188*, 199, 204

Bombay, 208, 225

Bonin Islands, 89–90

Bremer, Gordon, 213

259

Bridgman, Elijah Coleman, 184; and *Chinese Repository*, 11; criticizes Medhurst, 125; on footbinding, 160; on opium, 195, 196, 208
Brougham, Henry, 196
Buckinghamshire, Lord, 140

Calcutta, 81, 188, 212, 228
Canton, *4*, 7, *14*, *145*, 232; beggars in, 141–42; calls for alternative to, 89–92; character of people at, 40–41; foreign trade and residence confined to, 2, 4, 27, 29, 30, 32, 222; foreign women visit, 3, 4, 66, 166; fragile legal situation at, 116; observing and interpreting China from, 13–15; and opium, 183–84, 190, 194, 199, 200; population of, 144–45
Canton Chamber of Commerce, 19, 183, 196, 204
*Canton Press*, 193; establishment of, 11–12, 73, 195; publicizes opinion in Britain and India, 208–11; rivalry with *Canton Register*, 13, 52, 73, 228–30
*Canton Register*, 101, 193–95; founding of, 10–11, 12, 53; publicizes opinion in Britain and India, 208–11; rivalry with *Canton Press*, 13, 52, 73, 228–30
Canton System, 2, 6, 35, 115; criticized, 27, 28, 39, 46, 130; defended, 19, 46–47; end of, 12, 19, 221, 231; as historical anomaly, 29–30; prohibition against Western women, 2–3, 66, 81; restrictions of, 6, 7, 8, 19, 28, 38; strengths of, 89
China Association, 74
*Chinese Repository*, 13, 42, 193, 195, 208; founding of, 11
Chinnery, George, 156
Chuenpe (Chuanbi), 225
Chusan (Zhoushan), 30, 88, 89, 92–93, 222, 225, 227; footbinding at, 167,

170–72; Urmston on, 91–92, 93, 131, 190
Cohong, 2, 76, 111, 204
Confucius, 38, 123, 124, 142
country traders. *See* private traders
Court of Directors (of East India Company), 18, 35, 51, 84, 85
Crabbe, George, 198
Cree, Edward, 10, 167–68
Cumsingmoon (Jinxingmen), 188
Cunynghame, Arthur, 170, 172, 173

Dane's Island, 230
Daniell, James Frederick Nugent, 11–12
Daniell, Thomas, 10, 156, 160, 162
Daniell, William, 10, 156, 160, 162
Daoguang, Emperor, 27, 45, 71, 76, 190, 206, 223
Davis, John Francis, 9, 14, 19, *83*, 100, 123, 210; assesses earlier works on China, 119–20; on Canton System, 87–88; on character of Canton people, 13, 41; on Chinese business character, 16; on Chinese historical records, 30; and Chusan, 92–93; on despotism, 37; on early European traders, 51–52; on footbinding, 161, 162, 163, 165, 167; on infanticide, 153–54; on Jesuits, 106–7; on learning Chinese, 82–83; on Manchu conquest, 44–45; on opium, 15, 191; on population, 141, 142, 143, 144, 145; on Qing exclusion of foreigners, 29, 47; on Qing weakness, 45, 46, 224–25; on Staunton's translation of Qing code, 118; on understanding China, 18
de Guignes, Joseph, 120
Dealtry, Thomas, 201
Delano, Amasa, 58n97, 180n140
Deng Tingzhen, 204, 205
Dent, Lancelot, 9, 11–12, 183, 195
Dent, Thomas, 9
despotism, 35–41

## Index

Downing, Charles Toogood, 9, 19, 119, 221; on Canton, 14–15; on character of Canton people, 41; on confining foreigners to Canton, 47; criticized by Morrison, 121–22; on despotism, 37; on footbinding, 162, 163, 165, 167; on infanticide, 151, 154–55; on opium, 190, 196; on population of Canton, 145; on prejudice in Canton, 16; on Qing military, 224; on trade at Canton, 86; on understanding China, 18

Du Halde, Jean-Baptiste, 53, 59n117

East India Company, 9, 18, 51; criticized, 51, 52, 75, 201; in India, 6, 28, 187; monopoly defended, 92, 101, 107–13, 115–16; monopoly ends, 4, 11, 19, 20, 29, 68, 69, 73, 76, 107; and opium, 187, 190–91, 208; prohibition against missionaries, 9; weakening of, 12

Elgin, Lord, 232, 234

Elliot, Charles, 202, 212, 228; on China knowledge, 130, 132; criticized, 131, 225–27, 234; and Innes, 204–5; and opium crisis, 183–84, 200–201, 207, 209; on opium trade, 195, 200

Ellis, Henry, 8, 151; on Canton System, 47; on infanticide, 152; on Jesuits, 106; on Manchu conquest, 142; on monopoly, 111; on population, 147; on stagnation, 33, 35; on women, 161

factories, *4*, 14, 41, 81, 110, 145, 171, 194, 201, 205

Footbinding, 155–74, *157*, *158*

Forbes, Charles, 129

Forbes, Robert Bennet, 203–4

Formosa (Taiwan), 63, 72, 88, 89, 90, 91

Fryer, John 232

Giles, Herbert Allen, 232

Goddard, James, 30–31, 69–70, 100, 195

Gordon, G. J., 66–67

Gough, Hugh, 170

Grant, Charles, 29, 48, 68, 189

Grey, Earl, 31,

Gützlaff, Karl, 35, 56, *127*, 232; criticized, 126; on Manchus, 43; and opium, 192

Hall, Basil, 8, 13, 159, 160

Hart, Robert, 232

Hayne, Henry, 34, 40–41, 144, 156

Hislop, Emma, 130

Holman, James, 10, *65*, 120; on Baynes incident, 66; on character of Canton people, 40, 64; on despotism, 37; on opium, 190; on Qing government, 64–66

Holmes, Samuel, 8, 81, 150, 161

Honam (Henan), 29, 71, 159

Hong Kong, 1, 2, 40, 89, *229*; occupation of, 13, 20, 131, 222, 231; and disease, 92, 213; doubts about, 93, 131, 225, 227–30; and opium, 188, 199, 213

hong merchants, 2, 82, 109, 111, 112, 125, 158; accused of opium smuggling, 201, 218n102; Ellis on, 111; Marjoribanks on, 130; and opium crisis, 183, 200, 204, 205; Slade on, 111, 128; squeezed, 88; trade controlled by, 29, 71, 110, 128

Howqua, 49, 66, 159, 204

India, 1, 6, 12, 63, 78; British opinion in, 20, 21, 86, 186, 206–12, 226–27; Chinese trade with, 30; and opium, 6, 187, 190, 191, 192, 195, 202, 207, 234; Qing concerns about, 48, 51; Qing conflicts with, 142

infanticide, 37, 106, 139, 235–36; speculation about extent of, 20, 150–55

Inglis, Robert Hugh, 19, 28, 32, 35

Innes, James, 11, 201–5, *203*, 211

Jardine, Matheson & Co., 73, 111, 189, 192
Jardine, William, 8, 9, 11, 184, 194, 195, 211; influence on British policy, 7, 22n9; and opium, 197; and Palmerston, 6–7; on smuggling, 201; on value of Hong Kong, 227
Jesuits, 18, 71, 118, 119; challenged and criticized, 31, 50, 53, 102–7, 139, 151, 154, 161; mapmaking, 103
Jiaqing, Emperor, 45, 62, 100, 146–47
Jocelyn, Robert, 212
John, Griffith, 232
Johnson, James, 10, 119

Kangxi Emperor, 30, 31, 45, 103, 201
Keating, Arthur Saunders, 11, 46, 194, 202, 221
Kerr, William, 66
King, Charles W., 11, 184

Lay, George Tradescant, 9, 19, 232; calls for colonizing Bonin Islands, 89; on China freed, 231; on Chinese religions, 18; on footbinding, 158, 159, 161–62, 163, 165–66; on infanticide, 155; on opium, 192, 199
Lay, Horatio Nelson, 232
Legge, James, 232
Li Hongbin, 194
Li Houzhu, 165
Lin Zexu, 2, 6, 130, 183, 199, 202, 224
Lindsay, Hugh Hamilton, 9, 11, 12, 19, 35, 66, 74, 204; on coastal trade, 87; criticized 78–80; 123–24; letter to Palmerston, 4, 6, 76–77, 122; on *yi*, 122
Lintin (Lingding), 70, 130, *188*, *189*, 192, 211; and opium trade, 188–90, 191, 194, 195
Loch, Granville Gower, 170, *171*, 172–73
Lockhart, William, 167, *168*, 172
London Missionary Society, 9, 28, 45, 86, 195, 126, 232
Low, Harriett, 156
Lu Kun, 128

Macao (Macau), 4, *5*, 7, 10, 13, 33, 37; British factory at, 116; British move to, 1, 222; Catholic authorities in, 9; Company's press at, 33, 85, 119, 123; footbinding at, 156, 162, 167, 169, 170, 171; foreign community at, 12; and foreign trade, 2, 30; Lord Macartney on, 63; and opium distribution, 188; Western women confined to, 2, 66
Macartney, Lord, 8, *43*, 144, 150; on China knowledge, 99; on Chinese and Manchus, 42; on conflict between Britain and China, 63–64; on despotism, 39; on footbinding, 162, 164, 166; on learning Chinese, 81; on Macao, 63; on population, 145–46; on Qing decline, 45, 62; on reliability of Chinese sources, 149; on religion, 56n49
Macartney embassy, 8–9, 16, 64, 129, 151; and character of Canton people, 40–41; Davis on, 83; and footbinding, 161; and Jesuit impressions of China, 103; and Manchus, 42; Marjoribanks on, 69; Staunton on, 99
Mackenzie, Keith Stewart, 10, 213, 229
Mackintosh, James, 116–17
McLeod, John, 8, 126, 152
McPherson, Duncan, 10, 169, 172, 173, 212–13
Magniac & Co., 111
Malacca, 9, 131, 153, 232
Malthus, Thomas, 141, 149
Manchus, 19, 27, 28, 42–43; and Canton System, 29–30; and China's stagnation, 32–35; conquest of China, 43–45; and despotism, 35–40

Manila, 50, 90, 202
Marjoribanks, Charles, *36*, 48, 50; blames foreigners for Qing policy, 50, 51; on British ignorance of China, 130; on despotism, 35, 36, 37–38; letter to Charles Grant, 68–69, 89, 191, 199; on Lintin, 189; on opium, 191, 199
Marshman, Joshua, 120
Mason, George Henry, 115
Matheson, Alexander, 11, 207
Matheson, James, 6, 8, 9, 11, 19, *75*, 94n7; on British ignorance of China, 128; on British policy toward China, 7, 76; and *Canton Register*, 11, 193; on Canton System, 49, 76; on chance of peace, 212; criticized, 78, 80, 81, 123–24; demonstrates authority, 119; on Hong Kong, 227–28; letter to Palmerston, 4, 74–75; on opium, 197, 200; and opium crisis, 183, 184, 207, 211; on progress of war, 225–26; on *yi*, 122
Maxwell, Murray, 68
Medhurst, Walter Henry (father), 9, 19, 222, 232; on beggars, 142; on character of Canton people, 41; on Chinese sources, 149–50; criticized, 125; on despotism, 37; on footbinding, 163; on infanticide, 150, 154; on learning Chinese, 85; on opium, 15, 52, 191–92, 199; on population, 140, 143–44, 147–48; praises Chinese civilization, 17–18; on Qing restrictions, 48–49; on stagnation, 32, 35
Medhurst, Walter Henry (son), 233–37
Medical Missionary Society, 167, 168, 172
Melbourne, Lord, 7, 186, 207
Milburn, William, 187
Milne, William, 9, 153
missionaries, 9, 12, 82, 141, 174, 232, 233, 235

American, 125; criticized, 17; on footbinding, 166; on infanticide, 150, 151, 152; on opium, 191–92 *See also* Jesuits
Morrison, John Robert, 17, 85, 119, 130; and *Chinese Repository*, 19; criticizes Downing, 121–22; on despotism, 36–37; on earlier commercial enterprise, 30; on learning Chinese, 86
Morrison, Robert, 8, 18, *31*, 116, 129, 153; blames British, 51, 81–82; on British ignorance of China, 87, 126; on Canton System, 28, 30, 47, 141; changing views of China, 17; on character of Canton people, 40; on Chinese sources, 144–45, 149; establishes authority, 119; on footbinding, 156, 165; on learning Chinese, 84–85; on Lintin, 188; on Manchus, 42; on opium, 192; on population of Canton, 144; on Qing decline, 45; on stagnation, 33
Morse, Hosea Ballou, 187

Nanking (Nanjing), 71, 167; Treaty of, 92, 132, 222
Napier, Elizabeth, 4
Napier, Lord, 77, 78, 119, 123, 128, 227; humiliation of, 71, 74–75, 76, 129; mission and death of, 4, 9, 19, 61, 70, 80; on Qing government, 28–29, 31–32, 35–36
*Neptune* affair, 116
Ningpo (Ningbo), 30, 71, 88
Nye, Gideon, 134, 158

Olyphant, David Washington Cincinnatus, 11
Opium: British debates about, 20–21, 183–213; in British writings, 190–93; in Canton, 15, 190; and

Canton System, 6; and China, 184, 186; Chinese demand for, 6; in Company correspondence, 187–88; compensation for, 7; consumption and images of, 184, *185*; and corruption, 15, 199; criticism of, 11, 51; and Hong Kong, 131; and India, 6; and Innes fiasco, 202–5; Lin Zexu destroys, 2, 6, 184; and Lintin, 188–90, *189*; opinion in India and Britain of, 206–11; physiological effects of, 196–98; in the press, 193–96; Qing debates about, 186, 200; surrender of, 183

Opium War (First), 6, 7, 10, 20, 53, 130, 186, 230; and opening of China, 20, 167–74, 231; and opium debates, 211–13; as watershed, 222

Opium War (Second), 93, 232

Palmerston, Lord, *223*, 227; and British expedition to China, 7, 22n9, 186, 222; Elliot's dispatches to, 183, 195, 200, 204, 205; on Hong Kong, 131; Jardine advises, 6–7; Lindsay's letter to, 6, 76–77, 122, 124; Matheson's letters to, 4, 74; urged to compensate traders, 184, 207

Parsis, 201, 207

Pearl River, *14*, 69, 144, 155, 224, 230

Pearson, Alexander, 116

Peking (Beijing), *105*; Catholic missionaries in, 48, 106, 166; Convention of, 232; infanticide at, 152, 154

Penang, 9, 131

Philip, Robert, 195

pidgin English, 82

Polo, Marco, 165, 179n136

population, 30, 38, 44, 70; speculation about size of, 20, 47, 140–50

Pottinger, Henry, 131–32, 212, 234

private traders, 4, 6, 9, 53, 67; and opium 115, 186, 187, 188, 201, 208; Staunton on, 109–10

Qianlong, Emperor, 32, 39, 43, 45, 100, 101, 120, 149, 210

Reeves, John, 66
Reeves, John Russell, 66
Renaudot, Eusèbe, 165
Richard, Timothy, 232
Roberts, John William, 18
Ruan Yuan, 218n102
Russia, 63; and Chinese studies, 84, 86; despotism, 38; empire compared with Qing, 33; trade with China, 47

Select Committee (of East India Company), 8, 18, 19, 112, 187

Shanghai, 77, 88, 92; Medhurst on, 233–34

Singapore, 20, 131, 197, 223, 228–29, 230

sinology, 19, 232

Slade, John, 11; on British ignorance of China, 126, 128; on British policy toward China, 67, 87; on China knowledge, 130–31; on despotism, 37, 38; on monopoly, 101–2, 111, 112; on opium, 196; on population, 141; on Staunton's translation, 118–19; on *yi*, 124–25

stagnation, 32–35

Staunton, George Leonard, 8, *43*, 132n2, 156; on early British traders, 51; on footbinding, 163, 164, 166; on infanticide, 151–52; on monopoly, 107; on population, 146, 150

Staunton, George Thomas, 7, 8, 9, 55n31, *79*, 100, *108*, 222; on British ignorance of China, 126; on Canton System, 19, 46; criticized, 129, 222; criticizes Matheson and Lindsay, 78–81; defends monopoly, 107–10, 112, 113; on infanticide, 152–53; on Macartney embassy, 99–100; on opium, 191; on population, 147; on Qing decline, 146–47; on Terranova

case, 118; translates Qing code, 32–33, 106, 113–16, *114*, 118; on *yi*, 122–23
Su Dongpo, 122, 124

Taylor, Hudson, 232
Terranova, Francis, 111, 112, 118
Thelwall, Algernon Sydney, 209–10
Thoms, Peter Perring, 123–24
Tientsin (Tianjin), 77, 147; Treaty of, 232
Toone, Francis Hastings, 100
*Topaze* affair, 192
Treaty ports, 174, 232, 233
Tyerman, Daniel, 10; on beggars, 142; on footbinding, 158, 159, 160, 162, 164; on population, 144

Urmston, James Brabazon, 222; on British ignorance of China, 129; calls for taking Chusan, 90–92, 93; on China knowledge, 131; on opium, 190–91, 199; on population of Canton, 144

vaccination, 116, *117*
Vachell, George Harvey, 66

Wade, Thomas Francis, 232
Whampoa (Huangpu), 9, *10*, 68, 121, 189, 226; opium smuggling at, 188, 200, 201, 204
Whiteman, John Claremont, 12
Wilberforce, William, 198
William IV, King; 61–62, 66, 71, 74, 77
Williams, Samuel Wells, 7–8, 126
Wood, William Wightman, 11, 202

Xu Naiji, 200

*yi* (barbarian or foreigner), 122–25